"This is a thoroughly treated, must read book on local government/municipal finance and bankruptcy challenges. The book's uniqueness is its strength on emergency financial management stress, fiscal distress, and government bankruptcy with loss of financial capacity in modern times. The authors have done an excellent job of explaining and illustrating this highly significant feature of contemporary financial management; their work is admirably well done with adequate details without overwhelming the students, researchers, and instructors. The select case studies of the second half of the book supplement the theory, concept, and issues covered earlier, and are extremely useful to readers. Highly recommended for upper undergraduate and graduate MPA students, as well as for courses in public financial management, for its easy to read and substantive content".

– **Ali Farazmand**, Florida Atlantic University

"Ermasova and Guzman provide the reader with an approachable yet thorough understanding of the conceptual underpinnings of fiscal stress, its effects, and remedies that is augmented through the use of carefully selected case studies".

– **C. Kurt Zorn**, Indiana University

"Through a compelling review of current scholarship and a detailed discussion of case studies, the authors share with us their wealth of knowledge on the origins of fiscal malaise in U.S. cities and stimulate us to reflect on policy action that can counteract the economic, political, institutional and managerial environments that are conducive to local financial crises. A captivating read for scholars and practitioners interested in the management of local government financial condition!"

– **Evgenia Gorina**, University of Texas at Dallas

MUNICIPAL FISCAL STRESS, BANKRUPTCIES, AND OTHER FINANCIAL EMERGENCIES

It is difficult to find someone who has not heard about the Puerto Rico, Detroit, Michigan, or Orange County, California, bankruptcies. While guides for responsibly managing government finances exist, problems often originate not because of poor financial reporting or financial deficiencies but because issues external to financial wellbeing arise, such as economic, demographic, political, legal, or even environmental factors. Exacerbating the problem, there is not much advice in the existing literature on how to act when municipalities face financial struggles. Filling this important gap, this book explores fiscal health and fiscal hardships, municipal defaults and bankruptcies, and many other aspects to help guide local governments during fiscal distress.

Fiscal hardships negatively affect the quality and availability of public goods and services and, consequently, the wellbeing of residents and businesses living and working in distressed municipalities. Turned off streetlights, unmaintained public parks, potholes, inconsistent garbage pickup, longer response time from emergency services, and multiple other issues that residents of the struggling municipalities deal with, lead to higher crime rates, lower quality of K-12 education, dangerous road conditions, lower housing values, outmigration of wealthier population, and numerous other problems. The COVID-19 pandemic put additional unprecedented pressure on municipal finances nationwide.

In this book authors Tatyana Guzman and Natalia Ermasova evaluate distressed cities and municipalities and provide practical recommendations on improving their financial conditions. What are conditions and signs to look for to not to find yourself in similar situations? What can be done if your municipality is already experiencing fiscal hardships? What are the consequences of fiscal misfortunes? How does one exit a fiscal emergency? This book answers these and other questions and serves as a guide to fiscal health and prosperity for U.S.

municipal governments, students and researchers in public finance, and general public management fields.

Tatyana Guzman is Associate Professor in public finance and policy analysis at Cleveland State University. Dr. Guzman received her PhD in public affairs from O'Neill School of Public and Environmental Affairs at Indiana University and also holds an MA degree in economics. Dr. Guzman's primary research interests are in various aspects of the public finance field, including taxation, budgeting, and municipal bond markets. She has published over 20 journal articles and book chapters. Her research has appeared in such peer-reviewed journals as *Public Budgeting and Finance* (PBF), *Policy Studies Journal* (PSJ), *American Review of Public Administration* (ARPA), *Journal of Benefit-Cost Analysis* (JBCA), *Tax Notes*, and other outlets. Tatyana has 15 years of teaching experience at Cleveland State University, Indiana University Bloomington (IUB), and Indiana University Purdue University in Indianapolis (IUPUI), where she has taught undergraduate and graduate public finance and budgeting, research methods, economics, and statistics courses.

Natalia Ermasova is a Professor at Governors State University, Illinois, USA. She has a PhD in public affairs (SPEA, Indiana University, USA). Her primary research interests are capital budgeting, business ethics, public finance, leadership, risk-management, innovation management, and public education funding. She was Visiting Professor in Germany (Ludwigsburg Academy for Civil Services), Corvinus University (Hungary) and Fulbright Visiting Professor (SPEA, IU). Dr. Natalia Ermasova is a board member of the *International Journal of Public Administration* (IJPA) and Co-Editor of *Global Encyclopedia of Public Administration, Public Policy, and Governance*. More than 60 of her articles, books, and chapters were published in the USA, UK, and Australia. She is the author of six textbooks about budgeting systems, financial management, and risk-management. Her articles have been published in journals including *Public Finance and Management*, *State and Local Government Review*, the *International Journal of Public Administration*, and the *Journal of Management Development*.

MUNICIPAL FISCAL STRESS, BANKRUPTCIES, AND OTHER FINANCIAL EMERGENCIES

Tatyana Guzman and Natalia Ermasova

Routledge
Taylor & Francis Group
NEW YORK AND LONDON

Designed cover image: krisanapong detraphiphat (Getty Images)

First published 2023
by Routledge
605 Third Avenue, New York, NY 10158

and by Routledge
4 Park Square, Milton Park, Abingdon, Oxon, OX14 4RN

Routledge is an imprint of the Taylor & Francis Group, an informa business

Library of Congress Cataloging-in-Publication Data
Names: Guzman, Tatyana, author. | Ermasova, Natalia, author.
Title: Municipal fiscal stress, bankruptcies, and other financial emergencies / Tatyana Guzman and Natalia Ermasova.
Identifiers: LCCN 2022025936 | ISBN 9781032349374 (hardback) | ISBN 9781032349381 (paperback) | ISBN 9781003324553 (ebook)
Subjects: LCSH: Municipal finance—United States—Case studies. | Municipal bankruptcy—United States—Case studies.
Classification: LCC HJ9145 .G86 2023 | DDC 336.73—dc23/eng/20220907
LC record available at https://lccn.loc.gov/2022025936

ISBN: 978-1-032-34937-4 (hbk)
ISBN: 978-1-032-34938-1 (pbk)
ISBN: 978-1-003-32455-3 (ebk)

DOI: 10.4324/b23117

Typeset in Bembo
by Apex CoVantage, LLC

CONTENTS

PREFACE

In 2016, one of the authors, Dr. Tatyana Guzman, was approached by the cities of East Cleveland and Maple Heights, Ohio, with requests to assess potential ways of exiting the fiscal emergency situations these two cities were facing. Severe financial struggles meant that the municipalities did not have the funds to pay for expensive research. In the search for ways to help, Dr. Guzman engaged students in her graduate budgeting class to look for possible causes of the fiscal emergencies in these two cities and to study practices of other comparable cities that were in similar conditions and have improved their financial standing since then. While supervising the works of Dr. Guzman and Dr. Ermasova's students and observing how little research there is to explain causes of financial emergencies and give advice on potential ways out of fiscal stress, the idea came to write this book to provide an affordable guide for municipalities on exiting financial struggles.

While not a panacea for fiscal illnesses, this book consolidates, discusses, and evaluates general ways to measure fiscal health and then dives into assessments of fiscal stress situations for municipalities. The book discusses states' monitoring practices of local government finances, early warning signs, intervention policies, states' bankruptcy procedures, tax and non-tax incentives for economic development, budgeting approaches, and capital infrastructure maintenance during financially challenging times. The book also dives into case studies of several fiscally stressed municipalities to learn from the mistakes and successes of others. Most importantly, the book discusses major causes and positive practices in an attempt to prevent fiscal emergency in the municipalities in the first place and offers general recommendations on exiting fiscal emergency if it happens.

This book could serve as a desk reference for practitioners, especially now that the topic of fiscal emergency situations and bankruptcy is again taking center stage during the COVID-19 crisis, rising gas prices, high inflation, and predictions of the looming economic recession. This study is intended to be a valuable low-cost guide on exiting fiscal emergency for public administrators, financial directors, planners, zoning officials, city council members, mayors, developers, policy makers, and investors. University students will also benefit from applying the framework of this study to understand the causes and consequences of government practices during municipal fiscal emergencies and bankruptcies. The book should be of particular interest to graduate students who work for or plan to work for municipal governments as well as for urban planning students who take government finance courses.

The authors of the book want to thank Matt Cullen and Robert Pfaff for providing invaluable comments about Detroit bankruptcy, history, and behind-the-scenes developments in that city; anonymous reviewers for offering excellent comments and suggestions on the initial layout of the book; Amy and Janusz Kuzdowicz for showing some of Detroit's most valuable treasures; Alex Philip for sharing the photos that added so much life to this book; Arianna Killing for her help with edits. We are grateful to our families for their support, to our children and parents for guiding, questioning, criticizing, and simply for being there for us.

Tatyana Guzman and Natalia Ermasova

1
INTRODUCTION

It is difficult to find someone who has not heard about the Puerto Rico, Detroit, Michigan, or Orange County, California, bankruptcies. Even if these places are far away, their struggles touched the hearts of many Americans. As some of us face financial problems at some points in our personal lives, cities, counties, and sometimes even entire states find themselves facing financial difficulties of their own. Neither poor nor wealthy are protected against downfalls. Remember the high-profile bankruptcy cases of Enron, Blockbuster, or Kodak? Even Presidents Abraham Lincoln and Donald Trump; famous singers Toni Braxton, Cindy Lauper, Latoya Jackson, and David Bowie; actors Nicholas Cage, Kim Basinger, and Zsa Zsa Gabor; writer Mark Twain; sportsman Mike Tyson; radio host Larry King; car maker and business magnate Henry Ford; and Walt Disney all filed for bankruptcy. There is a plethora of recommendations on how to manage personal or corporate finances so as to not to find yourself in an ominous situation. While there is a lot to guide government finances too (for example, the Government Accounting Standards Board (GASB) sets up generally acceptable accounting principles for governments in the United States, the Government Finance Officers Association (GFOA) provides best practices in government reporting, and the Municipal Securities Rulemaking Board (MSRB) regulates the municipal bond market), problems often originate and are exacerbated not because of poor financial reporting or financial deficiencies per se but because of issues external to financial wellbeing such as economic, demographic, political, legal, or even environmental factors. At the same time, there is not much advice in the literature on how to act when municipalities face financial struggles. This is exactly what we discuss throughout this book. We talk about fiscal health and fiscal hardships, municipal defaults and bankruptcies, and many other aspects to help guide local governments during fiscal distress.

DOI: 10.4324/b23117-1

Fiscal hardships negatively affect the quality and availability of public goods and services and, consequently, the wellbeing of residents and businesses (and even passersby) of the distressed municipalities. They diminish the attractiveness of neighboring communities. How prevalent are fiscal downturns? Let's consider Ohio, a state that developed an excellent early monitoring system and a clear designation of what constitutes a fiscal emergency. In Ohio alone, there were eighty four recorded cases of fiscal emergency among local governments from the 1980's through the present. Of these, twelve governments are still in the fiscal emergency situation now (Ohio Auditor of State, 2022). Some fiscal emergencies lead to defaults (mostly due to a failure to pay interest or principle on issued bonds) or even bankruptcies (although not in Ohio because of peculiarities of the state legislature), while others do not. While municipal bankruptcies (so called Chapter 9 bankruptcies) and defaults are not as widespread as corporate ones, their extent, cost, and publicity make them quite notorious.

To put actual numbers behind these claims, Moody's Investors Services (2017) reported a 0.15 percent default rate on their rated municipal bonds between 2007 and 2012 (0.07 percent rate between 1970 and 2016) and a 6.92 percent default rate for the same period of time for corporate bonds. Despite the rarity of municipal defaults, the probability of their occurrence has increased in recent years. According to Appleson et al. (2012), there were 2,521 instances of government defaults between 1970 and 2011. Gao et al. (2019) claim that 2,063 municipal bond issues defaulted between 1999 and 2010, while Yang and Abbas (2020) report that only 2,563 local bond issues (by 679 issuers) experienced defaults between 2009 and 2015. Although the definition of default and, consequently, default counts likely differ between studies (see Chapter 2 for discussion) and, by presenting numbers from different research, we are potentially comparing apples to oranges, the trend is still evident.

If defaults are rare, municipal bankruptcies are even less common. Jeweler (2007) claims that only 72 Chapter 9 bankruptcies were filed between 1988 and 2005. Most of the filings were by special districts and other small municipalities. The most recent U.S. Census of Governments, 2017) reports indicate that there were 38,779 general purpose government units in the U.S. (counties, municipalities, and townships) and 51,296 special purpose governments (independent school districts and special districts). According to PEW Charitable Trusts (2020), between 2001 and 2017 there were 31 reported cases of Chapter 9 bankruptcy filings among general purpose governments and 92 among special purpose districts. The overall probability of special purpose government bankruptcy filing in 16 reported years was 0.18 percent, and general-purpose bankruptcy filing was 0.08 percent. Nebraska is worth a special mention, where 21 special-purpose districts filed for bankruptcy between 2000 and 2020. That is almost a quarter of all special-purpose districts' bankruptcy filings in that 20-year time period (PEW Charitable Trusts, 2020). Detroit became the largest U.S. city to ever file for bankruptcy in 2013, with 18 billion dollars in outstanding debt at the time of bankruptcy. Orange County, CA was the largest U.S. municipality to file for

Chapter 9 bankruptcy in 1994. At the time of bankruptcy filing, Orange County was the fifth most populous county in the U.S. According to the U.S. Census Bureau (2021), just under 3.2 million people resided in the county in 2019.

What municipalities defaulted on their bonds or even went bankrupt and why? While we devote a lot of attention to this matter later in the book, to give an initial glimpse of the causes of financial difficulties, if we consider the 150 largest U.S. cities (as defined by Lincoln Institute of Land Policy) in the 20 years between 1995 and 2019, 9 of them were or currently are in a dire fiscal situation, based on the opinions published by credit rating agencies (we rely on Moody's and Standard & Poor's (S&P's) for the matter of this exercise). These nine cities received a non-investment grade, or a "junk" rating during one or several years during the considered period.

- *Stockton, CA*: ratings were downgraded to junk in early 2012 after at least three years of running a substantial budget deficit. With the highest foreclosure rate in the country in 2008, hence lower property tax collections and 71 percent of general fund revenue earmarked for restricted purposes (City of Stockton, 2021), as well as very little flexibility to redirect money to the underperforming areas, the city filed for Chapter 9 bankruptcy on June 28, 2012 with a debt of about two billion dollars, a lot of which was in bond and pension obligations (Reuters, 2012, 2013a; Rivera, 2022). In 2012, Stockton was the most populous city to file for bankruptcy before the Detroit, MI bankruptcy in 2014
- *Hartford, CT*: rating agencies downgraded city bonds to junk in the summer of 2017, after the municipality announced that they were entertaining a possibility of filing for bankruptcy (which they never did). Unemployment, population loss, and the resulting substantial budget deficit were named as some of the reasons for the move. In Hartford, the capital of Connecticut, about half of all property belongs to the government or non-profit organizations that are tax exempt, which limits the amount of property tax revenue the city is able to raise. The state also does not allow for local sales or income taxes. High expenditures paralleled with limited ability to generate their own-source revenue (hence, high dependance on state transfers) resulted in a substantial budget deficit. Only by the summer of 2019 did rating agencies begin to change the outlook (not the ratings themselves) to positive, after the control of the city was overtaken by the state, which also paid the city's outstanding debt obligations. But the city was not out of the muddy waters yet. Yahoo Finance reports that 1 in 8,758 homes were foreclosed in Hartford in October 2020. The unemployment rate of 13.6 percent was the highest among all other cities in Connecticut in September 2020 and almost twice the average rate of 7.5 percent in the state (U.S. Bureau of Labor Statistics, 2021)
- *Washington D.C.*: ratings were downgraded to junk in February 1995 based on poor financial performance and a budget deficit resulting from high

expenditures and a shrinking tax base. High expenses were largely due to the fact that being a city without a state, Washington D.C. had to bear not only typical city-level expenses (like police and fire expenditures) but also expenses typically incurred by the state (like Medicaid or certain welfare expenses). Following severe unemployment and population loss during the economic recession of the early 1990s, Washington D.C. also lost a lot of its income and sales tax revenue. The severity of the revenue loss was worsened by multiple revenue limitations the city has had and the fact that 42 percent of the assessed value of D.C. properties had been exempt from property tax (Federal and other government buildings, foreign embassies, and non-profits). In 1997, the Federal Government passed the Revitalization Act that, among other things, shifted some expenditures (like courts, prisons, some Medicaid expenses, and others) from the district's responsibility onto the Federal government (Bouker, 2008). Both Moody's and S&P's lifted Washington D.C.'s credit ratings in early 1999

- *Chicago, IL*: ratings lowered to junk by Moody's standards (not S&P's) in May of 2015, due to the concern primarily about a high and growing pool of unfunded pension liabilities. These, according to Moody's, were eight times operating revenue in the fiscal year 2012, higher than any other local government in the U.S. (Moody's Investors Services, 2017). The city has also run a budget deficit almost every year in the past two decades. And, during the years with no deficit, Chicago used several financial legerdemains, such as recording borrowed money as revenue or selling (quite unsuccessfully) city assets (such as the Chicago Skyline, a toll road in the heart of Chicago in 2005 and parking meters in 2008) to balance its budget. While assets sales poured immediate cash into the city budget, the city lost the annual flow of revenue that these capital assets generated
- *New Orleans, LA*: rating downgraded to junk in the fall of 2005, following the historical flooding and destruction of the city by Hurricane Katrina and subsequent levees' failures. Interestingly, New Orleans later received more from insurance payments than what was lost from the hurricane. With the additional 130 million dollars in federal aid and funds the city was able to borrow from FEMA, the financial position of the city in the few years following the natural disaster became even better than before. Moody's started to lift the city's ratings in May 2007, while S&P's waited to upgrade theirs until April 2009. Today S&P's credit assessment of New Orleans is four notches higher than prior to Katrina
- *Detroit, MI*: although the downgrade stream by all major rating agencies started in 2005, Detroit's credit quality was only downgraded to junk in January 2009, four and a half years before the city filed for Chapter 9 bankruptcy on July 18, 2013. As one of the so-called "Rust-belt" or "Legacy" cities, the economy of Detroit has been heavily dependent on auto manufacturing with the three largest U.S. automakers, Chrysler, General Motors

(GM), and Ford, located in the city and its suburbs. As the auto making process became more automated and decentralized, the demand for auto workers in Detroit went down. The city lost 60 percent of its population during the 1950s (U.S. Census Bureau, 2021). High gasoline prices and low demand for American cars in the early 2000s and severe issues with the city's pension funds further exacerbated economic and demographic difficulties of the city. With an estimated 18–20 billion dollars in outstanding debt, Detroit was the most populous city to ever file for bankruptcy protection (see Chapter 9 for detailed case study of Detroit bankruptcy)

- *Flint, MI*: both S&P's and Moody's downgraded the city rating to junk in early 2000. The city renounced S&P's rating the same year and Moody's rating in 2006. Similar to Detroit, the economic downturn of the city was mainly due to the atomization and decentralization of car making processes, which resulted in a drop in employment by two major city employers, Buick Motor Company and GM. The financial problems were deepened by the famous Flint water crisis in 2014, when bankrupt Detroit privatized water operations and stopped providing it to the neighboring cities, including Flint. Flint switched to its own water purification system quite unsuccessfully. The city's drinking water was contaminated. Despite its already poor fiscal situation, Flint had to spend hundreds of millions of dollars to basically build the entire sewer system to deal with the issue
- *Pittsburgh, PA*: credit ratings lowered to non-investment grade toward the end of 2003 and in 2004 after the city was unable to further cut expenses or increase taxes to cover budget deficit. Pittsburgh applied for distressed municipality status in 2003. Similar to Detroit and Flint, Pittsburgh also lost a lot of manufacturing jobs by the mid-1980s and has never been able to fully recuperate. However, the financial situation somewhat improved after 2004, when Pittsburgh was given permission to increase its occupational tax, to create payroll tax, and to begin to phase-out the business privilege tax that allowed multiple businesses operating in the city to avoid paying taxes (Intergovernmental Cooperation Authority, 2009). The city additionally implemented cost saving strategies, especially for EMS and fire, and doubled the budget to demolish the city's abandoned buildings, among other cost saving actions. Due to the high legacy costs (especially pension and debt), Pittsburgh stayed in fiscal emergency for over 14 years until February 2018.

Of course, fiscal misfortunes do not only happen to large municipalities. On May 19, 2020, the city of Fairfield, Alabama, a suburb to AA-rated Birmingham, Alabama (the most populous city in the state), filed for bankruptcy after multiple local businesses closed their doors with the beginning of COVID-19 pandemic. This small city with a population of 11,117 residents (according to the U.S. Census Bureau, 2021) experienced a significant drop in tax revenue after two major employers left the city. U.S. Steel's Fairfield Works closed portions of their facility in 2015 and Walmart Supercenter closed in 2016. After these closures and millions in resulting debt obligations, the local transit authority stopped bus services, the city faced a shut-off of water services, and the county had to take over the police force (PEW Charitable Trusts, 2020).

East Cleveland, another small city of 13,792 residents (according to U.S. Census Bureau, 2021) and only three miles away from downtown Cleveland, in the beginning and midst of the 20th century used to be a highly desired neighborhood for businesses and residents alike. Inhabited by about 40 thousand people between the 1930s and 1970s, it housed the Rockefeller family and was a home to the world's first industrial park, the historical Nela Park bult by General Electric. Due to economic downgrade, real estate issues, corruption, and other circumstances, the economic and fiscal prosperity of East Cleveland received a notable downturn toward the last quarter of the century (Van Tassel & Grabowski, 1996). Over the past 34 years, the city of East Cleveland has been in a state of fiscal emergency for over 28 years (Ohio Auditor of State, 2022). Economic and fiscal issues additionally led to one of the most extreme cases of "white flight" in the nation. The Black population increased from 2 percent in 1960 to 67 percent in 1970 (Van Tassel & Grabowski, 1996), to 90 percent Black and 4.6 percent White in 2020 (U.S. Census Bureau, 2021).

Desert Hot Springs, California, a city of 32,512 (according to U.S. Census Bureau, 2021), is a home to numerous natural hot and cold mineral springs, spas and resorts, and summer temperatures almost all year around. Despite its potential, Desert Hot Springs was one of the poorest and most crime-ridden cities in California. "Seven gangs with up to 250 members call the place home, and at one point it had sixty-five percent of all parolees in the Coachella Valley despite having just five percent of the population" (Kelly, 2009). In 2001, the city applied for Chapter 9 bankruptcy after it lost a multimillion-dollar legal battle with a developer. In 2004, the city issued 9.7 million dollars in bonded debt to exit the bankruptcy. The situation, however, remained desperate for years to come. The crime condition became so bad that the city got involved in a major military style invasion. "Hundreds of law enforcement officers backed by armored cars and Black Hawk helicopters swept into the city . . . in a massive show of force that stunned the gangs, parolees and street thugs who had terrorized the community for years" (Kelly, 2009). In 2013, Desert Hot Springs declared a fiscal emergency once again when a new city finance director discovered a three-million-dollar deficit in the 13.5-million-dollar budget that occurred due to high debt service, pension obligations, and employee salaries (Reuters, 2013b).

This quick overlook of several financially struggling cities displays how different the causes of fiscal stress can be. Anything from the departure of or downsizing of the city's major employers, natural disasters in the area, racial tensions, lawsuits, or administrative corruption, to a national economic recession or even a world pandemic could lead to severe financial struggles for local governments. Most crises emerge over a rather long period of time, taking months if not years

FIGURE 1.1 Christmas Lights at Nela Park in East Cleveland.

Source: Photo credit Alex Philip

to develop (Lisa, 2021; Yang & Abbas, 2020). Others, mainly caused by natural disasters, occur in "ultra-short run" and are more difficult to foresee and prepare for (Kravchuk, 2021). Municipalities facing a crisis have a hard time making ends meet because they often lack the legal authority to introduce new or increase existing taxes. At times, downturns are less predictable as they may be caused by unforeseen events external to government operations. While causes of fiscal declines can be numerous, no matter what, municipalities can and should always be prepared for them. Any locality could save in designated rainy-day and natural and manmade disaster funds. The states can establish fiscal monitoring and intervention systems for local governments. The areas susceptible to natural disasters can institutionalize specific building standards and emergency evacuation procedures.

In this book we spend a lot of time discussing how even wealthy and desirable neighborhoods can downgrade drastically over time. What are conditions and signs to look for to not to find yourself in similar situations? What can be done if your municipality is already experiencing fiscal hardships? What are the consequences of fiscal misfortunes? How does one exit a fiscal emergency? This book tries to answer these and other questions and hopes to serve as a guide to fiscal health and prosperity for U.S. municipal governments, students and researchers in public finance, and general public management fields.

In this book we evaluate distressed cities and municipalities and provide practical recommendations on improving their financial conditions. Municipal fiscal stress puts a heavy burden on residents. Turned off streetlights, unmaintained public parks, potholes, inconsistent garbage pickup, longer response time from emergency services, and multiple other issues that residents of the struggling municipalities deal with lead to higher crime rates, lower quality of K-12 education, dangerous road conditions, lower housing values, outmigration of the wealthier population, and numerous other problems. The COVID-19 pandemic put additional unprecedented pressure on municipal finances nationwide. Municipalities face higher expenses and smaller tax revenue, while dealing with budgeting for economic and COVID-19 pandemic response activities.

We start off this book with a discussion of fiscal health and its measurements in Chapter 2, as well as the discussion and measurements of what are considered fiscal illnesses. In Chapter 3, we talk about preventative treatments and, when these do not work, we consider common prescriptions available for fiscally compromised local governments. Chapter 4 is dedicated to the most severe fiscal distress situations and municipal bankruptcies specifically. The following two chapters are devoted to the operating (Chapter 5) and capital (Chapter 6) budgeting practices for distressed municipalities. Chapter 7 discusses the most recent fiscal challenges that municipalities have faced during the COVID-19 pandemic. In the second half of the book, we consider six case studies of the U.S. cities and a county facing different degrees of financial distress. A more in-depth description of what every chapter has to offer is detailed next.

Chapter 2. "Municipal Fiscal Health" starts with definitions of "financial emergency", "fiscal distress", "fiscal stress", "fiscal hardship", and "fiscal health". We specify and discuss common measures of fiscal health. The chapter analyses and interprets financial indicators and explains how fiscal health and emergency can be understood through these indicators. It considers fiscal monitoring systems used by different states. The chapter additionally discusses how fiscal health can be understood through the lens of municipal credit ratings.

Chapter 3. The "Preventative Treatment and Federal, State, and Local Incentives for Unhealthy Municipalities" analyzes preventative practices and discusses an array of federal and state incentives for maintaining fiscal health and responding to fiscal illnesses, such as grants, tax advantages, administrative support, and others. The chapter discusses the actions localities take to get out of fiscal distress, like cuts in spending, local tax incentives, community partnerships, etc. Specifically, the chapter reviews preferential tax treatments, such as direct property tax relief mechanisms, the creation of TIF districts, Enterprise Zones, Opportunity Zones, and others. It also discusses indirect incentives (economic development tax incentives) that can also have a revitalizing effect on blighted areas, such as the New Markets Tax Credit (NMTC), Job Creation Tax Credit, Mega Project Tax Credit, Historical Preservation Tax Credit, other tax incentives that target specific geographical regions or industries, direct infrastructure investments, special bond issuance provisions, and other incentives. The chapter additionally looks at some noteworthy state intervention programs in distressed local government finances.

Chapter 4. "Legal Aspects of Municipal Bankruptcy" is devoted to the most critical cases of fiscal stress and specifically to municipal bankruptcies. In this chapter, we provide a distinction of Chapter 9 bankruptcy from other types of bankruptcy filings, offer a definition of fiscal emergency, review policies and the legal process of Chapter 9 bankruptcy, and review states' approaches to municipal bankruptcy. We discuss different types of emergency managers and responsibilities they have.

Chapter 5. "Fiscal stress and operating budget" evaluates operating budgets during fiscal stress and bankruptcy. The chapter characterizes and classifies changes in the operating budgeting process during fiscal stress and bankruptcy, including the main approaches to budget cuts. It explains the negative consequence of reducing expenditures for communities, economic development, and businesses. This chapter proposes the main strategies of restructuring operating budgets and exits from fiscal stress – such as emergent strategy, fiscal stress minimization strategy and the strategy of social budgeting – and budgeting strategies during more severe fiscal emergency and bankruptcy, such as austerity urbanism and pragmatic municipalism theories. We provide not only an analysis of budget cuts but also highlight fiscal stress minimization strategies and social-oriented operating budgeting during bankruptcy and fiscal stress in municipalities.

Chapter 6 "Fiscal Stress and Capital Infrastructure" introduces the reader to public capital management and the budgeting process during fiscal emergency and bankruptcy. The chapter depicts the current state, changes in public infrastructure conditions, public infrastructure needs, and capital financing issues during fiscal emergency and bankruptcy. The chapter reviews potential consequences of infrastructure inefficiency and includes recommendations for prioritization of capital projects, preventive maintenance, and administrative innovations during fiscal emergency and bankruptcy.

Chapter 7 "Fiscal Stress During the COVID-19 Pandemic" explores how the COVID-19 pandemic affected U.S. state and local governments and what their response to this fiscal stress has been so far. The chapter looks at financial losses in 2020 and their projection in 2021, major tax revenue decreases, cutback strategies used by local governments, and federal and state aid to municipalities.

The second half of the book includes six case studies of some interesting examples of bankruptcies and fiscal emergencies from around the United States and lessons learned from them. Of six cases, three are large central cities (Detroit, MI, Pittsburgh, PA, and Colorado Springs, CO), one is a medium-sized suburb (Vallejo, suburb of San Francisco, CA), one is a small city (Central Falls, suburb of Providence, RI), and the last case is a county (Jefferson County, AL). Of these six examples, four are bankruptcy cases (Detroit, MI; Vallejo, CA; Jefferson County, AL; and Central Falls, RI), one is an example of severe fiscal stress (Pittsburgh, PA), and one is a case of mild distress (Colorado Springs, CO). The case studies focus on causes of municipal bankruptcy, steps taken to exit the dire situations, and consequences of fiscal struggles.

The concluding chapter evaluates the case studies and analyzes the relationships between fiscal stress/bankruptcy practices and political, economic, and fiscal variables. The chapter summarizes the main causes of fiscal emergency situations in municipalities, the consequences of fiscal stress for communities, economic development, and businesses. This chapter proposes a tentative theory of fiscal stress behavior that includes three main strategies for restructuring and exiting from fiscal emergency situations and bankruptcy: the haphazard strategy, the emergency strategy, and the innovative strategy. The chapter also highlights administrative innovations in financial management and budgeting during bankruptcy and fiscal stress in considered municipalities.

References

Appleson, J., Parsons, E., & Haughwout, A. (2012). *The Untold Story of Municipal Bond Defaults*. New York City: Federal Research Bank of New York.

Bouker, J. (2008). *The DC Revitalization Act: History, Provisions, and Promises. Building the Best Capital City in the World A Report by DC Appleseed and Our Nation's Capital*. Retrieved November 15, 2020, from www.brookings.edu/wp-content/uploads/2016/07/appendix-1.pdf

City of Stockton (2021). *City News*. Retrieved August 9, 2021, from http://ww1.stocktonca.gov/

Gao, P., Lee, C., & Murphy, D. (2019). Municipal borrowing costs and state policies for distressed municipalities. *Journal of Financial Economics, 132*(2), 404–426.

Intergovernmental Cooperation Authority (2009). *A Summary Report of the Intergovernmental Cooperation Authority* (ICA) *and its Oversight Role with the City of Pittsburgh, 2004 to Present*. Philadelphia, PA: ICA.

Jeweler, R. (2007). *Municipal Reorganization: Chapter 9 of the US Bankruptcy Code*. Washington, D.C.: Congressional Research Service, Library of Congress.

Kelly, D. (2009). Desert Hot Springs is fighting for its life. *Los Angeles Times*, 25 August. Retrieved July 9, 2021, from www.latimes.com/archives/la-xpm-2009-aug-25-me-desert-hot-springs25-story.html

Kravchuk, R. (2021). *Municipal Budgets, Balance Sheets and Acute Fiscal Shock*. Presentation at the 2021 Annual Association for Budgeting and Financial Management. Washington, D.C.

Lisa, A. (2021). 40 cities that could be poised for a housing crisis. *Yahoo!Finance*, 13 March 2021. Retrieved December 9, 2021, from www.yahoo.com/now/40-cities-could-poised-housing-160000602.html

Moody's Investors Services (2017). *US municipal bond defaults and recoveries, 1970–2016*. Retrieved November 4, 2020, from www.moodys.com/researchdocumentcontentpage.aspx?docid=PBM_1059508

Ohio Auditor of State (2022). *Fiscal distress*. Retrieved July 12, 2022, from https://ohioauditor.gov/fiscal/LocalGovernmentFiscalDistress.pdf

PEW Charitable Trusts (2020). *State websites offer fiscal data on local governments*. Retrieved July 9, 2021, from www.PEWtrusts.org/en/research-and-analysis/articles/2020/10/20/state-websites-offer-fiscal-data-on-local-governments

Reuters (2012). *Stockton, California files for bankruptcy*, 28 June. Retrieved November 15, 2020, from www.reuters.com/article/us-stockton-bankruptcy/stockton-california-files-for-bankruptcy-idUSBRE85S05120120629

Reuters (2013a). *UPDATE 4-Court says city of Stockton, California may proceed with bankruptcy*. Retrieved July 9, 2021, from https://www.reuters.com/article/stockton-bankruptcy-idCNL2N0CO1AU20130402

Reuters (2013b). *CORRECTED-Another U.S. city mulls bankruptcy due to soaring wages and pensions*, 19 November. Retrieved July 9, 2021, from www.reuters.com/article/usa-municipality-hot-springs/corrected-another-u-s-city-mulls-bankruptcy-due-to-soaring-wages-and-pensions-idUSL2N0IY07420131119

Rivera, K. (2022). 'I would use the word terrifying'. Lessons learned 10 years later from Stockton's historic bankruptcy. *ABC10 NEWS*. June 28, 2022. Retrieved July 21, 2022, from https://www.abc10.com/article/news/local/stockton/stockton-bankruptcy-10-years-later/103-188125b5-ef3c-44e0-a523-c2ea77e74e81

U.S. Bureau of Labor Statistics (2021). *Local area unemployment statistics*. Retrieved July 9, 2021, from www.bls.gov/lau/

U.S. Census Bureau (2021). *Population*. Retrieved July 9, 2021, from www.census.gov/

U.S. Census of Governments (2017). *Census of governments*. Retrieved July 9, 2021, from www.census.gov/programs-surveys/cog.html

Van Tassel, D. D., & Grabowski, J. J. (1996). *The Encyclopedia of Cleveland History*. Bloomington, IN: Indiana University Press.

Yang, L. K., & Abbas, Y. (2020). General-purpose local government defaults: Type, trend, and impact. *Public Finance and Budgeting, 40*(4), 62–85.

2

MEASUREMENTS OF FISCAL HEALTH AND FISCAL HEALTH MONITORING SYSTEMS

Introduction

The art of government budgeting is a delicate balancing act between revenue and expenditures. Occasionally, even despite the best knowledge and craftsmanship, municipalities confront budget deficits when they lack sufficient revenue to cover expenses. Local governments often find ways to resolve temporary fiscal issues by, for example, borrowing money over the short term or postponing or cutting certain expenses. However, for some municipalities, budgetary challenges become more prolonged and serious, especially during economic downturns, such as the one caused by the COVID-19 pandemic. What is considered "healthy" for municipal finances, and how can one diagnose if a "runny nose" for a local government budget is a symptom of a simple "cold", "seasonal allergies", "flu", "COVID", "pneumonia", or even "cancer"? In this chapter we define fiscal health, offer a rather comprehensive diagnostic of municipal fiscal "illnesses", and discuss fiscal health monitoring systems adopted in some states.

Definitions

Let us start off by defining fiscal health. The most fundamental comprehension of *fiscal health* is the extent to which a local government generates more revenue than expenditures or needs to meet its ongoing obligations and provide services (Honadle et al., 2004). Others define fiscal health very similarly:

- "The ability of a government to balance its revenue-raising capacity and expenditure needs" (Ladd & Yinger, 1991). Ladd and Yinger (1991) further specify that "actual fiscal health" is the difference between "restricted

DOI: 10.4324/b23117-2

revenue capacity" that accounts for states' tax limitations and "actual expenditure needs"

- "The ability of government to meet its financial and service obligations" (Hendrick, 2004)
- "Government's ability to balance its financial obligations with its available revenue streams" (McDonald, 2019, pp. 83–84).

If the definition of fiscal health is quite straightforward, defining fiscal stress is more challenging as it has different meaning to different people (Campbell, 1970). The Advisory Commission on Intergovernmental Relations (ACIR) (ACIR, 1973), for example, highlights:

> To the residents of a city, a financial emergency may mean an increase in taxes or a curtailment of municipal services. To city employees, a financial crisis occurs if employees are laid off or pay raises are curtailed. To holders of a city's bonds, a financial crisis principal on its bonds. To members of civic organizations or minority groups in the community, a financial emergency occurs if there is a lack of funds to pay for urgently needed programs. And, finally, to city politicians, a financial emergency is any situation that generates voter concern at a level significant enough to affect the next election.
>
> *(p. 2)*

Figure 2.1 presents the stages in severity of fiscal challenges. The differences between fiscal (dis)stress situations can be very small, if there are any, but they basically diverge in depth and longevity.

Fiscal distress is a relatively mild fiscal disturbance, when a municipality cannot pay its bills by a due date, meet its payroll, balance its budget, or carry out essential public services for a short period. Fiscal distress situations are not reasons to panic but can result in major fiscal issues if not addressed quickly. Officials usually respond to fiscal distress with some combination of service cuts, worker layoffs, tax and fee increases, reserve spending, and borrowing.

Fiscal stress is a fiscal situation when a gap between projected revenue and expenditures is "short term, in the case of transitory economic shocks, or long term, in the case of structural budget imbalance" (CBO, 2010, p. 2). Such structural imbalance may arise from persistent economic shocks or other factors. The

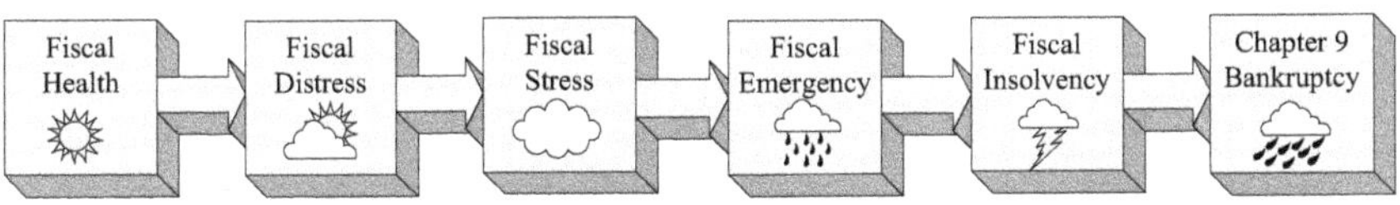

FIGURE 2.1 Fiscal Weather Monitoring System.

National Conference of State Legislatures (2010) provides the main reasons of the structural budget gaps: (1) ongoing revenue are insufficient to cover ongoing expenses; (2) "rising program costs coupled with revenue structures that do not often capture state economic growth" (p. 9).

Financial emergency, insolvency, or crisis is a fiscal situation when a municipality is: (1) unable to meet principal and/or interest payments on any of its debt obligations; (2) unable to pay any other financial obligations to employees, retirees, suppliers, banks, and other government agencies that are not represented by certificate of indebtedness; and (3) unable to provide services for its residents' needs.

ACIR (1973) defines fiscal emergency as the

> situations in which a city reaches the point at which it can no longer perform its existing levels of services because of inability to meet payrolls, pay current bills, pay amounts due to other government agencies, or pay debt service on bonds or maturing short-term notes because it lacks either cash or appropriations authority.
>
> *(p. 3)*

Overall, the following fiscal conditions may be a signal of fiscal emergency:

- "default on the principle or interest payment on bonded debt or other obligations
- failure for a specified time-period (two or more consecutive pay periods) to pay taxes and other contributions (such as those for social security)
- failure for a specified time-period to pay salaries or pensions
- a floating debt in the form of accounts payable and other unpaid obligations which after deduction of reserves for payment exceeds ten percent of the total appropriations of the last fiscal year".

(ACIR, 1973, p. 7)

ACIR (1973) defines fiscal emergency as:

1. an operating fund revenue-expenditure imbalance in which current expenditures significantly exceeded current revenue in one fiscal period
2. a consistent pattern of current expenditures exceeding current revenue by small amounts for several years
3. an excess of current operating liabilities over current assets (a fund deficit)
4. short-term operating loans outstanding at the conclusion of a fiscal year (or in some instances the borrowing of cash from restricted funds or an increase in unpaid bills in lieu of short-term operating loans)
5. a high and rising rate of property tax delinquency
6. a sudden substantial decrease in assessed values for unexpected reasons.

While fiscal emergency, crisis, or insolvency are often used interchangeably, we separate "insolvency" into its own category for the purposes of this research, as we consider insolvency as a more long-term fiscal emergency event. *Insolvency* is "a financial condition such that the municipality is (1) generally not paying its debts as they become due unless such debts are the subject of a bona fide dispute; or (2) unable to pay its debts as they become due" (11 U.S.C. §101(32)).

Chapter 9 is the worst and most terminal state in fiscal crisis. Only 12 states unconditionally authorize bankruptcies. Twenty-three states do not allow municipalities to apply for Chapter 9 bankruptcy protection at all and 15 states offer only conditional authorization (Moldogaziev et al., 2017). Bankruptcy proceedings allow struggling governments to restructure their debt, which provides protection from creditors by creating a plan between the municipality and its creditors to resolve the outstanding debt. Only municipalities may file for Chapter 9 bankruptcy (see Chapter 4 of this book for definition and details on municipal bankruptcies).

Measurements of Fiscal Health – Fiscal Ratios

There are no arguments about the definition of fiscal health; it is, nevertheless, an abstract term and there is still little agreement among researchers and policy makers on how to measure, forecast, or manage a state of financial decline (Jimenez, 2020; Levine et al., 2013; Gorina et al., 2018**a**; McDonald, 2019). Traditionally fiscal health has been measured through fiscal ratios (Gorina et al., 2018b; Gorina, Maher & Scorsone, 2019; Groves & Godsey, 1980; Groves et al., 2003; Hirsch & Rufolo, 1990; Kurtz, 2016; Maher, 2013; Maher & Deller, 2013; Maher, Oh & Liao, 2020; Mead, 2001; Leiser & Mills, 2019; Park, 2004; PEW Charitable Trusts, 2013; Public Policy Institute of California, 1998; Wassily, 1986; Watson et al., 2005). Later we study some of the more widely used metrics of fiscal health and emergencies developed by researchers and practitioners. While all these metrics have shortcomings, an overall review of them will help our reader understand what is available and what may be right for them.

ACIR made some of the first attempts to assess state and local finances and the relationship between them in a tool that became known as the Representative Revenue System (RRS) in 1962. RRS was periodically updated in 1971, 1979, 1981, 1988, and 1989. ACIR also produced an analysis of local bankruptcies and loan payment defaults from 1972 to 1983 (ACIR, 1979, 1981, 1985). ACIR reports identified several financial predictors of fiscal distress: operating expenditures exceeding revenue over time, current liabilities in excess of current assets, outstanding short-term loans, increases in property tax delinquency, decreased assessed valuation, and unfunded pension liabilities (ACIR, 1981, 1985, 1988, 1989). The system was eventually discontinued in 1996.

One of the important rating systems, the Financial Trends Monitoring System (FTMS) was created in 1980 by Groves and Godsey for the International

City/County Management Association (ICMA). In 2003, FTMS was updated by Nollenberger et al. It is comprised of 42 fiscal condition indicators. The FTMS is considered the most extensive and comprehensive source of municipal fiscal health assessment and includes most of the indicators found in the other condensed models (Brown, 1993; Chaney et al., 2002; Gao et al., 2019; Maher & Nollenberger, 2009; Wang et al., 2007). The FTMS monitors these indicators over five years and provides a dynamic rather than static approach to fiscal monitoring.

Groves et al. (1981) pioneered another popular assessment tool for local government fiscal health, the Financial Condition Index (FCI). The FCI contains four solvency measures, including cash, budgetary, long-term, and service-level solvency (Groves et al., 1981). We discuss the meaning and measures of solvency further in this chapter.

The ten-point test developed by Brown (1993) is still one of the highly discussed assessment tools in the literature. Brown suggested ten ratios, broadly classified into revenue, expenditure, operating position, and debt structure categories. The ratios were estimated for 167 cities with populations between 30 and 50 thousand people and 162 cities with populations between 50 and 100 thousand people and sorted by quartiles. The ratio in the lowest quartile received a score of 1 and in the highest quartile a 2. The higher the total number of upper quartiles, the higher the "health" score received by the city. Brown estimated lower and upper bounds for each quartile so that any city could easily compare themselves to their counterparts of similar population size. The estimates were, however, based on numbers from 1989 and are obsolete by now. We chose to discuss only the ratios (see Table 2.1) rather than their range as to not misguide our reader.

Kloha et al. (2005) developed their own ten-point fiscal assessment scale based on nine performance indicators: (1) population growth, (2) growth, or (3) decline in real property tax values; (4) the ratio between general fund expenditures and real property tax values in particular years; (5) the deficit or the difference between current general fund revenue and expenditures and (6) such deficit or difference over a certain number of years; (7) the size of general fund balance or reserves; (8) negative balances of general, special, capital, and debt service funds; and (9) the amount of long-term outstanding debt as a percentage of the local government's real property tax values. For every indicator that produced a negative result by the framework's standards, the authors assigned 1 point (2 points for indicator 6) to indicate the degree of fiscal distress. The closer the resulting number is to ten, the worse the fiscal situation is.

Wang et al. (2007) created a Financial Condition Index from 11 items measuring government-wide rather than just general fund information that included the cash, quick, current, and operating ratios, surplus per capita, net asset ratio, long-term liability ratio, long-term liabilities per capita, taxes per capita, revenue per capita, and expenditures per capita. Gorina et al. (2018a,b) found that the strongest predictors of fiscal distress were general fund balance as a percentage of expenditures, total debt as a percentage of revenue, and property taxes as a percentage of own-source revenue. Gorina et al. (2018**a**) used liquidity ratios, operating ratios, measures of longer-term obligations, measures of fiscal reserves, and government-wide measures of net assets and unrestricted net assets to develop a fiscal condition scoring system that can help predict financial emergencies.

There have been multiple other attempts to develop comprehensive measures of municipal fiscal health by think tanks and individual researchers like the U.S. Congressional Budget Office (2010), Aronson and King (1978), Ladd and Yinger (1991), McDonald (2019), Yang (2019), Yang and Abbas (2020), and others. The plethora of fiscal health assessment models is summarized by Gordon (2018) who provided a taxonomy of Municipal Fiscal Health Measures since the 1960s. Gordon distinguishes between the: (1) economic – fiscal capacity, indices of social, economic, and fiscal need; (2) fiscal and financial approach – liquidity, solvency, sustainability, diversification, capacity, and risk factors/ratios; (3) comprehensive approach – in addition to the first two includes assessment of political situation and general willingness to pay.

Some of the common financial indicators suggested by researchers to analyze fiscal health are reviewed in Table 2.1. The table by no means provides an exhaustive list of ratios, but it synthesizes some of the most important indicators suggested in the literature, many of which were mentioned previously.

Perhaps the most important fiscal health ratios are the assessments of organizations' solvency. *Solvency* is the ability of municipality to meet its medium- and long-term financial obligations, i.e. if revenue exceed liabilities. Similar to long-term solvency is the notion of *liquidity* or the ability to meet short-term obligations (often called short-term solvency). Solvency ratios include all government assets, whereas liquidity ratios focus only on cash and near-cash assets. Access to liquidity can play a crucial role, especially for unforeseen fiscal shocks caused by, for example, natural disasters. But keeping too much liquidity on hand is a double-edged sword because these assets could be invested in infrastructure needs, service provision, and other causes. Debt obligations, assets, and reserves' capacity are the other important factors to study to understand how healthy municipal finances are.

Depending on the needs and specifics of a municipality as well as available budgetary and financial information, the same ratios can be estimated for the total general government or for government and business-type activities separately (Johnson et al., 2012), only for the general fund revenue and expenses, for restricted use funds, for own-source tax and non-tax or intergovernmental revenue, and such. Many indicators are estimated in per capita terms (such as total taxes per capita, or total revenue per capita, or per capita total expenses) rather than ratios of one fiscal indicator to another.

It would be beneficial to not only know that the ratios should be positive or high (as specified in Table 2.1), but to indicate their actual magnitude. The reality is that such rules hardly exist. And, perhaps for a purpose. What looks good

TABLE 2.1 Fiscal Distress Indicators

Financial Indicators	*Definition*	*Magnitude*	*Formula*	*Study/Author*
I. Liquidity or Cash Solvency				
Government-wide cash ratio (most conservative)	The ability to generate sufficient revenue to meet payment obligations for 30 to 60 days	Between 0.5 and 1 is healthy If > 1 inefficient – too much cash on hand If < 0.5 not enough liquid assets	Government-wide cash and near cash assets/Government-wide current liabilities	Gorina et al. (2018a); McDonald, 2017; Clark, 2015; Stone et al., 2015; Nollenberger et al., 2003; Groves et al., 1981
Quick ratio	Financial indicator of short-term liquidity. Meaning there are sufficient cash and assets that can be turned into cash in a day or two to cover current liabilities	≥ is healthy < 1 may be issues with paying debts	(Cash + marketable securities + accounts receivable)/Current liabilities	Wang et al. (2007); Gordon (2018); Stone et al. (2015); Clark, 2015; Groves et al., 1981
Short-term liquidity or current ratio	Whether the government has the means available to cover its existing obligations in the short run	Between 1.5 and 3 is healthy ≤ 1 inefficient – liquidity problems ≥ 3 inefficient use of current assets	Current assets/Current liabilities	McDonald, 2017; Gorina et al. (2018**b**); Stone et al. (2015); Clark, 2015; Groves et al. 1981
II. Solvency or Leverage Ratios				
Operating/budgetary solvency ratio 1	Ability to generate sufficient revenue to provide desired level of service	High ratio	Government-wide revenue/Spending	Gorina et al. (2018**a**); Stone et al. (2015); Gorina and Maher (2016)
Operating ratio 2		High ratio	Governmental funds revenue/Spending	Gorina et al. (2018**a**)
Operating ratio 3		High ratio	General fund revenue/Spending	Gorina et al. (2018a)

Financial Indicators	*Definition*	*Magnitude*	*Formula*	*Study/Author*
Long-term solvency	The general and consistent ability to balance revenue and expenditures, meet future long-term debt obligations, such as pension obligations, and the capacity to deal with unforeseen fiscal challenges	High ratio	(Government-wide Net Assets – total government-wide liabilities)/ Government-wide expenditures	Gorina et al., 2018**b**; McDonald, 2017; Nollenberger et al., 2003
Operating position	Full cost of operating government. Expenses include paid and unpaid charges		Operating revenue/ Expenses	Johnson et al., 2012
Net revenue	Revenue available to satisfy liabilities	High ratio	Revenue/Liabilities	Brown (1993); Nollenberger et al. (2003); Wang et al. (2007); Maher (2009)
Own-source revenue ratio	Self-reliance	High ratio	Total general fund revenue from own sources/Total general fund revenue	Brown (1993)
General fund sources from other funds	Total general fund sources are the total of general fund revenue and operating transfers in	Low ratio	General fund sources from other funds/ Total general fund sources	Brown (1993)
Distance between current general fund revenue and expenditures	Deficit or the distance between current general fund revenue and expenditures	High ratio	(Current revenue – current expenditures)/ Current revenue	Kloha et al. (2005); Gordon (2018)

(Continued)

TABLE 2.1 (Continued)

Financial Indicators	*Definition*	*Magnitude*	*Formula*	*Study/Author*
Fiscal capacity	Revenue collections to revenue capacity	Close to 1.0	Revenue collections/ Revenue capacity	ACIR (1971)
Ratio of operating expenditures as % of total expenditures	Operating expenditures to total expenditures. Shows if infrastructure is adequately maintained	Low ratio	Operating expenditures/Total expenditures	Brown (1993)
Service solvency	Ability to deliver specific service like safety or health	High ratio	Program revenue/ Expenses	Johnson et al. (2012)
III. Relationship Among Assets, Expenditures, and Liabilities				
Net worth ratio	Restricted and unrestricted net assets as a share of total expenses	High ratio	Restricted and unrestricted net assets/Total expenses	Gordon (2018), Stone et al. (2015)
Continuing services ratio/financial Position	Unrestricted net assets as a share of total expenses	High ratio. Negative ratio means restricted assets are higher than total and government may shift part of the service expenses onto future generations.	Unrestricted net assets/ Total expenses	Gordon (2018), Johnson et al. (2012)
Return-on-assets ratio	Surplus (or deficit)/Total assets	Positive	Surplus (or deficit)/ Total assets	Gordon (2018)
IV. Debt Ratios				
Debt outstanding/ long-term solvency	Total value of debt outstanding/ Annual revenue	Low ratio	Total value of debt outstanding/Annual revenue	Trussel and Patrick (2009), Gorina and Maher (2016)

Financial Indicators	*Definition*	*Magnitude*	*Formula*	*Study/Author*
Debt service ratio 1	Debt service (interest + principal payments on debt)/Total expenses + principal	Low ratio	Debt service/Total expenditures + principal	Stone (2015)
Debt service ratio 2	Net direct debt service to total revenue	Low ratio	Net direct debt service/Total or GF revenue	Brown (1993); Gorina et al. (2018a)
Debt-to-asset ratio	Total debt divided by total assets	≤ 0.4	Total debt/total assets	Gordon (2018), Stone et al. (2015)
Longer-term obligations to government-wide revenue	Total long-term liabilities/Government-wide revenues	Low ratio	(Total long-term debt + pension obligations + other postemployment benefit estimates)/Government-wide revenue	Gorina et al. (2018**a**)
Short-term operating loans, bills	Failure to pay short-term operating loans	Low ratio	Borrowing from restricted funds + unpaid bills	ACIR (1973)
Long-term debt default	Default on payment of debt service	Zero	Default on payment of debt service	Act 47 (DCED, 1987)
Pension underfunding	Unfunded pension liability per capita	Low ratio	Unfunded pension liability/Population	Gordon (2018)

(Continued)

TABLE 2.1 (Continued)

Financial Indicators	*Definition*	*Magnitude*	*Formula*	*Study/Author*
V. Fiscal Reserves Ratios				
Fiscal reserves ratio 1	Total general fund balance as a share of general fund spending	High ratio	Total general fund balance/General fund spending	Gorina et al. (2018a)
Fiscal reserves ratio 2	General fund unreserved balance as a share of general fund spending	High ratio	General fund unreserved balance/ General fund spending	Gorina et al. (2018a)
Fiscal reserves ratio 3	Total governmental funds balance as a share of governmental fund spending	High ratio	Total governmental funds balance/ Governmental fund spending	Gorina et al. (2018a)
Fiscal reserves ratio 4	Governmental funds unreserved balance	High ratio	Governmental funds unreserved balance	Gorina et al. (2018a)

Source: Table created by authors

from the eyes of taxpayers (like lower taxes) may not be attractive in the eyes of creditors (ensuring a sufficient tax base to pay back the interest and principal on debt; Stone et al., 2015). The ratios may also differ given specific characteristics of the state or municipality itself. While understanding the causes and implications of the ratios' magnitudes are important, it is even more important to study trends over time to see if there are improvements.

A wide array of available ratios allows for evaluation of fiscal health from different angles, but they always have to be used carefully and thoughtfully. Stone et al. (2015) estimated a couple dozen ratios for the city of Detroit between 2002 and 2012, right before the city applied for Chapter 9 bankruptcy protection in 2013. Some ratios in the study confirmed a continuous decline, some pointed out a rapid deterioration right before the bankruptcy, and some (three out of four estimated liquidity ratios) did not show signs of distress at all. By engaging in this exercise, Stone and colleagues (2015) demonstrated how important it is to estimate multiple indicators to understand municipal fiscal health in its entirety. On a similar note, Clark (2015) used several approaches to evaluate validity and reliability of the FCI system discussed earlier. Specifically, he compared the FCI with the Ohio fiscal distress system and found a lot of inconsistencies between what the state considers unhealthy for local governments and FCI outcomes. Many of the most fiscally distressed cities rated quite well with the FCI system. The relationship between the FCI and socio-economic indicators was also determined to be weak, if any relationship is present at all. This being said, we reinstate that ratios should be used very cautiously and chosen carefully in assessments of municipal fiscal health.

Measurements of Fiscal Health – States' Actions

Local governments in most states are required to submit annual financial data to the states' auditors or other agencies. Thirty-eight states, excluding Alabama, Delaware, Hawaii, Idaho, Kentucky, Nevada, New Hampshire, New Mexico, North Dakota, Vermont, West Virginia, and Wyoming, have online platforms that collect financial reports, budgets, or other fiscal information on local governments (PEW, 2020). Of the states with online platforms, only three (Iowa, Maryland, and South Carolina) do not collect data on municipalities. Connecticut, Massachusetts, and Rhode Island do not collect county-level data. Seventeen states collect and publish similar information for special districts (visit PEW Charitable Trusts (2020) to access the links to state-sponsored websites with data on local government finances). While such centralized data collection provides a lot of transparency on local government finances, less than half of the states actually use this data to monitor the fiscal health of municipalities. Fiscal monitoring is, however, very beneficial as state governments have more resources and expertise to intervene with local government issues before the problems escalate.

Fiscal assessment ratios discussed in the previous section are widely applied in fiscal monitoring practices by many state and local governments. Some states (such as Colorado, Michigan, Ohio, and Pennsylvania, among others) implemented fiscal monitoring systems a while back, although their popularity grew widely already after the Great Recession of 2008–2009. According to PEW Charitable Trust (2016), 22 states (Colorado, Connecticut, Florida, Iowa, Kentucky, Louisiana, Maryland, Michigan, Minnesota, Nevada, New Hampshire, New Jersey, New Mexico, New York, North Carolina, Ohio, Oregon, Pennsylvania, Rhode Island, South Dakota, Tennessee, and Washington) currently have a formal system to monitor fiscal wellbeing. But, even among these states, the depth and extent of fiscal monitoring and state intervention diverges significantly. Only eight states (Louisiana, Nevada, New Jersey, North Carolina, Ohio, Pennsylvania, Rhode Island, and Tennessee) have both the laws that define fiscal stress and put early warning systems in place for local governments (PEW, 2016). Of these eight states Nevada is the only state without a public fiscal dashboard of municipal government finances (PEW, 2020).

States like Georgia, Minnesota, Missouri, and others collect financial reports from local government units, but this information is not systematically reviewed by the state's auditor or controller (like in Missouri), or even if they are reviewed (like in Minnesota) there are still no systems to recognize warning signs in place for local governments in these states.

In general, states identify municipalities as fiscally challenged if they default on interest or principal payments, delay payroll or pension contributions over certain period, or run a budget deficit among other conditions. We discuss states' fiscal monitoring practices of local governments now, and we cover states' intervention policies in Chapter 4 of this book.

After a series of municipal bankruptcies in ***California*** (Orange County bankruptcy in 1994, the cities of San Bernardino, Stockton, and Mammoth Lakes bankruptcies in 2012), the Treasurer of the State, Bill Lockyer, proposed an early fiscal warning system in 2012, similar to the New York model. The California State Auditor currently maintains the Local Government High-Risk Dashboard that presents debt, pensions, revenue, liquidity, population, and other data for California cities. The dashboard assigns points for every one of the following ten indicators:

- general fund reserves – up to 30 points
- debt burden – up to 15 points
- liquidity, pension obligations, and OPEB obligations – up to 10 points each
- revenue trends, pension funding, pension costs, future pension costs, and OPEB funding – up to 5 points each for a total of 100 points.

A score between 0 and 41.76 indicates a high probability of fiscal distress. A score between 41.77 and 71.23 is an indicator of moderate risk, and everything above 71.24 is considered a low risk of fiscal distress. The scoring card does not take into account any socio-economic or demographic indicators (California State Auditor, 2021).

Colorado developed the Fiscal Health Analysis Report system in 2013. The system estimates seven ratios, studies their three-year trends, and identifies the signs of concern. The state, however, does not have intervention programs for distressed municipalities.

- *Cash to Liabilities Ratio (CLR)*: shows cash position of the entity. When CLR = 1 there is exactly enough cash to pay for current liabilities. Continuous decline in CLR from one year to another or CLR < 1 for three years is a sign of cash flow problems or increased liabilities
- *Unrestricted Fund Balance*: the ratio of available fund balance and expenditures. It shows how long the entity can operate without new revenue. The recommended balance is two months of general fund expenditures or a ratio of 0.167. If the ratio declines for three consecutive years or goes below 0.167 from either increased expenditures or a decrease in fund balance, this may indicate distress
- *Debt Burden Ratio*: total revenue that supports debt payment, over debt payment. A ratio of 1 indicates that there are exactly sufficient revenue to cover current debt payments. A continuously declining ratio over the period of three years or a ratio below 1 are signs of distress since the municipality may not have sufficient revenue to pay debt
- *Tax Revenue per Capita*: shows the relationship between government revenue and population growth. A continuously declining ratio may be concerning as the government may not be collecting sufficient revenue to provide services to its residents.
- *Expenditures per Capita*: the ratio of expenditures to population are of concern if it continues to climb from one year to another and may indicate excessive government spending
- *Operating margin ratio*: the dollar amount added to government reserves when a municipality makes an additional one dollar in revenue. It is normal to have a negative ratio some years, for example, when large capital investments are made. But a negative or consistently declining ratio from one year to another indicates structural issues and, among other problems, can threaten a municipality's fiscal sustainability if long-term debt is used to pay for current expenditures
- *Enterprise fund net position*: looks at the health of enterprise funds (self-supporting government funds that account charges and fees from the sale of goods or services). The ratio is estimated by dividing the current and previous year's net position. A negative or continuously declining net position are signs of distress.

Every five years, the Office of Policy and Management (OPM) in ***Connecticut*** uses audited financial statements and data from different state agencies to estimate multiple "Municipal Fiscal Indicators" for every municipality in the state over the five-year period. These include financial, economic, tax, and demographic indicators, such as population, labor force, school enrollment, property tax revenue, intergovernmental revenue, total expenditures, annual debt service, total pension liability, and others. The indicators are estimated as totals, as averages, and in per capita terms but not as ratios of one indicator with respect to another. Municipalities are then ranked by many of these indicators.

Florida considers a local government or school district to be in an emergency if officials determine that state assistance will be needed to resolve or prevent a crisis (Florida Legislature, 2021; Florida Auditor General, 2021). Florida created an extensive monitoring system for local governments that requires a regular external financial audit, among other actions. Independent accountants evaluate the health of municipal finances based on 13 indicators: revenue and expenses, ability to raise cash to meet current needs, capacity to pay long-term debt, whether a city's tax structure can support its level of services over time, changes in outside revenue streams such as state aid, and whether the property tax rate is close to a state-imposed limit (Nollenberger et al., 2003). If the auditors determine that a city's financial condition is deteriorating, they are required to report this to city officials. The city administration, in turn, is required to convene this information to the governor and legislature if it meets one or more of the conditions needed for the governor to declare a financial emergency and offer state assistance (Spiotto et al., 2012; Spiotto, 2013). The conditions, spelled out in Florida statutes, include failure to pay short-term loans or debt service expenses because of the inability to cover a budget deficit (National Conference of State Legislatures, 2010). Florida's "Financial Emergency Guidelines" can be found at the state's auditor website.

The Department of Management in ***Iowa*** reviews all local budgets and the auditor's office examines some of them in-depth. But the state does not have any formal fiscal monitoring system beyond that and does not intervene in affairs of fiscally distressed municipalities (PEW, 2016).

The ***Louisiana*** Legislative Auditor (LLA) compiles a list of "Fiscally distressed municipalities". Municipalities are included in the list if they might be in danger of failing to provide basic services to residents or if they are delinquent on financial reporting with the state or the audit-performing certified public accountants (CPAs). A municipality is considered distressed if it has small or negative fund balances, loses utility operations, has cash flow problems, has unpaid obligations, or demonstrates other issues (Louisiana Legislative Auditor, 2021).

The Division of Local Services of the ***Massachusetts*** Department of Revenue operates a "Municipal Finance Trend Dashboard" for all cities and towns in the state. The dashboard currently depicts trends in fiscal indicators between 2018 and 2022, and the corresponding report allows for back-to-back comparison of indicators from 2017. The dashboard itself includes six categories of dashboards. The first category reflects on "Operating Position", including "trends in certified free cash, stabilization fund balances, overlay reserves, general fund unassigned fund balances, self-insured health insurance trust fund balances and uncollected real estate taxes" (Commonwealth of Massachusetts, 2021). Category two depicts trends in unfunded versus funded pension liabilities. The third category "Property Tax" includes "trends in average single-family tax bills, new growth, levies, tax rates, assessed values, excess and override capacity, Proposition 2½ ballot questions, and tax classification". Category four is for general and enterprise funds' revenue and expenditures. The category five dashboard is for socio-economic and demographic indicators, and category six is for "trends in outstanding debt, debt service, bond ratings, and authorized but unissued debt" (Commonwealth of Massachusetts, 2021).

In 2010, the Citizens Research Council of ***Michigan*** prepared a 74-page, in-depth study of the financial position of the city of Detroit, identifying many similar factors that have contributed to its declining financial position (Citizens Research Council of Michigan, 2010). Following the request from the state's Department of Treasury, Michigan State University researchers developed a set of nine measures the state uses to evaluate local governments' financial health, including population trends, increases and decreases in property tax value, general fund spending as a percentage of property tax value, budget deficits in current and two prior years, and long-term debt as a percentage of property tax value. Unsatisfactory performance on any given indicator receives 1 point, and preferable performance is assigned a score of 0. A municipality "distress" level that is 4 points or less is considered "fiscally neutral" and no state intervention is needed. If a locality receives 5 to 7 points it is placed on "fiscal watch", while considered at "fiscal stress" with 8 to 10 points. These ratios are the predecessors of what is now published in the Community Financial Dashboard.

The Michigan Department of Treasury maintains a "Community Financial Dashboard" where it depicts time trends (from 2010) of multiple fiscal health indicators for Michigan counties, cities, townships, and villages estimated from the local Annual Financial Reports (Michigan Division of Local Governments, 2021). The dashboard includes expenditure, revenue, pension liability, long-term debt, and multiple other trends (Michigan Department of Treasury, 2020, 2021). Municipalities are then ranked based on seven ratios. The higher the percentile, the stronger the position of the locality in a given ratio. The seven ratios are:

- *General Fund Health*: per capita total general fund balance
- *General Fund Ratio*: unrestricted general fund (savings account) balance over general fund revenue. Higher ratio indicates a better preparedness of the municipality to fiscal shocks
- *General Fund Cash Ratio*: general fund cash and cash equivalents over total current liabilities. Higher ratio indicates that municipality has money to pay short-term obligations
- *Pension Health*: per capita total unfunded pension liability
- *Property Tax Health*: per capita total taxable value

- *Debt Health*: per capita total debt
- *Government Net Position Ratio*: government net position over government fund revenue. This ratio indicates long-term solvency. The higher the ratio the more capable the municipality is to pay long-term obligations.

Nevada lists 27 conditions (Nevada Legislature, 2021) that the state weighs before determining if a local government is in "severe financial emergency", including (but not limited to) the following:

- Required financial reports have not been filed or are consistently late,
- The audit report reflects the unlawful expenditure of money,
- The audit report shows funds with deficit fund balances,
- Local government has incurred debt beyond its ability to repay,
- Local government has not corrected violations as noted in the audit report,
- Local government has a record of being late in its payments for services and supplies,
- Local government has had insufficient cash to meet required payroll payments in a timely manner,
- Local government has borrowed money or entered into long-term lease arrangements without following the provisions of the NRS or regulations,
- The governing body of the local government has failed to correct problems after it has been notified of such problems by the department,
- An employer in the county that accounts for more than fifteen percent of the employment in the county has closed or significantly reduced operations,
- Local government has experienced a cumulative decline of ten percent in population or assessed valuation for the past two years,
- The ending balance in the general fund of the local government has declined for the past two years or is less than four percent of the actual expenditures from the general fund of the local government for the immediately preceding fiscal year,
- The local government has failed to pay, in a timely manner, contributions to the Public Employees' Retirement System, workers' compensation or payroll taxes.

(Nevada Legislature, 2021)

The ***New York*** Comptroller established the "Fiscal Stress Monitoring System", in which cities and school districts share financial data throughout the year. Nine financial indicator categories are estimated based on such data, including (1) year-end fund balance, (2) total fund balance, (3) operating deficits, (4) cash ratio, (5) cash as a percentage of monthly expenditures, (6) short-term cash-flow debt issuance, (7) short-term cash-flow debt issuance trend, (8) personal services and employee benefits, and (9) debt service as a percentage of revenue. These indicators are then used to classify the levels of fiscal distress into significant (65–100 points), moderate (55–64.9 points), "nearing fiscal stress" (45–54.9 points), or no fiscal distress (less than 44.9 points). The Comptroller's office offers technical assistance such as early-stage budget planning to help the city or school district foresee problems, correct them, and try to avoid a deeper crisis (New York State Comptroller, 2021).

North Carolina is another state with a sophisticated financial tracking system. Local governments submit financial data extracted from state-mandated reports by independent auditors. The state's Local Government Commission is working with the U.S. Census Bureau to develop a financial profile of each city and county that is shared in a public database. North Carolina uses many of the same financial indicators as Florida.

An initial fiscal distress monitoring system was developed in ***Ohio*** in 1979 after an infamous default on debt obligations by the city of Cleveland (Ohio Auditor of State, 2020). Since 1996, the emergency protection has become available for townships and counties as well. In 2011 a "fiscal caution" designation was added to the fiscal distress list. The current system of Financial Health Indicators is aimed to help local officials better predict their communities' health and identify those that show signs of elevated fiscal stress (Table 2.2). Such indicators are routinely calculated for all local government units, and, if the financial situation deteriorates, municipalities are placed into one of three escalating categories: fiscal caution, fiscal watch, and fiscal emergency. The Auditor of the State also precisely stipulates the requirements to be met to exit every category.

The Audits Division of the Secretary of State's Office in ***Oregon*** collects independent audits of local government units, but the state itself rarely audits local financial statements.

In ***Pennsylvania*** the Department of Community and Economic Development (DCED) administers the Municipalities Financial Recovery Act, Act No. 47 (1987) (Pennsylvania Municipalities Financial Recovery Act, 2021). Under Act 47, DCED has a responsibility to assist Pennsylvania municipalities that are experiencing severe financial difficulties to ensure health, safety and welfare of their citizens. Act 47 defines 11 financial indicators of fiscal stress for local governments that, in general, include a 30-day or more delayed payroll, payments to the creditors, payment to the pension plan, a 1% or higher budget deficit each consecutive year over a three-year period, default on payment of interest or principal on municipal bonds, and other similar characteristics. The presence of any one of the eleven indicators is sufficient to define a municipality as "distressed".

Rhode Island provides state-sponsored fiscal oversight and administration if a municipality's credit rating falls below investment grade or if it runs a budget deficit (the state adopted a balanced budget requirement in 1981).

In ***South Dakota***, the Department of Legislative Audits conducts either full or limited internal control audits of local governments that are then published on the state's website.

TABLE 2.2 Financial Health Indicators in Ohio

Financial Indicators	*Calculation*	*Explanation of Indicator*	*Critical Outlook*	*Cautionary Outlook*
Unrestricted Net Assets/Position of Governmental Type Activities (GTA)	The difference between unrestricted government assets and liabilities	If an entity's unrestricted net assets/position is declining or negative, it leaves little or no room for unexpected expenses and is a sign of fiscal stress	Zero or negative	Decline between the current and prior year by more than 1%
Unassigned Fund Balance of the General Fund	Unassigned fund balance is the portion of fund balance that has no related liabilities	Identifies if fund balance is available for unrestricted purposes	Zero or negative	Decline between the current and prior year by more than 1%
Change in Unrestricted Net Assets/Position for GTA	Changes (increases or decreases) in unrestricted net assets/position from the prior year to the current	Identifies a trend of deteriorating unrestricted net assets/position, as well as how rapidly it is deteriorating	At least two of the three prior periods are at zero or negative or a rapidly declining trend defined as a decline in each of the last three periods with a 20% or higher drop	Declining trend defined as a decline in each of the last three periods with a drop of 10% to 20%
Change in General Fund Unassigned Fund Balance	Increases or decreases in unassigned fund balance from the prior year to the current year	Identifies a trend of a deteriorating unassigned fund balance, as well as how rapidly it is deteriorating	At least two of the three prior periods are at zero or negative or a rapidly declining trend defined as a decline in each of the last three periods with a 20% or higher drop	Declining trend defined as a decline in each of the last three periods with a drop of 10% to 20%

Financial Indicators	*Calculation*	*Explanation of Indicator*	*Critical Outlook*	*Cautionary Outlook*
Total General Fund (GF) Balance/GF Revenue	GF Balance/GF Revenue	Identifies reserves available in the General Fund	Negative very low percentage (< 4%) or if fund balance is less than a two-month carryover (17%), a rapidly declining trend defined as a drop of 10% or more over a three-year period	Low percentage (< 8%), a declining trend defined as a drop of 5%–10% over a three-year period
Decline in General Fund Property Tax Revenue	Percentage change from year to year for property tax revenue	Identifies declines in property tax revenue and is an indication that an entity may be facing financial hardship due to declines in significant revenue sources	If property tax revenue 7–20% of total General Fund revenue, a trend of declining tax revenue over the last three years exceeding 20% – or if property tax revenue is more than 20% of total revenue, a trend of declining tax revenue over the last 3 years exceeding 10%	Decrease in tax revenue from the current to the prior year by more than 1%
Decline in General Fund Tax Revenue	The percentage change from year to year for sales tax revenue for counties and income tax revenue for cities	Identifies declines in this revenue and is an indication that an entity may be facing financial hardship due to declines in significant revenue sources	If income or sales tax revenue represents 7–20% of total general fund revenue, a trend of declining tax revenue over a three-year period exceeding 20% or if income tax or sales tax revenue represents more than 20% of total general fund revenue, a trend of declining tax revenue over the last 3 years exceeding 10%	Decrease in tax revenue from the current to the prior year by more than 1%

(Continued)

TABLE 2.2 (Continued)

Financial Indicators	*Calculation*	*Explanation of Indicator*	*Critical Outlook*	*Cautionary Outlook*
Percentage of General Fund Revenue that Exceeds General Fund Expenditures	(Total general fund revenues – total general fund expenditures)/Total general fund revenues	Identifies shortage in current budget. A trend of operating deficits indicates potential financial hardships	Negative percentage	Low percentage (< 5%)
General Revenues of GTA/Net Expenses of GTA	General Revenues of GTA/ Net Expenses of GTA	This indicator determines if, on a government-wide basis, expenses are exceeding revenues	Ratio less than 100%	Declining trend of at least three years
General Fund Intergovernmental Revenues as a Percentage of Total General Fund Revenues	General Fund Intergovernmental Revenues/Total General Fund Revenues*100%	Reflects an over-reliance on intergovernmental revenues that are subject to state and federal budget cuts	Ratio greater than 20%	Ratio between 15–20%
Condition of Capital Assets	Accumulated depreciation as a percentage of depreciable capital assets	Identify situations in which repair or replacement of the local government's assets will be necessary	Ratio greater than 70%	Ratio between 50–70%
Percentage of the Budget Used/ Needed for Repayment of Debt	Debt Service Expenditures/ Total Revenues	High debt service expenditures to total revenues is unfavorable since the entity spends more of its current budget on debt payment	Ratio greater than 15%	Ratio between 12%–15%

Financial Indicators	*Calculation*	*Explanation of Indicator*	*Critical Outlook*	*Cautionary Outlook*
Average Daily Expenses or Expenditures Ratio 1	Unrestricted Net Assets/ Average Daily Expenses of GTA	The number of days the local government's unrestricted net assets/position can sustain the entity	Zero days or below	Fewer than 30 days
Average Daily Expenses or Expenditures Ratio 2	Unassigned General Fund Balance/Average Daily General Fund Expenditures	The number of days the local government's unassigned fund balance can sustain the entity	Zero days or below	Fewer than 30 days
Average Daily Expenses or Expenditures Ratio 3	General Fund Cash and Investments/Average Daily General Fund Expenditures	The number of days the local government's cash and investments can sustain the entity	Zero days or below	Fewer than 30 days

Source: Table is compiled by authors from Ohio Auditor of State (2020)

Tennessee takes fiscal monitoring and intervention very seriously and emphasizes the importance of early actions. The state's Comptroller audits local budgets and financial documents and estimates fiscal ratios to identify signs of distress.

In 2015, ***Washington*** State's Auditor's Office developed a Financial Intelligence Tool (FIT), an interactive open data portal that displays five fiscal health ratios for every locality in the state and their trends over time (Washington State Auditor's Office, 2016):

- *Cash Balance Sufficiency* is the number of days that the general fund balance can cover operating expenditures. It measures government ability to deal with fiscal emergencies and is recommended to be at minimum of 60 days
- *Operating Margin* is the difference between operating revenues and expenses divided by total revenues. If the ratio is positive, government activities are sustainable
- *Percent Change in Cash Position.* If the indicator is positive, liquidity position improved
- *Debt Load* is the ratio of debt to revenues. The Washington auditor's office guides municipalities to spend not more than 12% of revenue on debt payments
- *Enterprise Fund Self-Sufficiency* is the ratio of net enterprise fund income to total revenues. The ratio should be positive.

FIT was created to give an opportunity to local governments, especially smaller ones with fewer resources to self-monitor, but Washington does not have intervention policies.

Some financial monitoring triggers are unique to certain states; it would be helpful for all states to develop objective criteria that everyone could use to detect fiscal stress in municipalities.

Measurements of Fiscal Health – Credit Ratings

The attentive reader probably noticed that in Chapter 1 the fiscal situation in municipalities was assessed with credit ratings. When it came to actual measurement of fiscal health in Chapter 2, however, we have only discussed fiscal ratios so far, although we noted that Rhode Island, for instance, relies on credit ratings to distinguish healthy from distressed municipalities. While fiscal ratios provide internal assessment of fiscal health, credit ratings can also serve as determinants of city fiscal wellbeing, as they incorporate outside perception on the fiscal, economic, demographic, and political performance of local governments. Credit ratings are independent and informed judgements about an issuer's (in our case the bond issuer is a municipality) ability and willingness to pay principal and interest on debt on time and in full (Kriz, 2003). A high credit rating indicates a low probability of default, hence the high quality of an asset.

To pay for new roads, school buildings, ports, stadiums, and other capital projects, government entities can use current revenues or can borrow. To borrow, governments issue bonds – legal obligations to pay back the amount borrowed, the principal, and the accompanying interest rate. And, to borrow at lower rate, as we, individuals, are concerned about our own credit ratings, municipalities care about their credit ratings as well. With better credit ratings more borrowed money can be used for capital infrastructure projects and less to pay interest to investors,[1] which the public usually considers as a better use of taxpayers' dollars. Just like TransUnion, Experian, and other rating agencies use certain characteristics about our personal life and finances, such as the amount of credit card and other debt we have, credit usage, and payment history among other factors, to assign individual credit ratings, Moody's Investor Services (2017, 2021), Standard & Poor's (S&P's), Fitch and other smaller credit rating agencies, assign credit ratings to corporate and government issuers.

While the rating of corporate bonds is based on the risk of loss, the rating for government bonds is generally based on overall fiscal strength of the issuing municipality (Municipal Bond Fairness Act, 2008). In contrast to corporate bonds, new municipal bonds receive the rating of existing GO debt[2] or the issuer's credit rating. Rating agencies issue third party reputable views on the health of a municipality that are, at the same time, based on insiders' information that may not be available to investors or residents.

There are four general groups of factors that determine government credit ratings. In addition to fiscal ratios outlined before, credit rating agencies are concerned about overall health of the economy, demographical situation, and managerial performance. As discussed earlier, from the fiscal perspective, healthier municipalities in general have a lower debt burden, rely more heavily on their own source revenues rather than state or federal transfers, have fewer spending and revenue limits, and have a more diversified revenue portfolio. From an economic angle, lower unemployment rate and higher per capita personal income serve as indicators of a healthier economy and, therefore, a more stable tax base. Demographically, population size and growth serve as proxy for a strong tax base and indicate a healthier economy. From a credit ratings perspective, fiscal, economic, and demographic factors serve as indicators of a municipality's ability to pay debt (Appleson et al., 2012). Finally, political and general managerial factors such as corruption, margin of mayoral win, or even mayoral and city council party affiliation indicate political stability and may even serve as proxies for fiscal choices and ultimately show a municipality's willingness to pay debt.

Table 2.3 discusses some of the important indicators in more detail. While the table provides a general overview of factors that are considered important for fiscal health and better credit worthiness, it by no means provides a complete review of the literature on the topic. However, it is a good reference to understand what is important and what sources to consider if more information is needed.

TABLE 2.3 Indicators of Municipal Health

Indicators	*How They Measure Municipal Health*	*Direction of Effect*	*References*
Fiscal Factors			
Ratio of Debt Outstanding to General Revenue (or, to Personal Income)	Long-run risk of return on investment	Negative	Uyar & Escarraz, 1995; Depken & LaFountain, 2006; Krueger & Walker, 2008
Gross Debt Minus Debt Issued for or on Behalf of Other Agencies (Conduit Debt)	Net direct debt burden	Negative	Liu & Thakor, 1984; Marlowe, 2007
Unfunded Pension Liabilities	Long-run risk of return on investment	Negative	Benson & Marks, 2016
State Per Capita Tax Burden as a Percent of Per Capita Personal Income	Ability of the states to collect higher tax revenues to finance future debt and other expenses	Negative	Depken & LaFountain, 2006; Krueger & Walker, 2008
Own Source Revenues	Fiscal independence	Positive	Denison et al., 2007; Johnson & Kriz, 2005
Tax and Expenditure Limitations	Limitations on taxing or spending authority	Negative	Johnson & Kriz, 2002; Moldogaziev & Guzman, 2015; Maher et al., 2016
Revenue Diversification	Revenue stability	Positive	Yan, 2011
Economic Factors			
Unemployment Rate	Economic stress	Negative	Liu & Thakor, 1984, Johnson & Kriz, 2002, Johnson & Kriz, 2005, Depken & LaFountain, 2006, Krueger & Walker, 2008,
Per Capita Personal Income	Strength of the economy	Positive	Marlowe, 2007; and Krueger & Walker, 2008; Clark & Guzman, 2022; Guzman & Clark, 2022
Demographic Factors			
Population Growth	Demographic position	Positive	Liu & Thakor, 1984; Capeci, 1991; Marlowe, 2007
Population Size	Proxy for tax base or sophistication in capital market access		Marlowe, 2007; Palumbo & Zaporowski, 2012; Johnson et al., 2012; Guzman & Clark, 2022

TABLE 2.3 (Continued)

Indicators	*How They Measure Municipal Health*	*Direction of Effect*	*References*
Political Factors			
Divided Government	Increased competition between parties, lower commitment, or policy gridlock	Negative	Krueger & Walker, 2008; Jimenez, 2011
Margin of Win	Voter approval	Positive	Johnson & Kriz, 2005; Grizzle, 2010
Government Turnover	New administration may reconsider existing commitments or act to reward supporters	Negative	Krueger & Walker, 2008; Jimenez, 2011
Managerial Factors			
311 systems Implementation	Innovative nature of municipal practices	Positive	Clark & Guzman, 2022
Violent Crime Rate	How well a city is managed	Negative	Guzman & Clark, 2022

Conclusions

We started off this book by defining and measuring fiscal health of municipalities. The array of developed fiscal indicators provides all kinds of approaches for estimating different aspects of municipal fiscal health. But administrations worried about reelections are often accused of cherry-picking the indicators that make their municipalities look good. To illustrate how this is possible, one can refer to the Stone et al. (2015) study, for example, that estimated several key financial indicators for Detroit, MI over an 11-year period. Some of the indicators showed the worsening of economic conditions and even substantial changes right before bankruptcy, while others demonstrated no signs of deterioration.

When it comes to fiscal health, fiscal ratios undoubtedly play an important role in measuring financial wellbeing and offering warning signs when things don't go well. But fiscal ratios can, unfortunately, be manipulated and even if not, they alone provide a rather narrow view of municipal wellbeing. In addition to financial indicators, municipal health is shaped by such factors as how well a municipality is managed, the political situation, as well as demographic and economic conditions. Credit ratings incorporate all these other indicators and represent a third-party opinion rather than an internal assessment of fiscal health, which is an unbiased yet highly informed view since agencies are required to provide any internal information deemed necessary by credit rating agencies to form their opinion about credit worthiness. But some, especially smaller or really unhealthy municipalities, never apply and do not receive credit ratings. So, the usage of credit ratings in the assessment of fiscal health may be limited.

Notes

1 There are, of course, other factors that affect borrowing costs, such as certain bond issue features – issue size, the bond type (revenue, general obligation, or other), term of the bond (so-called term to maturity), call or put features (provisions that allow to buy or sell bond back to the issuer before it matures), whether the bond is taxable, and others; type of bond sale on a primary market (negotiated or competitive); bond insurance (so-called enhanced credit ratings); and multiple other factors (Moldogaziev et al., 2017; Moldogaziev and Guzman, 2015; Robbins and Simonsen (2007); Peng (2002)). But, issuers' (so-called "underlying") credit ratings remain one extremely important determinant of borrowing costs (Guzman and Moldogaziev, 2012; Johnson and Kriz, 2002, 2005; Peng and Brucato, 2004).

2 There are basically two types of bonds that governments issue: General Obligation (GO) and revenue bonds. The principal and interest on GO bonds (also called full faith and credit bonds) is paid out of general fund, while revenue bonds are repaid out of specific project revenues (such as revenues from ticket sales to pay for stadiums or parking fees to pay for meters or parking lots). While GO and revenue bonds are by far most preferred by government issuers, there are also tax-backed bonds (repaid from specific tax revenue, such as property tax), double-barrelled bonds (secured by both project and general fund revenues), and moral obligation bonds (secured typically by project revenue and issuers' moral obligation).

References

Advisory Commission on Intergovernmental Relations (ACIR) (1971). *Measuring the Fiscal Capacity and Effort of State and Local Areas*. Washington, D.C.: US Government Printing Office.

Advisory Commission on Intergovernmental Relations (ACIR) (1973). *City Financial Emergencies: The Intergovernmental Dimension*. Washington, D.C.: U.S. Government Printing Office.

Advisory Commission on Intergovernmental Relations (ACIR) (1979). *State-Local Finances in Recession and Inflation: An Economic Analysis*. Washington, D.C.: US Government Printing Office.

Advisory Commission on Intergovernmental Relations (ACIR) (1981). *Measuring Local Discretionary Authority*. Washington, D.C.: US Government Printing Office.

Advisory Commission on Intergovernmental Relations (ACIR) (1985). *Bankruptcies, Defaults, and Other Local Government Finance Emergencies*. Washington, D.C.: US Government Printing Office.

Advisory Commission on Intergovernmental Relations (ACIR) (1988). *Local Revenue Diversification: Local Income Taxes*. Washington, D.C.: US Government Printing Office.

Advisory Commission on Intergovernmental Relations (ACIR) (1989). *Local Revenue Diversification: Local Sales Taxes*. Washington, D.C.: US Government Printing Office.

Appleson, J., Parsons, E., & Haughwout, A. (2012). *The Untold Story of Municipal Bond Defaults*. New York City: Federal Research Bank of New York.

Aronson, J. R., & King, A. E. (1978). Is there a fiscal crisis outside of New York? *National Tax Journal, 31*(2), 135–155.

Benson, E. D., & Marks, B. R. (2016). Does the level of funding of city government pension liabilities affect tax-exempt bond insurance premiums and credit ratings? *Municipal Finance Journal*, *37*(1), 37–54.

Brown, K. W. (1993). Ten-point test of financial condition: Toward an easy-to-use assessment tool for small cities. *Government Finance Review*, *9*(6), 21–26.

California State Auditor (2021). *California state auditor's methodology for ranking California cities based on fiscal risk*. Retrieved November 15, 2020, from https://california-auditor.connect.socrata.com

Campbell, A. (1970). *The States and the Urban Crisis*. New York: Columbia University Press.

Capeci, J. (1991). Credit risk, credit ratings and municipal bond yields: A panel study. *National Tax Journal*, *44*(4), 41–56.

Chaney, B. A., Mead, D. M., & Schermann, K. R. (2002). The new governmental financial reporting model: What it means for analyzing government financial condition. *Journal of Government Financial Management*, *51*, 26–34.

Citizens Research Council of Michigan (2010). *The Fiscal Condition of the City of Detroit, Report 361*. Livonia, MI: Citizens Research Council of Michigan, April 2010.

Clark, B. (2015). Evaluating the validity and reliability of the financial condition index for local governments. *Public Budgeting & Finance*, *35*(2), 66–88.

Clark, B. Y., & Guzman, T. (2022). Is a more transparent, connected, and engaged city a smarter investment? A study of the relationship between 311 systems and credit ratings in American cities. *Government Information Quarterly*, Published online 9 July 2022, 101744, ISSN 0740-624X, https://doi.org/10.1016/j.giq.2022.101744.

Commonwealth of Massachusetts (2021). *Municipal finance trend dashboard key municipal fiscal health indicators*. Retrieved November 16, 2021, from www.mass.gov/service-details/municipal-finance-trend-dashboard

DCED (1987). *The municipalities financial recovery act, Act of 1987, P.L. 246, No. 47*. Retrieved December 10, 2021, from https://dced.pa.gov/local-government/act-47-financial-distress/

Denison, D. V., Yan, W., & Zhao, Z. (2007). Is management performance a factor in municipal bond credit ratings? The case of Texas school districts. *Public Budgeting & Finance*, *17*(1), 86–98.

Depken, C. A., & LaFountain, C. (2006). Fiscal consequences of public corruption: Empirical evidence from state bond ratings. *Public Choice*, *126*(1), 75–85.

Florida Auditor General (2021). *Financial Emergency Guidelines*. Retrieved July 9, 2021, from https://flauditor.gov/pages/pdf_files/financial%20emergency%20guidelines%20-%20lg.pdf

Florida Legislature (2021). *Florida statutes, Sec. 218.503, determination of financial emergency*. Retrieved July 9, 2021, from www.flsenate.gov/Laws/Statutes/2012/218.503.

Gao, P., Lee, C., & Murphy, D. (2019). Municipal borrowing costs and state policies for distressed municipalities. *Journal of Financial Economics*, *132*(2), 404–426.

Gordon, T. (2018). *Predicting Municipal Fiscal Distress: Aspiration or Reality?* Cambridge, MA: Lincoln Institute of Land Policy.

Gorina, E., Joffe, M., & Maher, C. (2018a). *Using Fiscal Ratios to Predict Local Fiscal Distress. Mercatus* [Working Paper]. Arlington, VA: Mercatus Center at George Mason University.

Gorina, E., & Maher, C. (2016). *Measuring and modeling determinants of fiscal stress in US municipalities*. 11/17/2016. Mercatus Working Paper, Retrieved July 11, 2021, from https://ssrn.com/abstract=3211662 or http://dx.doi.org/10.2139/ssrn.3211662

Gorina, E., Maher, C., & Joffe, M. (2018b). Local fiscal distress: Measurement and prediction. *Public Budgeting & Finance, 38*(1), 72–94
Gorina, E., Maher, C., & Scorsone, E. (2019). *How Can We Conceptualize and Measure Local Fiscal pressure?* ABFM Conference Presentation. Washington, D.C.
Groves, S. M., & Godsey, W. M. (1980). *Evaluating Local Government Financial Condition. International City Management Association.* New York: ICMA.
Groves, S. M., Godsey, W. M., & Schulman, M. (1981). Financial indicators for local government. *Public Budgeting and Finance, 1*(2), 5–19
Groves, S. M., Valente, M. G., & Schulman, M. (2003). *Evaluation Financial Condition: A Handbook for Local Government.* Washington, D.C.: International City/County Management Association.
Grizzle, C. (2010). The impact of budget stabilization funds on state general obligation bond ratings. *Public Budgeting and Finance, 30*(2), 95–111.
Guzman, T., & Clark, B. (2022). Crime and credit: The empirical study of how crime affects credit ratings of large U.S. cities. *Social Science Quarterly*, Forthcoming.
Guzman, T., & Moldogaziev, T. (2012). Which bonds are more expensive? The cost differentials by debt issue purpose and the method of sale: An empirical analysis. *Public Budgeting & Finance, 32*(3), 79–101.
Hendrick, R. (2004). Assessing and measuring the fiscal heath of local governments: Focus on Chicago suburban municipalities. *Urban Affairs Review, 40*(1), 78–114.
Hirsch, W. Z., & Rufolo, A. M. (1990). *Public Finance and Expenditure in a Federal System.* San Diego, CA: Harcourt Brace Jovanovich.
Honadle, B. W., Costa, J. M., & Cigler, B. A. (2004). *Fiscal Health for Local Governments: An Introduction to Concepts, Practical Analysis, and Strategies.* Boston, MA: Elsevier Academic Press.
Jimenez, B. S. (2011). Management quality and state bond ratings: Exploring the links between public management and fiscal outcomes. *International Journal of Public Administration, 34*(12), 783–799.
Jimenez, B. S. (2020). Municipal government form and budget outcomes: Political responsiveness, bureaucratic insulation, and the budgetary solvency of cities. *Journal of Public Administration Research and Theory, 30*(1), 161–177.
Johnson, C., Kioko, S., & Hildreth, B. (2012). Government-wide financial statements and credit risk. *Public Budgeting & Finance, 32*(1), 80–104.
Johnson, C. L., & Kriz, K. (2002). Impact of three credit ratings on interest rates of state GO bonds. *Municipal Finance Journal, 23*(1), 1–16.
Johnson, C. L., & Kriz, K. (2005). Fiscal institutions, credit ratings, and borrowing costs. *Public Budgeting & Finance, 25*(1), 84–103.
Kloha, P., Weissert, C. S., & Kleine, R. (2005). Developing and testing a composite model to predict local fiscal distress. *Public Administration Review, 65*(3), 313–323.
Kriz, K. A. (2003). Comparative costs of negotiated versus competitive bond sales: New evidence from state general obligation bonds. *The Quarterly Review of Economics and Finance, 43*(2), 191–211.
Krueger, S., & Walker, R. (2008). Divided government, political turnover, and state bond ratings. *Public Finance Review, 36*(3), 259–286.
Kurtz, L. (2016). Responses to local governmental fiscal distress: An analysis of municipal utilization of bankruptcy, asset monetization and debt financing. [PhD Dissertation, Pennsylvania State University].
Ladd, H., & Yinger, J. (1991). *America's Ailing Cities. Fiscal Health and the Design of Urban Policy*. Baltimore, MD: Johns Hopkins University Press, Charles Village.

Leiser, S., & Mills, S. (2019). Local government fiscal health: Comparing self-assessments to conventional measures. *Public Budgeting & Finance, 39*(3), 75–96.

Levine, H. C., Justice, J. B., & Scorsone, E. A., (Eds.). (2013). *Handbook of Local Government Fiscal Health*. Burlington, MA: Jones and Bartlett Learning.

Liu, P., & Thakor, A. (1984). Interest yields, credit ratings, and economic characteristics of state bonds: An empirical analysis. *Journal of Money, Credit, and Banking, 16*(3), 344–352.

Louisiana Legislative Auditor (2021). *Audit Reports*. Retrieved December 10, 2021, from https://lla.la.gov/reports-data/index.shtml

Maher, C. S. (2013). Measuring financial condition: An essential element of management during periods of fiscal stress. *The Journal of Government Financial Management, 62*(1), 20.

Maher, C. S., & Deller, S. C. (2013). Assessing the relationship between objective and subjective measures of fiscal condition using government-wide statements. *Public Budgeting & Finance, 33*(3), 115–136.

Maher, C. S., Deller, S. C., Stallmann, J. I., & Park, S. (2016). The impact of tax and expenditure limits on municipal credit ratings. *The American Review of Public Administration, 46*(5), 592–613.

Maher, C. S., & Nollenberger, K. (2009). Revisiting Kenneth Brown's "10-point test." *Government Finance Review, 25*(5), 61–66.

Maher, C. S., Oh, J. W., & Liao, W. J. (2020). Assessing fiscal distress in small county governments. *Journal of Public Budgeting, Accounting & Financial Management, 32*(4), 691–711.

Marlowe, J. (2007). Much ado about nothing? The size and credit quality implications of municipal other postemployment benefit liabilities. *Public Budgeting and Finance, 27* (2), 104–131.

McDonald, B. (2019). The Challenges and Implications of Fiscal Health. *South Carolina Journal of International Law and Business, 15*(2), 78–99.

McDonald III, B. (2017). *Measuring the Fiscal Health of Municipalities* (Working Paper WP17BM1). Cambridge, MA: Lincoln Institute of Land Policy.

Mead, D. M. (2001). *An Analyst's Guide to Government Financial Statements*. Norwalk, CT: Governmental Accounting Standards Board (GASB).

Michigan Department of Treasury (2020). *Fiscal health indicators*. Retrieved July 9, 2021, from www.michigan.gov/treasury/0,1607,7-121-1751_47023-171423--,00.html

Michigan Department of Treasury (2021). *MI community financial dashboard*. Retrieved from https://micommunityfinancials.michigan.gov/#!/dashboard/COUNTY/

Michigan Division of Local Governments (2021). *Municipal finance trend dashboard. Key municipal fiscal health indicators*. Retrieved December 10, 2021, from www.mass.gov/service-details/municipal-finance-trend-dashboard

Moldogaziev, T. T., & Guzman, T. (2015). Economic crises, economic structure, and state credit quality through-the-cycle. *Public Budgeting & Finance, 35*(4), 42–67.

Moldogaziev, T. T., Kioko, S. N., & Hildreth, W. B. (2017). Impact of bankruptcy eligibility requirements and statutory liens on borrowing costs. *Public Budgeting & Finance, 37*(4), 47–73.

Moody's Investors Services (2017). *US municipal bond defaults and recoveries, 1970–2016*. Retrieved November 4, 2020, from www.moodys.com/researchdocumentcontentpage.aspx?docid=PBM_1059508

Moody's Investor Services (2021). *Rating action press releases for the variety of years*. Retrieved July 9, 2021, from www.moodys.com

Municipal Bond Fairness Act. (2008). *Municipal bond fairness act September 9 2008*. Retrieved December 10, 2021 from https://frwebgate.access.gpo.gov/cgi-bin/getdoc.cgi?dbname=110_cong_reports&docid=f:hr835.110

National Conference of State Legislatures (2010). *State measures to balance FY 2010 budgets,* May 2010. Retrieved December 10, 2021, from www.ncsl.org/documents/fiscal/november2010sbu_free.pdf

Nevada Legislature (2021). *Nevada revised statutes, Chapter 354 – Local Financial Administration. Sec. 354.685, Severe financial emergency: Conditions.* Retrieved December 12, 2021, from www.leg.state.nv.us/NRS/NRS-354.html#NRS354Sec685

New York State Comptroller (2021). *Fiscal stress monitoring system.* Retrieved December 12, 2021, from https://wwe1.osc.state.ny.us/localgov/fiscalmonitoring/fsms.cfm

Nollenberger, K., Groves, S. M., & Valente, M. G. (2003). *Evaluating Financial Condition: A Handbook for Local Government.* Washington, D.C.: International City/County Management Association.

Ohio Auditor of State (2020). *Financial health indicators booklet,* pp. 12–18. Retrieved from www.ohioauditor.gov/FHI/fhi%20report%20descriptions.pdf

Palumbo, G., & Zaporowski, M. P. (2012). Determinants of municipal bond ratings for general-purpose governments: An empirical analysis. *Public Budgeting and Finance, 32*(2), 86–102.

Park, K. (2004). To file or not to file: The causes of municipal bankruptcy in the United States. *Journal of Public Budgeting, Accounting & Financial Management, 16*(2), 228–242.

Peng, J. (2002). Do investors look beyond insured triple – A rating? An analysis of standard & poor's underlying ratings. *Public Budgeting & Finance, 22*(3), 115–131.

Peng, J., & Brucato, P. Jr. (2004). An empirical analysis of market and institutional mechanisms for alleviating information asymmetry in the municipal bond market. *Journal of Economics & Finance, 28*(2), 226–238.

Pennsylvania Municipalities Financial Recovery Act (2021). Act of 1987, P.L. 246, No. 47. Retrieved July 9, 2021, from www.legis.state.pa.us/WU01/LI/LI/US/HTM/1987/0/0047.HTM

PEW Charitable Trusts (2013). *The state role in local government financial distress.* Retrieved July 9, 2021, from www.PEWtrusts.org/~/media/assets/2016/04/PEW_state_role_in_local_government_financial_distress.pdf

PEW Charitable Trusts (2016). *State Strategies to Detect Local Fiscal Distress.* Washington, D.C.: PEW Charitable Trusts.

PEW Charitable Trusts (2020). *State websites offer fiscal data on local governments.* Retrieved July 9, 2021, from www.PEWtrusts.org/en/research-and-analysis/articles/2020/10/20/state-websites-offer-fiscal-data-on-local-governments

Public Policy Institute of California (1998). *When government fails: The Orange county bankruptcy, a policy summary,* 18 March 1998. Retrieved July 9, 2021, from www.ppic.org/content/pubs/op/op_398op.pdf

Robbins, M. D., & Simonsen, B. (2007). Competition and selection in municipal bond sales: Evidence from Missouri. *Public Budgeting & Finance, 27*(2), 88–103.

Spiotto, J., Acker, A., & Appleby, L. (2012). *Municipalities in Distress? How States and Investors Deal With Local Government Financial Emergencies.* New York: Chapman & Cutler LLP.

Spiotto, J. E. (2013). The role of the state in supervising and assisting municipalities, especially in times of financial distress. Municipal Finance Journal, 33/34(4/1), 1–31.

Stone, S. B., Singla, A., Comeaux, J., & Kirschner, C. (2015). A comparison of financial indicators: The case of detroit. *Public Budgeting and Finance, 35*(4), 90–111.

Trussel, J. M., & Patrick, P. A. (2009). A predictive model of fiscal distress in local governments. *Journal of Public Budgeting, Accounting & Financial Management, 21*(4), 16–28.

U.S. Congressional Budget Office (2010). *Fiscal stress faced by local governments*. Retrieved December 10, 2021, from www.cbo.gov/sites/default/files/111th-congress-2009-2010/reports/12-09-municipalitiesbrief.pdf

Uyar, B., & Escarraz, D. (1995). Rank order analysis of state general obligation bond ratings. *Journal of Economics and Finance, 19*(2), 91–105.

Wang, X., Dennis, L., & Tu, Y. S. (2007). Measuring financial condition: A study of U.S. states, *Public Budgeting and Finance*, *27*(2), 1–21.

Washington State Auditor's Office (2016). *2016 NSAA Awards Program: Outstanding Special Project Award*. Seattle, WA: Local Government Performance Center.

Wassily, L. (1986). *Input Output Economics*. New York: Oxford University Press.

Watson, D. J., Handley, D., & Hassett, W. (2005). Financial distress and municipal bankruptcy: The case of Prichard, AL. *Journal of Public Budgeting and Financial Management*, *17*(1), 129–50.

Yan, W. (2011). The interactive effect of revenue diversification and economic base on US local government revenue stability. *Public Money & Management*, *31*(6), 419–426.

Yang, L. (2019). Not all state authorizations for municipal bankruptcy are equal: Impact on state borrowing costs. *National Tax Journal*, *72*(2), 435–464.

Yang, L. K., & Abbas, Y. (2020). General-purpose local government defaults: Type, trend, and impact. *Public Finance and Budgeting*, *40*(4), 62–85.

3

PREVENTATIVE TREATMENT AND FEDERAL, STATE, AND LOCAL INCENTIVES FOR UNHEALTHY MUNICIPALITIES

Introduction

We spent a lot of time and attention in Chapter 2 on defining fiscal health and diagnostics of fiscal illnesses. In Chapter 3 we talk about preventative medicine. At the end of the day, maintaining fiscal wellbeing is the most reliable and cost-efficient way to ensure municipal health, because even a seemingly insignificant illness may become chronic and highly devastating if not addressed on time. If the municipality is nevertheless getting financially sick, we introduce our reader to various treatments and therapies available for these municipal illnesses. In this chapter we discuss federal and state incentives available for distressed municipalities and actions that localities can take themselves to exit a financial crisis. An additional overview of available programs can be found in Bartik (2017), Francis and Randell (2017), Mallah (2017), Rappa (2017), PEW Charitable Trusts (2013), Coe (2008), Maher and Deller (2007), Kloha et al. (2005), Honadle (2003), and other sources.

Federal programs usually come in the form of grants or tax preferences, targeting economically disadvantaged areas or individuals. State assistance for distressed municipalities can be a lot more versatile and include legal (such as tax and/or expenditure limits, balanced budget requirements, debt ceilings, reserve requirements, or limitations on municipal investment decisions), educational, or administrative support (when states provide fiscal monitoring, appoint a fiscal controller, offer grants or tax incentives to municipalities, etc.).

States' intervention programs vary based on the fiscal distress conditions they address. Mallach (2017) classifies states' intervention programs by intended outcomes, programs that: (1) increase economic competitiveness, (2) strengthen housing markets, (3) improve quality of life, (4) develop human capital, and (5)

DOI: 10.4324/b23117-3

improve capacity to fund and deliver services. Francis and Randell (2017) suggest that investment in economic development falls into three categories: (1) investment in marketplace (general business support and financial assistance, small-business procurement programs, and tax incentives), (2) workforce development (developing and training the local labor force), and (3) investment in community (investment in public goods).

Ensurance of Municipal Fiscal Health

Before we begin a conversation about available treatments, it is important to understand how to maintain fiscal health and prevent fiscal illnesses in the first place. Kravchuk (2021) emphasizes that the best way to prepare for fiscal shocks is to "strengthen balance sheets under normal operating conditions" (p. 18). Accounting and financial reporting practices established by the Government Accounting Standards Board (GASB), the Government Finance Officers Association (GFOA), and other organizations serve as a primary guide to good financial practices for local governments. State governments play an exceptionally important role in ensuring the fiscal health of their local governments by providing technical advice and training to local governments and institutionalizing certain requirements that municipalities should adhere to.

The prohibition of running a budget deficit or over-relying on debt are two examples of such state-imposed constraints on local governments. All states besides Vermont are required to balance their budgets (municipalities are legally not allowed to carry on a deficit from one year into another). But even Vermont, despite not legalizing a *balanced budget requirement (BBR)*, does not carry out the deficit from one year to another (NASBO, 2021). Forty states have policies that *limit the amount of debt* that can be issued (NASBO, 2021). In Michigan, debt issuance must additionally be approved by vote. 27 states publish debt affordability documents. Some of these 27 states do not have legislative debt caps, so the debt limitations have more of an advisory than legislative nature (Alaska, California, Kentucky, Minnesota, Mississippi, New Mexico, North Carolina, Oklahoma, Oregon, and South Dakota). Twenty-nine states have policies that limit debt service.

While often extremely painful, in the short-term balanced budget requirements and debt limitations can alleviate and even prevent future fiscal distress. If a municipality is simply legally not allowed to run a deficit or issue new debt, a small fiscal distress can be solved by cutting current expenses, redistributing funds, or raising additional revenues (usually not tax revenues such as fees and charges for services). Besides legal limitations, budget deficit and excessive debt burden are viewed negatively by creditors, residents, and other interested parties. Unfortunately, financially strained governments sometimes rely on miscellaneous "tricks" to balance budgets artificially, such as overly optimistic revenue forecasts or misclassification of certain operating expenses into capital, among others.

Some government entities establish an independent fiscal authority to issue bonds (and run certain operations) on their behalf to overcome debt limitations or issue Certificates of Participation (COPs) or warrants, instead of bonds, that do not require voters' approval for debt issuance.

Another important constructive practice is the creation of budget stabilization, also known as *"rainy-day" funds*, *natural disaster funds*, or any other *stabilization funds* that may be useful based on a municipality's geographical location, access to natural resources, and current socio-economic conditions. Positive general (or other) fund balances can play the same role as rainy-day funds and are sometimes even more preferred by municipalities because undedicated funds are easier to access and spend when there is a need (access to rainy-day funds is usually restricted by legislative action and other requirements that limit expenditures to prevent unnecessary spending). Such funds are basically savings accounts where the government puts aside money in better financial times for potential future breakdowns (see Chapter 5 for further discussion of countercyclical and multi-year budgeting). While there is no uniform agreement on the size of rainy-day funds, it is suggested that such budget stabilization funds have enough cash to provide the same level of services for several months. On a state level, the minimum and maximum size of rainy-day funds is set up by a constitutional and/or statutory requirement and is tied most often to the current or previous year's general fund revenues or appropriations (NASBO, 2021).

Another advisable practice to help create a stronger fiscal environment for a municipality is a *diversified revenue structure*. Just like personal investment advisors suggest diversifying individual portfolios, governments should diversify their revenue portfolios as well, to include a healthy mix of different tax and non-tax revenues. This is often a difficult task for local governments that tend to rely heavily on a single tax revenue, usually property tax. Tax and non-tax revenues have different elasticities, meaning that some of them are very sensitive to changes in economic activity (elastic taxes, such as personal and corporate income taxes), and other taxes are inelastic and their revenues do not change substantively with fluctuations in the economy, such as many excises or property taxes. Income tax revenues, for example, tend to significantly increase during economic recoveries when the tax base (the number of employed, per capita income, and corporate profits) increases, and they go down during economic recessions when the tax base shrinks. Many excise tax revenues (alcohol, tobacco, gasoline, and others) and property tax revenues, on the other hand, remain inelastic as people continue to buy certain products despite economic changes and cannot easily sell their properties, even if they are unemployed and their household income is down (widespread foreclosures during Great Recession of 2008–2009 potentially made property tax revenues more elastic during that time frame). It is advisable for municipalities whenever possible (this possibility is often restricted by state tax limitations) to diversify their revenues to include a healthy mix of elastic revenue sources that can generate additional funds when the economy is in better shape (and save some of these surpluses in rainy-day funds) and inelastic tax and non-tax revenues that can provide stability during recessions.

Similar to the idea of diversified revenue portfolio is the advice to *diversify municipal economy* in general. It is sometimes a hard task especially for smaller cities that often rely heavily on one or two big businesses that pay the majority of taxes and employ most people in the town. If such businesses depart or simply downsize, it may have a devastating effect on local government finances.

The introduction of *performance* measures into budgeting practices can be another input to strengthen government financial performance. While there is a body of literature that argues that performance, even if measured, is not appropriately utilized in decision-making and even worse is used to sugarcoat government reports and redirect funds (Bischoff & Blaeschke, 2016; Montesinos et al., 2013), there are multiple studies that, on the other hand, find performance budgeting to be a quite useful tool in ensuring municipal fiscal health. Performance budgeting is believed to increase transparency – hence accountability and control of public entities – and improve response to constituents' needs. Availability of performance data may provide tools for comparison between public organizations, which may help further improve performance (Mizrahi & Minchuk, 2020; Nielsen & Moynihan, 2017; Moynihan, 2006). The use of performance budgeting may lead to better resource allocations and cost savings (De Jong & Ho, 2019; Ho, 2018).

Some suggestible practices stay somewhat separate from the accounting, financial, or budgeting realms but may, nevertheless, play an important role in strengthening city finances by providing cost savings or creating favorable revenue-generating environment.

For example, the introduction of so-called *smart city technological innovations* – such as smart streetlights, smart sensors, 311 systems (phone and web-based technologies used for non-emergency requests and information inquiries, such as reporting potholes, graffiti, or dead animals or requesting information about city buses or the garbage pick-up schedule), and other technologies – is another option for municipalities to consider. While smart city innovations require initial investments, they are usually connected to important services or infrastructure needs (Nam & Pardo, 2011, p. 286) and, once implemented, provide cost efficiency and lead to a more effective, transparent, and collaborative government (Nam & Pardo, 2014; Puron-Cid et al., 2019). Availability of web- or mobile-based 311 systems in cities and the length of time since their adoption are found to be positively related to the cities' credit ratings (Clark & Guzman, 2022) but are not known to affect the budget allocations of departments that use 311 systems (such departments do not spend more or less after implementation of 311 systems) (Clark & Guzman, 2017).

Public-private partnerships and *cooperation between different government units* may serve as great tools to share – and, hence, cut – costs of providing government services. Multiple examples of such partnerships and the roles they played in recovery of fiscally stressed municipalities are discussed in the case studies in chapters 9–14 of this book.

Other important preventative practices are *economic development programs* aimed at attracting and retaining businesses and individuals in the area. One of the crucial elements of such programs is the tax incentives offered by federal, state, and local governments.

Federal, State, and Local Tax Incentives

There are many economic development tax incentives that governments use. The list of such tax preferences discussed in this chapter is by no means comprehensive. There are literally thousands of grants and tax incentive programs offered by federal, state, and local governments as well as philanthropy and corporations for income security, job training, transportation, social services, community development, and other purposes. These programs target specific people or locations or both. New ideas and incentives are created on a regular basis, and the older ones are not used anymore. It is simply not feasible to describe all programs, but we aim at discussing what we consider more popular and perhaps more successful tax preferences used by local governments.

It should be emphasized that any incentives should be used cautiously. Every tax incentive means forgone tax revenues for municipalities, and the benefits from using them in attracting businesses, elevating poverty, urban revitalization, improving fiscal health, and other intended outcomes are often trivial. Tax incentives are frequently coupled with direct subsidies (to attract certain companies in the neighborhood or provide infrastructure needs for them), which further increases expenditures for the granting municipality (Scally et al., 2018). The competitive edge and, consequently, the effectiveness of tax incentives may also be lower if neighboring, especially wealthier, communities also rely extensively on such incentives.

Many tax preferences target only blighted areas, such as opportunity zones, New Markets Tax Credits (NMTC), tax increment financing (TIF) districts, renaissance and enterprise zones, and multiple others. Other tax preferences, such as property tax abatements, historic preservation tax credits, Job Creation Tax Credits, and others are aimed at attracting and retaining businesses and residents, overall economic development projects, preserving historical structures, or other purposes. These tax preferences are available to anyone and do not target blighted areas specifically, but they might be more beneficial and, perhaps, utilized more heavily in declining areas.

Table 3.1 provides classification of some of the more popular and relevant tax incentives, and we discuss these and other preferences in details later.

Federal Incentives for Local Governments

By some estimates, a total of 1,616 federal grants were available for state and local governments in 2018 (Congressional Research Service, 2019). Websites like sam.gov or grants.gov provide descriptions of federal assistance programs for state and

TABLE 3.1 Types of Tax Incentives

	Income Tax	*Property Tax*	*Capital Gains Tax*	*Any Tax*	*Other Incentives*
Federal Incentives					
Opportunity Zones			✓		
New Markets Tax Credit (NMTC)	✓				
Low-Income Housing Tax Credit (LIHTC)	✓				
Hardest Hit Fund					✓
Rebuilding American Infrastructure with Sustainability and Equity (RAISE) Grant					✓
Federal and State[1]					
Brownfield Tax Preferences	✓			✓	
Historic Preservation Tax Credit	✓			✓	
Low-income Housing Tax Credit					
State and Local					
Tax Increment Financing		✓			
Business Improvement District		✓			
Enterprise Zone				✓	✓
Renaissance Zone				✓	
Industrial Development Bonds (IDBs)		✓			✓
Community Redevelopment/ Reinvestment Areas		✓			
Tax Exemptions or Abatements for Industrial Facilities, Commercial Facilities, Personal Property, etc.		✓			
Limitations on Tax Rates, Levies, or Assessed Values		✓			
Vertical Housing Program		✓			

Source: Table created by authors

local governments. In addition to grants, the federal government offered hundreds of tax incentives to individuals and businesses to support community revitalization and economic development initiatives. The Federal Office of Management and Budgeting (OMB) publishes a description of all federal tax preferences in the "Tax Expenditure" section of "Analytical Perspectives" www.whitehouse.gov/omb/analytical-perspectives/ U.S. Department of Treasury reprints OMB Tax Expenditure reports: https://home.treasury.gov/policy-issues/tax-policy/tax-expenditures On the legislative side, similar "Tax Expenditure" reports with description of all federal tax incentives are prepared by the Joint Committee on taxation of U.S. Congress: www.jct.gov/publications/?category_name=Tax+Expenditures.

While the intent of every federal tax incentive and grant program is to benefit local communities in one way or another, the uptake on these programs might be low, especially among financially deprived local governments that would otherwise benefit from such federal assistance programs first and foremost. Unfortunately, financially struggling municipalities may not know about available opportunities in the first place, and even if they do they often simply do not have the financial, administrative, or legal capacity to take advantage of such programs.

Some of the common federal incentives for local governments are discussed next.

Empowerment Zone (EZ), Enterprise Community (EC), and Renewal Community (RC) Initiatives provide federal tax credits and deductions, grants, bonding authority, and other benefits to economically distressed and rural communities.

Opportunity Zones (OZ) is the federal capital gains tax advantage program that allows deferring and even lowering federal capital gains tax liability when funds are invested in low-income communities designated as Opportunity Zones. This program was created in 2017 by the Tax Cuts and Jobs Act. In total, 8,764 census tracts in the U.S. were designated as Opportunity Zones (Guzman & Lefebre, 2020).

New Markets Tax Credit (NMTC): Similar to Opportunity Zones, the NMTC program offers a federal income tax credit toward investments in communities with a poverty rate of at least 20 percent. The program was created in 2000 and is set to expire in 2021.

The ***Low-Income Housing Tax Credit (LIHTC)*** program offers a nonrefundable income tax credit for acquisition and rehabilitation or construction of new, affordable rental properties for lower-income residents. The credit can be claimed beginning from the year the property becomes available for renters and up to ten years in future. The LIHTC program is administered by the IRS through State Housing Finance Authorities (Stamm & LaJoiemore, 2020). Under this program, private investors receive a federal income tax credit as an incentive to make equity investments in affordable rental housing. The LIHTC program offers enhanced benefits in two types of geographical areas: Qualified Census Tracts (QCTs) and Difficult Development Areas (DDAs). QCTs are census tracts that have high poverty rates or many residents with incomes below the regional median. DDAs tracts are the areas where construction costs are high relative to median incomes, which can make housing expensive for many residents. The federal government identifies QCTs and DDAs. States have the discretion to determine the extent to which they prioritize those areas when allocating credits and can also supplement the QCTs and DDAs with additional geographic targeting. In addition, many states have also created their own affordable housing tax credits programs that "generally piggyback on the federal credit, offering additional state tax breaks to projects that qualify for the federal program" (PEW Charitable Trusts, 2021, p. 16).

Brownfield Tax Preferences can be granted by federal, state, and local governments. At the federal level the program allows for income tax deductions of hazardous brownfields' cleanup expenses. On the state level, the preference is usually offered in the form of a tax credit that can be claimed toward different taxes as specified by the granting state (Bartik & Erickcek, 2014). The brownfield tax preferences can be claimed during the year the qualifying expenses occurred.

Michigan, for example, provides Brownfield Redevelopment TIFs (read about TIFs below) and Michigan Business Tax (MBT) credits for projects that redevelop a contaminated, blighted, or functionally obsolete property on a case-by-case basis (Michigan Economic Development Corporation, 2008). Credits are available for up to 10 percent of eligible investments but cannot exceed 30 million dollars. Projects with total credits greater than one million dollars require approval by the Michigan Economic Growth Authority (MEGA) Board.

The ***Historic Preservation Tax Credit (HPTC)*** program offers a tax credit toward rehabilitation of historic buildings. The federal program has existed since 1976 and currently allows investors in historic buildings to claim a federal income tax credit for 20 percent of qualified rehabilitation expenditures. Several states, including Alabama, California, Colorado, Iowa, Michigan, Missouri, New York, Ohio, Oklahoma, Pennsylvania, Rhode Island, Virginia, Wisconsin, and others administer additional generous HPTC programs that can be combined with federal benefits. The Ohio HPTC, for example, offers an additional 25 percent credit that can be claimed toward any state tax liability and, combined with the federal HPTC, provides a 45 percent tax credit for rehabilitation of historic buildings (Guzman, 2018, Lendel et al., 2015).

The ***Hardest Hit Fund (HHF)*** established in 2010 by President Obama provides funding to the states' Housing Finance Agencies (HFAs) for mortgage and down payment assistance and other relevant activities for homeowners. For municipalities, the fund provides financing for blight elimination. The funding opportunities vary by state.

Rebuilding American Infrastructure with Sustainability and Equity (RAISE) is a brand-new discretionary merit-based grant program established by President Biden's administration in 2021. It is a successor of President Obama's administration the Transportation Investment Generating Economic Recovery (TIGER) program. RAISE provides grants to local governments for investments in rail, roads and highways, bridges, transit, and port projects with substantial local or regional impact. The program among other areas targets rural communities and Areas of Persistent Poverty and Historically Disadvantaged Communities.

State and Local Incentives for Local Governments

Such tax incentives are typically enabled by a state but administered locally. Most of them offer some sort of property tax relief, which is exclusively local tax in most (but not all) states. Incentives have grown enormously over the past 25 years. Most of the increase occurred from 1990 to 2001. Tennessee, New Jersey, Wisconsin, and Minnesota substantively expanded their incentive programs between 2007 and 2015. Business incentives today average over 30 percent of state and local business taxes (W.E. Upjohn Institute for Employment Research, 2021). The W.E. Upjohn Institute for Employment Research created a new database with information on state and local business taxes and economic development incentives. According to Bartik (2017), of all states in 2015, on average the largest incentive program was the Job Creation Tax Credit (JCTCs), which accounted for 44.9 percent of total incentive costs. The second-largest tax expenditure[2] (27.4 percent) came from property tax abatements. Solar Investment Tax Credit (ITCs), R&D tax credits, and customized job training jointly constituted about one-quarter of incentive costs (p. 89).

As of 2015, New Mexico, New York, and Louisiana's use of incentives added up to over 3 percent of value added. Tax incentives in Tennessee, New Jersey, Indiana, Iowa, Nebraska, South Carolina, Kentucky, and Michigan were over 2 percent of value-added or over 2,000 dollars per worker. Washington State, Nevada, Virginia, Maryland, and California provide only small incentives (W.E. Upjohn Institute for Employment Research, 2021). The incentives are lower for firms offering higher wages and higher for low-wage firms in 12 states, including Virginia, New Jersey, Massachusetts, Maryland, California, Texas, Michigan, Nevada, Minnesota, Wisconsin, Georgia, and the District of Columbia (W.E. Upjohn Institute for Employment Research, 2021).

Next we discuss major state and local incentives individually.

Tax Increment Financing (TIF): When TIF is established, the taxing jurisdiction continues to collect the property tax within the TIF area, but the tax is imposed only on the base existing at the time of TIF creation. The tax on any increments of the base property value is then reinvested in a TIF district – usually in infrastructure improvements – which is supposed to promote economic development in the area. A typical TIF lasts 23 years. The first TIF was established in California in 1952. Today, all states except Arizona have TIFs. Illinois is the most reliant of all other states on tax increment financing. The Illinois Controller reported 1,397 TIFs established by 514 municipalities in the state in 2016. In Chicago alone, there were 146 TIFs in 2015 (20.18 percent of all parcels in Chicago) and accounted for 461 million dollars in forgone property tax revenue in 2015 (Cook County Clerk, 2016). For comparison, as of now, there are 1,260 TIF districts in Ohio. Sixty-nine of them are in Cuyahoga County. The city of Cleveland, the largest city in Cuyahoga County, currently has 22 TIFs (Ohio Development Services Agency).

A ***Business Improvement District (BID)*** is a geographical area, where businesses are required to pay higher (property) taxes to subsidize projects within the BID. All states, except Wyoming, including Washington D.C., have BIDs.

Business Retention and Expansion Investment is financing through loans and loan guarantees to businesses expanding or relocating in the state.

An ***Enterprise Zone*** is an economically distressed geographical area where investors are offered tax breaks, infrastructure preferences, or reduced regulations to encourage business attraction and retention. Forty-three states have enterprise zones.

The ***Enterprise Zone Jobs Tax Credit*** is a corporate income tax credit for companies creating new jobs in designated enterprise zones.

A ***Renaissance Zone*** is Michigan and North Dakota's version of enterprise zones and is basically a blighted geographical area that is given a tax-free redevelopment zone status for a certain period of time.

Community Redevelopment/Reinvestment Areas: Any property improvements or construction of new properties in designated Community Redevelopment/Reinvestment Areas are exempt from property taxation for a defined period of time.

Industrial Development Bonds (IDBs) are tax-exempt government bonds issued on behalf of firms (so-called conduit bonds) for redevelopment projects. The government usually holds title to the properties (re)developed with BIDs and these properties are, therefore, tax-exempt. Some states (Kentucky, Louisiana, Mississippi, Missouri, New Jersey, New Mexico, New York, North Dakota, Ohio, South Carolina, Tennessee, Texas, and West Virginia) require firms-beneficiaries to compensate the government for losses in property taxes through a "payment in lieu of taxes" ("PILOT"; Kenyon, Langley & Paquin, 2012).

Property tax abatements are typically given for ten years but can be extended beyond this period. The abatements can be given on land, structures, improvements, personal property, and others. They can be offered to commercial, industrial, agricultural, or residential properties.

Statutory state property tax ***limitations on tax rates, levies, or assessed values*** available in one form or another in every state can be another layer of reassurance for residents and businesses willing to invest in property improvements (McClure, 2019).

Several cities in Oregon and Wisconsin offer a ***Vertical Housing Program*** that provides property tax abatements for up to ten years for a certain percentage of expenses spent on property improvements on mixed-use multistory multifamily housing in designated ***Vertical Housing Zones*** (Mallah, 2017).

Keystone Innovation Zone (KIZ) is an incentive program in Pennsylvania that provides income (personal and corporate) tax credits to young (less than eight years old), for-profit companies in life sciences and technology sectors within the boundaries of a KIZ. (Pennsylvania Department of Community and Economic Development, 2021).

A ***Development Fund*** provides gap financing through loans and equity investments for companies requiring a lender of last resort.

The ***Job Creation Tax Credit*** is a corporate income tax credit for companies creating new jobs.

Income Tax Exemption for New or Expanding Businesses allows for up to a five-year exemption from state corporate income taxes for companies relocating or expanding in the state.

The ***Transportation Economic Assistance Program (TEA)*** is a funding tool for transportation improvements for a company expanding or relocating in the state.

A ***Motion Picture Production Tax Credit*** is an income tax credit for up to 25 percent of production costs of movies and other electronic media projects. This tax incentive started in the 1990s in response to the flight of movie productions to other countries, such as Canada. Since then, states have offered increasingly competitive incentives to lure productions away from other countries and states (Luther, 2010). The structure, type, and size of the incentives vary from state to state. For example, in Louisiana, the maximum credit that can be offered is 150 million dollars per fiscal year claimed toward personal or corporate income tax liability (Louisiana Economic Development, 2021). In Rhode Island, there is a corporate income tax credit for up to 25 percent of production costs for films and other electronic media projects (Good Jobs First, 2021).

The ***Jobs Training Program*** provides reimbursements for training costs, withheld from new employees' wages and salaries.

The ***High-Quality Jobs Program*** provides various tax credits, exemptions, and/or refunds for firms meeting specific job creation, wages, and benefits requirements.

The ***Wage and Salary Credit*** is a corporate income tax credit for new or relocating companies based on payroll costs.

The ***Job Training Tax Credit*** is a corporate income tax credit of up to 50 percent of training costs for new or existing employees.

The ***Research Activities Credit (RAC)*** is a refundable state income tax credit for qualified research and development expenditures.

Property tax abatements are particularly significant in D.C., Michigan, New Mexico, Pennsylvania, and Tennessee. Investment tax credits play a more important role in Alabama, Kentucky, Nebraska, and South Carolina. R&D tax credits were a large share of incentives in California, Maryland, and Massachusetts. Customized job training programs are well above the national average (greater than 0.30 percent versus national average of 0.07 percent) in New Mexico, Iowa, and Missouri (Bartik, 2017). Table 3.2 summarizes main tax incentives by state.

TABLE 3.2 States' Main Incentives

	Enterprise Zones	*Job Creation Tax Credit*	*TIFs*	*Jobs Training Programs*
Alabama		✓	✓	✓
Alaska			✓	
Arizona	✓	✓		✓
Arkansas			✓	
California	✓	✓	✓	✓
Colorado	✓	✓	✓	✓
Connecticut	✓	✓	✓	✓
Delaware		✓	✓	✓
Florida	✓		✓	
Georgia	✓	✓	✓	✓
Hawaii	✓	✓	✓	✓
Idaho	✓	✓	✓	✓
Illinois	✓	✓	✓	✓
Indiana	✓	✓	✓	✓
Iowa	✓		✓	✓
Kansas	✓	✓	✓	✓
Kentucky	✓	✓	✓	✓
Louisiana	✓	✓	✓	✓
Maine	✓		✓	
Maryland	✓	✓	✓	✓
Massachusetts	✓	✓	✓	✓
Michigan	✓	✓	✓	✓
Minnesota	✓	✓	✓	✓
Mississippi	✓	✓	✓	✓
Missouri	✓	✓	✓	✓
Montana		✓	✓	✓
Nebraska		✓	✓	✓
Nevada		✓	✓	✓
New Hampshire	✓		✓	✓
New Jersey	✓	✓	✓	✓
New Mexico		✓	✓	✓
New York	✓	✓	✓	✓
North Carolina	✓	✓	✓	✓
North Dakota	✓	✓	✓	✓
Ohio	✓	✓	✓	✓
Oklahoma	✓		✓	✓
Oregon	✓	✓	✓	✓
Pennsylvania	✓		✓	✓
Rhode Island	✓	✓	✓	✓
South Carolina	✓	✓	✓	✓
South Dakota	✓	✓	✓	✓
Tennessee	✓	✓	✓	✓
Texas	✓	✓	✓	✓

(*Continued*)

TABLE 3.2 (Continued)

	Enterprise Zones	*Job Creation Tax Credit*	*TIFs*	*Jobs Training Programs*
Utah	✓	✓	✓	✓
Vermont	✓	✓	✓	✓
Virginia	✓	✓	✓	✓
Washington	✓	✓	✓	✓
West Virginia	✓	✓	✓	✓
Wisconsin	✓	✓	✓	✓
Wyoming	✓	✓	✓	✓

Source: Created by authors from Good Job First (2021)

The empirical evidence about the effectiveness of all sorts of tax incentives has rendered mixed results. Greenstone and Moretti (2004) found that attracting a large company increased property values in winning counties by 6.6 to 10.2 percent relative to runner-up counties over the course of six years. However, incentives were more likely to be awarded by communities in states with more corrupt political cultures (Felix & Hines, 2010). Tax incentives have also been criticized because they are frequently used in the areas where economic development would happen even without incentives. The growth in TIF districts is often found to be accompanied by declines in nearby communities as employment opportunities, inventories, etc. simply relocate from one place to another (Man, 2001; Dye & Merriman, 2006). Even if TIFs are successful in one geographical location, they might be ineffective in another. Sentiments similar to those about TIFs are shared about the effectiveness of Enterprise Zones (Hirasuna & Michael, 2005; Hanson & Rohlin, 2013). The success of property tax abatement programs has been found to be limited as well, working only short-term, and they are more effective if offered in combination with other incentives (Dalehite et al., 2005; Wassmer, 2009).

State Actions in Assisting Insolvent Municipalities

PEW Charitable Trusts (2020) suggests that the three most important steps states can make to ensure the fiscal health of its local governments are to (1) provide constant monitoring of municipal finances and implement an early warning system, (2) provide technical assistance and training to local government officials, and (3) intervene if things are not going well. Table 3.3 summarizes states' intervention strategies. Fiscal monitoring was discussed in Chapter 2. We discuss states' involvement in the most severe cases of fiscal stress and specifically Chapter 9 bankruptcy in Chapter 4. General states' intervention strategies for distressed municipalities are reviewed here.

States differ dramatically in variety and depth of assistance they provide to insolvent municipalities. Francis and Randell (2017) suggested that "every state has an economic development strategy composed of several program tools . . . most states have more than one strategy with actions formulated, funded, and implemented by different agencies at different levels of government" (p. 1). Some states limit their involvement with local government finances by collecting certain fiscal data or reports on state sponsored web portals (like Alaska or Montana). Other states do not even do this (like Alabama or Wyoming) (Alabama Economic Development Alliance, 2020). If municipalities face fiscal hardships, certain states step back and leave municipalities to resolve their own fiscal issues (like in the cases of Stockton, CA or Jefferson County, AL). Others take a very active part in municipal recovery efforts (during Detroit, MI or Central Falls, RI bankruptcies or the Buffalo, NY fiscal emergency). Some adopted a detailed formal plan of actions (like Rhode Island, Pennsylvania, and Connecticut). Others assist on an ad hoc basis and do not have established formal procedures (like Massachusetts). Some states adopted more proactive intervention programs (like Maine, Michigan, Nevada, New York, Pennsylvania, and others). Actions of other states are more reactive – states acknowledge the problem and assist localities when they are already deep in crisis (like with the Hillview, KY bankruptcy).

Proactive states have adopted regulations that allow them to provide financial and technical assistance to distressed municipalities (Gao et al., 2019). Proactive states often appoint an authority to help manage local finances (discussed in Chapter 4). Given the ordered and defined nature of proactive states and their steps to protect credit worthiness of local governments, unsurprisingly, research found that borrowing costs are generally lower and default events are less common in proactive states. In the following paragraphs, we discuss states individually to examine state intervention policies available for distressed municipalities.

In ***Connecticut***, when municipalities experienced financial distress, the state acted on an ad hoc basis until very recently. In 2017 the state adopted the *Public Act 17–2* that established four tiers of fiscal stress levels based on Municipal Fiscal Indicators (see Chapter 2) and created a Municipal Accountability Review Board (MARB). In 2019 another legislature, the *Public Act 19–193* was adopted, which established a process for early detection of fiscal distress based on seven indicators (see Chapter 2). Municipalities in Tier I are overseen by the Municipal Finance Advisory Committee (MFAC) staffed by professionals in different spheres and are required to develop a three-year financial plan. If a municipality moves to the second tier it is overseen by MARB, which not only includes specialists in different financial spheres in its board but also includes public finance officials. Tier II municipalities, in addition to a three-year plan, have to submit certain financial information and approve elements of their municipal budget with MARB. These municipalities are also eligible for restructuring funds. In addition to all Tier II requirements, MARB approves most labor contracts by Tier III municipalities

TABLE 3.3 States' Intervention Strategies

	Online Data Portals	*Fiscal Monitoring*	*Laws Defining Fiscal Distress*	*Early Warning*	*State Intervention*
Alabama					
Alaska	✓				
Arizona	✓				
Arkansas	✓				
California	✓				
Colorado	✓	✓			
Connecticut	✓	✓			✓
Delaware					
Florida	✓	✓	✓		✓
Georgia	✓				
Hawaii					
Idaho					
Illinois	✓		✓		✓
Indiana	✓		✓		✓
Iowa	✓	✓			
Kansas	✓				
Kentucky		✓			
Louisiana	✓	✓	✓	✓	✓
Maine	✓		✓		✓
Maryland	✓	✓			
Massachusetts	✓				✓
Michigan	✓	✓	✓		✓
Minnesota	✓	✓			
Mississippi	✓				
Missouri	✓				
Montana	✓				
Nebraska	✓				
Nevada		✓	✓	✓	✓
New Hampshire		✓	✓		✓
New Jersey	✓	✓	✓	✓	✓
New Mexico		✓			✓
New York	✓	✓			✓
North Carolina	✓	✓	✓	✓	✓
North Dakota					
Ohio	✓	✓	✓	✓	✓
Oklahoma	✓				
Oregon	✓	✓	✓		✓
Pennsylvania	✓	✓	✓	✓	✓
Rhode Island	✓	✓	✓	✓	✓
South Carolina	✓				

TABLE 3.3 (Continued)

	Online Data Portals	*Fiscal Monitoring*	*Laws Defining Fiscal Distress*	*Early Warning*	*State Intervention*
South Dakota	✓	✓			
Tennessee	✓	✓	✓	✓	✓
Texas	✓				✓
Utah	✓				
Vermont					
Virginia	✓				
Washington	✓	✓			
West Virginia					
Wisconsin	✓				
Wyoming					

Source: Created by authors from PEW Charitable Trusts (2013) and PEW Charitable Trusts (2021)

and reviews debt issuance, labor contracts, and other functional elements of such municipal governments. MFAC additionally reviews employee benefits, demographics, tax base, fund balances, audit reports, debt and cash management and general operating practices, and provides a general budget analysis of Tier III municipalities. For the most distressed, Tier IV municipalities, MARB shifts from advisory practices to control and intervention, which includes an appointment of a financial manager, the authority to approve or disapprove budget transfers, to impose binding arbitration on labor contracts, and other actions (Government Fiscal Sustainability Workgroup Meeting, 2019).

In ***Kentucky,*** the state government monitors county but not city finances. The Kentucky Department for Local Government under the Office of the Governor approves counties' annual budgets, reviews quarterly financial statements, and advises fiscally distressed counties. Some of the financial services (payroll, personnel, administrative, and social security) for larger government units (the state and county governments with populations over 70,000) are offered by the State's Division of Local Government Services under the Office of the Controller. Fiscal monitoring on the city level and advice for distressed cities and towns are provided by a voluntary Kentucky League of Cities, not the state (Pew, 2016).

In ***Louisiana,*** fiscal intervention is more discretionary rather than mandatory in nature. Struggling municipalities may be referred to the Fiscal Review Committee that consists of the auditor, attorney general, and the treasurer. The committee and the Louisiana Legislative Auditor (LLA) give advice to struggling municipalities and, in extreme cases, the committee may recommend the court to appoint a financial administrator to undertake the administration of the insolvent municipality. Incompliant municipalities, however, still receive transfers from the state.

The ***Maryland*** Office of Legislative Audits (OLA) publishes a Review of Local Government Audit Report. The report looks for potential financial problems identified by unfavorable fiscal ratios or trends and incompliance with reporting requirements. Distressed municipalities are asked to discuss with the Office of Legislative Audits (OLA) the corrective actions that will be taken.

The ***Minnesota*** Office of the State Auditor (OSA) collects and reviews local governments' financial statements, but the state does not take over the finances of fiscally challenged municipalities (Minnesota Employment and Economic Development, 2017; PEW Charitable Trusts, 2016).

In 1921, the ***New Hampshire*** governor created a commission to oversee Manchester's troubled finances, which became one of the earliest examples of a state intervention using a financial control board. Nowadays, the New Hampshire Department of Revenue's Municipal and Property Division (MPD) collects certain financial data on local governments and advises financially distressed municipalities. The advice is non-binding. Municipalities can also apply to the governor for financial assistance. This practice was, however, used only once since established in 1935 (PEW Charitable Trusts, 2016).

New Jersey has one of the oldest and utmost state-involved fiscal monitoring systems in the U.S. The beginning of the state oversight is dated back to the Great Depression. The Division of Local Government Services (DLGS) reviews all local budgets and audit reports for compliance, assists in budget preparations, financial reporting, and procurement (Division of Local Government Services, 2021). The division is responsible for "the financial integrity" of all government units in the state (Division of Local Government Services, 2021). The Division can reject the budget if, for example, the locality did not allocate enough money to cover debt obligations or its revenue estimates are too optimistic (PEW Charitable Trusts, 2016). The Local Finance Board that is also a part of DLGS reviews and approves applications from local governments that want to issue debt, to make sure the debt capacity is not met and that the municipality has funds to pay interest and principal on issued bonds (ibid). Financially struggling municipality can apply for state funding, called "transitional aid", but in return it may lose some of its financial independence as the state assigns a fiscal monitor, whose oversight continues as long as the local government receives state aid. After years of escalating state aid, the program has contracted under Governor Chris Christie, going from about 200 million dollars when he took office in 2010 to about 95 million dollars in fiscal 2014 (New Jersey Legislature, 2013). New Jersey also has a program that connects distressed area residents participating in job training programs with jobs created by state assisted economic development projects (Rappa, 2017).

The Division of Local Government under the ***New Mexico*** Department of Finance and Administration reviews and approves local budgets and financial reports, provides revenue projections, and conducts early monitoring of municipal finances. At any signs of fiscal distress, the state sends the auditor, provides recommendations, and requests a "corrective action plan" (PEW Charitable Trusts,

2016). If violation or fraud are detected, the state may suspend a locality or a person and take charge of the entity.

The 1975 the city of New York financial crisis resulted in ***New York*** state and federal involvement in debt restructuring, pension obligations, and tax revisions. The state "advanced money to New York City in 1975 and set up an independent corporation to sell bonds backed by state taxes to help the city avoid bankruptcy" (PEW Charitable Trusts, 2013, p. 11). "This intervention resulted in the creation of the Municipal Assistance Corporation (MAC) that was authorized to issue debt on behalf of the city, and the Financial Control Board (FCB), which assumed oversight of the city's financial matters" (National Association of Bond Lawyers, 2015, p. 11). New York's Emergency Financial Control Board authorizes the municipality or the board to file a petition in the New York Supreme Court for approval of a repayment plan. New York does have one common intervention tool that applies to all cities and school districts; the state allows local governments to borrow money to plug operating budget gaps, but the bond sales are subject to the strict oversight of the state comptroller (New York Local Finance Law, section 10.10).

In 1931, the ***North Carolina*** Legislature responded to a wave of municipal defaults at the start of the Great Depression by creating a commission to advise troubled cities and impose budget controls if necessary. This commission had a professional staff and a nine-member board. It examined local governments' financial reports to recognize fiscal distress and financial problems. The municipality in fiscal distress goes on a watch list of this commission. According to PEW Charitable Trusts (2013), if municipalities "cannot correct their difficulties, the commission can step in and run their day-to-day operations, including raising taxes, until local officials resolve the underlying crisis" (p. 31). North Carolina's commission keeps local debt in check by approving and selling bonds issued by cities, counties, and special districts for capital projects such as fire stations, water plants, and parks (PEW Charitable Trusts, 2013, p. 30). Since 1942, no North Carolina city, county, or special district has failed to meet a bond obligation. North Carolina is a proactive state, so local officials can work out their problems before the commission is forced to assume control.

When the ***North Carolina*** Local Government Commission recognizes a potential fiscal distress in a local government, they send city officials a letter asking about plans to correct the financial problems. The state has the authority to intervene and run the city's day-to-day operations if local leaders are reluctant to changes (North Carolina Environmental Quality, 2021; PEW Charitable Trusts, 2013).

New Jersey's incentive program targets four major cities with the lowest median family income (as identified by the 2009 U.S. Census Bureau American Community Survey). From late 2013 through 2015, the state allocated 1.1 billion dollars in tax incentives under this program to 16 projects in the city of Camden alone (Nurin, 2015).

In 1978, after Cleveland became the first major city since the Great Depression to default on short-term notes, the ***Ohio*** Legislature allowed the city to borrow money from the state to avert bankruptcy. Since then, Ohio has developed an advanced system for monitoring local government finances. The Auditor of State's Local Government Services Division, established in the mid-1980s, has been assisting distressed municipalities with financial, budgeting, and accounting reporting, advice, and training. The consulting is free for the municipality if the auditor has placed the city, county, or school district under a fiscal caution, watch, or emergency, the three designations of financial distress (Ohio Auditor of State, 2021a). Ohio's fiscal distress system was created in 1979, when the original municipal fiscal emergency law was enacted as a response to a financial crisis in the city of Cleveland. Since that time, financial planning and supervision commissions have aided over 50 Ohio local governments declared to be in fiscal emergency (Ohio Auditor of State, 2021a). In 1996, fiscal emergency protection was extended to counties and townships (House Bill 462). HB 462 modified the fiscal emergency statute to create the "fiscal watch" status to provide an early warning to faltering entities whose finances are approaching emergency status. In 2011, House Bill 153 further modified the fiscal emergency statute to create the "fiscal caution" designation to identify fiscal practices and budgetary conditions that, if not corrected, could result in a declaration of fiscal watch or fiscal emergency (Ohio Auditor of State, 2021a).

"Fiscal Caution" designates the lowest degree of fiscal distressed (mainly for municipalities with small budget deficit – see Chapter 2 for detailed discussion of the fiscal monitoring system in Ohio). Once a locality is placed in this category, it has 60 days to submit a written proposal to the Auditor of the State on how it plans to resolve the situation. The Auditor may visit and consult the municipality. If their fiscal health continues to deteriorate (the budget deficit keeps climbing and the accounts are not paid for 30 days or more) the municipality is placed under "Fiscal Watch". The municipality has 120 days to submit a plan of corrective actions that has to be approved by the State Auditor. If it does not happen in that time frame, the locality is placed in "Fiscal Emergency". To be moved in this category the municipality should have deficit and other unfavorable conditions for four months or fail to make payroll or debt payments for 30 days or more. Municipalities in fiscal emergency are placed under the oversight of the "Financial Planning and Supervision Commission" chaired by the State Auditor and staffed by the Treasurer of the State, the Director of Ohio Office of Budgeting and Management, and the head and three residents (with a business background) of the struggling locality. The commission reviews and approves a financial recovery plan, revenue and expenditure estimates, the amount and purpose of debt issue, etc. (Ohio Auditor of State, 2021b).

The fiscal monitoring of local governments in ***Pennsylvania*** started in the late 1980s with Pennsylvania's Municipalities Financial Recovery Act (Act 47) of 1987, which provided criteria for identifying fiscal stress,[3] the powers and duties of the Department of Community and Economic Development in assisting a community to alleviate its fiscal stress status, a procedure for declaring a fiscal stress and authorizing the appointment of a municipality's coordinator, a requirement that a fiscally stressed municipality develops a fiscal plan to remedy its fiscal stress status, the option for a fiscally stressed municipality to formulate its own fiscal plan, a requirement that the state withholds all nonessential state funds if a fiscally stressed municipality refuses to adopt a fiscal solvency plan, and an authorization for a fiscally stressed municipality to file under Chapter 9 bankruptcy law (Pennsylvania General Assembly, 2006).

Twenty-seven cities and towns in Pennsylvania have qualified for the state intervention program aimed at rescuing the most struggling local governments with chronic budget deficits, in danger of failing to pay employees, and those facing a default on bond payments (Pennsylvania Department of Community & Economic Development, 2021). Once a community is identified as fiscally stressed, an Act 47 coordinator is appointed and paid for by the state. In 1991, Pennsylvania created an Intergovernmental Cooperation Authority to help Philadelphia, PA overcome its budget crisis. This Authority has the power to review and approve cities' five-year financial plans. If the authority rejects a five-year plan, it has the power to withhold a share of the city wage tax (Spiotto et al., 2012). In 2014, the state additionally designed an early intervention program that now serves as an example of the effectiveness of early actions. At the first signs of distress, Pennsylvania offers voluntary technical and monetary assistance with budgeting and financial issues, as well as training for local government officials. Between 2014 – when the early intervention program was created in Pennsylvania – and 2016, 80 localities participated in the program. Only five of them were moved to the fiscally stressed municipality list (Act 47 discussed later; PEW Charitable Trusts, 2020). If a municipality is designated as fiscally stressed, a coordinator appointed by the state develops a suggestive recovery plan, but the municipality is not required to adhere to the plan. Pennsylvania provides matching grants to fiscally stressed municipalities for developing multi-year financial plans (Mallah, 2017).

Pennsylvania provides financial support to municipalities and requires developing a recovery plan to remedy fiscal stress. The coordinator assists with implementation of the recovery plan, but the municipality continues to be responsible for day-to-day operations. From 2015 to 2022, seven municipalities recovered from the fiscal emergency status in Pennsylvania (Act 47 oversight): Scranton, the city of Farrell, Mercer County, Plymouth, Luzerne County; Nanticoke, Luzerne County; Clairton, Allegheny County; Pittsburgh, Allegheny County; and Altoona, Blair County. Scranton is the most recent community to exit Act 47 status on January 25, 2022 (Pennsylvania Department of Community and Economic Development, 2022).

Rhode Island established a budget and review commission in 1993 to oversee municipalities whose bond ratings went below the investment grade (Rhode

Island Public Laws, 2001). The commission is empowered to impose taxes and make certain appropriations to help struggling municipalities. In 2003 the state mandated municipalities to additionally submit a budget, an audit report, and a five-year forecast on an annual basis. If the budget shows a deficit, the municipality is required to submit a corrective plan. From 2010, the Fiscal Stability Act provides an appointment of a "fiscal overseer" for insolvent municipalities, who develops three-year financial plans for the locality, monitors all contracts and financial obligations, and provides monthly deficit reduction reports. If the actions of the overseer are not sufficient, the state creates a "budget committee", which can also exercise powers of local elected officials. If both the overseer and the budget committee are not sufficient, the final stage is the appointment of a "receiver" who can additionally apply for Chapter 9 bankruptcy on behalf of the municipality and represent the municipality during the bankruptcy process. In 2016, after the city of Central Falls, RI bankruptcy, the state additionally created a centralized "Municipal Transparency Portal" where municipalities are required to publish their budgets (Rhode Island Public Expenditure Council, 2021). Rhode Island provides grants to municipalities with the highest property tax burdens relative to taxpayers' wealth (Mallah, 2017).

Rhode Island additionally provides some of the most aggressive employment and training tax incentives' programs in the nation (Rhode Island Department of Labor and Training, 2022). To name a few, the Work Opportunity Tax Credit offers a tax credit to employers of 2,400 dollars per hired employee from one of the target groups, including Temporary Assistance to Needy Families (TANF) recipients, some veterans, recipients of vocational rehabilitation services, food stamp recipients, qualified ex-felons, and Supplemental Security Income (SSI) recipients (Rhode Island Department of Labor and Training, 2022). The New Employment Tax Incentive is a deduction or modification of 40 percent of the employee's first year wages up to 2,400 dollars per employee (Rhode Island Department of Labor and Training, 2022). This incentive is available to businesses that hire previously unemployed Rhode Island residents. Once each employee has been employed by the business for a minimum of 52 consecutive calendar weeks, has a minimum of 1,820 hours of paid employment, and is certified by the Department of Labor and Training, the business becomes entitled to take this incentive. The Job Training Tax Credit is a corporate income tax credit of up to 50 percent of training costs for new or existing employees (Good Jobs First, 2021).

In ***Tennessee,*** if fiscal ratios indicate the possibility of fiscal distress, the locality is asked to prepare a corrective plan and is referred to the State and Local Finance Office. Since 1986, localities with outstanding debt are required to submit their budgets for state approval (PEW Charitable Trusts, 2016). The state emphasizes the importance of early monitoring and prevention of fiscal disturbances in the first place. The state comptroller not only directs local governments to submit all sorts of financial reports for audits and review, but since 2007 all local recorders, treasurers, and finance directors are required to go through a required annual training provided by the Municipal Technical Advisory Service and take certification exams. To promote healthy fiscal behavior, Tennessee also created incentives where counties can apply for and receive grants for economic development, fiscal strength and an efficient government through a state-subsidized program called ThreeStar.

Virginia created accelerated, five-year, capital investment incentive grants for businesses in distressed areas. Virginia has discretionary grants for creating jobs and stimulating investment in tobacco industry-dependent communities. The state provides low-interest loans for businesses in qualified regions (Rappa, 2017).

Local Economic Development Incentives for Struggling Municipalities

Many incentives for distressed municipalities come from outside of the struggling districts. But local governments themselves can and should create incentives to attract new businesses and residents and encourage retention and expansion of the existing economic development base. Some of these incentives include:

- tax preferences
- direct subsidies
- provision of functioning infrastructure and access to utilities
- fee waivers
- regulation waivers
- offering land at low or even no cost for certain time
- discounts on utilities
- expedited paperwork, permitting, and other processes
- low interest loans
- state and federal grants and loans.

These incentives do not come without sacrifices. When a tax advantage, a subsidy, a fee waiver, or another incentive is offered to certain individuals or businesses, first and foremost it reduces the municipal revenue base or increases expenditures, which might be especially difficult to afford for a government unit that already experiences severe financial problems. For example, Detroit reported over 39 million dollars in forgone tax revenue among 11 tax abatement programs in 2020 (City of Detroit, 2020). It also provides redistribution of resources, which may create political and moral tensions when decisions about allocation of incentives are made, especially among those who do not benefit from the incentives. School districts, the largest recipients of local funds, also often suffer most financially when tax incentives are given for economic development. But, despite their high cost, economic incentives are especially important for struggling municipalities as they provide a long-term investment in the fiscal health of local communities. Case-studies later discussed in this book show one after another how fiscal issues originated and were exacerbated when major employers left and residents followed them in the search of employment and a safer place to live. Poor overall economic conditions, structural changes in the economy, local corruption, demographic changes, and other factors could be contributing factors to why businesses close or simply move away, but such exodus could often be avoided if tax or other incentives are offered on time.

Local Actions for Fiscally Distressed Municipalities

When local governments face fiscal difficulties, the array of actions that can be taken to improve the situation are essentially limited to cutting expenses, raising revenues, or using a combination of these.

Tax revenue is a product of the tax rate and tax base. Economic development tools discussed extensively in this chapter create an opportunity to expand a tax base, as localities are often limited in their ability to create new or raise existing tax rates. In fact, 38 states have municipal tax or expenditure limits, or TELs (Stallmann et al., 2012). Most of these states have tax limits, and only four have expenditure limits. The states without municipal TELs are Connecticut, Delaware, Georgia, Hawaii, Kansas, New Hampshire, South Carolina, Tennessee, Utah, Vermont, and Virginia. Minnesota has municipal TELs some years. The oldest existing TELs that have not been changed are from 1911 in Wyoming. The states with the strictest restrictions on local governments are California (Proposition 13), Colorado (TABOR; Taxpayer Bill of Rights), and Michigan (Headlee Amendment). TELs are typically tied to inflation, or population growth, growth in personal income, or a combination of thereof. The goal of TELs is also to establish fiscal control and responsibility, but the inability to raise local taxes to generate required revenues often puts an excessive strain on struggling local governments. If a tax increase is not an option, revenues can be raised from non-tax revenue sources, such as new or increased fees and charges, sale of government assets, state transfers, and such.

On the expenditure side, fiscally distressed "less well-managed governments will adopt 'across-the-board' cuts; while more enlightened entities will pursue more targeted cuts and equitable revenue measures" (Kravchuk, 2021, p. 7). Partnerships between public entities and the private sector (Public-Private Partnership, PPP, or 3P) or cost-sharing of certain government operations (such as fire protection, recycling and waste management, etc.) with nearby municipalities can be among these cost-saving alternatives. We discuss real-life examples and the theories behind cost-cutting and revenue generating strategies for distressed municipalities in Chapter 5 of this book.

Conclusions

This chapter examined how federal, state, and local governments' laws, policies, and practices affect the course of municipalities' revitalization. It also discussed what policies, incentives, and programs can be designed to improve financial conditions in a number of distinct but interrelated spheres: building fiscal and service delivery capacity, granting tax exemptions, requiring developers to provide affordable housing units, building a stronger real estate market, ensuring economic competitiveness, investing in local human capital, and enhancing quality of life. We discuss what preventive programs states have to ensure municipal fiscal health and the extent to which states make funds available to supplement limited municipal resources.

In the next chapter, Chapter 4, we review actions and policies aimed at municipalities in severe fiscal stress and bankruptcy situations. And in the following Chapters, 5 and 6, we continue the conversation by discussing budget specific approaches during different stages of fiscal stress. Chapter 5 focuses on operating budgets and Chapter 6 discusses capital infrastructure and capital budgets.

Notes

1 On a state level the credit can be applied to any taxes.
2 Tax expenditures are the tax revenues lost due to tax credits, abatements, deduction, exemptions, exclusions, and other preferences embedded in the tax code. In other words, these are the revenues that could've been collected if tax preferences did not exist.
3 Act 47 uses the term "fiscal distress" to identify fiscal stress and fiscal emergency situation. In this book, we consider "fiscal distress" as the most mild fiscal stress situation (see Chapter 2 for details). Act 47, however, is mainly concerned with what we refer to in this book as "fiscal emergency" or a lot more severe and detrimental fiscal stress situation. For the sake of consistency with the terminology used in the book any mention of Act 47 situation is refered to as fiscal stress or fiscal emergency in this book.

References

Alabama Economic Development Alliance (2020). *Accelerate Alabama 2.0.* Retrieved December 23, 2021, from www.madeinalabama.com/assets/2017/01/Accelerate-Alabama-2.0.pdf

Bartik, T. (2017). A new panel database on business incentives for economic development offered by state and local governments in the governments in the United States. *W.E. Upjohn Institute for Employment Research.* Retrieved December 23, 2021, from https://research.upjohn.org/cgi/viewcontent.cgi?referer=&httpsredir=1&article=1228&context=reports

Bartik, T. J., & Erickcek, G. (2014). Simulating the effects of the tax credit. Program of the Michigan economic growth authority on job creation and fiscal benefits. *Economic Development Quarterly, 28*(4), 314–327.

Bischoff, I., & Blaeschke, F. (2016). Performance budgeting: Incentives and social waste from window dressing. *Journal of Public Administration Research and Theory, 26*(2), 344–358.

City of Detroit (2020). Financial reports. *CAFR 2020*. Retrieved December 2, 2021, from https://detroitmi.gov/departments/office-chief-financial-officer/financial-reports

Clark, B. Y., & Guzman, T. S. (2017). Does technologically enabled citizen participation lead to budget adjustments? An investigation of Boston, MA, and San Francisco, CA. *The American Review of Public Administration*, 47(8), 945–961.

Clark, B. Y., & Guzman, T. (2022). Is a more transparent, connected, and engaged city a smarter investment? A study of the relationship between 311 systems and credit ratings in American cities. *Government Information Quarterly*, Published online 9 July 2022, 101744, ISSN 0740-624X, https://doi.org/10.1016/j.giq.2022.101744.

Coe, C. K. (2008). Preventing local government fiscal crises: Emerging best practices. *Public Administration Review, 68*(4), 759–767.

Congressional Research Service. (2019). *Federal Grants to State and Local Governments: A Historical Perspective on Contemporary Issues*. Washington, D.C.: Congressional Research Service, 22 May 2019. Retrieved December 2, 2021, from https://crsreports.congress.gov/product/details?prodcode=R40638

Cook County Clerk (2016). *TIF Reports*. Retrieved December 2, 2021, from https://www.cookcountyclerkil.gov/property-taxes/tifs-tax-increment-financing/tif-reports

Dalehite, E. G., Mikesell, J., & Zorn, C. K (2005). Variations in property tax abatement programs among states. *Economic Development Quarterly, 19*(1), 157–173.

De Jong, M., & Ho, A. T.-K. (2019). Lessons about integrating performance with budgeting in high-income countries: An evolving exercise. In *Performance Budgeting Reform* (pp. 110–130). New York: Routledge.

Division of Local Government Services (2021). *Division of local government services New Jersey*. Retrieved December 23, 2021, from www.nj.gov/dca/dlgs/dlgs/index.shtml

Dye, R. F., & David, F. M. (2006). Tax increment financing: A tool for local economic development. *Land Lines 18*(1), 2–7.

Felix, R., & Hines, J. (2010). *Who Offers Tax-based Business Development Incentives?* [Working Paper No. 17466]. Cambridge, MA. National Bureau of Economic Research.

Francis, N., & Randell, M. (2017). *State economic development strategies. A discussion framework*. Retrieved December 23, 2021, from www.urban.org/sites/default/files/publication/89906/2001243-state-economic-development-strategies-a-discussion-framework_2.pdf

Gao, P., Lee, C., & Murphy, D. (2019). Municipal borrowing costs and state policies for distressed municipalities. *Journal of Financial Economics, 132*(2), 404–426.

Good Jobs First (2021). *Tracking subsidies, promoting accountability in economic development*. Retrieved December 23, 2021, from www.goodjobsfirst.org/accountable-usa

Government Fiscal Sustainability Workgroup Meeting. (2019). *Monitoring and oversight of municipal fiscal health in Connecticut*, 21–22 October. Retrieved December 23, 2021, from www.canr.msu.edu/center_for_local_government_finance_and_policy/uploads/files/CT_-_Fiscal_Sustainability_Workshop_Oct_2019__-__Read-Only.pdf

Greenstone, M., & Moretti, E. (2004). *Bidding for Industrial Plants: Does Winning a "Million-Dollar Plant" Increase Welfare?* Cambridge, MA: National Bureau of Economic Research.

Guzman, T. (2018). Cost-benefit and fiscal impact analysis of Ohio historic preservation tax credit (OHPTC). *Journal of Benefit-Cost Analysis, 9*(2), 342–373.

Guzman, T., & Lefebre, R. (2020). Are there opportunities in opportunity zones? *Urban Publications, 12*(3), 1682.

Hanson, A., & Rohlin, S. (2013). Do spatially targeted redevelopment programs spillover? *Regional Science and Urban Economics, 43*(1), 86–100.

Hirasuna, D., & Michael, J. (2005). *Enterprise Zones: A Review of the Economic Theory and Empirical Evidence*. St. Paul, MN: Minnesota House of Representatives Research Department. Retrieved February 1, 2022, from www.house.leg.state.mn.us/hrd/pubs/entzones.pdf

Ho, A. T.-K. (2018). From performance budgeting to performance budget management: Theory and practice. *Public Administration Review, 78*(5), 748–758.

Honadle, B. W. (2003). The states' role in US local government fiscal crises: A theoretical model and results of a national survey. *International Journal of Public Administration, 26*(13), 1431–1472.

Kenyon, D. A., Langley, A. H., & Paquin, B. P. (2012). *Rethinking Property Tax Incentives for Business*. Cambridge, MA: Lincoln Institute of Land Policy.

Kloha, P., Weissert, C. S., & Kleine, R. (2005). Developing and testing a composite model to predict local fiscal distress. *Public Administration Review, 65*(3), 313–323.

Kravchuk, R. (2021). *Municipal Budgets, Balance Sheets and Acute Fiscal Shock*. Presentation at the 2021 Annual Association for Budgeting and Financial Management. Washington, D.C.: District of Columbia.

Lendel, I., Clouse, C., Coran, E., Guzman, T., Piazza, M., Ryberg, W., Post, C., & Kalynchuk, K. (2015). Ohio historic preservation tax credit economic impact study. *Urban Publications*. Paper 1334.

Louisiana Economic Development (2021). *Motion picture production program*. Retrieved December 23, 2021, from www.opportunitylouisiana.com/business-incentives/motion-picture-production-program

Luther, W. (2010). Movie production incentives: Blockbuster support for lackluster policy, special report. *Tax Foundation, 173*, 4–20.

Maher, C. S., & Deller, S. C. (2007). Municipal responses to fiscal stress. *International Journal of Public Administration, 30*(12–14), 1549–1572.

Mallah, A. (2017). *State Government and Urban Revitalization: How States Can Foster Stronger, More Inclusive Cities*. [Working Paper WP17AM1. Lincoln Institute of Land Policy]. Retrieved December 23, 2021, from www.lincolninst.edu/sites/default/files/pubfiles/mallach_wp17am1.pdf

Man, J. (2001). Effects of tax increment financing on economic development. In Johnson, C. L., & Man, J. Y. (Eds.), *Tax Increment Financing and Economic Development* (pp. 101–109). SUNY Press.

McClure, K. (2019). What should be the future of the low-income housing tax credit program? *Housing Policy Debate, 29*(1), 65–81.

Michigan Economic Development Corporation (2008). *Brownfield redevelopment*. Retrieved December 23, 2021, from www.michigan.gov/documents/deq/deq-ess-bgl-BrownfieldMBThandout_224411_7.pdf

Minnesota Employment and Economic Development (2017). *Minnesota job creation fund*. Retrieved December 23, 2021, from http://mn.gov/deed/business/financing-business/deed-programs/mn-jcf/.

Mizrahi, S., & Minchuk, Y. (2020). The relevance and reliability of performance information for accountability: A survey experiment exploring citizens' views. *Public Administration, 98*(1), 140–158.

Montesinos, V., Brusca, I., Rossi, F. M., & Aversano, N. (2013). The usefulness of performance reporting in local government: Comparing Italy and Spain. *Public Money & Management, 33*(3), 171–176.

Moynihan, D. P. (2006). What do we talk about when we talk about performance? Dialogue theory and performance budgeting. *Journal of Public Administration Research and Theory, 16*(2), 151–168.

Nam, T., & Pardo, T. A. (2011). *Conceptualizing smart city with dimensions of technology, people, and institutions*. Proceedings of the 12th Annual International Digital Government Research Conference. Digital Government Innovation in Challenging Times, pp. 282–291. https://doi.org/10.1145/2037556.2037602

Nam, T., & Pardo, T. A. (2014). The changing face of a city government: A case study of Philly311. *Government Information Quarterly, 31*(Suppl. 1), S1–S9. Retrieved December 23, 2021, from www.doi.org/10.1016/j.giq.2014.01.002

NASBO (2021). *Overview: Fiscal 2019–2021*. Retrieved December 23, 2021, from https://www.nasbo.org/reports-data/state-expenditure-report

National Association of Bond Lawyers (2015). *Municipal bankruptcy: A guide for public finance attorneys* (3rd ed.). Retrieved October 12, 2021, from www.bradley.com/-/media/files/insights/publications/2018/12/municipal-bankruptcy-a-guide-for-public-finance-attorneys-3rd-edition.pdf

New Jersey Legislature (2013). *Appropriations act FY 2013, summary totals*. Retrieved October 12, 2021, from www.njleg.state.nj.us/legislativepub/budget_2013/fy13_scoring.pdf

Nielsen, P. A., & Moynihan, D. P. (2017). How do politicians attribute bureaucratic responsibility for performance? Negativity bias and interest group advocacy. *Journal of Public Administration Research and Theory, 27*(2), 269–283.

North Carolina Environmental Quality (2021). *Related tax incentives*. Retrieved December 23, 2021, from https://deq.nc.gov/about/divisions/waste-management/brownfields-program/program-information/tax-incentives/related-tax-incentives

Nurin, T. (2015). *The List: Camden Banks on Millions in Tax Subsidies to Help Fund Its Future*. New Jersery: Spotlight.

Ohio Auditor of State (2021a). *Local government fiscal caution/watch/emergency law fact sheet*. Retrieved October 12, 2021, from https://ohioauditor.gov/fiscaldistress.html

Ohio Auditor of State (2021b). *Fiscal caution*. Retrieved October 12, 2021, from https://ohioauditor.gov/fiscal/local.html

Pennsylvania Department of Community and Economic Development (2021). *Keystone Innovation Zone (KIZ) tax credit program*. Retrieved December 23, 2021, from https://dced.pa.gov/programs/keystone-innovation-zone-tax-credit-program/

Pennsylvania Department of Community and Economic Development (2022). *Wolf administration announces scranton has successfully terminated distressed municipality status under act 47*, 25 January 2022. Retrieved February 7, 2022, from https://dced.pa.gov/newsroom/wolf-administration-announces-scranton-has-successfully-terminated-distressed-municipality-status-under-act-47/

Pennsylvania General Assembly (2006). *Local Government Commission, Pennsylvania Legislator's Municipal Deskbook* (3rd ed., pp. 185–186). Harrisburg, PA: Local Government Commission. Retrieved December 23, 2021, from https://www.lgc.state.pa.us/deskBook.cfm

PEW Charitable Trusts (2013). *The state role in local government financial distress*. Retrieved December 23, 2021, from www.pewtrusts.org/~/media/assets/2016/04/pew_state_role_in_local_government_financial_distress.pdf

PEW Charitable Trusts (2016). *State Strategies to Detect Local Fiscal Distress*. Washington, D.C.: PEW Charitable Trusts.

PEW Charitable Trusts (2020). *3 Steps states can take to strengthen localities' fiscal health*, 30 June. Retrieved December 23, 2021, from www.pewtrusts.org/en/research-and-analysis/fact-sheets/2020/06/3-steps-states-can-take-to-strengthen-localities-fiscal-health

PEW Charitable Trusts (2021). *How states can direct economic development to places and people in need*. Retrieved December 23, 2021, from www.pewtrusts.org/-/media/assets/2021/01/how_states_can_direct_economic_development_to_places_and_people_in_need.pdf

Puron-Cid, G., Reddick, C. G., & Ganapati, S. (2019). Public value of online financial transparency: Financial sustainability and corruption of public officials in the US state governments. *International Journal of Public Sector Management, 32*(5), 467–488. https://doi.org/10.1108/IJPSM-03-2018-0073

Rappa, J. (2017). *Other states distressed municipalities programs*. Research Report. Office of Legislative Research. www.cga.ct.gov/2017/rpt/pdf/2017-R-0214.pdf

Rhode Island Department of Labor and Training (2022). *Rhode Island tax credits*. Retrieved December 23, 2021, from https://dlt.ri.gov/employers/rhode-island-tax-credits

Rhode Island Public Expenditure Council (RIPEC). (2021). *An introduction to municipal finance in Rhode Island*. Retrieved December 23, 2021, from https://ripec.org/wp-ontent/uploads/2021/04/2021_Intro_Municipal_Finance.pdf

Rhode Island Public Laws (2001). Chapter 180, Section 141. Enacted 07/13/2001. Retrieved December 23, 2021, from http://webserver.rilin.state.ri.us/PublicLaws01/law01180.htm

Scally, C., Gold, A., & DuBois, N. (2018). *The low-income housing tax credit: How it works and who it serves*. Urban Institute. Retrieved December 23, 2021, from www.urban.org/sites/default/files/publication/98758/lithc_how_it_works_and_who_it_serves_final_2.pdf.

Spiotto, J., Acker, A., & Appleby, L. (2012). *Municipalities in Distress? How States and Investors Deal With Local Government Financial Emergencies*. Charlotte, NC: Chapman & Cutler LLP.

Stallmann, J., Deller, S., & Amiel, L. (2012). Tax and expenditure limitations and state credit ratings. *Public Finance Review, 40*(5), 643–669

Stamm, E.& LaJoiemore, T. (2020). An overview of the low-income housing tax credit. *Tax Foundation*. Retrieved May 3, 2021, from https://files.taxfoundation.org/20200810100355/An-Overview-of-the-Low-Income-Housing-Tax-Credit.pdf

Wassmer, R. W. (2009). Property tax abatement as a means of promoting state and local economic activity. In Augustine, N. Y., Bell, M. E., Brunori, D., & Youngman, J. M. (Eds.), *Erosion of the Property Tax Base: Trends, Causes, and Consequences* (pp. 221–269). Cambridge, MA: Lincoln Institute of Land Policy.

W.E. Upjohn Institute for Employment Research (2021). *Findings from the business incentives database*. Retrieved May 3, 2021, from www.upjohn.org/bied/mapall.php

4

LEGAL ASPECTS OF MUNICIPAL BANKRUPTCY

Introduction

Chapter 2 was dedicated to fiscal health and diagnostics of fiscal illnesses. In Chapter 3, we discussed mild cases of fiscal distress and available treatments and therapies for them. The current chapter is devoted to intensive care treatments of the most severe fiscal illnesses, such as the designation of struggling municipalities in a fiscal emergency category, the overhauling of administration of such municipalities by emergency managers, and municipal bankruptcy.

Despite popular belief, municipal bankruptcies happen not because local governments accumulate a large amount of debt but because they lack sufficient liquidity to cover all current expenses, including debt payments. Municipalities can get into financial problems in various ways, "sometimes through economic or social misfortune; sometimes through incompetence or malevolence; sometimes through a stubborn unwillingness to make tough budgetary choices; and often through a combination of these causes" (Mikesell, 2002, p. 1). Businesses bankruptcy often means liquidation (or selling) of property to be able to pay the creditors. If a city, a county, or a school district experiences a fiscal emergency it cannot be sold or liquidated to pay back debt. So, what does municipal bankruptcy really mean?

There are six types of bankruptcy in the U.S. Federal "Bankruptcy Code". Only one of them pertains to municipalities (FindLaw (2021). Bankruptcy. Retrieved from www.findlaw.com/bankruptcy.html FindLaw, 2021 www.findlaw.com/bankruptcy.html).

- *Chapter* 7 bankruptcy is for individuals and businesses that due to financial challenges have to "close their doors". This type of bankruptcy presumes liquidation of assets to pay debt.

DOI: 10.4324/b23117-4

- *Chapter 9* of the Federal "Bankruptcy Code" is the chapter for municipal bankruptcies. This is what we discuss here in this book.
- *Chapter 11* bankruptcy is for businesses that seek restructuring, not exiting (as with Chapter 7).
- *Chapter 12* is the bankruptcy protection law specifically for farmers.
- *Chapter 13* bankruptcy is to some degree similar to Chapter 9 bankruptcy for municipalities (or Chapter 11 for businesses), but Chapter 13 applies to individuals who seek bankruptcy protection to be able to restructure and pay back debt within three to five years. Chapter 13 bankruptcy (unlike Chapter 7) allows individuals to keep their property.
- *Chapter 15* bankruptcy is for individuals with assets in foreign countries.

During the Great Depression in the 1930s, Detroit, Miami, and other local governments in 41 states were in default. In 1938, over 3,000 units of government were in a fiscal emergency situation (Lewis, 1994). However, since the Great Depression, municipal bankruptcies have been rare – only 636 municipal bankruptcy cases were filed from 1937 to 2012 (De Angel & Xiaowei, 2013).

While the primary focus of this chapter is the explanation of Chapter 9 municipal bankruptcy, we also describe the availability, mechanics, advantages, and disadvantages of Chapter 9 in different states. What are the goals and the principal policies of municipal bankruptcy laws? Why can municipalities not apply for Chapter 9 in some states while they can in others? What distinguishes these states' granting express authority, compared to states subject to court-determined eligibility?

History of Municipal Bankruptcy Laws

Municipal bankruptcy law has a long history. In 1898, Congress enacted a general long-term bankruptcy statute. The statute underwent substantial revisions beginning in the 1930s and remained in effect until the enactment of the 1978 Bankruptcy Code (Bankruptcy Act of July 1, 1898, c. 541, 30 Stat. 544, as amended; repealed by P.L. 95–598, Nov. 6, 1978, eff. October 1, 1979). In 1934, Congress enacted a reorganization law targeting municipalities (Congressional Research Service, 2007). This initial law was, however, overturned by the Supreme Court in 1936, citing interference with the Tenth Amendment, which proclaims sovereignty of the states as unconstitutional. Congress revised the municipal reorganization provisions in 1937.

The fiscal crises in New York, Cleveland, Detroit, and other cities in the late 1970s showed that Chapter 9, as it existed in the Bankruptcy Act, was not realistically available to municipalities. According to the Congressional Research Service (2007), "the petitioning municipality was thus required to locate its creditors, draw up a plan, and negotiate and obtain the required consents before it could even file its reorganization" (p. 3). In April of 1976, just ahead of the 1978

Bankruptcy Code, Congress enacted "major substantive revisions pursuant to P.L. 94–260 to chapter IX of the Bankruptcy Act of 1898. The procedures effected by P.L. 94–260 were incorporated as chapter 9 of the current law, the Bankruptcy Reform Act of 1978, P.L. 95–598, as amended" (Congressional Research Service, 2007, p. 3).

The 1978 Bankruptcy Code incorporated recently revised Chapter 9. Major revisions were further enacted in 1988, substantially shaping the current language of Chapter 9. The 1994 amendments (§402 of the Bankruptcy Reform Act of 1994, P.L. 103–394) require state authorization of Chapter 9 bankruptcy filing by municipalities. Chapter 9 provides court protection for fiscally distressed municipalities. The municipality receives the power to adjust its debts through the bankruptcy plan negotiated with creditors (Mikesell, 2002).

In 1994, the Bankruptcy Reform Act created a National Bankruptcy Review Commission to study the Bankruptcy Code and provide recommendations for its improvements. Two of the principal policies of bankruptcy law are the protection or preservation of creditors' rights and the relief of the debtor from financial burdens, which may take the form of reorganization and the modification of its obligations.

Legal Process of Chapter 9 Bankruptcy

Article I, Section 8, Clause 4 of the U.S. Constitution states that: "Congress shall have Power . . . [t]o establish . . . uniform Laws on the subject of Bankruptcies throughout the United States". In addition to Clause 4, two other constitutional provisions play important roles in municipal bankruptcy legislation. First is the "Contract Clause" of Article I, Section 10: "No State shall . . . pass any . . . Law . . . impairing the Obligation of Contracts" (U.S. Constitution, art. I, §10). Second is the Tenth Amendment: "All powers not delegated to the United States by the Constitution, nor prohibited by it to the States, are reserved to the states, respectively, or to the People" (U.S. Constitution, amend. X.).

The Bankruptcy Code broadly defines a "municipality" as a "political subdivision or public agency or instrumentality of a State" (11 U.S. Constitution, §101(40)). Section 109I(2), Title 11 of the United States Bankruptcy Code requires that a municipality be "specifically authorized, in its capacity as a municipality or by name, to be a debtor under such chapter by State law, or by a governmental officer or organization empowered by State law to authorize such entity to be a debtor under such chapter".

Section 109(c) provides five eligibility requirements to become a Chapter 9 debtor. An entity qualifies if it:

1 is a municipality,
2 is specifically authorized, in its capacity as a municipality or by name, to be a debtor under such chapter by State law, or by a governmental officer or

organization empowered by State law to authorize such entity to be a debtor under such chapter,

3 is insolvent,[1]

4 created a plan to adjust municipal debts, and

5 [the municipality]

a has obtained the agreement of creditors holding at least a majority in amount of the claims of each class that such entity intends to impair under a plan in a case under such chapter,

b has negotiated in good faith with creditors and has failed to obtain the agreement of creditors holding at least a majority in amount of the claims of each class that such entity intends to impair under a plan in a case under such chapter,

c is unable to negotiate with creditors because such negotiation is impracticable, or

d reasonably believes that a creditor may attempt to obtain a transfer that is avoidable under section 547 of this title.

(National Association of Bond Lawyers, 2015, p. 37)

According to 11 U.S.C. § 109, "A Chapter 9 petitioner must satisfy each of the mandatory provisions of § 109(c)(1)-(4), and one of the requirements under §109(c)(5) to be eligible for relief under the Code".

The bankruptcy courts rule that a municipality does not meet the insolvency requirement if it is merely economically distressed or, even if distressed, retains a favorable cash position. For example, Boise County, Idaho failed to show an inability to pay debt in 2011 with surplus funds and a borrowing capacity. Hamilton Creek Metro District in Summit County, Colorado was refused Chapter 9 bankruptcy protection in 1998 because it was found not to be severely economically distressed. Bridgeport, Connecticut was refused Chapter 9 protection in 1991 when the federal judge ruled that the city, despite financial struggles, had sufficient reserves to pay back its creditors.

After filing an objection to Chapter 9 petition, Section 921(c) stipulates that a municipality itself bears the burden of proving its insolvency on the petition date. The ***automatic stay*** protects the debtor against creditor lawsuits, foreclosures, attempts to terminate leases, and collection phone calls and emails. According to Knox et al. (2020), the automatic stay is

> triggered by the filing of the bankruptcy petition, and the protection in Chapter 9 cases to officers and inhabitants goes beyond the protection afforded only to debtors in Chapter 11 cases . . . the automatic stay provides the municipality the opportunity to focus on a comprehensive solution rather than simultaneously fighting multiple brushfires.
>
> *(pp. 7–8)*

The municipality must show that it satisfies at least one of the "creditor negotiation" tests of Section 109(c)(5), which "include requirements that the municipality has made efforts to negotiate with its creditors regarding the impairment of their claims or that such an effort is impracticable" (National Association of Bond Lawyers, 2015, p. 41). In addition to filing the petition, the municipality (Chapter 9 debtor) must provide

> the list of creditors and a list of the twenty largest creditors, must also give notice of the case filing (and any subsequent dismissal of the case) through publication at least once a week for three successive weeks in a newspaper of general circulation in the district where the case is commenced and in such other newspapers having general circulation among bond dealers and bondholders.
>
> *(National Association of Bond Lawyers, 2015, p. 56)*

Information about how to file a bankruptcy petition as well as access to previous court records can be found though the Public Access to Court Electronic Records (PACER) syste m: https://pacer.uscourts.gov/

After filing a Chapter 9 petition, the management of the municipality remains the same as before the filing. Elected officials and legislative bodies continue to perform their daily duties. "The municipality is free to incur post-petition debt, borrow funds, and buy or sell property without authorization of the court" (National Association of Bond Lawyers, 2015, p. 57). The bankruptcy court has the power to grant or deny relief, confirm or dismiss the debtor's plan, approve or deny the assumption of contracts and leases, and dismiss the case entirely for ineligibility, lack of good faith, or failure to achieve confirmation. Otherwise, the court's oversight role is limited. Specifically, the bankruptcy court cannot order municipalities to raise taxes or fees during the Chapter 9 process. The municipalities are not subject to liquidation or strict judicial control. In addition, development of the reorganization plan is largely the initiative of municipal authorities.

Pursuant to 11 U.S.C. §§362(a) and 922(a), the filing of a Chapter 9 petition will operate as a stay of all litigation and debt collection activities against a municipality and its property. A general policy of Chapter 9 is to give the municipal debtor a relief from debt collection efforts in order to develop a plan to restructure its debts (National Association of Bond Lawyers, 2015). Different types of debt obligations receive different treatment in the Chapter 9 process:

1 general obligation bonds are treated as general debt. A municipality is not required to make principal or interest payments during the bankruptcy process. The obligations created by general obligation bonds are subject to negotiations and possible restructuring under the adjustment plan
2 revenue bonds continue to be secured and paid with earmarked revenues if these revenues are available.

According to 11 U.S.C. §928, "in a Chapter 9 bankruptcy case, revenue bonds, as secured obligations, often receive treatment that is superior to the treatment afforded to single-barrel GOs, which may be treated as unsecured debt" (National Association of Bond Lawyers, 2015, p. 47). Section 902(2) of the Bankruptcy Code defines special revenues as revenues derived from (1) the operation or ownership of transportation or utility projects, (2) special excise taxes, (3) incremental taxes attributable to a special project, (4) certain municipal functions, and (5) taxes levied to finance a specific project (11 U.S.C. §902(2)).

The municipality must propose the plan for adjustment in good faith and in accordance with the law. The plan must be in the best interests of the creditors of the municipality (11 U.S.C. §943(b)(7)). The Bankruptcy Code specifies that the debtor shall file the adjustment plan either with the petition or at a later court-defined time. There is no provision in Chapter 9 allowing creditors or other third parties to file the plan (Mikesell, 2002). The payments to creditors proposed by the plan should be no less than what would be obtained through the dismissal of the case when creditors are free to exercise their non-bankruptcy remedies. The debtor must demonstrate that it would have the ability to make the payments and perform the obligations required by the plan and maintain a level of operations necessary for its ongoing municipal duties. This may require the court to make a careful examination of the debtor's projected revenues and expenses (National Association of Bond Lawyers, 2015, p. 88). The court must confirm a plan when the following conditions are met: (1) the plan complies with the general provisions of the overall bankruptcy code, (2) all amounts to be paid by the debtor have been fully disclosed and are reasonable, (3) the debtor is not prohibited by law from taking any action necessary to carry out the plan, (4) any regulatory or electoral approvals necessary to carry out the plan have been obtained, and (5) the plan is in the best interests of creditors and is feasible (Mikesell, 2002).

After the adjustment plan is confirmed, the municipality emerges from Chapter 9 protection and is required to fulfill its obligations to creditors under the terms of the bankruptcy plan. Usually, reorganization of municipal debt is accomplished by extending debt maturities, reducing the amount of principal or interest, or refinancing the debt by obtaining a new loan (Mikesell, 2002).

> The municipality is discharged from all debts when (1) the plan is confirmed; (2) the debtor deposits with the disbursing agent any consideration to be distributed under the plan by such agent; and (3) the court has determined that any security to be distributed and any provision made to pay or secure payment of such obligations under the plan are valid.
>
> *(National Association of Bond Lawyers, 2015, p. 88)*

The bankruptcy court may retain the jurisdiction of the municipality's case, even after confirmation, for a period of time necessary to ensure the successful implementation of the plan. "Where a Chapter 9 debtor has failed to perform its obligations under a confirmed plan, the court has post-confirmation jurisdiction to deny the debtor's motion to close the case and find that the plan has not been substantially consummated" (National Association of Bond Lawyers, 2015, p. 89).

Advantages and Downsides of Bankruptcy

During bankruptcy municipalities may still borrow, raise taxes (if they have legal authority by the state to do so), spend money as they see fit, adjust non-debt contractual obligations, and use its property (Mikesell, 2002, p. 5). An important advantage of Chapter 9 bankruptcy is that a municipality is awarded time to adjust financial obligations. Section 362 of the Bankruptcy Code "the automatic stay" stops all collections from any debtors as soon as a Chapter 9 bankruptcy petition is filed. The unpaid claims of creditors can be then either reduced and/or extended and restructured. During bankruptcy process municipalities may reject collective bargaining agreements and retiree benefit plans. According to Knox et al. (2020), "the plan of adjustment can provide a fresh start and the ability to achieve long-term financial stability for the municipality by deferring and/or reducing past obligations" (p. 8).

Another important immediate advantages of a bankruptcy filing is that "bankruptcy judges are experts in financial restructuring, negotiations and arbitrating complex debtor/creditor and intercreditor disputes", which can aid municipalities tremendously in facilitating negotiations with the creditors and restructuring efforts (Knox et al., 2020, p. 8).

Bankruptcy is, however, typically a last resort option as a remedy for ailing municipalities, due to its sizeable side effects. Perhaps the largest one is the negative image (stigma) of municipal bankruptcy that, among other aspects, has an adverse impact on the business climate in the municipality. Empty storefronts, abandoned buildings, unmoved grass, and simply the perception of bankruptcy can be very unattractive for businesses and residents alike who may never want to move to a city that was once bankrupt. Municipal bankruptcies hurt existing businesses that depend on municipal contracts as well.

This stigma and other factors underlying bankruptcy negatively affect not only the struggling municipality itself, but there is a ripple effect on nearby municipalities. In one such ripple effect example, in April 2013, approaching bankruptcy, Detroit, MI in a cost-saving move terminated its water contract with the city of Flint that for 46 years received water from Detroit Water and Sewerage Department (DWSD) leading to the infamous Flint Water Crisis. In another example, sewer problems that started to backfire in the 1990s were at the heart of the Jefferson County (Jeffco) bankruptcy in 2013 (read Chapter 11 about the Jeffco bankruptcy). Interestingly, a much earlier sewer scandal (related to the same Jeffco sewer system) was at the epicenter of the 1991 bankruptcy scandal of a small town of Lipscomb in Jefferson County, a suburb of Birmingham. The two bond issues that Lipscomb held at the time of bankruptcy were both backed by residential sewer and water levies. But the residents were reportedly unable to pay an additional assessment, hundreds of accounts had collectively tens of thousands of dollars in delinquent payments, and the sewer system (the same sewer system in the center of Jefferson County bankruptcy) itself was in a desperate need of repairs. The city defaulted on its payments and later that year applied for bankruptcy. Already after Jeffco bankruptcy, COVID-19 closures added to the fiscal stress of Fairfield, AL in Jefferson County, another suburb of Birmingham. Fairfield already experienced difficulties after the major city's employer and taxpayer, Walmart, closed its doors and another one, U.S. Steel's Fairfield Works, substantively downsized. The city applied for Chapter 9 bankruptcy protection on May 19, 2020 (see also the discussions of Fairfield bankruptcy in Chapter 1).

Another disadvantage is the cost of filing and pursuing a Chapter 9 case. Legal and financial consulting fees can easily reach millions of dollars. Jefferson County, Alabama reportedly spent about 30 million dollars in legal and other bankruptcy-related fees (Wright, 2019). The cost on lawyers and consultants in Detroit's bankruptcy totaled almost 178 million dollars (Reuters, 2014). And

> every dollar spent on these costs is a dollar that cannot go toward solving the underlying financial problem. It is therefore in the interest of all stakeholders to realize that unless they can come to a negotiated settlement that avoids bankruptcy, these costs ultimately will consume funds that otherwise could be more productively used.
>
> *(Knox et al., 2020, p. 9)*

Another major downside of municipal bankruptcy is the credit ratings' downgrade. Low credit ratings negatively affect credit history and, consequently, the government's ability to borrow at lower costs, for many years to come (Guzman & Moldogaziev, 2012, Capeci, 1991). Bankruptcy can have a "contagion effect" on other municipal issuers in the state, as their borrowing costs may increase too, even if they themselves never applied for bankruptcy (Yang, 2019a, 2019b; Yang & Abbas, 2020). Not even bankruptcy per se but mere access to bankruptcy is found to negatively affect municipal borrowing costs. Moldogaziev et al. (2017) estimated that, independently of credit ratings or any other factors, municipalities in states that allow for Chapter 9 bankruptcy unconditionally pay yields six basis points higher, and they pay four basis points higher in the states that allow for conditional bankruptcy authorization (read more about conditional and unconditional bankruptcy authorization in the next section). Finally, a moral hazard problem is possible in Chapter 9 states, as easy access to bankruptcy can potentially result in borrowers carelessly issuing more debt (Yang, 2019a).

States' Interventions

In the most severe cases of fiscal distress, 20 states implemented various intervention strategies into local government finances (see Table 4.3). The intervention is carried out generally by one of three groups of state appointed ***intervenors*** or

emergency managers or a combination of thereof: a receiver, state agency, or a financial control board or commission (PEW Charitable Trusts, 2013).

Receiver, Emergency Manager, Financial Manager, Overseer, or Coordinator

Some states choose to appoint an outside person, usually a legal and financial expert, to lead the distressed city over a certain period, until the municipality exits bankruptcy. Rhode Island Governor Lincoln Chafee, for example, hired Robert G. Flanders, Rhode Island Supreme Court Associate Justice and a specialist in municipal restructuring, to lead Central Falls, RI, out of bankruptcy from 2011 to 2012. Michigan Governor Rick Snyder similarly turned for help to Washington D.C. bankruptcy lawyer Kevyn Orr to guide Detroit out of bankruptcy in between 2013 and 2014.

State Agency

Instead of hiring an outsider, some states designate a state agency or appoint a state employee to perform the role of financial manager for the distressed municipality. For example, the Nevada Department of Taxation oversees fiscal emergencies in this state. In 1999, the Nevada Department of Taxation took control over the small city of Gabbs after concluding that increasing property taxes and water and sewer fees would not raise enough money to balance Gabbs' budget. Two years later, the Nevada Legislature, which originally incorporated Gabbs, voted to dissolve and dis-incorporate the city and place it under control of the county government.

Financial Control Board

Other states appoint a financial control board or commission consisting of state and local government officials to facilitate municipal recovery efforts. For example, the state of New York created a Buffalo Fiscal Stability Authority, a nine-member board, in 2003 to oversee a financial recovery in the city of Buffalo. The authority is still active. In 1988, Connecticut appointed a nine-member State Financial Review Board to handle the fiscal emergency of the city of Bridgeport, the largest municipality in Connecticut. The board dissolved itself in 1995.

Some states use a combination of fiscal managers and often approach fiscal emergency on a case-by-case basis. Pennsylvania, for example, designates the Pennsylvania Department of Community and Economic Development to conduct fiscal monitoring and intervention for fiscally distressed cities. Yet, two cities in the state have their fiscal emergencies handled differently. In 2004, the Pittsburgh Intergovernmental Cooperation Authority (ICA), a five-member board, was created to oversee their city's financial insolvency (Guzman, 2019). The

Pennsylvania Intergovernmental Cooperation Authority (PICA), a five-member board, was created in 1991 to handle the city of Philadelphia's finances. Both fiscal authorities are still actively managing these cities' finances. Massachusetts appointed a receiver to financially struggling Chelsea in 1991. The receiver left in 1995 after the situation improved. When Springfield, Massachusetts, the third-largest city in the state, was distressed in 2004, the state lawmakers established a five-member financial control board consisting of state and local appointees. The board was dissolved after the city ended the 2009 budget year with 35 million dollars in reserves (PEW Charitable Trusts, 2013).

The intervention practices for severely distressed and bankrupt cities include restructuring of finances (including debt, labor contracts, taxes, fees, and credits), emergency financing, technical assistance, loans and grants, and dissolving or consolidating local government involuntarily (Jeweler, 2007; Lockwood, 2013; PEW Charitable Trusts, 2013; White & Gordon, 2014).

Restructuring of Finances, Including Debt

Fifteen of the twenty states that institutionalized state intervention policies allow an emergency manager to renegotiate the terms of existing bonds on behalf of the city government (PEW Charitable Trusts, 2013). The Municipal Assistance Corporation (MAC), a public-private corporation, was created by the state of New York in 1975 to aid New York City in an extreme financial crisis. The city had exhausted all lending opportunities and was no longer able to have any debt issuances underwritten. MAC helped to sell the bonds and raise money for the city. In 1990, the Illinois legislature similarly created a package of loans, established a state bonding authority, and appointed a financial manager and a five-member Financial Advisory Authority to rescue the city of East St. Louis (Illinois Auditor Authority, 2021).

Labor Contracts

Seven states permit emergency managers to reduce labor costs in distressed municipalities, authorizing them to renegotiate existing labor contracts, including multiyear commitments to increase salaries, benefits, or other compensations (PEW Charitable Trusts, 2013, p. 16).

Taxes, Fees, and Credits

Eleven states give emergency managers the authority to introduce new taxes, fees, and charges or increase existing ones.

Emergency Financing

Legislature in 14 states permits state loans (usually offered at zero or low interest), grants, or credit guarantees. Massachusetts allocated 52 million dollars to

Springfield in 2004 to support this city during its fiscal emergency. Michigan and Rhode Island transferred state funds to support Detroit and Central Falls respectively during their bankruptcies.

Technical Assistance

Nineteen out of twenty states with intervention programs offer budgeting, financial, and other technical advice to fiscally challenged municipalities.

Dissolving or Consolidating Local Government Involuntarily

Michigan, Nevada, and Tennessee give the power to an emergency manager to disincorporate or dissolve a city and consolidate it with another nearby jurisdiction (PEW Charitable Trusts, 2013).

States' Legal Frameworks for Municipal Bankruptcy

As mentioned earlier, the U.S. Bankruptcy Code allows municipalities to file for bankruptcy protection only with state authorization. Twenty-seven states authorize some form of bankruptcy filing with varying conditions. Twelve of these states authorize bankruptcy filing unconditionally, twelve other states have conditional authorization, and the remaining three provide limited authorization (Spiotto et al., 2012). Georgia and Iowa explicitly prohibit cities from seeking Chapter 9 protection, and the remaining 21 states do not have regulations allowing or prohibiting local government bankruptcies (See Table 3.1 for details; PEW Charitable Trusts, 2013). The District of Columbia is not authorized to use Chapter 9 bankruptcy protection because it is not a municipality as defined in the Bankruptcy Code.

Effective January 1, 2012, the ***California*** Government Code, Section 53760, specifies eligibility for Chapter 9 protection. Municipalities should either complete a 60–90-day mediation process or face an immediate financial crisis that threatens the health or welfare of its residents. Federal judges lead municipal bankruptcy cases, but a judge cannot liquidate a city as the court can liquidate a corporation with Chapter 11, for example. Instead, the judge's role is limited to determining the fairness of the city's plan to adjust debts and pay creditors after negotiations among stakeholders. As Christopher M. Klein, the chief judge of the U.S. Bankruptcy Court for the Eastern District of California says, Chapter 9 filings are "intensely a negotiation model because the judge's powers are greatly limited" (Klein, 2012, p. 1).

Multiple cities in California have applied for Chapter 9 bankruptcy: Stockton and San Bernardino in June and July of 2012 respectively, Vallejo in May 2008, Desert Hot Springs in December 2001, and infamous Orange County in December 1994.

In ***Connecticut***, the governor must approve Chapter 9 filings. The state deals with fiscal distress in an ad hoc manner. Four special acts have been enacted to restore the fiscal sustainability of municipalities (LCO 4532 (Waterbury); SA 92–5 (West Haven); SA 88–80, 89–23, 89–47, 90–31, 91–40 (Bridgeport); and SA 93–4 (Jewett City; http://cga.ct.gov/2001/rpt/2001-R-0312.htm).

A 1979 Financial Emergency Act in ***Florida*** established a financial emergency board to oversee fiscally stressed municipalities and reserved the right to file for bankruptcy to the governor (Lang & Stulz, 1992).

In accordance with current bankruptcy law, municipalities in ***Illinois*** cannot voluntarily petition for Chapter 9 bankruptcy without state authorization (65 ILCS 5/8–12–1 through 65 ILCS 5/8–12–24 (Financially Distressed City Law) and 50 ILCS 320/1 through 50 ILCS 320/14 (Local Government Financial Planning and Supervision Act)). So far, such authorization was granted exclusively to the Illinois Power Agency (20 Ill. Comp. Stat. Ann. 3855/1–20(b)(15). Section 3855/1–20(b)(15).

Municipalities in ***Iowa*** may only file a Chapter 9 petition if they are rendered insolvent "as a result of a debt involuntarily incurred" (Iowa Code §76.16A).

Michigan is one of the states that conditionally authorizes Chapter 9 bankruptcy filings. Specifically, MCL141.1558 authorizes a local government for which an Emergency Manager (EM) has been appointed to become a Chapter 9 debtor if the governor approves the emergency manager's recommendation to commence a Chapter 9 case. Michigan Public Act 436 of 2012, the Local Financial Stability and Choice Act, which took effect on March 28, 2013, replaced the Local Government and School District Fiscal Accountability Act, Public Act 4 of 2011. Act 436 offers municipalities experiencing fiscal emergencies a choice of four options: to accept the state-appointed emergency manager, apply for Chapter 9 bankruptcy, enter into the mediation process, or join a "consent agreement" with the state. If the governor appoints an EM for the municipality or a school district in fiscal emergency, the EM assumes the power and duties of the chief administrative officer and legislative body (Egan & Gallagher, 2012). According to Kasdan (2014), "the emergency manager (EM) exercises a level of legal-rational authority necessary to wield the hatchet that cuts through financial entanglements" (p. 1093). Governor Rick Snyder appointed an emergency manager to take over the day-to-day operation of Detroit in March 2013 (Davey, 2013).

In 2014, four municipalities and three school districts in Michigan were under control of an EM, while an additional nine local governments entered or exited the process through a review or consent agreement with the state (Department of Treasury, State of Michigan, 2014). During his tenure, Governor Rick Snyder appointed 22 emergency managers in Michigan. But, in 2018, no city or school district was under emergency manager control in the state (Maher, 2018). Governor Snyder said, "The fact that the state now has no emergency managers in place for the first time in eighteen years shows how well that commitment has worked" (Maher, 2018, p. 1).

Montana allows a "local entity" to file for bankruptcy, but specifically excludes counties from this definition (Montana Code. Ann. §7–7–132).

Nevada does not allow for Chapter 9 bankruptcy, but the state's "severe financial emergency" law permits an appointment of an emergency manager, by the state Department of Taxation, to negotiate and approve most collective bargaining agreements for a city in crisis (N.R.S. 354.686–725).

Oregon allows only irrigation districts to seek reorganization (National Association of Bond Lawyers, 2015). Oregon additionally passed several legislations that allow the state to take over certain local government services, such as elections or tax collection, in counties during fiscal emergency situations.

To apply for bankruptcy in ***Pennsylvania,*** a municipality has to be a part of the Act 47 program (Pennsylvania's Municipalities Financial Recovery Act of 1987, discussed in Chapter 3) and obtain a written approval from the State Department of Internal Affairs (National Association of Bond Lawyers, 2015). Only the receiver can apply for bankruptcy. The city of Harrisburg, for example, entered the Act 47 program on December 15, 2010. In 2011, the city council rejected a recovery plan developed by the coordinator and a second plan developed by the mayor. State legislature restricted the ability of the financially distressed Harrisburg to file for bankruptcy. The Harrisburg city council without mayor's consent, nevertheless, authorized the filing, but the petition was ultimately dismissed by the federal Bankruptcy Court for failure to satisfy the Chapter 9 eligibility requirements (i.e. state approval) (National Association of Bond Lawyers (2015, p. 10).

Rhode Island became the most recent state to adopt bankruptcy regulations on June 11, 2010, in response to fiscal emergency situation in the city of Central Falls, RI and a limited ability of the state to intervene at that time. The state intervention system includes three tiers based on the severity of fiscal stress situation. At the first tier, the state appoints an *overseer* to advise locality on how to avoid a budget deficit. If situation does not improve, at the second tier, the state appoints a *budget committee* that includes both local officials and state appointees. Finally at the third tier, the state appoints a *receiver* to take over local government. Only the receiver is authorized to apply for Chapter 9 bankruptcy (Yang, 2019a, 2019b).

The municipal bankruptcy laws are summarized in Table 4.1, and all Chapter 9 municipal bankruptcy filings in the past 20 years are summarized in Table 4.2.

Conclusions

The bankruptcies in Detroit, MI; Jefferson County, AL; Central Falls, RI; and Vallejo, CA demonstrated the effectiveness and practical necessity of Chapter 9. In general terms, a municipality can apply for Chapter 9 bankruptcy only if it is in the state that allows for Chapter 9 bankruptcy in the first place, if it is insolvent and is unable to come to an agreement with creditors (Section 109 (c) of the Bankruptcy Codes). Twelve states authorize Chapter 9 filings unconditionally; twelve other states permit bankruptcy filings under state-specified conditions. Three other states authorize only certain municipalities to file for

TABLE 4.1 Municipal Bankruptcy Laws in Different States

	Municipality Can Apply for Chapter 9 Bankruptcy	*Year Municipal Bankruptcy Law Was Adopted*	*Corresponding Laws*[2]
Federal		1934, 1937, 1978, 1988, 1994	The Bankruptcy Act of 1898; Bankruptcy Reform Act of 1978, P.L. 95–598; 1988 Amendment, P.L. 100–597; §402 of the Bankruptcy Reform Act of 1994, P.L. 103–394
Alabama	Yes	1935	Ala. Code §11–81–3
Alaska	No		
Arizona	Yes	1955	Ariz. Rev. Stat. Ann. § 35–603
Arkansas	Yes	1939	Ark. Code Ann. § 14–74–103
California	Conditional	1949, 2012 (revised)	Cal. Gov't Code § 53760
Colorado	Limited		CRS § 37–32–102
Connecticut	Conditional	1993	Conn. Gen. Stat. Ann. § 7–566
Delaware	No		
Florida	Conditional	1933, 1979 (revised)	Fla. Stat. Ann. § 218.01
Georgia	No		
Hawaii	No		
Idaho	Yes	1939	Idaho Code Ann. § 67–3903
Illinois	Limited		20 Ill. Comp. Stat. Ann. 320/9(b)(4)
Indiana	No		
Iowa	No		
Kansas	No		
Kentucky	Conditional	1942	Ky. Rev. Stat Ann. § 66.400
Louisiana	Conditional	1950	La. Rev. Stat. Ann. § 39–619
Maine	No		
Maryland	No		
Massachusetts	No		
Michigan	Conditional	1988	Mich. Comp. Laws § 141.1222
Minnesota	Yes	1997	Minn. Stat. Ann. § 471.831
Mississippi	No		
Missouri	Yes	1995	Mo. Ann. Stat. § 427.100
Montana	Yes	1939	Mont. Code Ann. § 7–7–132

(Continued)

TABLE 4.1 (Continued)

	Municipality Can Apply for Chapter 9 Bankruptcy	*Year Municipal Bankruptcy Law Was Adopted*	*Corresponding Laws*[2]
Nebraska	Yes	1943	Neb. Rev. St. § 13–402
Nevada	No		
New Hampshire	No		
New Jersey	Conditional	1938, 1999 (revised)	N.J. Stat. Ann. § 52:27–40
New Mexico	No		
New York	Conditional	1975	N.Y. Local Finance Law § 85.80
North Carolina	Conditional	1939, 1971 (revised)	N.C. Gen. Stat. Ann. § 23–48
North Dakota	No		
Ohio	Conditional	Before 1953, 1979 (revised)	Ohio Rev. Code Ann. § 133.36
Oklahoma	Yes	1935	Okla. Stat. Ann. Tit. 62 §§ 281, 283
Oregon	Limited		Or. Rev. Stat. § 548.705
Pennsylvania	Conditional	1987	53 Pa. Cons. Stat. Ann. § 11701.261
Rhode Island	Conditional	2010	R.I. Gen. Laws §45–9–7
South Carolina	Yes	1939	S.C. Code Ann. § 6–1–10
South Dakota	No		
Tennessee	No		
Texas	Yes	1987	Tex. Loc. Gov't Code § 140.001
Utah	No		
Vermont	No		
Virginia	No		
Washington	Yes	1935	Wash. Rev. Code § 39.64.040
West Virginia	No		
Wisconsin	No		
Wyoming	No		

Source: Compiled from Spiotto, 2013

Note: *Limited provision* means that only certain municipal government entities may apply for Chapter 9 bankruptcy protection. In Illinois, for example, such authority belongs only to the Illinois Power Agency, and in Oregon, only irrigation districts can apply for Chapter 9 bankruptcy. *Conditional authorization* means that to be able to apply for bankruptcy, the municipality has to secure support from the state legislature.

TABLE 4.2 Chapter 9 Municipal Bankruptcy from 2001 to 2021

Chapter 9 Municipal Bankruptcy Cases	*State*	*Date Filed*	*Date Closed*
City of Fairfield	AL	5/19/2020	no closing date
City of Perla	AR	5/26/2019	no closing date
City of Hillview	KY	8/20/2015	5/24/2016
City of Detroit	MI	7/18/2013	12/10/2014
City of San Bernardino	CA	8/1/2012	06/15/2017
Town of Mammoth Lakes	CA	7/3/2012	12/5/2012
City of Stockton	CA	6/28/2012	2/25/2015
Jefferson County	AL	11/9/2011	06/04/2013
City of Central Falls	RI	8/1/2011	10/24/2012
Boise County	ID	3/1/2011	2/10/2012
City of Prichard	AL	10/27/2009	3/13/2017
Town of Moffett	OK	10/22/2009	4/23/2012
Village of Washington Park	IL	7/6/2009	1/10/2011
Westfall Township	PA	4/10/2009	6/4/2010
City of Vallejo	CA	5/23/2008	11/01/2011
City of Gould	AR	4/21/2008	6/18/2010
Town of Marion	MS	2/6/2007	7/17/2007
Town of Moffett	OK	12/20/2006	12/16/2008
Town of Marshall Creek	TX	1/23/2006	3/7/2012
City of Camp Wood	TX	8/5/2005	6/27/2007
Village of Alorton	IL	1/6/2005	4/9/2007
Town of Millport	AL	12/14/2004	7/31/2008
Village of Washington Park	IL	5/7/2004	9/23/2005
City of Westminster	TX	4/16/2004	8/11/2004
City of Iron Mountain Lake	MO	10/14/2003	12/20/2005
Village of Brooklyn	IL	10/13/2003	5/24/2010
City of Reeds Spring	MO	11/8/2002	10/7/2004
City of Rio Bravo	TX	6/23/2002	10/2/2014
City of Desert Hot Springs	CA	12/19/2001	6/2/2005
Village of Hillsdale	MO	11/21/2001	12/12/2002
City of Kendleton	TX	6/27/2001	4/1/2004

Source: Compiled by the authors from PEW Charitable Trusts (2020). Retrieved from https://www.pewtrusts.org/en/research-and-analysis/articles/2020/07/07/by-the-numbers-a-look-at-municipal-bankruptcies-over-the-past-20-years

bankruptcy. Twenty-three states do not authorize municipal bankruptcy under any circumstances.

While there are downsides associated with Chapter 9 bankruptcy filing, the benefits can sometimes outweigh the negatives like the opportunity to restructure debt obligations and renegotiate contracts with creditors. The bankruptcy court cannot force a municipality to make certain expenditure cuts, solicit new revenues, or sell assets. The functions of the bankruptcy court are generally limited to approval of the bankruptcy petition (if the debtor is eligible), confirmation of a plan of debt adjustment, and ensuring implementation of the plan. Chapter 9 provides guidance for a major municipal reorganization. Under Chapter 9, municipalities are not subject to liquidation or strict judicial control. The development of the reorganization plan is largely the initiative of municipal authorities (Congressional Research Service, 2007). Chapter 9 reorganization and intervention practices usually include restructuring of finances; negotiation of labor contracts; increase of taxes, fees, and credits; emergency financing; technical assistance; provision of loans and grants; and dissolving or consolidating local government involuntarily. These practices are shaped by the constraints of the federal and state laws under which a municipality operates.

Notes

1 Municipal insolvency is defined as a "financial condition" in which a municipality is: (1) generally not paying its debts as they become due unless such debts are the subject of a bona fide dispute; or (2) unable to pay its debts as they become due. (11 U.S.C. §101(32)(C). The insolvency tests are applied as of the time of the filing.)

2 www.bradley.com/-/media/files/insights/publications/2018/12/municipal-bankruptcy-a-guide-for-public-finance-attorneys-3rd-edition.pdf

References

Capeci, J. (1991). Credit risk, credit ratings and municipal bond yields: A panel study. *National Tax Journal, 44*(4), 41–56.

Congressional Research Service (2007). Municipal reorganization: Chapter 9 of the U.S. bankruptcy code. *CRS Report for Congress*. Retrieved August 5, 2021, https://www.everycrsreport.com/reports/R41738.html

Davey, M. (2013, March 14). Bankruptcy lawyer is named to manage an ailing Detroit. *The New York Times*. Retrieved August 5, 2021, https://www.nytimes.com/2013/03/15/us/gov-rick-snyder-kevyn-orr-emergency-manager-detroit.html

De Angel, M., & Xiaowei, T. (2013). United States: Chapter 9 municipal bankruptcy – utilization, avoidance, and impact. In Canuto, O., & Liu, L. (Eds.), *Until Debt Do Us Part Subnational Debt, Insolvency, and Markets* (pp. 323–345). New York: Stand Alone Books.

Department of Treasury, State of Michigan. (2014). *Local government fiscal health*, 11 April. Retrieved August 5, 2021, from www.michigan.gov/treasury

Egan, P., & Gallagher, J. (2012). Michigan voters reject all proposals; emergency manager law repealed. *Detroit Free Press*, 7 November. Retrieved August 5, 2021, from www.freep.com/article/20121107/NEWS15/311070105/Michigan-proposals-emergency-manager-law.

FindLaw (2021). Bankruptcy. Retrieved from www.findlaw.com/bankruptcy.html

Guzman, T. (2019). Fiscal conditions of largest legacy cities. In *The Legacies of Legacy Cities: Continuity and Change amid Decline and Revival*. Pittsburgh, PA: University of Pittsburgh Press.

Guzman, T., & Moldogaziev, T. (2012). Which bonds are more expensive? The cost differentials by debt issue purpose and the method of sale: An empirical analysis. *Public Budgeting & Finance, 32*(3), 79–101.

Illinois Auditor Authority (2021). *East St. Louis financial advisory authority*, 30 June. Retrieved August 5, 2021, from www.auditor.illinois.gov/Audit-Reports/East-St-Louis-Financial-Advisory-Authority.asp

Jeweler, R. (2007). *Municipal Reorganization: Chapter 9 of the US Bankruptcy Code*. Washington, D.C.: Congressional Research Service, Library of Congress.

Kasdan, O. (2014). A tale of two hatchet men: Emergency financial management in Michigan. *Administration & Society*, *46*(9), 1092–1108.

Klein, C. (Ed.). (2012). *U.S. Bankruptcy Court judge, remarks at California Fiscal Crisis conference, University of California, Berkeley Institute of Governmental Studies,* 21 September 2012. Retrieved October 12, 2021, from http://igs.berkeley.edu/events/fiscalstress.

Knox, J., Levinson, M., & Brennan, D. (2020). *Municipal Bankruptcy: Avoiding and Using Chapter 9 In Times of Fiscal Stress* (3rd ed.). San Francisco, CA: Orrick, Herrington & Sutcliffe LLP

Lang, L., & Stulz, R. (1992). Contagion and competitive intra-industry effects of bankruptcy announcements: An empirical analysis. *Journal of Financial Economics, 32*(1), 45–60.

Lewis, C. (1994). Municipal bankruptcy and the states. *Urban Affairs Quarterly*, *30*(1), 3–26

Lockwood, J. (2013). Scranton council adopts 22% tax hike, *The Times Tribune*, 11 January. Retrieved October 12, 2021, from http://thetimes-tribune.com/news/scranton-council-adopts-22-tax-hike-1.1428287

Maher, K (2018). Michigan Cities Move Off the State's Critical List. *The Wall Street Journal*, 12 July. Retrieved October 12, 2021, from www.wsj.com/articles/michigan-cities-move-off-the-states-critical-list-1530446401

Mikesell, J. (2002). *Subnational Government Bankruptcy, Default, and Fiscal Crisis in the United States*. [Working Paper 02–21]. Atlanta, GA: International Studies Program Georgia State University.

Moldogaziev, T., Kioko, S., & Hildreth, B. (2017). Impact of bankruptcy eligibility requirements and statutory liens on borrowing costs. *Public Budgeting & Finance, 37*(4), 47–73.

National Association of Bond Lawyers (2015). *Municipal bankruptcy: A guide for public finance attorneys* (3rd ed.). Retrieved October 12, 2021, from www.bradley.com/-/media/files/insights/publications/2018/12/municipal-bankruptcy-a-guide-for-public-finance-attorneys-3rd-edition.pdf

PEW Charitable Trusts (2013). *The state role in local government financial distress*. Retrieved October 12, 2021, from www.pewtrusts.org/~/media/assets/2016/04/pew_state_role_in_local_government_financial_distress.pdf

PEW Charitable Trusts (2020). *By the numbers: A look at municipal bankruptcies over the past 20 years*. Retrieved October 12, 2021, from https://www.pewtrusts.org/en/research-and-analysis/articles/2020/07/07/by-the-numbers-a-look-at-municipal-bankruptcies-over-the-past-20-years

Reuters (2014). *Fees, expenses for Detroit bankruptcy hit nearly $178 million*. Retrieved February 19, 2022, from www.reuters.com/article/usa-detroit-bankruptcy-fees/fees-expenses-for-detroit-bankruptcy-hit-nearly-178-million-idUSL1N0UE1LJ20141230

Spiotto, J. E. (2013). The role of the state in supervising and assisting municipalities, especially in times of financial distress. *Municipal Finance Journal*, *33/34*(4/1), 1–31.

Spiotto, J., Acker, A., & Appleby, L. (2012). *Municipalities in Distress? How States and Investors Deal With Local Government Financial Emergencies*. Charlotte, NC: Chapman & Cutler LLP.

White, E., & Gordon, C. (2014). Governing law for municipal bankruptcy in Illinois. *Pratt's Journal of Bankruptcy Law*, *9*, 16–21. Retrieved October 12, 2021, from www.

chapman.com/media/publication/316_Chapman_Governing_Law_Municipal_Bankruptcy_Illinois_JournalBankruptcyLaw_010114.pdf

Wright, B. (2019). *One year ago Jefferson County emerged from bankruptcy. Did Wall Street fleece the County Commission?* Retrieved from www.al.com/news/birmingham/2014/12/one_year_later_jefferson_count.html

Yang, L. (2019a). Negative externality of fiscal problems: Dissecting the contagion effect of municipal bankruptcy. *Public Administration Review, 79*(2), 156–167.

Yang, L. (2019b). Not all state authorizations for municipal bankruptcy are equal: Impact of bankruptcy authorizations on state primary market borrowing costs. *National Tax Journal, 72*(2), 435–464.

Yang, L. K., & Abbas, Y. (2020). General-purpose local government defaults: Type, trend, and impact. *Public Finance and Budgeting, 40*(4), 62–85.

5

FISCAL STRESS AND OPERATING BUDGET

Introduction

Local governments provide a vast array of services that affect everyone in the jurisdiction every single day. The way these services are provided and budgeted for are, however, unique: one municipality may offer a highly sophisticated system of fire suppression, emergency rescue, trash collection, recycling, and emergency medical services, while another local government may be limited to providing only basic law enforcement while outsourcing other services to nearby municipalities. Local governments often overlap. One city may be independent, whereas another might be fully or partially consolidated with the local county. School districts can be similarly independent or city or county dependent. Every overlapping jurisdiction decides through their budgeting process what services will be provided, to whom, at what level, and how they will be paid for.

Under fiscal stress, when revenues are reduced dramatically, municipalities have no choice but to cut expenditures. They have to do it wisely to avoid service interruptions, especially those threatening public safety and health. Expenditure cuts create a wide array of new questions. Should such cuts be across the board or more targeted? Which services should be provided and at what level, and which should be abolished? What would be the optimal mix of healthcare, education, recreation, welfare, and law enforcement programs in the municipality? What departments (Police Department, Fire Department, Public Works Department, etc.) will sustain the largest cuts? Should public safety or social services have priority in the operating budget? How would such cuts affect communities during fiscal stress? What other overlapping governments are affected by the cuts?

The COVID-19 crisis and the corresponding economic decline exacerbated the gap between available fiscal resources and needs (Felix, 2020; Miller et al.,

DOI: 10.4324/b23117-5

2021; Romanov & Thatcher, 2020) and introduced even more questions, while solutions have become more scarce and choices more difficult. The effect of COVID-19 on municipalities' fiscal capacity over time proved to be increasingly negative, indicating that revenue systems remain vulnerable and less flexible under fiscal stress (PEW Charitable Trusts, 2020). The National Association of Counties (2020) estimated an overall 144 billion dollars in budgetary impact across all U.S. counties through fiscal year 2020–2021 – 114 billion dollars in lost revenue and 30 billion dollars in additional expenditures, with the median county spending around 8 percent of its total budget on their COVID-19 response.

In this chapter, we study operating budgeting practices that municipalities employ when they face fiscal struggles. Operating budgets are used for recurring expenses, such as wages and salaries, benefits, payment for utilities, materials, etc. In Chapter 6 we discuss capital budgeting and infrastructure finance needs during fiscal stress. Capital budgeting is used for long-term, non-recurring, and high-ticketed expenditures, such as new constructions and capital improvements of buildings, roads, bridges, dams, etc.

Important Theoretical Approaches to Operating Budgeting

There have been numerous budget theories developed to the day. We believe several of these traditional budgeting approaches need to be addressed to provide a general understanding and basic theoretical background to operating budgeting. By no means can we cover all of these theoretical approaches in this book, but, by addressing some important and relevant ideas, we open room for further discussion of budgeting practices for municipalities during fiscally challenging times.

1) Incrementalism

We start off our discussion with the earlier and perhaps the most well-known budget theory, *incrementalism*, which argues that "budgeting is incremental, not comprehensive. An agency's budgets based on last year's budget with special attention given to a narrow range of increases or decreases" (Wildavsky, 1964, p. 15). Incrementalism suggests that agencies act as advocates, protecting their budget base and requesting small ("incremental") increases from the previous year (Davis et al., 1966; Lindblom, 1959; Wildavsky, 1961).

While incrementalism gained a lot of support in earlier budget studies, especially around the 1950s and 1960s, recent budget literature is less enthusiastic about it. LeLoup (2002), for example, says that "incrementalism was built on a series of analytical choices that severely limited its applicability as a theory and made it unsuitable for explaining the kinds of changes that were taking place in budgeting in the 1970s and 1980s" (p. 5). LeLoup (2002) distinguishes between *microbudgeting* and *macrobudgeting*[1] in incrementalism and, based on these, defines the following drawbacks of incrementalism: (1) a theory of microbudgeting concentrating on the parts, not the whole; (2) the definition of budgeting as

> a bottom-up process of making marginal adjustments to estimates on an annual basis, without considering macrobudgetary attempts to shape the budget from the top down, (3) budgets by agency rather than by function or broader aggregates. It looked at change over a year rather than over longer time periods.

LeLoup (2002) says that

> in the new century, if the economy remains positive, one might expect budgeting to return to a greater emphasis on microbudgeting and less on macrobudgeting. The changes in the composition of the budget, its sensitivity to the economy, and the long experience with deficits have changed budgeting forever. But if surpluses continue, the budget process will see renewed emphasis on program and policy issues as well as on how to balance the totals.
>
> *(p. 15)*

LeLoup (2002) suggests an emerging new paradigm of budgeting in terms of budgeting scope and nature as: (1) a balance between macro- and micro-level and (2) less comprehensive – but broad – multi-year budgeting. In his opinion, however, these changes in budgeting can occur only during positive economic growth. In positive budgeting, strong-growth environments, the public needed little reassurance of the value of public spending. In negative budgeting, weak or slow-growth (sometimes called *slowth*) environments, the nexus between tax payments for public revenues and budget benefits for public expenditures must be reestablished (Hyde, 2002, pp. 458–459).

2) Multi-year Budgeting and Counter-cyclical Fiscal Policies

LeLoup's thinking is similar to *Keynes's* idea of *countercyclical fiscal policies*, which are designed to act against the business cycle flow: deficit spending during recessions or when recovery is long-delayed, and unemployment is persistently high – and the suppression of inflation in boom times by either increasing taxes or cutting back on government outlays. Keynes (1924) argued that governments should solve problems in the short run rather than waiting for the market to adjust itself in the long run, because, in the long run, we would all be dead.

Hou and Moynihan (2008) calls for a countercyclical policy approach in which budgeting for stability involves saving during an economic boom to meet elevated expenditures during economic recessions (refer to Chapter 3 for discussion of balanced budget requirements, rainy-day funds, etc.). Such a countercyclical policy assumes a multi-year rather than annual budgeting approach. An annual budgeting approach's strength lies in its spending controls and its management of day-to-day operations, but it is not adequate for facing economic distress. Hou and Moynihan (2008) and Hou (2006) pointed out that politically, the annual budget was a governance tool to promote democracy; managerially, it was intended to coordinate the legislative and executive branches; and technically, it aimed to improve administrative efficiency of budgeting.

To prepare for future recessions, the best annual budgeting approach would be to accumulate annual surpluses. However, annual budgets are not designed to deal with political and legal demands associated with running surpluses. Hence, surpluses generally tend to be small, if there are any. Hou (2006) argued that the annual budgeting cycle cannot guarantee a balanced budget and makes it more difficult for state and local governments to ensure balanced budgets in the long run. Boex et al. (2000) also advocate for multi-year budgeting (medium-term financial plans) that "can offer significant benefits, such as forewarning potential fiscal imbalances in future years and enhancing aggregate budget discipline, and to evolve the multi-year budget framework into a more integrated approach over time" (p. 110). Boex et al. (2000) emphasize such benefits of a multi-year budget approach as: (1) placement of a more explicit and consistent statement of policy goals and priorities, (2) a signal whether current policies and their future implications are in line with the current fiscal strategy, (3) provision of continuity to the budget process by placing the annual budget discussion in the context of the government's medium-term fiscal strategy and policy priorities, (4) improving efficiency in public resource allocation by enhancing transparency and accountability in the budget process, (5) providing a mechanism for the systematic review of spending priorities and commitments, and (6) providing a means for cooperation between various government agencies (Boex et al., 2000, p. 92).

Premchand (2007) agrees with the importance of the multi-year budget framework. He highlights the necessity of the following changes in expenditure management: (1) preparation of a medium-term fiscal outlook, (2) preparation of medium-term rolling expenditure budgets, (3) formulation of functional or program resource ceilings, (4) recognition of risks and associated measures, (5) formulation of priorities and strategies, (6) explicit recognition of performance links, (7) fundamental or periodic reviews, and (8) introduction of accrual budgeting and accounting.

Kovner and Lusk (2010) propose a *sustainable budgeting model* that suggests a way to combine budgeting and the planning process to achieve inflows relative to outflows that ensure long-term budget balance and, thus, a sustainable fiscal position. This model calibrates the revenue inflows and outflows for various time horizons using present value concepts. The model calls for three scenarios for each project or focus of funding: best-case (inflows/revenues high and outflows/costs relatively low), average-case (revenues and costs fall somewhere in between best case and worst case), and worst-case scenarios (highest relative outflows/

costs and lowest relative inflows). The expected value is calculated by estimating the likelihood of these best-, average-, and worst-case scenarios. The expected value projection for a project or funding focus can then be compared to a defined breakeven range. This sustainable budgeting model is related to variability, and the balancing of inflows/revenues and outflows/costs is analogous to planning for budgetary responses in the event of budget shortfalls brought on by economic downturns. Klase and Dougherty (2008) suggested that this model provides an interesting and conceptually useful approach for making choices between projects or funding areas in planning an operating budget to keep it balanced in the long-term. The PEW Charitable Trusts (2009) and National League of Cities (2010) identify four important components of establishing an effective long-term budget: (1) estimate revenues and expenditures into the future, (2) consider the long-term impact of tax and expenditure decisions, (3) manage long-term liabilities, and (4) maintain a reasonable level of debt.

On the other hand, Boex et al. (2000) highlight potential drawbacks associated with multi-year budgeting. They point out that

> (1) excessive reliance on the forward estimates in the annual budget formulation process could result in inflexibility and inertia in fiscal policies; (2) overly optimistic multi-year projections could be used as a justification for otherwise unjustifiable public spending programs; (3) a full-blown, multi-year budget approach may be a complex and administratively costly tool which may divert attention and resources from the more fundamental task of developing adequate annual budgets.
>
> *(pp. 91–92)*

3) Economic Decline as Innovations' Trigger

The third approach suggests that budgeting changes occur as organizations either internally generate innovations or adapt to them. These are vital to organizational learning and adaptation to external conditions, including fiscal emergency situations (Barnett, 1953; Becker & Whisler, 1967; Fernandez & Rainey, 2006). Adopted or *"ingested" innovations* are the processes, technologies, and products that are invented elsewhere and learned about and implemented by the organization for the first time (Knight, 1967; Lewis & Seibold, 1993; Pierce & Delbecq, 1977; Sandford, 2003; Walker, 1969, 2008). According to March and Simon (1993), "most innovations in an organization are a result of borrowing rather than invention" (p. 209). By borrowing innovations, organizations save on the invention and testing costs and minimize evaluation risks.

Sandford (2003) argues that

> public management innovation awards do not recognize new but unproven ideas: they choose the best applications based on results and replications as

> well as originality. Thus, some of the best applications are relatively recent inventions that have been in operation long enough to show results and be replicated.
>
> *(pp. 46–47)*

Some innovations may be combinations of known ideas in novel ways or applications of known ideas to new settings, provided they too have shown results (Levin & Sanger, 1992).

An *administrative innovation* is the implementation of an internally generated or a borrowed idea – whether pertaining to a product, system, process, policy, program, or service – that was new to the organization at the time of adoption (Thompson, 1965; Zaltman et al., 1973). Damanpour (1996) defines administrative innovations as innovations in organizational structure, administrative practices, and human resources, whereas *technical innovations* are the innovations in products, services, and the technology used to produce them. Administrative innovations result from human interactions that occur during accomplishing organizational goals or tasks (Cummings & Srivastva, 1977, Damanpour & Evan, 1984). They include those rules, roles, procedures, and structures that are related to the communication and exchange among people and between the environment and people (Cummings & Srivastva, 1977). Administrative innovations can come from the implementation of a new way to recruit personnel, allocate resources, and structure tasks, authority, and rewards (Evan, 1966). These include innovations in organizational structure and human resource management (Knight, 1967). Cyert and March (1964) gave the definition of a problem-oriented innovation – "search, like decision making, is problem oriented . . . search is stimulated by a problem . . . and is directed toward finding a solution to that problem" (p. 169).

The importance of the *external environment* has long been emphasized in public management literature. Organizational actions need to fit with the external environment, and when the environment changes, organizations have to change (Chattopadhyay et al., 2001; Wise, 1999, 2002) because existing strategies may become suboptimal when the opportunities and threats associated with those strategies become redefined and the performance outcomes are altered (Audia et al., 2000). The transformation process is even more rapid and drastic in the case of an *environmental jolt* (Meyer, 1979, 1980, 1994; Meyer & Goes, 1988; Meyer & Rowan, 1977; Meyer et al., 1990; Park & Mezias, 2005). Meyer (1982) defined environmental jolts as "transient perturbations whose occurrences are difficult to foresee and whose impact on organizations are disruptive and often inimical" (p. 515).

According to Starbuck et al. (1978), "The Chinese symbol for crisis combines two simpler symbols, the symbol for danger and the one for opportunity. Crises are times of danger, but they are also times of opportunity" (p. 135). Public organizations improve their effectiveness and efficiency when they undergo rational adaptive changes in response to a changing environment (Fernandez & Rainey,

2006; Halligan, 1999; March & Olsen, 1989; Lane, 1999; Kaufman, 1991; Wise, 1999, 2002; Zaltman et al., 1973). According to Cyert and March (1992), "slack provides a source of funds for innovations that would not be approved in the face of scarcity but that have strong subunit support . . . such innovations typically include improvements in the technology (better engineering, newer forms of products)" (p. 189). They also claimed that this proposition is not applicable to the problem-oriented innovations. The problem-oriented innovations would be approved in the face of scarce financial resources as the result of these innovations' necessity.

Theoretical Approaches to Operating Budgeting During Economic Decline and Mild Fiscal Stress

As it was briefly mentioned in Chapter 3, fiscally distressed local governments have very limited options to get back on track financially. They can cut spending, increase taxes (which are often limited or even impossible due to state-imposed tax and/or expenditure limits), enact additional user fees or charges, or use a combination of thereof (Behn, 1985; Deschenaux & Juppe, 2015; Graaf et al., 2016; Istrate & Handy, 2016). These options, in some shape or form, come from theoretical and empirical research in operating budgeting during fiscal stress, and these studies can be broadly divided into the following categories:

1 studies that propose an emergent strategy, specifically, cutback management practices
2 studies that recommend fiscal stress minimization strategies as the midpoint on the emergent-to-planned strategy continuum
3 studies that endorse social budgeting.

1) Emergent Strategy

The first approach suggests using an emergent strategy. Rivera (2012) provides the definition of an emergent strategy as "a pattern of action that develops over time in an organization in the absence of a specific mission and goals, or despite a mission and goals" (p. 1). An emergent strategy develops when an organization takes a series of actions that, with time, turn into a consistent pattern of behavior – regardless of specific intentions – and implies that an organization is learning what works in practice.

The primary example of an emergent strategy is *cutback management* that is particularly applicable in budget literature. From its earliest origins in the 1970s, cutback management theory has focused on government response to economic declines and tactics used to manage cutbacks. Research on cutback management largely draws upon Charles H. Levine's (1978) study on "Organizational Decline and Cutback Management", which suggests the end of more than a half-century of "positive budgeting" (i.e., incremental budgeting theory discussed earlier) and the beginning of a "negative budgeting" era.

Various techniques in cutback management can be employed to address fiscal stress. Levine (1978) lays out the main administrative "methods" for cutback management: (1) "stretching the budget" to get through the fiscal year; (2) "rationing demands" by limiting service or charging fees; (3) "selective withdrawal" by redrawing geographic divisions of the organization or terminating specific programs; (4) "retrenchment" by permanently altering the structure, programs, and staffing of the organizations; (5) cutting programs based on low productivity; and (6) cutting personnel according to seniority or engaging in hiring freezes.

Cutback management was not intended to be a budgetary system; rather, it is a process. Its objective is to fuse political-economic realities with management strategies that reestablish in the public mind the value of public-sector programs and services. Cutback budgeting was initiated in many states during the recession of 1981–1983 that disrupted budgetary incrementalism practices and its norms of conflict-avoidance (Behn, 1985). Controlling expenditures again became the dominant orientation of central budget offices. Miller (1983) points out the variation of state responses to recessions in the early 1980s, such as travel restrictions, space utilization, hiring freezes, across-the-board cuts, and use of bonds.

General cutback strategies, such as hiring freezes, pay freezes, furloughs, layoffs, and productivity improvements, were found to be used at the same rate and scope by states between 1984 and 2004, but Bowling and Burke (2006) conclude that states with tax limits utilized a broader and deeper set of cutback strategies (Scorcone & Plerhoples, 2010).

Levine et al. (1981) proposed the *administrative response model of cutback management*, where the cutback management process begins with broad, across-the-board cuts and then moves onto elimination of targeted programs and major budget reductions as the severity of revenue restrictions increases. Thurmaier and Gosling (2008, p. 121) note that politicians increasingly ran on platforms to cut government expenditures and taxes and let markets have a larger role in shaping society.

There has been plenty of empirical evidence of cutback management responses by state and local governments to economic recessions of 2001 and 2008–2009 and emerging evidence of this response to the economic slowdown caused by the COVID-19 pandemic. Scorscone and Plerhoples (2010) noted that during the 2008 recession, states used budget cuts and restructuring over tax-raising efforts to a much larger extent than during previous recessions. Klase and Dougherty (2008) examined cutback strategies in eight mid-Atlantic and eastern states during the 2001 recession and found support for the administrative response model of cutback management that was advocated by Levine et al. (1981). Rubin and Willoughby (2009) concluded that the choice of the cutback strategies depends on economic circumstances, as expected due to fiscal pressure and resulting administrative responses.

Following the Great Recession of 2008–2009, the National Conference of State Legislatures (2010) estimated that "almost 40 states cut spending for K – 12 educations in fiscal year 2010, and 31 governors proposed to cut such funding in their budgets for 2011" (p. 2).

2) Fiscal Stress Minimization Strategies

The second approach to operating budgeting during fiscal stress focuses on *stress minimization strategies*, such as (1) feasibility of an expanded budget process, (2) raising additional revenue, (3) allowing the deficit to grow, and (4) improving organization design. According to Premchand (2007), "the nature and dimensions of the fiscal stress was such that it became abundantly clear that the traditional methods of nip and tuck, or a cut here or there in the sectoral allocations, would not serve the purpose" (p. 27). Cutback management had to be augmented with other deficit reduction strategies. Back in the day, the Advisory Commission on Intergovernmental Relations (ACIR) (1973) talked about the changing urban population dynamics and, as a result, the necessity to change municipal revenue structure –

> central cities meanwhile are increasingly characterized by declining population, increasing concentration of poor, nonwhite and elderly, obsolescent housing, and above-average rates of crime. The fiscal implications for central cities are high and rising demands for expenditures, especially for non-school purposes and related to the poor, nonwhite, and elderly. These demands require continually increasing tax revenues from bases that are being undermined by the flight of affluent citizens to the suburb.
>
> *(p. 34)*

Titus et al. (2011) and Mintzberg (1990) propose that the effective strategy formation process should include both orientations: emergent strategy orientation and planned strategy orientation. In the private sector, "neither purely emergent nor purely planned strategy should be regarded as inherently desirable" (Titus et al., 2011, p. 451). This emergent-to-planned strategy continuum can also be effective in the public sector, particularly in the operating budgeting process. Pure cutback management can lead to *ad hoc* and non-purposeful strategies. Likewise, a strong planning orientation may contribute to a false sense of control (Mintzberg, 1990).

If a municipality finds itself in fiscal crisis, Premchand (1993) argues that "the first task is to determine the nature of the crisis, the factors contributing to it, whether it is short term or medium term" (p. 57). It is important to analyze whether it is a general problem affecting the whole economy or only the state or locality. Premchand (1993) provides a good analogy of strategic management during fiscal stress as "the role of an aircraft pilot who has to determine whether the turbulence is short and temporary or likely to be prolonged. If it is the latter, a decision on whether any change in the flying altitude is necessary would prove useful" (p. 57).

There are multiple illustrations of fiscal stress minimization strategies in action. During the COVID-19 crisis, for example, "state and local governments have cut their workforces by 5% during the pandemic, and some of the states that performed best in regard to revenue enacted tax increases during 2020" (Gascon & LaBelle, 2021, p. 3). In 2014, to overcome fiscal distress, Homewood, IL instituted a new "restaurant tax" that placed an additional two percent charge on any vendors that sell food and provide space to eat it (like restaurants, cafeterias, etc.).

3) Social Budgeting

The social budgeting approach places a higher emphasis on social protection. Social protection includes pensions, healthcare, dependent care, and other variables (Scholz et al., 2000). Social budgeting encompasses the analysis of public market failures, provision of public goods and services, safety, health, and environmental laws to develop communal social policy (Nakray; 2015; Scholz et al., 2000; Richardson, 2011; Watkins, 2019). Cichon et al. (2001) define social budgeting as changes in prioritizations of social expenditures and financing social protection programs and public education. Scholz et al.'s (2000) definition of social budgeting is "the forecast of income and expenditure (budget projection), normally for a medium-term period, and/or simulations of social expenditures and revenues under alternative economic, demographic and/or legislative assumptions" (p. 4).

Scholz et al. (2000) point out that during fiscal distress "more than ever, governments need to develop steering mechanisms for the social sector to make sure that scarce resources are allocated where they are most needed" (p. 4). PEW Charitable Trust (2020) similarly acknowledges that "in the face of declining revenue, the ability to effectively and accurately prioritize spending on programs and services that have beneficial outcomes is crucial" (p. 1).

The need for support and protection for financially vulnerable and adversely influenced communities becomes even more important during fiscal stress. Social budgeting is critical for entities that provide public goods with social implications to the communities they serve. We suggest local governments use social budgeting as a primary tool during fiscal stress. By relying on social budgeting features, local governments could make budget adjustments yet prioritize protection of social and/or safety projects during fiscal stress. The lack of financial resources, which decreases funding for programs, projects, and services, would lead to ranking of social programs and projects.

As PEW Charitable Trust (2020) emphasizes, policymakers

> can use an evidence lens to drive funding decisions and deploy key strategies to be more deliberate about targeted cuts. Using these tools, state and local officials can get the information they need to determine whether programs and services are effective. At a time of limited resources, taxpayer dollars need to be directed in a way that has the highest impact.
>
> *(p. 9)*

Social budgeting represents an important step in identifying spending priorities through a social lens during fiscal stress.

Social protection spending on a national and state level unavoidably increases during economic declines due to higher unemployment rates, hence a higher number of unemployment insurance claims and lower income resulting in higher eligibility for food stamps, Medicaid, and other social insurance and entitlement programs. The National Conference of State Legislatures (2010) discusses multiple examples of increases in social protection spending during the Great Recession of 2008–2009:

- corrections or public safety programs were above budgeted levels in five states
- California reported overspending in social service programs, including the in-home support services program
- Kansas increased social service caseloads
- Texas had around 400 million dollars (2.1 percent) over budget for K-12 formula funding.

"Other programs over budget included employee compensation in California, the state public defender/indigent defense program in Iowa and the homestead exemption program in Nebraska" (National Conference of State Legislatures, 2010, p. 5).

In the face of a fiscal decline, when financially vulnerable populations are affected first and foremost, local governments should more than ever emphasize the importance of social budgeting.

Theoretical Approaches to Operating Budgeting During Severe Fiscal Stress and Chapter 9 Bankruptcy

Fiscal stress makes municipalities rethink their budgeting approaches and priorities. The more severe the signs of stress are, the more drastic budgeting changes must be. Public finance literature emphasizes two approaches to budgeting during severe fiscal stress and bankruptcy, *austerity urbanism* and *pragmatic municipalism*.

The idea of *austerity urbanism* is similar to the notion of cutback management, which implies cuts in expenses, but it is a lot more dramatic because municipalities face severe emergency or bankruptcy (Davidson, 2019; Abott & Singla, 2021). The quality of service-delivery and availability of government services suffer profoundly when austerity urbanism is implemented, and it often leads to a lower quality of life for residents. Expenditures for many discretionary purposes, especially social services, such as parks and rec or libraries, are usually affected first and foremost. Abott and Singla (2021) found empirical evidence that bankrupt municipalities turn to austerity urbanism practices significantly more than similar non-bankrupt municipalities. Detroit, MI and Jefferson County, AL bankruptcies in many ways resembled the austerity urbanism approach (see Chapter 9 on Detroit and Chapter 11 on Jefferson County case studies).

The second approach to budgeting in severe fiscal emergency, *Pragmatic Municipalism*, in some sense resembles ideas of *Fiscal Stress Minimization Strategies*. Pragmatic municipalism implies a resentment to cuts and focuses more on a search for new revenues such as user charges and fees, cost-saving strategies such as restructuring, and innovation (Kim and Warner, 2016). During fiscal emergency, fiscal stress becomes a function of declining revenues subject to hard budget constraint. Chapter 9 bankruptcy then can be seen by municipalities as the means of softening such constraint (Abott & Singla, 2021). It was extensively discussed in Chapter 4 of this book that bankruptcy offers temporary protection against creditors and secures some time for the municipality, during which it does not have to pay interest and principal on debt or make some other payments. Such a break, made possible by softening budget constraints, allows struggling municipalities to rethink, reorganize, and simply reset yet retain control of their operations. Pragmatic municipalism thus prioritizes "consistency in service provision" (Abott & Singla, 2021, p. 11).

The post default or bankruptcy practices employed by the cities of Cleveland, OH; Vallejo, CA; Stockton, CA; or Jefferson County, AL can serve as examples of pragmatic municipalism. In 1978, Cleveland became the first large city to default on financial obligations since the Great Depression of the 1930s (Guzman, 2019). In 1971, to deal with its fiscal stress, Cleveland, OH initially referred to austerity urbanism by announcing layoffs totaling over 2,000 employees and a reduction in their workforce by 22 percent (ACIR, 1973). However, the voter-approved income tax increases in 1979 and 1981 were some of the major contributors to Cleveland's emergence from the default and, several years later, a successful exit from the fiscal emergency situation. The City of Vallejo, CA increased their sales tax rate after filing for Chapter 9 bankruptcy on May 17, 2008. Stockton, CA created more resource efficiency in service delivery and started to rely a lot more on community-based policing after bankruptcy.

Abott and Singha (2021) found that filing for bankruptcy results in "a shrinking public sector" (p. 1; consistent with the austerity urbanism theory) but also in "improved service delivery" (p. 1), an idea consistent with pragmatic municipalism. So, "Chapter 9 bankruptcy may provide governments with the space to improve operations while still cutting costs" (p. 1).

Conclusions

In this chapter we discussed several budgeting approaches that have been used by municipalities during different stages of fiscal distress situations. *Cutback management* rests on the idea of expenditure cuts when municipalities experience fiscal distress. Since the essence of government responsibilities is service provision, the majority of government expenses usually fall on labor costs, including public pensions. So, under cutback management, municipalities rely heavily (but not exclusively) on hiring and pay freezes, furloughs, layoffs, pension and benefit cuts, and cuts in other personnel expenses. *Austerity urbanism* takes cutback management to a more extreme level when localities face fiscal emergency or bankruptcy. In both cases, expenditure cuts usually affect service delivery and have an overall negative affect on the community.

Fiscal Stress Minimization Strategies assume that under fiscal stress, governments cannot solely rely on expenditure cuts and should look for opportunities to raise additional revenues, improve planning and organization design, etc. Under fiscal emergency and bankruptcy, *pragmatic municipalism* similarly emphasizes the importance of other non-expenditure cutting strategies. It also considers bankruptcy as time that municipalities use to restructure and rethink their priorities and organizational structure, as well as to renegotiate debt with their creditors. Both fiscal stress minimization and pragmatic municipalism ideas prioritize consistent service delivery.

The *social budgeting approach* implies that during fiscal stress, budgeting should focus on changes that have social implications. Since financially vulnerable populations are usually affected first and foremost during economic declines, the uninterrupted service delivery to such populations should be prioritized in the budgeting process. The social budgeting approach, therefore, diverges even further away from the cutback management and austerity urbanism ideas and adds on an important implication to the fiscal stress minimization strategies and pragmatic municipalism ideas.

Note

1 *Microbudgeting* is defined as low to intermediate-level decisions on agencies, programs, and line items, usually made from the bottom up – characterized by the stable and predictable budget processes after World War II described by Fenno (1966) and Wildavsky (1964). *Macrobudgeting* is defined as high-level decisions on spending, revenue, and deficit totals and relative budget shares, often made from the top down; these became increasingly prevalent because of the historically large, chronic deficits (LeLoup, 2002, p. 1).

References

Abott, C., & Singla, A. (2021). Service solvency and quality of life after municipal bankruptcy. *Journal of Political Institutions and Political Economy*, *2*(2), 249–280.

Advisory Commission on Intergovernmental Relations (ACIR) (1973). *City Financial Emergencies: The Intergovernmental Dimension*. Washington, D.C.: U.S. Government Printing Office.

Audia, P., Locke E.A., & Smith K.G. (2000). The Paradox of Success: An Archival and a Laboratory Study of Strategic Persistence Following Radical Environmental Change, The *Academy of Management Journal*, 43 (5), 837–853
Barnett, H. (1953). *Innovation*. New York: McGraw-Hill.
Becker, S. W., & Whisler, T. L. (1967). Some determinants of organizational success. *Journal of Business, 40*, 511–18.
Behn, R. (1985). Cutback budgeting. *Journal of Policy Analysis and Management, 5*(2), 155–177.
Boex, J. L., Martinez-Vazquez, J., & McNab, R. M. (2000). Multi-year budgeting: A review of international practices and lessons for developing and transitional economies. *Public Budgeting & Finance, 6*(3), 91–112.
Bowling, C. J., & Burke, B. F. (2006). *Levine's Legacy: Comparing State Administrator Strategies to Treat Fiscal Stress, 1984 and 2004*. Austin, TX: 7th State Politics and Policy Conference.
Cichon, M., Hagemeyer, K., & Scholz, W. (2001). Central and Eastern Europe: Social budgeting in transition economies. *International Security Review, 54*(2), 191–215.
Chattopadhyay, P., Glick, W.H., & Huber, G.P. (2001). Organizational actions in response to threats and opportunities. Academy of Management Journal, 44, 937–955.
Cummings, T. G., & Srivastva, S. (1977). *Management of Work: A Socio-Technical Systems Approach*. Kent, OH: Kent State University Press.
Cyert, R.M., & March, J.G. (1992). A Behavioral Theory of the Firm. 2th ed. Upper Saddle River, NJ: Prentice Hall.
Cyert, R.M. & March J.C. (1964). A Behavioral Theory of Organizations. In Faris R.E. (ed.), Handbook of Modern Sociology (pp. 485–529). Chicago, IL: Prentice Hall.
Damanpour, F. (1996). Organizational complexity and innovation: Developing and testing multiple contingency models. *Management Science, 42*, 693–716.
Damanpour, F., & Evan, W. M. (1984). Organizational innovation and performance: The problem of "organizational lag". *Administrative Science Quarterly, 29*(3), 392–409.
Davidson, M. (2019). Extreme municipal fiscal stress and austerity? A case study of fiscal reform after Chapter 9 bankruptcy. *Environment and Planning C: Politics and Space*. 38(3), 522–538.
Davis, O., Dempster, A. H., & Wildavsky, A. (1966). A theory of the budgetary process. *The American Political Science Review, 60*(3), 529–547.
Deschenaux, W. G., & Juppe, D. B. (2015). It's always something: Maryland's path through the "great recession". *Public Budgeting and Finance, 3*(1), 106–125.
Evan, W. M. (1966). Organizational lag. *Human Organizations, 25*, 51–53.
Felix, A. (2020). *COVID-19 challenges state and local government finances By Alison Felix*. Retrieved from kansascityfed.org/documents/5438/2020-eb20felix0513.pdf
Fenno, R. (1966). The Power of the PurseAppropriations Politics in Congress. New York City, USA: Little, Brown and Company
Fernandez, S., & Rainey, H. G. (2006). Managing successful organizational change in the public sector: An agenda for research and practice. *Public Administration Review, 66*, 168–176.
Gascon, C., & LaBelle, J. (2021). COVID-19 and states' revenues: An analysis. *Federal Reserve Bank of Saint Louis*. Retrieved from www.stlouisfed.org/publications/regional-economist/first-quarter-2021/covid-19-states-revenues-analysis
Graaf, S. (2016). The impact of the great recession on county human-service organizations: A cross-case analysis. *Human Service Organizations: Management, Leadership, & Governance Journal, 40*(2), 152–169

Guzman, Tatyana (2019). Fiscal conditions of largest legacy cities. In *The Legacies of Legacy Cities: Continuity and Change amid Decline and Revival*. Pittsburgh, PA: University of Pittsburgh Press.

Halligan, J.(1999). New Public Sector Models: Reform in Australia and New Zealand', in J. Lane (ed.), Public Sector Reform. Thousand Oaks, CA: Sage, pp. 17–46.

Hou, Y. (2006). Budgeting for fiscal stability over the business cycle: A countercyclical fiscal policy and the multiyear perspective on budgeting. *Public Administration Review, 66*(5), 32–41.

Hou, Y., & Moynihan, D. (2008). The case for countercyclical fiscal capacity. *Journal of Public Administration Research and Theory, 18*(1), 139–159.

Hyde, A. C. (2002). *Government Budgeting. Theory, Process, and Politics* (3rd ed.). Washington, D.C.: The Brookings Institution Center for Public Policy Education.

Istrate, E., & Handy, D. (2016). "The state of county finances: Progress through adversity, "*NACo Trends Analysis Paper Series*. October 2016. Retrieved from www.naco.org/sites/default/files/documents/2016t20Countypercent20Report_10.07.16.pdf

Kaufman, H. (1991). Time, Chance, and Organizations, 2nd ed. Chatham, NJ: Chatham House.

Keynes, J. M. (1924). *The Theory of Money and the Foreign Exchanges. A Tract on Monetary Reform*. New York: Business & Economics.

Klase, K. A., & Dougherty, M. J. (2008). The impact of performance budgeting on state budget outcomes. *Journal of Public Budgeting, Accounting & Financial Management, 20*(3), 277–298.

Knight, K. E. (1967). A descriptive model of the intra-firm innovation process. *The Journal of Business, 40*, 478–496.

Kovner, C., & Lusk, E. (2010). The sustainability budgeting model: Multiplemode flexible budgeting using sustainability as the synthesizing criterion. *Nursing Economics, 28*(6), 377–385.

Lane, J. (ed.). (1997). Public Sector Reform: Rationale, Trends and Problems. Thousand Oaks, CA: Sage, pp. 17–46.

LeLoup, L. (2002). Budget theory for a new century. In Khan, A., & Hildreth, B. (Eds.), *Budget Theory in the Public Sector* (pp. 2–18). New York, NY: Quorum Books.

Levin, M., & Sanger, M. (1992). Using old stuff in new ways: Innovation as a case of evolutionary tinkering. *Journal of Policy analysis and Management, 11*(1), 88–115.

Levine, C. H. (1978). Organizational decline and cutback management. *Public Administration Review, 38*(4), 316–325.

Levine, C. H., Rubin, I. S., & Wolohojian, G. (1981). *The Politics of Retrenchment: How Local Governments Manage Fiscal Stress*. Beverly Hills, CA: Sage Publications.

Lewis, L. K., & Seibold, D. R. (1993). Innovation modification during intraorganizational adoption. *Academy of Management Review, 18*, 322–354.

Lindblom, C. E. (1959). The science of "Muddling Through". *Public Administration Review, 19*(2), 79–88.

March, J. (1978). Bounded Rationality, Ambiguity, and the Engineering of Choice. *The Bell Journal of Economics*, 9 (2), 587–608.

March, J., & Simon, H. (1993). *Organizations* (2nd ed.). Oxford: Blackwell.

Meyer, A. D. (1982). Adapting to environmental jolts. *Administrative Science Quarterly, 27*, 515–537.

Meyer, A. D., Brooks, G. R., & Goes, J. B. (1990). Environmental jolts and industry revolutions: Organizational responses to discontinuous change. *Strategic Management Journal, Summer special Issue 11*, 93–110.

Meyer, A. D., & Goes, J. B. (1988). Organizational assimilations and innovation: A multi-level contextual analysis. *Academy of Management Journal*, *31*, 897–923.

Meyer, J. W. (1980). The world polity and the authority of the nation-state. In Bergesen, A. (Ed.), *Studies of the Modern World-System* (pp. 109–137). New York: Academic Press.

Meyer, J. W. (1994). Rationalized environments. In Scott, R., & Myer, J. (Eds.), *Institutional Environments and Organizations* (pp. 28–54). Newbury Park, CA: Sage.

Meyer, J. W., & Rowan, B. (1977). Institutionalized organizations: Formal structure as myth and ceremony. *American Journal of Sociology*, *83*, 340–363.

Meyer, M. W. (1979). *Change in Public Bureaucracies*. Cambridge: Cambridge University Press.

Miller, G.R. (1983). Taking stock of a discipline. *Journal of Communication*, 33(3), 31–41.

Miller, R. A., Klouda, N., & Fisk, J. M. (2021). Concrete evidence: Infrastructure challenges and the COVID-19 pandemic. *Public Works Management & Policy*, *26*(1), 19–25.

Mintzberg, H. (1990). The design school: reconsidering the basic premises of strategic management. *Strategic Management Journal*, 11 (3), 171–195.

Nakray, K. (2015). Gender budgeting & public policy; the challenges to operationalizing gender justice in India. *Policy & Politics, 43*(4), 561–577

National Association of Counties (2020). *Analysis of the fiscal impact of Covid-19 on counties*. May 2020. Retrieved October 12, 2021, from https://www.naco.org/resources/analysis-fiscal-impact-covid-19-county-finances

National Association of State Budget Officers (NASBO) (2009). *Budget process in the states*. Retrieved October 12, 2021, from http://www.nasbo.org/publications.php.

National Conference of State Legislatures (2010). *State measures to balance FY 2010 budgets*, May 2010. Retrieved October 12, 2021, from www.ncsl.org/documents/fiscal/november2010sbu_free.pdf

National League of Cities (2010). *Cities can't cut their way to prosperity*. Retrieved October 12, 2021, from www.nlc.org/article/2010/02/11/cities-cant-cut-their-way-to-prosperity/

PEW Charitable Trusts (2009). *States' Budget Woes Register With Public*. Retrieved October 12, 2021, from https://www.pewtrusts.org/en/research-and-analysis/reports/2009/03/05/news-interest-index-states-budget-woes-register-with-public

PEW Charitable Trusts (2020). *How public officials can use data and evidence to make strategic budget cuts*. Retrieved from www.pewtrusts.org/en/research-and-analysis/issue-briefs/2020/09/how-public-officials-can-use-data-and-evidence-to-make-strategic-budget-cuts

Pierce, J. L., & Delbecq, A. L. (1977). Organization structure, individual attitudes and innovation. *Academy of Management Review*, *2*(1), 27–37.

Premchand, A. (1993). *Government Budgeting and Expenditure Controls – Theory and Practice*. Washington, D.C.: International Monetary Fund.

Premchand, A. (2007). Capital budgets: Theory and practice/budgeting and budgetary institution. In Shah, A. (Ed.). (pp. 91–113). Budgeting and Budgetary Institutions. Washington, D.C.: The International Bank for Reconstruction and Development.

Richardson, J. (2011). *From Recession to Renewal the Impact of the Financial Crisis on Public Services and Local Government*. Bristol: The Policy Press University of Bristol.

Rivera, G. (2012). Emergent strategy. *Interaction Institute for Social Change*. Retrieved from https://interactioninstitute.org/emergent-strategy/

Romanov, E., & Thatcher, D. (2020). School officials await potential COVID-19-related budget cuts. *National Conference of State Legislatures*. Retrieved from www.ncsl.org/research/education/school-officials-await-potential-covid-19-related-budget-cuts-magazine2020.aspx

Rubin, M.M., & Willoughby, K.G.. (2009). State budget balancing strategies: riding into the future on lessons learned from the past. 5th TAD Conference, Washington, DC.

Sandford, B. (2003). What border? Public management innovation in the United States and Canada. *Journal of Policy Analysis and Management, 19*(1), 46–74.
Scholz, W., Cichon, M., & Krzysztof, H. (2000). *Social Budgeting Quantitative Methods in Social protection. International Labour Office (ILO).* Geneva: International Labour Office (ILO). Retrieved from www.social-protection.org/gimi/RessourcePDF.action?ressource.ressourceId=8022
Scorscone, T., & Plerhoples, E. (2010). *An Assessment of Michigan's Local Government Fiscal Indicator System*. Washington, D.C.: Senate Fiscal Agency.
Starbuck, W. H., Greve, A., & Hedberg, B. (1978) Responding to crisis. *Journal of Business Administration*, 9(2), 112–137.
Thompson, V. A. (1965). Bureaucracy and innovation. *Administrative Science Quarterly, 10*(1), 1–20.
Thurmaier, K., & Gosling, J. (2008). *Public Budgeting. Policy, Process, and Politics* (Edited by Irene S. Rubin). New York, NY: ME Sharpe Inc.
Titus, V., Covin. J. & Slevin, D. (2011). Aligning strategic processes in pursuit of firm growth. *Journal of Business Research*. 64, 446–453
Walker, J. L. (1969). The diffusion of innovations among the American States. *The American Political Science Review, 63*(3), 880–899.
Walker, R. (2008). An empirical evaluation of innovation types and organizational and environmental characteristics: Towards a configuration framework. *Journal of Public Administration Research and Theory, 18*, 591–615.
Watkins, B. R. (2019). *Budgeting in times of fiscal stress: An analysis of the budget Process and resource allocation of social programs in a large urban county from 2006–2017* [PhD Dissertation, University of Texas at Arlington]. Retrieved from https://rc.library.uta.edu/uta-ir/bitstream/handle/10106/28882/WATKINSBABERS-DISSERTATION-2019.pdf?sequence=1&isAllowed=y
Wildavsky, A. (1961). Political implications of budgetary reform. *Public Administration Review, 21*(4), 183–190.
Wildavsky, A. (1964). *The Politics of the Budgetary Process*. Toronto: Little, Brown and Co.
Wise, L.R. (1999). The Use of Innovative Practices in the Public and Private Sectors: The Role of Organizational and Individual Factors. Public Productivity and Management Review, 23, 150–68.
Wise, L.R. (2002).Public Management Reform: Competing Drivers of Change. Public Administration Review, 62, 543–54.
Zaltman, G., Duncan, R., & Holbek, J.(1973). Innovations and Organizations. New York: Wiley.

6

FISCAL STRESS AND CAPITAL INFRASTRUCTURE

Introduction

Similar to homeowners with limited budgets and a long list of needed repairs, U.S. municipalities often face tough choices when deciding what to renovate, replace, or build new. These high-price choices become even more difficult in times of fiscal distress. How should municipalities rank capital projects during fiscal stress or bankruptcy? How should municipalities decide what is a higher priority – repairing a school, jail, or something else? What would benefit a municipality more – a new community center or a library? Should the city or municipality upgrade the HVAC system and install energy efficient windows in an aging administrative hall or plan to replace the building? When should it be replaced? These and multiple other questions commonly asked during the capital budget process become even more acute at the times when municipalities experience fiscal stress.

Extensive and efficient public infrastructure is a crucial component of municipal economic growth and development. *Public infrastructure* denotes basic physical assets and structures that facilitate economic activity through provision of services to households and enterprises. In this chapter, we discuss capital spending and the current state of infrastructure and review capital budgeting challenges. We advocate for the importance of the effective development of multi-year capital plans for municipalities and discuss how to align those plans with a municipality's mission, objectively prioritize competing capital priorities, understand the impact of different funding scenarios, and ensure cost-effective capital projects.

DOI: 10.4324/b23117-6

FIGURE 6.1 Demolishing a building in Cleveland, Ohio.

Photo credit: Alex Philip

Capital Spending

According to the Congressional Budget Office (2019a), the federal government spent 256 billion dollars on physical capital, including structures (government buildings, transportation infrastructure, water and power projects, etc.), major equipment (such as computers, machinery, and vehicles), and software in 2018. The federal government invested 110 billion dollars in nondefense physical capital, including 64 billion dollars in transportation. Ninety-two percent of this transportation funding was distributed as grants to state and local governments that helped pay for construction and rehabilitation of highways, mass transportation, and airports. The remaining 8 percent was invested primarily in major equipment for airports and the Coast Guard (Congressional Budget Office, 2019b, p. 19).

In addition to the federal government, state governments expended over 135 billion dollars and local governments over 243 billion dollars in capital outlays in 2018 (U.S. Census Bureau, 2020). Interestingly, in Rhode Island, New Hampshire, and New Jersey the share of capital outlays in overall direct expenditures in 2018 was only a third of that share in Hawaii, North Dakota, and Utah (see Figure 6.2.).

Even if capital outlays may seem large in absolute values, the total federal investments declined as a share of total federal spending, from about 30 percent in the

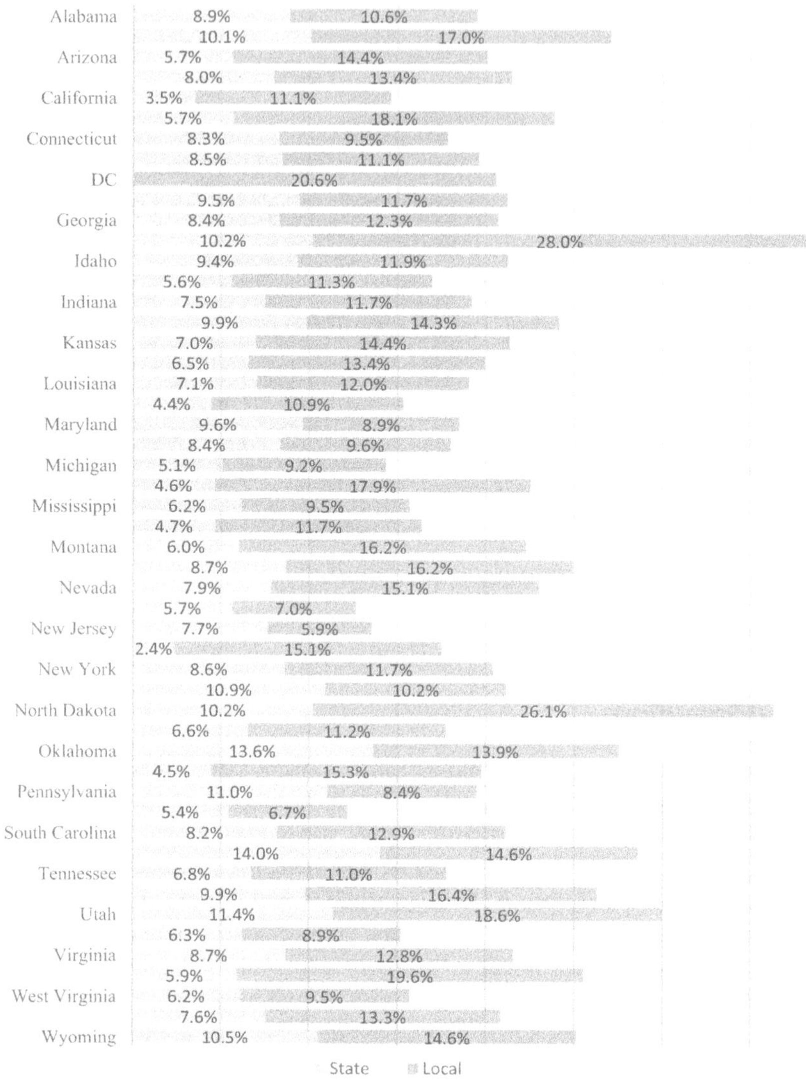

FIGURE 6.2 State and Local Capital Outlays as a Share of Direct Expenditures in 2018 (U.S. Census Bureau, 2020).

1960s to about 15 percent between 2010 and 2018 (GovInfo, 2018, 2019, 2020; Congressional Budget Office, 2019b, p. 12). Most of the decline of federal investments occurred by the early 1980s (Stewart & Atkinson, 2013). Federal spending in transportation infrastructure alone was 38 percent of total public investment in 1977 and declined to less than 25 percent by 2016 (Business Roundtable, 2016). Spending by state and local governments on all types of capital also fell from its high of

3 percent of the nation's gross domestic product (GDP) in the late 1960s to 2.4 percent of the GDP in the early 2000s and then to 1.87 percent by 2017 (McNichol, 2019). According to Ermasova and Ebdon (2019), this situation was "partly due to the divergence between major capital expenditures and spending on operations and maintenance" (p. 31). The gap between spending on basic upkeep versus major system improvements is consistent with the growing gap between federal versus state and local infrastructure spending in these areas (Congressional Budget Office, 2015).

Lower spending had negative consequences for the national economy, as expected. In 2017, The American Society of Civil Engineers (ASCE) estimated that 500,000 jobs would be lost from 2018 to 2025 (ASCE, 2017). The COVID-19 pandemic has initially exacerbated existing challenges in underinvestment in public infrastructure, delaying investments in infrastructure in the short term. While "budgets are buckling under unprecedented demands, meaning less support is available for infrastructure investments, precisely at the time we should be investing" (ASCE, 2020, p. 1). But recent federal infrastructure bills bring high hopes for the future of infrastructure.

One of the COVID-19 major stimulus packages, the American Rescue Plan, the 1.9 trillion-dollar economic stimulus bill signed into law by President Biden on March 11, 2021, "provides $10 billion for payments to States, territories, and Tribal governments to carry out critical capital projects that directly enable work, education, and health monitoring, including remote options, in response to the public health emergency" (U.S. Treasury, 2021, p. 1). These capital projects include investments in depreciable assets and the ancillary costs needed to put the capital assets in use and must be critical in nature. The Capital Projects Fund as part of American Rescue Plan allows for investment in high-quality broadband as well as other connectivity infrastructure, devices, and equipment and provides flexibility for each state, territory, and Tribal government to make other investments in critical community hubs. All capital projects must demonstrate that they meet the critical connectivity needs highlighted and amplified by the COVID-19 pandemic.

The Infrastructure Investment and Jobs Act signed into law by President Biden on November 15, 2021 includes additional 550 billion dollars in new spending on the nation's physical infrastructure and represents the largest investment in roads, bridges, ports, water, and rail in years (CBC News, 2021). This infrastructure plan would support modernization of "20,000 miles of highways, roads, and mainstreets. It will fix the ten most economically significant bridges in the country in need of reconstruction. It also will repair the worst 10,000 smaller bridges, providing critical linkages to communities" (White House, 2021, p. 1). The spending provides 110 billion dollars for roads, bridges, and major projects; 39 billion for public transit; and 66 billion for railways. It also includes 65 billion dollars to expand broadband infrastructure and 55 billion for clear water investments. According to Kosich (2022), 97 million dollars are coming to Ohio in 2022, which is "going to make a big difference in Cuyahoga County and really across the state in making it possible to improve those bridges that we count on every day" (p. 1).

State of Infrastructure

The recent leap in federal infrastructure spending is encouraging, but the decades of underinvestment in capital needs have not passed unnoticed. Already back in 1983 Choate and Walter emphasized that public infrastructure was deteriorating faster than it could be repaired or replaced. Rivenbark et al. (2018) observed that even municipalities that consistently invest in capital assets have a hard time maintaining the pace with depreciation. In turn, "declining quality and poor performance of public infrastructure system impose huge costs on US businesses and individuals and create bottlenecks that constrain economic development" (Chen, 2018, p. 126).

ASCE (2017) estimates that two trillion dollars needs to be invested over five years to bring the condition of the nation's infrastructure up to a good condition. The 2021 Report Card for America's Infrastructure, released by ASCE, assigns a highly concerning overall grade of C− to the nation's infrastructure (ASCE, 2021a). In 2017, Transit was rated D−; Aviation, Dams, Drinking Water, Inland Waterways, and Roads rated D; Energy, Hazardous Waste, and Schools rated D+ (poor condition); Bridges, Solid Waste, and Ports rated C+; and Rail, Public Parks, and Recreation rated C (mediocre condition) (ASCE, 2017, 2021a). In 2021, the Rail rating increased to B, Ports to C+, Energy to C, Drinking Water to C−, and Aviation to D+, while the Solid Waste rating remained at C+, Schools and Hazardous Waste stayed at D+, Roads and Dams were still rated D, Bridges downgraded to C, and Public parks to D+ (ASCE, 2021a).

America's surface transportation system is extensive, including over four million miles of roads and about 614,000 bridges; 46,100 of these bridges are currently structurally deficient and 40 percent of all bridges are at least 50 years old. According to ASCE (2020), at current investment rates, it would take 50 years to repair these bridges. The decades of underinvestment have led to a 90-billion-dollar transit maintenance backlog nationally (ASCE, 2020). Frankel and Wachs (2017) pointed out that "unless the crisis was addressed soon, deterioration would accelerate in coming decades leading to steadily worsening conditions of roads, bridges, water supply, and sewage systems" (p. 1). Approximately 20 percent of road pavement is also in poor condition, although the total miles rated as poor have decreased in recent years (Ermasova & Ebdon, 2019). Increases in the number of cars on the roads coupled with often unsatisfactory road conditions led to higher congestion in recent years. Due to the lack of funding for maintenance, over 2,170 high-hazard potential dams were deficient in 2017. The National Park Service estimated 12 billion dollars in deferred maintenance costs. By 2025, around one million jobs are expected to be lost due to the economic impacts of deteriorating transportation infrastructure (ASCE, 2017, House Committee on Transportation and Infrastructure, 2020a, 2020b).

Aging water and wastewater systems are another problem the nation faces. Nearly 156,000 public drinking water systems and 15,000 wastewater treatment

FIGURE 6.3 The Kinzua Bridge. A historic railroad bridge in Allegheny, Pennsylvania.

Source: Photo credit Alex Philip

plants are located across the United States. There are an estimated 240,000 water main breaks each year that result in a discharge of about 900 billion gallons of untreated sewage (ASCE, 2020, Ermasova & Ebdon, 2019). A main break of water occurs every two minutes, and an estimated six billion gallons of treated water are lost each day in the U.S., enough to fill over 9,000 swimming pools (ASCE, 2021b). Allen et al. (2018) highlight that

> the opportunity for microbial contamination from decades to century old water distribution systems is increasing with time. Thus, increased health risk to consumers should be a driving factor in accelerating reinvestment in America's aging water distribution water systems.
>
> *(p. 301)*

At current rates, it would take 200 years to replace the water pipes, which is double their useful life. Despite all these concerns, U.S. drinking water quality is still considered to be the safest in the world. And there are signs of progress as federal financing programs expand and water utility companies increase reinvestment rates in their networks. It is estimated that more than 12,000 miles of water pipes were planned to be replaced by drinking water utilities across the country in 2020 (ASCE, 2021b).

Capital Management and Budgeting

To cope with public infrastructure challenges, governments rely on capital budgeting practices. Capital budgeting serves as the primary instrument for analyzing the condition of infrastructure, evaluating needs for capital improvement, and consequently stimulating economic growth and development. It legally binds capital spending to remain within the funds allocated for this purpose. As a managerial and administrative document, capital budgeting specifies the ways and means to provide public services and establishes criteria by which they are monitored, measured, and evaluated (Khan & Hildreth, 2002). McClain (1966, p. 10) calls capital budgeting not "a one-shot plan to solve physical facilities problems, but a continuous program with a new year added as the current budget year is completed".

Ammar et al. (2001) specify four essential components of capital budgeting: preparation of a planning document, creation of an operating budget link, project selection, and the capital planning process. Much earlier 1965 work by Robert Anthony (1965, pp. 16–18) specified three distinct administrative processes in capital budgeting:

- *strategic planning* – the process of decision-making in regards to an organization's objectives, changes in the objectives, the capital resources used to attain these objectives, and the policies that will govern the acquisition, use, and disposition of investment resources
- *operational control* – the process of assuring that specific investment tasks are carried out effectively and efficiently
- *management control* – the process by which managers assure that investment resources are obtained and used effectively and efficiently to accomplish an organization's objectives.

Given the long-term nature of the life of capital projects and their long-term financing, the *multi-year budget process* and *countercyclical fiscal policies* (discussed in Chapter 5) are as, if not more, important in capital as in operating budgeting processes. According to Auerbach et al. (2020), capital expenditures are

> surprisingly cyclical, perhaps because spending required to plan and maintain capital projects comes out of operating budgets, governments may wish to avoid the costs of servicing debt during times of economic stress, and because many areas require voter approval for any bond issuance, which is less likely to be forthcoming during an economic downturn.
>
> *(p. 22)*

The long-term nature of capital budgeting is reflected in capital improvement plans (CIPs) that municipalities prepare, typically for a period of five to seven years. CIPs list all capital improvement projects to be pursued during the budgeted time frame, along with the financing sources, completion years, and other relevant details.

Changes in Capital Budgeting During Economic Decline and Fiscal Stress

Fiscal emergency makes systematic strategic planning (discussed in Chapter 5) more difficult. Hamel and Prahald (1989) note that "uncertainty requires that strategy is concerned less with specific actions and the more with establishing clarity of direction within which short-term flexibility can be reconciled with overall coordination of strategic decisions" (pp. 67–68). There has been some *rapprochement* to capital budgeting during fiscal emergencies. Rapid changes necessitate strategies that are flexible and creative – characteristics that, according to Hamel and Prahalad (1989), are rarely associated with formalized planning.

During economic declines the gap between available fiscal resources and needs widens. It can lead to situations when capital expenditure commitments made during more stable years can no longer be continued (Choate & Walter, 1983).

External Environment, COVID-19 Pandemic, and Capital Infrastructure

The COVID-19 pandemic is a broad-scale and very distinct example of environmental jolt discussed in Chapter 5. On one hand it provided a unique opportunity to pursue capital projects, such as capital repairs to vacant capital buildings and road repairs and construction (especially during Spring of 2020) when quarantine lockdowns kept people at home. Historically, low interest rates have also allowed for cheap borrowing to finance capital projects. There are two ways governments use to finance capital projects, the *pay-as-you-go* approach, when capital projects are financed out of current revenues and the *pay-as-you-use* approach, when governments borrow to finance capital expenses. COVID-19 put a big halt on many government revenues, so there have been fewer proceeds available for pay-as-you go financing. Despite access to low interest rates, any crisis generates uncertainty and, perhaps, fear to borrow so, pay-as-you-use financial mechanisms may have also been underutilized. Bureaucracy might have been another impediment in pursuing capital projects. Too little time has elapsed to understand the actual impact of COVID-19 on capital investment, but the government has provided a lot of stimulus dollars and secured low interest rates (until winter of 2022; interest rates have been increasing since) to encourage such investments, so the effect can go either way.

Preliminary observations on the effect of COVID-19 on capital infrastructure show a 49 percent decline of receipts in May 2020 compared to May 2019 in the federal Highway Trust Fund (ASCE, 2020, p. 4). According to the American Road and Transportation Builders Association (2020), at least nine billion dollars of construction work on transportation projects was deferred in 2020. The COVID-19 crisis caused a 20 to 30 percent decline in total annual receipts of ports. The drinking water sector is estimated to lose nearly 14 billion dollars (around 17 percent) in annual revenue "as a result of the current pandemic, including more than $5 billion in losses related to suspending water service disconnections and increased customer delinquencies" (ASCE, 2020, p. 6). By 2020, the COVID-19 crisis resulted in a 12.5-billion-dollar shortfall for the nation's wastewater utilities (20 percent loss of revenue) due to the decline in usage from commercial and industrial users and a temporary halt on shutoffs on delinquent payments (Congressional Budget Office, 2020, p. 14). According to Phillips (2020), "65% of cities are being forced to delay or cancel capital expenses and infrastructure projects" (p. 1).

ASCE (2020) suggests that Congress should make an infrastructure investment a main goal of its immediate response and long-term economic recovery strategy. ASCE (2020) recommends to: (1) fully fund the High Hazard Potential Dam Rehabilitation (HHPDR) program at the authorized amount of 60 million dollars in 2021, (2) provide an additional ten billion dollars for airports to mitigate the growing pandemic industry impacts in the aviation industry, (3) remove the federally imposed cap on Passenger Facility Charges (PFCs) to offer airports an option to invest in their own facilities, (4) support the inclusion of the Rebuild America's School Infrastructure Act in any economic relief package, (5) create a 70 billion dollar federal grant program and a 30 billion dollar tax credit bond program targeted at schools in economically disadvantaged communities with facilities that pose health and safety risks to students and staff (ASCE, 2020, p. 12), and (6) allocate four billion dollars a year in federal grants for the Clean Water State Revolving Fund to help communities with much needed wastewater infrastructure projects (ASCE, 2020, p. 14).

Federal stimulus dollars are extremely important, but without effective implementation of capital projects on a local level, such federal stimulus programs can never be fully effective. The COVID-19 crisis not only revealed deficiencies in some infrastructure sectors, such as health and digital connectivity, but also lowered the demand and/or ability to pay for some infrastructure needs. The crisis boosts the necessity for more and better public investment to support recovery after what is evolving into a deep and potentially long-lasting recession (Tandberg & Allen, 2020). Indeed, public investment is a common fiscal stimulus tool that gained popularity thanks to its high multiplier effect – especially during recessions – and its discretionary nature.

The Adoption of Administrative Innovations in Capital Budgeting During Fiscal Stress

As mentioned earlier, the COVID-19 crisis (and the Great Recession of 2008–2009) have served as environmental jolt for budget offices. Environmental jolt can prompt financial crisis, that is, perceptions by field actors (public organizations, legislators, citizen, etc.) that fundamental outcomes contrast with expectations and can consequently trigger actions to avoid dramatic negative outcomes. Public organizations could obtain significant benefits from some administrative innovations by improving their forecasting, coordination process, capital budgeting, and debt financing to endure revenue shortfalls during economic decline and fiscal emergency.

These changes have emphasized the necessity to increase a planning period, use long-term or medium-term planning, develop formal mechanisms to set aside funds to preserve existing facilities, use computer programming to increase automation of the process, increase collaboration between departments, and link capital planning decisions to statewide performance goals and strategic plans.

The coordination of the capital and operating budgets is another important element of the capital budgeting process. The same set of program needs drives both capital and operating budget requests, and the two budgets affect each other. Projects and spending approved in the capital budget influence future operating budgets as principal and interest on capital borrowings are paid out of operating funds. Decisions made in the operating budget to improve or expand services can necessitate future expansion of capital facilities or the acquisition of new equipment. Dual budgeting practices balance budget office's workload and reduce the amount of information that must be processed by lawmakers at any time. The separation of the capital and operating budgets encourages government capital formation. If, however, a government has a separate staff dedicated exclusively to capital budget matters, then preparing the two budgets concurrently is not merely feasible but highly preferable. According to Mikesell (2007), a separation of capital budgets can improve both the efficiency and equity of providing and financing nonrecurrent projects with long-term service flows, facilitate financial planning, and integrate their plans with the social, financial, and political environment.

Recent Adopted Administrative Innovations in Capital Budgeting Processes

Many states changed their capital planning process during the economic downturn of 2008–2009 and the COVID-19 crisis by (1) implementing administrative innovations in capital budgeting, (2) the utilization of cutback management (discussed in Chapter 5), and (3) changing capital projects' selection process (with a focus on projects that provide economic stimulus).

Some specific administrative innovations in capital management and budgeting that are worth mentioning are:

- a more comprehensive analysis of the capital budget needs of state agencies that also provide greater transparency for taxpayers and legislature
- an increased emphasis on repair and renovation and capital renewal, rather than new construction. Capital planning focuses on "shovel-ready" projects that can immediately get started and provide economic stimulus

- an evolution of multi-year budget framework into a more integrated approach over time
- greater emphasis on the prioritization and selection process
- emphasis on improved governance through greater fiscal transparency and enhanced framework for financial and program accountability and collaborative initiatives and teamwork
- improved budget-making process through dedicated computer databases
- development of a comprehensive analysis of the capital budget needs
- the use of two separate bills for pay-as-you-go and pay-as-you-use financing
- improved coordination with the operating budget and cash-monitoring controls.

PEW Trust Fund (2020) emphasizes that during COVID-19 crisis, "budget priorities can then be focused on the programs that are both serving the populations with the greatest needs and are evidence-based" (p. 5). Tennessee, for instance, created the Office of Evidence and Impact to begin using evidence to make budget changes and to complete a statewide program inventory (Tennessee Department of Finance & Administration, 2020).

Prioritization and Ranking of Public Capital Projects

A central component of the capital budgeting process is the establishment of priorities within the extensive array of proposed projects. With resources constrained, funding is limited for fiscally challenged municipalities, with few exceptions, to critical infrastructure projects, such as fire/life/safety and court-ordered projects. When municipalities have a basis for making informed decisions about project prioritization and capital budget allocation, they are less vulnerable to emergency failures. Emergency repair projects typically result in hefty premiums for labor during non-standard work hours, rushed shipments, and unplanned but necessary one-off purchases.

Whereas private firms often make capital spending decisions based on analytic techniques such as benefit-cost analysis, the government has been slow to apply these methods because of the amount of time involved, the problem of determining a dollar value for government services, and incompetence in application of these techniques within government organizations (Wiggins, 1980, pp. 19–20). Unlike private spending decisions, public sector decisions involve "political and social considerations in addition to purely economic and legal constraints" (Snyder, 1977, p. 268).

In 2019, about a third of all utilities had a robust asset management program in place to help prioritize their capital and operations/maintenance investments, which is a 20 percent increase from 2016. With scarce resources and limits on financing options in many municipalities during the COVID-19 crisis, establishing a set of priorities is a crucial task. Municipal governments employ different methods to set priorities in deciding on their capital expenditures, using project-by-project, case-by-case, or formal mechanisms, either in statute or by practice or by setting priorities on a functional basis (i.e., allocating expenditures for higher education, transportation, aiding local governments, or protecting natural resources) or by setting priorities for certain activities, such as health and safety.

According to Chan (2004), capital projects in the public sector should be prioritized based on relevant criteria, including hazard elimination, legal mandates, regulatory compliance, commitment to project completion, preservation of existing assets, service improvement, and cost-benefit justification. A variety of categories are used for project prioritizations, with common ones being resource use and economic development, emergency situations, legal reasons, and health and safety considerations. Alaska, Montana, and Indiana employ health and safety, critical maintenance, improvements, and new construction categories to prioritize their capital project needs. New York ranks priorities based on the potential for permanent job creation, revenue generation, and risk assessment (i.e., any risks to the project in terms of scope, cost, time, safety, and social and environmental impacts). Massachusetts' criteria for capital project prioritization include: job creation, improving the economy and strengthening the infrastructure, legal compliance, preservation of a facility, improvement in operational efficiency, investing in public education, and supporting the innovation industries. Alaska's Office of Management and Budget (2010) uses the following prioritization criteria: resource development, education, public safety, transportation/infrastructure, and military support. Virginia's Department of Planning and Budget and the Governor's Cabinet Secretaries categorize its capital requests based on supplemental funding needed for equipment or other reasons, emergencies and code compliance, broken infrastructure, renovations and improvements, and acquisitions and new construction. Capital needs in Virginia are ranked by: (1) safety, health, regulatory, security, environmental requirements, or accreditation, (2) upgrading or replacing major mechanical systems and utility infrastructure, (3) renovation or maintenance of existing facilities, (4) construction, expansion, or acquiring facilities to meet programmatic needs, (5) improving energy efficiency.

Since municipalities tend to underinvest in infrastructure, they need to evaluate the tradeoffs involved in choosing one investment over others. According to Pagano (1986, p. 96),

> ensuring strict control over capital project selection can be attained both by establishing rigid project selection criteria and by specifying a precise ordinal ranking of those criteria. The more automatic the selection, the less likely it is that a bureaucrat can alter the process and impose his or her imprint on the capital budget.

With responsibility for tens or hundreds of buildings totaling millions of square feet, budget directors and facility managers need to keep track of municipal facilities and use objective criteria to make decisions about their physical assets. To do so, they need to be able to answer these questions about their facilities:

- What is the best way to validate our building portfolio?
- What are the existing physical and functional conditions?
- What do municipalities need to change to correct existing conditions?
- What will the changes cost (both now and in the future)?
- What are our priorities?
- What information can we use to strengthen funding requests?
- What is the optimal allocation of facilities dollars?
- What metrics/benchmarks/reports can we use to measure success of capital projects?

Budget director and managers and facilities managers will need to prioritize infrastructure projects and weigh their value against other municipality needs.

The following Balanced Scorecard Project Development Timeline can be used for project prioritization purposes:

Step 1: Establish Strategic Goals
Step 2: Identify 3 to 5 Strategic Themes
Step 3: Build a Strategic Map
Step 4: Define Metrics and Targets
Step 5: Identify and Provide Ranking of Capital Programs
Step 6: Create an Implementation Plan

Municipalities must comply with codes, regulations, and standards. For example, buildings must be accessible, schools must meet safety guidelines, and the facilities must be equipped to properly dispose of fuel and other hazardous materials. In addition, data needed to make decisions about renovating or renewing facilities may not exist, and if it does exist, it may be outdated.

Local governments should develop comprehensive, multi-year plans that indicate which facilities need maintenance, renovations, and replacement. To develop such plans, it would be a suggestible practice to create an automated system that provides:

- current data on the condition of buildings, so that decisions could be made more rigorously
- a method for objectively setting priorities across the portfolio
- project planning tools that turn requirements into actions
- reporting tools that will give both finance and facilities departments the data they need.

The process of prioritization begins by categorizing identified facility requirements. These categories typically include major operations and maintenance projects, including system renewal, strategic capital projects such as construction of a new library, and mandated projects such as those involving regulatory compliance. Some funding sources are restricted to certain categories or project levels, while others can fund projects regardless of type.

With projects categorization, municipalities must create consistent criteria for evaluating each project and a consistent process for applying these criteria. Applying weights based on overall organizational objectives yields a comprehensive picture of how projects should be prioritized for budget allocation. Statistical ranking methods, such as pair-wise comparisons, can be used to facilitate the process, effectively tying requirements to organizational priorities. After each capital request is enumerated individually, all funding requests can be ranked by score.

Municipalities should use the facility self-assessment practices that employ a consistent, repeatable process for internal staff. By leveraging existing facility resources to quickly assess assets of all types and portfolios of all sizes, organizations can greatly enhance the management of facilities. The self-assessment process should be rapid and cost-effective, resulting in data that can identify "hot spots" within the portfolio that require a more detailed professional condition assessment and help develop quick budgetary estimates. According to VFA (2011), "lifecycle renewal costs can be a significant percentage of major operational and maintenance expenses. A detailed understanding of renewal timelines and costs is important to effectively prioritize systems requirements and avoid unanticipated spikes in required funding over time" (p. 5). A good facility self-assessment also maintains data captured in previous assessments to ensure that strategic decisions are based on factual information. Self-assessment empowers organizations to close the loop on portfolio knowledge gaps and gain immediate insight into their most pressing facility needs.

In summary, the following steps could be utilized by local governments to organize capital projects prioritization process efficiently and effectively:

- provide cost estimation for capital assets' renewal and replacement
- estimate system renewal costs and timelines based on both facility condition and asset age
- forecast long-term costs and explore the impact of different spending levels on facility conditions
- create multi-year budgets based on organization-wide priorities and strategies
- develop multiple ranking strategies for different types of assets and compare various budget scenarios
- evaluate different project scenarios and develop cost-effective capital projects from prioritized capital needs
- evaluate and prioritize green options by incorporating sustainability requirements into long-term capital plans.

Maintenance of Public Infrastructure

Public infrastructure asset maintenance is the weakest area in capital management for many, if not most, municipalities (Chen, 2014, 2016, 2017, Chen & Bartle, 2017, Ebdon, 2007, Ermasova, 2012, 2013, 2016, 2020, Ermasova & Ebdon, 2019, Ermasova & Mikesell, 2019, Guzman, 2019, Jacobs, 2008, Munnell, 1990, Srithongrung et al., 2019). Political support for a capital project can be more important than benefit-cost analysis. Besides, politicians prefer new constructions to maintenance of existing infrastructure. Separate planning of capital expenditures and related current maintenance expenditures led to multiple negative outcomes, such as uncompleted construction projects, prolongation of construction terms, and high exploitation costs of existing projects.

Ebdon (2007) accentuates that "capital assets need to be maintained in good working order to prevent excessive long-term costs and safety hazards" (p. 66). For this an improved capital infrastructure management is needed, including maintenance of up-to-date information systems, comprehensive assessments of capital assets' condition, and available financing to pay for the maintenance needs. Pagano (1984) similarly suggests that maintenance planning should be tied directly to the assessment of the condition of the capital stock with the asset management system (AMS). Pagano (1984) highlights some advantages of using maintenance planning in capital budgeting, such as combining information about condition of capital assets with typical depreciation schedules and information on replacement costs, developing estimates of both full costs of bringing infrastructure up to a good condition and a mix of repairs versus replacements of capital assets, and developing detailed maintenance plans with adequate funds for maintenance.

For example, decades old drinking water infrastructure systems, declining water use, costs of regulatory compliance, and stagnant federal funding has resulted in many water utilities struggling to fund the cost of operations and maintenance of drinking water systems. Maintenance costs reached an all-time high of 50.2 billion dollars in 2017, in part due to deferred capital projects (ASCE, 2021b). ASCE survey (ASCE, 2021b) found that 47 percent of the maintenance work undertaken by utilities is reactive and done after systems fail.

One of the measures that utilities are taking to improve operations and maintenance and shore up resilience and affordability, which shifts decision-making from reactive to proactive, is the development of asset management programs. Facility Condition Index (FCI) is the industry-standard metrics that is suggested to be used to evaluate the necessity for facility improvements.

$$FCI = \frac{\textit{Total Cost of Existing Requirements}}{\textit{Current Replacement Value}}$$

$0 \leq FCI < 5$ *percent* – excellent capital asset condition
$5 \leq FCI < 10$ *percent* – good capital asset condition
$FCI \geq 10$ *percent* – fair to poor capital asset condition

The FCI is basically the ratio of deferred maintenance dollars to replacement dollars. To calculate the FCI for a building, divide the total estimated cost to complete deferred maintenance projects for the building by its estimated replacement value. The lower the FCI, the lower the need for remedial or renewal funding relative to the facility's value. For example, an FCI of 0.05 signifies a 5 percent deficiency, which is generally considered low, and an FCI of 0.8 means that a building needs extensive repairs or replacement. Metrics such as the FCI allows for comparison of similar buildings and establishing target condition ratings. Comparing buildings analytically also highlights the assets in the greatest need for updates, repairs, or replacements.

The majority of municipalities differentiate between routine maintenance as an operating expenditure and deferred or major maintenance as a capital expenditure. During fiscally challenging times, maintenance expenses are often moved from the operating to capital budgets as the former usually are legally not allowed to carry deficit (which becomes a difficult task for fiscally strained municipalities) and the latter are simply required to be financed. Some municipalities developed a system to rate maintenance projects as part of the effort to preserve facilities. Many municipalities place additional emphasis on the planning and execution of preventive maintenance.

Conclusions

Public infrastructure is critical to economic and social wellbeing and development of municipalities. The effective management and budgeting of capital expenditures are among the most pressing challenges of municipal governments. The efforts require comprehensive and systematic planning, centralized execution and project management, and efficacy of infrastructure maintenance. The capital investment planning processes are complicated and often not well coordinated. The intergovernmental coordination, however, could be crucial in solving the crumbling infrastructure problem. For example, the highway system has the largest level of federal involvement. Nonetheless, even this system is characterized by great complexity in terms of ownership, operation, and finance falling largely under the responsibility of state and local governments. Achieving a consensus on any type of national policy proves difficult and complicates efforts aimed at coordinating systems across jurisdiction boundaries.

To address infrastructure needs quickly and efficiently, governments at all levels need to prepare and consistently update a comprehensive capital investment plan that would include a list of construction-ready infrastructure projects covering dams, inland waterways, clean and drinking water, and highways. COVID-19 crisis has offered a unique opportunity to reinvest in capital infrastructure and jumpstart the U.S. economy. Some major capital investment efforts have been undertaken, but federal government would need to consider further consistent infrastructure spending by finding the balance between the short-term need to maintain employment and economic activity and the large-scale capital projects of transformative nature.

There has been an increased need to institutionalize recommended practices in capital budgeting at all levels of government, particularly related to long-term planning, project management, and prioritization. The overall increase in planning and data-driven decisions should help to reduce long-term life-cycle costs and result in more efficient and effective use of resources. With capital projects prioritized and FCI data in place for maintenance, it is possible to justify both short- and long-term capital budget requirements by demonstrating the impact of different funding levels on the condition of an individual facility or the entire portfolio. Turning municipal strategic plans into actionable annual budgets can be a challenge, but funding scenarios can reduce risks and highlight financial consequences if the work is not completed.

The ultimate result is a budget based on an objectively ranked list of capital needs, with clear assumptions about funding and costs. If available funding levels change, the budget scenario may be reapplied to determine the impact on funded projects. If priorities of municipalities change during fiscal distress, ranking of the strategies should also be quickly modified to reflect new priorities. During fiscal distress, it is even more critical than ever for municipalities to effectively prioritize where limited capital funding should be spent, weighing the costs and benefits of competing projects and understanding the implications of deferred construction and maintenance.

References

Allen, M., Clark, R., Cotruvo, J. A., & Grigg, N. (2018). Drinking water and public health in an era of aging distribution infrastructure. *Public Works Management & Policy, 23*(4), 301–309.

American Road & Transportation Builders Association (2020). *Economics & market analysis.* Retrieved December 28, 2020, from www.artba.org/economics/

American Society of Civil Engineers (2017). *The infrastructure report card.* Retrieved December 28, 2020, from www.infrastructurerportcard.org/wp-content-uploads/2016/10/Grades-Chart.png

American Society of Civil Engineers (2020). *COVID-19's impacts on America's infrastructure.* Retrieved December 28, 2020, from www.infrastructurereportcard.org/wp-content/uploads/2020/06/COVID-19-Infrastructure-Status-Report.pdf

American Society of Civil Engineers (2021a). *The 2021 report card for America's infrastructure.* Retrieved April 8, 2021, from https://infrastructurereportcard.org/

American Society of Civil Engineers (2021b). *The 2021 report card: Drinking water.* Retrieved April 8, 2021, from https://infrastructurereportcard.org/wp-content/uploads/2020/12/Drinking-Water-2021.pdf

Ammar, A., Duncombe, R., & Wright, A. (2001). Evaluating capital management: A new approach. *Public Budgeting and Finance, 2*(1), 47–69.

Anthony, R. (1965). *Planning and Control Systems, A Framework for Analysis.* Boston, MA: Harvard University.

Auerbach, A., Gale, B., Lutz, B., & Sheiner, L. (2020). Fiscal effects of COVID-19. Brookings papers on economic activity. *The Brookings Institution*, 23 September. www.brookings.edu/bpea-articles/fiscal-effects-of-COVID-19/

Business Roundtable (2016). *Road to Growth: The Case for Investing in America's Transportation Infrastructure*. Retrieved December 28, 2020, from http://businessroundtable.org/sites/default/files/2015.09.16%20Infrastructure%20Report%20-%20Final.pdf

CBC News (202). *Biden signs $1.2 trillion infrastructure bill into law, hailing bipartisan breakthrough*, 16 November. www.cbsnews.com/live-updates/infrastructure-bill-biden-signing-ceremony-white-house/

Chan, Y. (2004). Use of capital budgeting techniques and an analytic approach to capital investment. Decisions in Canadian municipal governments. *Public Budgeting & Finance, 3*(2), 47–54.

Chen, C. (2014). Measuring state highway sustainability: Taking the fiscal dimension into account. *Public Works Management and Policy, 19*(3), 255–276.

Chen, C. (2016). Effects of fiscal stress on state highway infrastructure finance: A composite index approach. *Municipal Finance Journal, 37*(2), 1–28.

Chen, C. (2017). Does money matter for infrastructure outcomes? The effects of public infrastructure finance on state infrastructure quality. *Journal of Public Budgeting, Accounting and Financial Management, 29*(3), 375–408.

Chen, C. (2018). Public infrastructure finance: Symposium introduction. *Journal of Public Budgeting, Accounting and Financial Management, 30*(2), 126–134.

Chen, C., & Bartle, J. R. (2017). *Infrastructure Finance: A Guide for Local Government Managers*. Washington, D.C.: A Policy Issue White Paper for International City/County Management (ICMA) and Government Finance Officers Association (GFOA). Retrieved from https://icma.org/documents/infrastructure-financing-guide-local-government-managers

Choate, P., & Walter, S. (1983). *America in Ruins: The Decaying Infrastructure*. Durham, NC: Duke Press Paperbacks.

Congressional Budget Office (2015). *Public spending on transportation and water infrastructure: 1956 to 2014*. Retrieved from www.cbo.gov/publication/49910

Congressional Budget Office (2019a). *Capital budgeting*. Retrieved from www.cbo.gov/sites/default/files/cbofiles/ftpdocs/91xx/doc9167/maintext.3.1.shtml

Congressional Budget Office (2019b). *Federal investment 1962 to 2018*. Retrieved from www.cbo.gov/publication/55375

Congressional Budget Office (2020). *An update to the economic outlook: 2020 to 2030*. Retrieved February 4, 2022, from https://www.cbo.gov/system/fi outlook.pdf

Ebdon, C. (2007). Underpinning government: Capital and infrastructure management in state and local government. In Ingraham, P. (Ed.), *Pursuit of Performance: Management Systems in State and Local Government* (pp. 57–81). Hoboken, NJ: Johns Hopkins University Press.

Ermasova, N. (2012). *Capital budgeting at the state level: An empirical analysis from the economic downturn through the present*. [PhD Dissertation, SPEA, IU].

Ermasova, N. (2013). Capital budgeting in the states after the great recession. *State and Local Government Review, 45*(2), 119–130.

Ermasova, N. (2016). *Budget Systems in Russia* (2nd ed.). Moscow: UNITY.

Ermasova, N. (2020). The 35 years of public capital budgeting: A review and future research agenda. *Public Finance and Management, 20*(4), 1–32.

Ermasova, N., & Ebdon, C. (2019). Public capital budgeting and management processes in the United States. In Srithongrung, A., Ermasova, N., & Yususf, W. (Eds.), *Capital Management and Budgeting in the Public Sector*. Hershey, PA: IGI Global.

Ermasova, N., & Mikesell, J. (2019). Public capital budgeting and management: The concept and its application in three important federations. *Public Finance and Management. 19*(3), 207–231.

Frankel, E., & Wachs, M. (2017). More than money: Infrastructure and governance. *Public Works Management and Policy, 22*(1), 6–11.

GovInfo (2018). *Federal Investment in 2018*. Retrieved from https://budgetcounsel.files.wordpress.com/2018/02/ap17-investment-fy2019.pdf

GovInfo (2019). *Federal investment in 2019*. Retrieved from www.govinfo.gov/content/pkg/BUDGET-2019-PER/pdf/BUDGET-2019-PER-7-4.pdf

GovInfo (2020). *Federal investment in 2020*. Retrieved December 28, 2020, from www.whitehouse.gov/wp-content/uploads/2020/02/ap_16_investment_fy21.pdf

Guzman, T. (2019). The case of public capital budgeting and management process in Uzbekistan. In Srithongrung, A., Ermasova, N., & Yususf, W. (Eds.), *Capital Management and Budgeting in the Public Sector*. Hershey, PA: IGI Global.

Hamel, G., & Prahalad, C. K. (1989). Strategic intent. *Harvard Business Review, 6*(3), 67–76.

House Committee on Transportation and Infrastructure (2020a). *Committee leaders unveil the invest in America act, a transformational surface transportation bill to bring nation's infrastructure into a new era*. Retrieved on June 3, 2020, from https://transportation.house.gov/news/press-releases/committee-leaders-unveil-the-invest-in-america-act-a-transformational-surface-transportation-bill-to-bring-nations-infrastructure-into-a-new-era

House Committee on Transportation and Infrastructure (2020b). *Investing in a new vision for the environment and surface transportation in America act*. Retrieved June 3, 2020, from https://transportation.house.gov/imo/media/doc/2020%20INVEST%20in%20America%20Bill%20Summary.pdf

Jacobs, D. F. (2008). *A Review of Capital Budgeting Practices*. IMF Working Paper of Fiscal Affairs Department. Retrieved from http://blog-pfm.imf.org/pfmblog/files/a_review_of_capital_budgeting_practices1.pdf

Khan, A., & Hildreth, B. (Ed.). (2002). *Budget Theory in the Public Sector*. New York: Quorum Books.

Kosich, J. (2022). President Biden to tout Infrastructure and Investment Act money heading to Ohio in Thursday visit. *News5Cleveland*, 16 February 2022. Retrieved February 17, 2022, from www.news5cleveland.com/news/local-news/oh-lorain/president-biden-to-tout-infrastructure-and-investment-act-money-heading-to-ohio-in-thursday-visit

McClain, J. M. (1966). *Capital budgeting in selected states*. Lexington, KY: Bureau of Business Research, College of Commerce, University of Kentucky.

McNichol, E. (2019). It's time for states to invest in infrastructure. *CBPP Report*. www.cbpp.org/sites/default/files/atoms/files/2-23-16sfp.pdf

Mikesell, J. (2007). *Fiscal Administration: Analysis and Applications for the Public Sector* (8th ed.). Belmont, CA: Thomson Wadsworth.

Munnell, A. H. (1990). *How does public infrastructure affect regional economic performance?* In Munnell, A. A. (Ed.), *Is There a Shortfall in Public Capital Investment?* (pp. 23–34). Boston, MA: Federal Reserve Bank of Boston.

Pagano, M. (1984). Notes on capital budgeting. *Public Budgeting & Finance, 4*(2), 31–40.

Pagano, M. A. (1986). State capital budgeting: Controls and constraints over project selection. *State & Local Government Review, 18*(3), 94–106.

PEW Trust Fund (2020). *The impact of the coronavirus*. Retrieved on June 3, 2022, from https://www.pewtrusts.org/en/trust/archive/summer-2020/the-impact-of-the-coronavirus

Phillips, Z. (2020). Report: US cities' massive budget cuts impact infrastructure, capital expenses. *Construction Dive*. Retrieved on June 3, 2020, from www.constructiondive.

com/news/report-us-cities-massive-budget-cuts-impact-infrastructure-capital-expen/580793/

Rivenbark, W. C., Afonso, W., & Roenigk, D. J. (2018). Capital spending in local government: Providing context through the lens of government-wide financial statements. *Journal of Public Budgeting, Accounting and Financial Management*, *30*(4), 402–414.

Snyder, J. C. (1977). *Fiscal Management and Planning in Local Government*. Lexington, MA: Lexington Books.

Srithongrung, A., Ermasova, N., & Yusuf, W. (2019). *Capital Management and Budgeting in the Public Sector*. Hershey, Pennsylvania: IGI Global.

Stewart, L., & Atkinson, R. (2013). *The Greater Stagnation: The Decline in Capital Investment is the Real Threat to U.S. Economic Growth*. The Information Technology & Innovation Foundation. Retrieved from https://www2.itif.org/2013-the-greater-stagnation.pdf

Tandberg, E., & Allen, R. (2020). *Managing Public Investment Spending during the Crisis. Special Series on COVID-19, Fiscal Affairs Department, May 11, International Monetary Fund, Washington, D.C.* Retrieved December 28, 2020, from www.imf.org/~/media/Files/Publications/COVID19 – special-notes/en-special-series-on-COVID-19-managing-public-investment – spending-during-the-crisis.ashx?la=en

Tennessee Department of Finance & Administration (2020). *The office of evidence and impact*. Retrieved from www.tn.gov/finance/oei/program-inventory.html

U.S. Census Bureau (2020). *2018 Annual Surveys of State and Local Government Finances*. Retrieved December 28, 2021, from https://www.census.gov/programs-surveys/gov-finances.html

U.S. Treasury (2021). *Capital projects fund*. Retrieved May 3, 2022, from https://home.treasury.gov/policy-issues/coronavirus/assistance-for-state-local-and-tribal-governments/capital-projects-fund

VFA (2011). *Data-Driven Decisions Increase Effectiveness of Facility Management at Colleges and Universities*. VFA White Paper. Greenville, SC: GORDIAN. Retrieved May 3, 2022, from https://www.gordian.com/resources/state-of-facilities-in-higher-education-9th-edition/

White House (2021). *FACT SHEET: The American jobs plan,* 31 March. Retrieved April 28, 2021, from www.whitehouse.gov/briefing-room/statements-releases/2021/03/31/fact-sheet-the-american-jobs-plan/

Wiggins, D. C. (1980). A case study in governmental capital budgeting. *Governmental Finance*, *9*, 19–22.

7

FISCAL STRESS DURING THE COVID-19 PANDEMIC

Introduction

From a national perspective, the COVID-19 pandemic has had the biggest effect on the economy and municipal finances since the Great Depression (Congressional Budget Office, 2020a). During March and April 2020, as the COVID-19 crisis gathered steam, 40 million people in the United States lost their jobs due to layoffs and bankruptcies across the economy. The unemployment rate in April 2020 increased by 10.3 percentage points to 14.7 percent, the highest single month increase since January 1948. The number of unemployed persons rose from 15.9 million to 23.1 million in April due to the effects of the COVID-19 pandemic and efforts to contain it (U.S. Bureau of Labor Statistics, 2020). The COVID-19 crisis has impacted all local governments across the United States, having "a major impact on cities of all sizes" (National League of Cities, 2020a; Romm, 2020a, p. 1).

This chapter aims to explore how the COVID-19 pandemic has affected U.S. state and local governments and what their responses to this fiscal stress have been. What have been the financial losses and gains for the local governments in 2020 and 2021? How have tax revenues been affected? How have the size and the purpose of expenditures changed? What aid for municipalities was offered by federal and state governments to address economic fallout and lay the foundation for a strong and equitable fiscal recovery?

Fiscal Shock from the COVID-19 Pandemic

During economic downturns the federal government uses fiscal policy tools such as lower taxes and higher expenditures to stimulate the economy and turn it back on a path toward recovery. Federal and local fiscal actions, however, often work

DOI: 10.4324/b23117-7

in the opposite directions during economic recessions. The majority of state and local governments face annual balanced budget requirements, and as such they confront fiscal shocks on both the revenue and spending sides. Practices show that after the 2001 and 2007–2009 recessions, for instance, state revenues (inflation adjusted) remained stagnant for multiple quarters before reaching pre-recession levels (Gascon & LaBelle, 2021). When an economic downturn reduces revenues, state and local governments are forced to either cut spending or raise other taxes and non-tax revenues to make up for the budget's shortfall (Clemens & Miran, 2012; Dadayan, 2020a,b; Mikesell, 2007, Poterba, 1994). As a result, state and local government actions contradict federal government recovery efforts, deepen the recession, and slow down the recovery process.

The COVID-19 crisis affected state and local fiscal conditions in similar ways as previous downturns. However, several unique features have put immediate pressure on state and local government finances. First, government spending has risen significantly as states were buying medical supplies and setting up temporary healthcare facilities to combat the spread of COVID-19. Local governments provided preventive and supportive actions that had impacts on both the revenue and expenditure sides of their budgets. Municipalities had to purchase necessary protective equipment to disinfect their own premises in addition to public spaces. They also provided specific services to residents, such as delivering food and goods to the elderly and other vulnerable populations or purchasing and distributing face masks.

Second, state and local governments voluntarily delayed the payment of state and local taxes and provided several tax exemptions to businesses. Most states have postponed income tax filing deadlines from April 15, 2020 to July 15, 2020 and from April 15, 2021 to May 17, 2021 to align with the new federal deadlines, creating a temporary liquidity challenge.

Third, shelter-in-place orders in many states toward the beginning of the pandemic reduced consumer spending, thereby lowering sales tax collections. Although food purchases for home consumption have increased, many states exempt groceries from sales taxes. Consumer spending bounced almost all the way back relatively quickly but shifted by a hefty margin from in-person to online shopping. Online shopping for certain essentials such as over-the-counter medicine, groceries, household supplies, and personal-care products grew more than 35 percent. Even online shopping for discretionary categories such as skin care and makeup, apparel, and jewelry and accessories increased by more than 15 percent at the beginning of the pandemic (McKinsey & Company, 2020).

One of the consequences of COVID-19 fiscal responses for local governments was the budget deficit that "in 2020 reaches 16 percent of GDP – more than 11 percent of GDP larger than was predicted in the pre-COVID baseline, and much higher than even the peak deficit in the Great Recession – about 10 percent of GDP" (Auerbach et al., 2020, p. 10). McNichol and Leachman (2020) estimated that states alone would face 290 billion dollars in combined budget shortfalls in fiscal year 2021. In California, for example, the Department of Finance projected a 9.2 percent increase in Medicaid enrollees, a 51.1 percent increase in SNAP participation, and an unprecedented 75.6 percent increase in public assistance participation through fiscal year 2021 (California Health Care Foundation, 2021). San Francisco, CA reported an additional 375 million dollars in COVID-related spending in fiscal year 2020 and projected costs of up to 470 million dollars in fiscal year 2021, although these projections were subject to considerable uncertainty about the course of the pandemic, as well as state and federal policy responses (San Francisco Office of the Mayor, 2020).

Revenue Shortage

In April 2020, 92 percent of North Carolina's municipalities reported that they were expecting a general-fund shortfall for fiscal year 2021; additionally, over 20 percent of municipalities in the state expected to see shortfalls to exceed 10 percent of their general funds (Afonso, 2021, p. 159). Revenue shortages were expected by all state and local governments in the early days of the COVID-19 pandemic.

The COVID-19 restrictions on local and regional transportation resulted in decreased municipal revenues from transportation services, especially in larger cities. Less travel meant lower gasoline and lodging tax revenues and lower parking fees. The ban on mass gatherings impacted local budgets by decreasing collections from admission excises. Closed schools meant that revenues from catering and other paid services provided by schools disappeared from local budgets. Some measures aimed at supporting the economy had a derogatory effect on local budgets as well. The option to postpone the payment of income taxes in 2020 and 2021, for example, provided a much-needed relief to taxpayers but further strained state and local government finances.

The main tax revenues that state and local governments collect are personal income tax, property tax, and sales tax. According to the U.S. Census Bureau (2021), right before COVID the total general own-source revenues of state and local governments were 2.7 trillion dollars. Twenty-one percent of all state and local own-source revenues came from property tax. Property tax is of a great importance for local governments that collected over 46 percent of total revenues from this tax alone. Sales taxes generated just under 24 percent of total revenues for states and localities in 2019. And personal income tax made up 16.5 percent of revenues. Of non-tax revenues, 21 percent of total state and local revenues was generated by user charges. These numbers are, of course, different in every state. New Hampshire, for example, collected 46 percent of their total own-source revenue from property tax alone in 2019. The share of property tax in total tax revenues for this state was 62.5 percent. New Hampshire, however, does not collect general sales tax and generates almost no revenue from the excises at either the state or local level. Washington State on the other hand collected 40 percent of all own-source revenues, almost

TABLE 7.1 Estimations of State and Local Revenue Losses During COVID-19 Pandemic

References	*Estimations of State and Local Governments Revenue Losses*
White et al. (2020)	$130 billion fiscal losses over the two fiscal years
Bartik (2020)	$875 billion fiscal losses over the two fiscal years
Whitaker (2020)	$141 billion of revenue losses from all sources in fiscal year 2020
Clemens and Veuger (2020a,b)	$240 billion a total state and local government revenue loss due to the COVID-19 pandemic of $240 billion in fiscal year 2021
Dadayan (2020a)	a $200 billion combined two-year revenue shortfall
Chernick et al. (2020)	"a shortfall in revenues of 5.5 percent under the less severe scenario and 9 percent under the more severe scenario. The hardest hit cities face revenue losses of 15 percent or more" (p. 699).

63 percent of total tax revenues, from sales taxes in 2019. At the same time, neighboring Oregon, similar to New Hampshire, does not collect general sales tax at either the state or local level (U.S. Census Bureau, 2021).

While Census data following the COVID-19 stroke is not yet available, many scholars have estimated the likely effects of the pandemic on the fiscal health of state and local governments. Table 7.1 provides the estimations of state and local revenue losses.

Many scholars estimate that the decline in tax collections was historic and exceeded the declines during the Great Recession of 2008–2009 (Clemens & Veuger, 2020a,b; Gordon et al., 2020; Whitaker, 2020). The state revenues declined by nearly 14 billion dollars or 1.8 percent between April and December 2020 compared with the same period in 2019 (Dadayan, 2020a, p. 1). Colorado projected a budget shortfall of up to three billion dollars in fiscal year 2021, about 10 percent of their total annual budget (Burness, 2020).

Accurate estimations for income and sales tax revenue losses associate with the COVID-19 pandemic are difficult to make, due to the large variation in unemployment rates across the states. Pagano and McFarland (2020) found that

> cities with both a vulnerable economic composition (greater than 15% share of employment in high-risk industries) and a tax structure that is highly reliant on elastic sources of revenue (greater than 25% share of general fund revenues) will feel a dip in revenues more quickly than those with alternative economic and fiscal structures.
>
> *(p. 1)*[1]

Fiedler et al. (2020) estimate that a one percentage point increase in the unemployment rate lowers real per capita total state revenues by 3.7 percent. Clemens and Veuger (2020a) used the historical relationship between changes in personal income and income tax collections and changes in personal consumption and sales tax collections.

Income tax contributes, on average, 38 percent of total states' revenues, with a range of 0 percent to 74 percent in different states (Gascon & LaBelle, 2021, p. 3).

> New Hampshire, California, New Jersey, and New York are projected to record the largest 2020 percentage declines, with income taxes falling 9 percent, 8.5 percent, 8 percent, and 6.7 percent, respectively. In contrast, Illinois, Kansas, Kentucky, North Carolina, and West Virginia are projected to suffer declines of less than 1.5 percent.
>
> *(Auerbach et al., 2020, pp. 37–38)*

Six states (Florida, Nevada, South Dakota, Tennessee, Texas, and Wyoming) do not collect personal income tax at either the state or local level. Alaska does not collect personal income tax on the state level but allows municipalities to collect it on a local level. In two other states, New Hampshire and Washington, personal income tax collections are minuscular, because New Hampshire limits its income tax base to dividends and interest income only and Washington taxes only capital gains and only of high-income earners.

The sales tax revenues decreased by more than six billion dollars, or 21 percent, in May 2020 compared to one year earlier (Dadayan, 2020b). Auerbach et al. (2020) projected that sales tax revenues would decline by 49 billion dollars in 2020, 45 billion dollars in 2021, and 46 billion dollars in 2022. Sales tax contributes on average 34.4 percent to state and local tax revenues, with a range of 0–63 percent of tax revenues in 2019 (U.S. Census Bureau, 2021) because some states do not collect sales taxes and others rely on them quite heavily. Forty-five states collect general sales tax on a state level, and forty permit local governments to collect their own sales taxes. Arkansas, Illinois, Missouri, Tennessee, Utah, and Virginia tax sales of grocery food at a reduced rate. Alabama, Mississippi, and South Dakota tax grocery food sales at the full rate. Hawaii, Idaho, Kansas, and Oklahoma tax grocery food sales at the full rate, but low-income households may receive rebates or income tax credits against the tax (Federation of Tax Administrators, 2020). Idaho, South Dakota, and Utah suffered very modest sales tax declines, in part because they tax the sale of groceries. Auerbach et al. (2020) projected that the largest percentage declines of sales tax revenues would be "in the District of Columbia (18%) and Rhode Island (16%) while the smallest declines are in Alabama, Idaho, and Arkansas (4%, 5%, and 6%)" (p. 43).

Corporate taxes constitute a small proportion of state and local tax revenues, only about 2.4 percent of own-source revenues in 2019 (U.S. Census Bureau, 2021). Yet, the projected decreases of state corporate income tax revenues by "$2 billion in 2020, $29 billion in 2021, and $14 billion in 2022" (Auerbach et al., 2020, p. 44) would substantively undermine the 65.6-billion-dollar tax revenues collected in 2019 (U.S. Census Bureau, 2021).

Initial lockdowns that closed factories in March 2020 adversely affected the demand for natural resources, such as coal, oil, and natural gas. As mentioned, restricted travel reduced demand for gasoline, as well. Consequently, severance taxes – taxes assessed on extracted natural resources such as coal, oil, and natural gas – declined sharply in the states that rely heavily on them, such as Colorado, Kansas, western Missouri, Nebraska, northern New Mexico, Oklahoma, and Wyoming.

> In New Mexico, Oklahoma, and Wyoming, severance taxes make up 20 percent, 10 percent, and 31 percent of general fund tax revenues, respectively. Through the first nine months of the current fiscal year, severance tax collections fell by 22 percent in Colorado and 27 percent in Oklahoma.
>
> *(Felix, 2020, p. 3).*

Auerbach et al. (2020) additionally estimate that the pandemic will "lower revenues from 'other taxes' and fees, excluding fees to public hospitals and institutions of higher education, by $82 billion this year, $55 billion next year, and $45 billion in 2022" (p. 46). The authors predicted higher losses in "other taxes" and fees than one would anticipate because "the decline in use of transportation services alone seems likely to depress revenues by over $45 billion in 2020" (p. 4).

Overall Auerbach et al. (2020) estimate

> that state and local own source revenues, excluding fees to public hospitals and institution of higher education – which we view as somewhat distinct – will decline $155 billion in 2020, $167 billion in 2021, and $145 billion in 2022. Including lower fees to hospitals and higher education would bring these totals to $188 billion, $189 billion, and $167 billion
>
> *(p. 4)*

Local revenues from hotel occupancy taxes, real estate transfer taxes, utility user taxes, and other miscellaneous sources were all reduced as a result of the pandemic (Pagano & McFarland, 2020). The National League of Cities (2020a, 2020b) reports that city finance officers expect a combined fiscal 2020 and 2021 general fund revenue decline of up to 13 percent. Cities with fewer than 50,000 residents were expected to face the largest shortfalls (Chernick et al., 2020; Pagano & McFarland, 2020). Statistics show, however, that despite gloomy predictions, the economy bounced almost all the way back quite quickly, and, at least on the state level, already in 2021 tax revenues were much higher than anticipated (NASBO, 2021; Rivkin & Karoub, 2021).

Budgeting Responses to Fiscal Losses During COVID-19

To deal with budget deficits (caused mainly by declining tax and non-tax revenues) and to respond to other emerging fiscal shocks, especially in the beginning of the pandemic, state and local governments had to turn to the *Cutback Management*, *Fiscal Stress Minimization Strategies*, and *Social Budgeting* mechanisms we discussed in Chapter 5. The NLC and the U.S. Conference of Mayors conducted a survey of 2,100 U.S. cities in March and April of 2020 to analyze the economic effects of the novel coronavirus and found that many local governments had "sharp declines in tax revenue as businesses shutter, workers lose their jobs in record numbers and tourism grinds to a halt" (Romm, 2020a, p. 1). Romm (2020a) reported that "nearly 9 in 10 cities surveyed – from smaller hubs with populations of fewer than 50,000 to the largest metropolitan areas in the country – signaled they expect a revenue shortfall" (p. 1).

State and, especially, local governments that were already in fiscal distress before 2019 and lacked a fiscal buffer faced painfully deep service cuts (Fiedler et al., 2019). Not only operating but capital expenses were slashed. In some cases, simple budget cuts were substituted by cost savings through shared services or public-private partnership agreements or simply improving the budget processes. Some municipalities tried to raise additional revenues to patch looming budget deficits. The federal government also chipped in by passing several legislative acts to provide relief to state and local governments.

Operating Budget Cuts

Whitaker (2020) estimated that "state and local governments will need to cut expenditures by between $59 billion and $350 billion in fiscal year 2021 (FY21) to offset impending losses of revenue" (p. 1). According to Gordon et al. (2020), "in finalizing their fiscal 2021 budgets, states mainly relied on one-time actions, including hiring freezes, cancelled program expansions, drawing down reserve funds, internal borrowing, and deferring expenses into the next fiscal year" (p. 749). The National Conference of State Legislatures (2021) reports that about half of all states have instituted across-the-board spending cuts. NASBO (2021) argues that on a state level

> during fiscal 2021, 19 states reported making targeted spending cuts, seven states reported making across-the-board cuts, 17 states imposed hiring freezes and/or eliminated vacant positions, four states imposed furloughs, two states reported salary reductions, and one state offered employees early retirement.
> *(p. IX)*

According to Romm (2020a) over 1,100 cities in Michigan were preparing to scale back public services. Besides, "almost 600 cities predicted they may have to

TABLE 7.2 Data on Planned Spending and Estimated Revenue for the City of Philadelphia, Pennsylvania's General Fund for Fiscal Year 2021 ($ million)

Category of pending	*FY2021 Proposed ($ mln)*	*FY2021 Revised ($ mln)*	*Percent Change*
Budget Stabilization Reserve	36.5	0	– 100%
Arts, Culture, and Creative Economy	14.5	0	– 100%
Commerce	9.60	1.45	– 85%
Finance	40.1	18.4	– 54%
Planning and Development	15.7	$7.63	– 51%
Sustainability	2.47	1.2	– 51%
Homeless Services	60.8	48.0	– 21%
Community College Subsidy	54.5	44.1	– 19%
Streets	170	151	– 11%
Human Services	179	162	– 9%
Public Health	167	159	– 5%

Source: Table created by authors from City of Philadelphia, Pennsylvania Controller's Office (2020)

lay off some government workers amid the crunch. Local leaders in 1,000 cities said the reductions probably would affect their local police departments and other public safety agencies" (Romm, 2020a, p. 1). Over three-quarters of North Carolina's municipalities reported they were not budgeting for any new positions, and over half instituted hiring freezes (Afonso, 2021, p. 159). According to Afonso (2021), "reducing capital expenditures was the second-most-common strategy, followed by increasing fees, with only one jurisdiction reporting an intent to increase taxes" (p. 166). This allows for expanding programming in some key areas, such as public health and housing.

The Budget of San Antonio in 2021 included 87 million dollars in cuts over two years due to pandemic-related revenue reductions. The cuts included "a hiring freeze, compensation adjustments for existing city employees, suspension of economic development incentives, and reductions to the Police Department overtime budget and Cadet Hiring Bonus program" (FEMA, 2021, p. 15). The Village of Bolingbrook, IL cut road projects and saved money on mosquito abatement services, equipment maintenance, and tree replacements. Revised spending for fiscal year 2021 for the city of Philadelphia, Pennsylvania's general fund was 341 million dollars (see Table 7.2).

Capital Budget Cuts

The COVID-19 pandemic and associated financial crisis required many municipalities to decrease their capital spending (Romm, 2020b). "The National League of Cities reported in June that more than 700 cities have halted plans to improve roadways, buy new equipment, and complete upgrades to water systems and other critical infrastructure" (Romm, 2020b, p. 1). Washington D.C. decreased its capital budget by about 13 percent in 2020. Washington D.C. had a database of its assets and a priority ranking of its capital projects, "it was able to revise its nearly $8 billion capital budget in a matter of weeks to reflect the reduced revenues, while maintaining core priorities and delivering high-quality infrastructure for District of Columbia residents" (FEMA, 2021, p. 14). Chattanooga, TN

> cuts $7 million from capital expenses in 2021, nixing the purchase of a new firetruck and other government vehicles. And the city's financial blueprints no longer include a water-pipe replacement program, reflecting officials' fears about paying for improvements using new local fees in the middle of a recession.
>
> *(Romm, 2020b, p. 1)*

Increase of Taxes and Fees

To cover the budget deficit caused by the pandemic, some local governments implemented other *Fiscal Stress Minimization Strategies* (see Chapter 5 for discussion), by choosing to increase taxes and fees, for instance. In Chicago, IL, taxpayers were "hit with $94 million in property tax increases and $38 million in higher fines and fees, including a policy for speed cameras to ticket drivers for going just 6 mph over the speed limit, to help close the city's budget deficit" (Carlson, 2021). In Ohio, where tax limitations make it difficult to institute tax increases, several counties increased the property tax base instead, to raise additional revenues and to offset declining sales and income tax bases. The value of homes for property tax purposes in Cuyahoga County, OH, home to the City of Cleveland, increased by 16 percent during 2021 reappraisals (Cleveland.com, 2021). Montgomery County, OH, the home to the city of Dayton, similarly increased the value of the properties for tax purposes by an average of 15.5 percent countywide during 2020 reappraisals (Stewart, 2021).

Improved Budgeting

While some "ad hoc solutions" and *cutback instruments* are needed for crisis management, they should be combined with other more permanent budgeting mechanisms. In addition to tax increases, during the COVID-19 pandemic, municipalities turned to other *Fiscal Stress Minimization Strategies* and *Social Budgeting* mechanisms. After all, the goal of municipal governments is to provide vital services to residents through the efficient and effective use of taxpayer money. Throughout the COVID-19 crisis, municipalities have faced unemployment, a complicated environment for local business retention and expansion, declining tax revenues, and inflation, among multiple other challenges, making strategic budget decisions more important than ever.

According to Anessi-Pessina et al. (2020) the most immediate response to a budget deficit during the COVID-19 pandemic was rebudgeting, i.e., the possibility to amend the budget during the financial year:

> several forces are urging governments to embrace a more strategic approach in order to pursue a dual set of goals: on the one hand, spend effectively in the short run, making good use of the looser budgetary constraints and the extensive emergency funds; on the other, lay the foundations to recover from the mounting debt that will inevitably be produced by increased spending and by shrinking tax and fee revenues.
>
> *(pp. 958–959)*

As an example of rebudgeting practices, in New York State the overview of the Comptroller's Fiscal Stress Monitoring System of municipal government finances (discussed in Chapter 2) showed that in fiscal year 2020 municipalities in this state made up for lost revenues by closing recreational facilities and summer camps and reducing the number of special events due to COVID-19 precautions, diverting funds from these to other purposes.

Fiscal risk management has proved to be another important budgetary tool during the COVID-19 crisis. Fiscal risk management provides management control, comprehensive information on fiscal risks, mitigation measures, scenario analyses, and stress testing that can support the discussion of potential fiscal policy implications during the COVID-19 crisis.

As previously mentioned, for some states and municipalities, the COVID-19 pandemic became an *environmental jolt* that triggered administrative or other innovations. On May 5, 2020, the city of Philadelphia, Pennsylvania Controller's Office, for example, released a visualization tool to better understand the major changes in the revised budget released in response to declining tax revenues resulting from the COVID-19 pandemic (City of Philadelphia, Pennsylvania Controller's Office, 2020). This tool brought transparency to the city's budgeting process. The visualization tool includes data on planned spending and estimated revenue for the City of Philadelphia general fund for fiscal years 2020 through 2025. The spending data is broken down by fiscal year, city department, spending class, and spending category. Additionally, revenue data can be viewed by fiscal year and revenue source (City of Philadelphia, Pennsylvania Controller's Office, 2020).

Fund Balances and Rainy-day Funds

Adding to the budgeting decisions discussed in the previous section, some of the tax revenue losses during COVID-19 were offset by the rainy-day funds or positive fund balances that state and local governments set aside during economic expansion. Afonso (2021) suggests that "budget-balancing strategies, including the appropriation of fund balance, a common way to smooth expenditures in the face of declining revenues" (p. 165). When the COVID-19 pandemic hit, state and local governments entered the recession in a relatively strong financial position with funds and surpluses around "$119 billion in fiscal year 2019, equal to 14 percent of general fund expenditures – a historic high" (Auerbach et al., 2020, p. 21). Cities reported reserves had around 30 percent of annual spending, compared to 25 percent before the Great Recession (National League of Cities, 2020a).

FEMA (2021) suggests that COVID-19 has affected municipalities in an unequal manner and that communities that already had fewer resources than their counterparts were facing a larger burden due to the pandemic. Researchers find that positive general fund balances and the size of rainy-day funds have, indeed, been correlated more strongly with the ability to save rather than with the need to save (Afonso, 2021; Gorina et al., 2019). On a state level, in early 2020 right before the beginning of the pandemic, the rainy-day fund in Wyoming had a balance of 109.0 percent of state general fund expenditures, 52.6 percent in Alaska, 30.0 percent in North Dakota, and 26.8 percent in New Mexico (Tax Foundation, 2020). On the other hand, Illinois and Kansas had basically emptied their reserve funds, even before the pandemic. New Jersey and Pennsylvania both had rainy-day fund balances at only 1 percent of their general fund expenditures. According to the National Association of Budget Officers (NASBO) "Fiscal Survey of States" report (NASBO, 2021), 12 states tapped into their rainy-day funds, 9 states used fund balances, 13 states transferred money to general fund from other funds, and 4 deferred payments in 2020 to deal with the revenue shortage caused by the COVID-19 pandemic. However, better than expected revenue growth in 2021 led to a substantial increase in state rainy-day funds, by a total of 112.7 billion dollars at year-end across the states.

Shared-service Agreements

Some municipalities improved efficiency and found cost-savings through shared-service agreements or consolidation of services with neighboring cities, towns, or counties. Multiple neighboring communities partnered with each other as COVID-19 commenced to provide emergency, social, and public safety services (FEMA, 2021). Some states, such as New York, New Jersey, and Illinois, among others, offered support for shared services for municipalities. According to FEMA (2021), "as the COVID-19 pandemic places additional strain on local government capacity, including staff cuts or hiring freezes, such collaborative projects may be of particular benefit for bolstering local government capacity" (p. 12). For example, five communities within Walworth County, WI created a combined EMS to respond to calls in their communities in 2021. The partnership cost was split among the six communities, totaled around 500,000 dollars a year, and was paid for through an increase in property taxes in those communities (FEMA, 2021).

A Public-private Partnership

Local governments have also used public-private partnerships in response to the COVID-19 crisis as a funding mechanism to support local business communities and for workforce development and job placement initiatives (FEMA, 2021). In the city of Birmingham, AL, a group of 30 organizations formed a public-private partnership to expand COVID-19 relief and recovery efforts called "Bham Strong" (FEMA, 2021). "Bham Strong" had two main objectives: (1) to create an emergency loan fund for small businesses to bridge the gap before the Small Business Association (SBA) aid would arrive and (2) to create the Birmingham Service Corps that matched recently unemployed individuals with paid volunteer opportunities related to the pandemic. According to FEMA (2021), "Bham Strong collected survey data from local businesses and started an emergency loan fund of $2.4 million dollars funded by the City of Birmingham, the Community Foundation of Greater Birmingham, and corporate donors" (p. 17).

In another example demonstrating a response to the COVID-19 pandemic, in Fairfield County, CT, Housatonic and Norwalk Community Colleges created a no-cost, fast-track healthcare training pilot program thanks to a partnership between the colleges' foundations, Bank of America and Social Venture Partners (SVP; Roberts, 2020). This job retraining program directly targeted those who became unemployed as a result of the COVID-19 pandemic by an adaption of healthcare worker training programs already in place at the community colleges participating in this program (FEMA, 2021). The goal of this innovative public-private partnership was to quickly retrain displaced or unemployed workers – particularly from the hospitality field – and arrange employment within hospitals for in-demand healthcare jobs. Partnerships for clinical and hiring arrangements were with Stamford, Norwalk, Greenwich, Bridgeport, Norwalk/Nuvance Health, and Yale New Haven Hospitals (Roberts, 2020).

Federal Transfers During the COVID-19 Pandemic

To prevent major fiscal problems, municipalities turned their heads to the federal government to help compensate for the revenue losses and higher expenditures caused by the COVID-19 pandemic. According to Anessi-Pessina et al. (2020),

> a related issue is whether to allow individual subnational governments to run deficits and build-up debt, the alternative being for the central government to increase transfers to subnational governments, concentrate all deficits and debt at the national level and take sole responsibility for debt creation and management.
>
> *(p. 959)*

In spring 2021, The Michigan Public Policy Survey found that many municipalities across Michigan have been able to weather COVID-19 impacts only because of external federal assistance (Horner & Ivacke, 2021). The New York State Comptroller (2021) similarly acknowledges that "the American Rescue Plan Act of 2021 supplemented revenues lost due to COVID-19 with direct payments to most local governments" (p. 2).

The Coronavirus Preparedness and Response Supplemental Appropriations Act (P.L. 116–123, signed into law on March 6, 2020) was the first federal bill passed by Congress in response to COVID-19. This relatively small, immediate increase in domestic discretionary spending included eight billion dollars in funds to develop vaccines and for various other mitigation and epidemiological efforts (Congressional Budget Office, 2020b; Joyce & Prabowo, 2020).

On March 18, 2020, President Trump signed the Families First Coronavirus Response Act (P.L. 116–127) with an estimated cost of 192 billion dollars. The Families First Coronavirus Response Act allocated 105 billion dollars for paid sick leave, expanded family and medical leave, provided free testing, and enhanced Medicaid matching funds for state and local governments. This act was expected to bring an additional 40 billion dollars for states annually (Fiedler et al., 2020).

> A total of $140 billion in funds made available to federal agencies for funding to provide assistance to businesses and governments affected by COVID-19. This includes $44 billion to the Federal Emergency Management Agency (FEMA) to support state and local response and recovery, $35 billion in assistance to airports and transit systems, $31 billion to state and local governments and higher education institutions, and $25 billion for various nutritional programs and rural programs.
>
> *(Joyce & Prabowo, 2020, p. 747)*

This bill included an extension of unemployment benefits, with the federal government picking up 100 percent of the costs of these benefits, rather than the usual 50 percent. The law also loosened the requirements for receiving Supplemental Nutrition Assistance Program (SNAP; food stamp) benefits and provided alternate ways for states to provide meals to children affected by school closures (Congressional Budget Office, 2020b).

The major federal government COVID-19-related stimulus program, the Coronavirus Aid, Relief, and Economic Security Act (H.R.748 – CARES Act), was signed into law by President Trump on March 27, 2020. "At over $2 trillion, this has been the largest rescue package in U.S. history" (Investopedia, 2021). The CARES Act provided 349 billion dollars for the "Paycheck Protection Program" that could be used by any business or non-profit organization with fewer than 500 employees per physical location to cover payroll, salaries, utilities, and other day-to-day expenses. The program waived the fees and included loan forgiveness terms. The "Pandemic Unemployment Insurance" program of the CARES Act provided 600 dollars a week to the unemployed on top of regular unemployment compensation. The CARES Act provided 1,200 dollars per taxpayer plus

500 dollars per child in tax rebates for eligible taxpayers, assistance with mortgage payments, and loans and guarantees to the hardest-hit industries, such as airlines, among other provisions. An additional 150 billion dollars, about 7.5 percent of the total CARES Act bill, was directed to the "Coronavirus Relief Fund" for state and local governments.

> Three billion dollars was reserved for federally administered territories and $8 billion was reserved for tribal governments. Payments to states and local governments were divided proportionally according to population. These were large, open-ended block grants that were directed toward costs associated with controlling the pandemic and mitigating its economic damage.
>
> *(Investopedia, 2021)*

While the CARES Act offered hefty assistance to state and municipal governments, these efforts are believed to have been neither sufficient nor well-targeted. "The federal response has not sufficiently addressed the state and local fiscal effects of the COVID-19 recession" (Gordon et al., 2020, p. 742). States and municipalities have received "significant compensation for COVID-19 – related costs under the CARES Act, though most of this aid is time limited and not particularly well targeted to those cities and counties with the highest incidence of COVID-19 cases" (Chernick et al., 2020, p. 724). The federal support for programs serving individuals directly affected by the recession were also falling short (Bitler et al., 2020).

In April 2020, the Federal Reserve established the Municipal Liquidity Facility, which helped to alleviate short-term liquidity issues that arose for local governments with delayed tax collections. Through this facility, larger U.S. counties (with population of at least half a million) and cities (with at least 250,000 residents) could sell short-term notes to the Federal Government and get cash for daily operations. The Municipal Liquidity Program concluded in the end of 2020.

Another major 1.9-trillion-dollar stimulus package, the American Rescue Plan Act (ARPA) of 2021, also known as the COVID-19 Stimulus Package or American Rescue Plan (P.L. 117–2), was signed into law by President Biden on March 11, 2021. According to the U.S. Treasury (2021a), "the American Rescue Plan provides $350 billion in emergency funding for eligible state, local, territorial, and Tribal governments to respond to the COVID-19 emergency and bring back jobs" (p. 1). It allows states and local governments to spend on activities related to fighting COVID-19, restore public services, rehire or increase compensation for some types of public service workers, and invest in selected infrastructure. The American Rescue Plan Act included provisions for establishing two funds, the Coronavirus State Fiscal Recovery Fund (CSFRF) and the Coronavirus Local Fiscal Recovery Fund (CLFRF). ARPA funds have been allocated to tens of thousands of eligible state, local, territorial, and Tribal governments to respond to the COVID-19 crisis and bring back jobs. Table 7.3 provides information about these allocations from CLFRF in 2021.

TABLE 7.3 Allocations from Coronavirus State and Local Fiscal Recovery Funds

Type	*Amount ($ billions)*
States and District of Columbia	$195.3
Counties	$65.1
Metropolitan Cites	$45.6
Tribal Governments	$20.0
Territories	$4.5
Non-entitlement Units of Local Government	$19.5
Total	$350

Source: U.S. Treasury (2021b,c)

The funds to municipalities are allocated mainly based on population size. Eligible local governments that are classified as non-entitlement units of local government receive funding through their applicable state government. The ARPA funds will allow most states facing budget challenges to avoid steep cuts in services or restore funding to areas they were cut in the beginning of the COVID-19 pandemic. "States hope their economies and revenues will rebound quickly and they are able to replace one-time federal funds with state general fund revenues in future fiscal years" (National Conference of State Legislature, 2021, p. 1). States need to review tax structures to address the new reality caused by the COVID-19 pandemic and change tax rules in response to new trends in consumer behavior, such as ecommerce and the growing role of the digital economy (Dadayan, 2020b).

Of course, federal stimulus programs do not come without sizeable side effects. The major one is the obscene amount of debt burden the government is shifting onto future generations. In the two years following the beginning of pandemic, national debt increased by almost seven trillion dollars from 23.3 trillion in February 2020 to over thirty trillion in February 2022 (U.S. Debt Clock). Besides, even though much needed, stimulus programs provide only temporary, not structural, solutions to the problem. "These programs may provide relief in the short run, but they are unlikely to fill budget gaps in the next couple of fiscal years as the decline in state and local tax collections intensifies" (Auerbach et al., 2020, p. 3).

Conclusions

The COVID-19 crisis poses strong challenges to governmental budgeting at the local level. As a consequence of the COVID-19 pandemic, municipalities face problems on both the revenue and expenditure sides of their budgets. The impacts of COVID-19 on subnational finance are highly diverse, and the varying effects depend on five main factors: the scope of local government responsibilities, the sensitivity of local finance to economic fluctuations, the ability of subnational governments to absorb exceptional stress, the fiscal health, and the scope and efficiency of support policies from higher levels of government.

To cope with fiscal crisis and reductions in revenue, municipalities instituted hiring freezes and layoffs, reduced capital expenditures, increased fees and taxes, and closed facilities among multiple other measures. These strategies are similar to those used nationally in previous economic downturns (Ammons & Fleck, 2010; Afonso, 2013, 2014, 2021; Gorina et al., 2019).

The COVID-19 pandemic does not only impact local governments while it lasts, but it will also affect the direction of fiscal policy after it is over given the projection of rising debt and the long-lasting effects on the national economy and local governments. Municipalities acting under stress, such as the COVID-19 pandemic, are less likely to have the flexibility to adapt to challenging fiscal situations (New York State Comptroller, 2021). The notion that local governments' budgets may be impacted by the pandemic for years to come is supported by a New York State Comptroller report of 2021, stating that

> over time, low fund balances, weak cash positions, and lost revenues make sustaining the functions of government or providing constituent services untenable. Thus, while most local governments managed to avoid a stress designation in the initial year of the economic crisis, fiscal stress may increase for them in the next few years if the economic recovery falters.
>
> *(p. 2)*

To tackle fiscal challenges during and after the COVID-19 pandemic, budgeting processes have to adopt the following changes:

1. become more strategic
2. promote greater flexibility of resource allocation (rebudgeting), reallocate financial and nonfinancial resources according to emerging needs in a timely and transparent fashion
3. pursue greater coordination across different levels of governments
4. use innovative methods of planning and information exchanges
5. pursue full transparency in budget documents through explanatory notes on the calculation details
6. create strong collaborations and networks.

This chapter takes an important first step in understanding the fiscal stress during the COVID-19 pandemic and its effect on municipalities. It is a snapshot of municipal approaches to budgeting under the unique challenges presented by the pandemic. Information presented here could help inform future budgeting practices and point to where additional scholarship is needed.

Note

1 Read about elastic and inelastic tax revenues in Chapter 3.

References

Afonso, W. (2013). Coping with the great recession: Theory and practice for county governments. *International Journal of Public Administration, 36*(11), 768–779.

Afonso, W. (2014). Local government capital spending during and after recessions: A cause for concern? *International Journal of Public Administration, 37*(8), 494–505

Afonso, W. (2021). Planning for the unknown: Local government strategies from the fiscal year 2021 budget season in response to the COVID-19 pandemic. *State and Local Government Review, 53*(2), 159–171.

Ammons, D., & Fleck, T. (2010). *Budget-Balancing Tactics in Local Government*. Chapel Hill, NC: School of Government, The University of North Carolina, North Carolina.

Anessi-Pessina, E., Barbera, C., Langella, C., Manes-Rossi, F., Sancino, A., Sicilia, M., & Steccolini, I. (2020). Reconsidering public budgeting after the COVID-19 outbreak: Key lessons and future challenges. *Journal of Public Budgeting, Accounting & Financial Management, 32*(5), 957–965. https://doi.org/10.1108/JPBAFM-07-2020-0115

Auerbach, A., Gale, B., Lutz, B., & Sheiner, L. (2020). *Fiscal Effects of COVID-19. Brookings Papers on Economic Activity*. The Brookings Institution. Retrieved September 4, 2020, from www.brookings.edu/bpea-articles/fiscal-effects-of-COVID-19/

Bartik, Timothy. (2020). *A Proposal for Timely, Responsive Federal Aid to State and Local Governments During the Pandemic Recession*. W.E. Upjohn Institute for Employment Research. Retrieved December 4, 2020, from www.upjohn.org/research-highlights/proposal-timely-responsive-federal-aid-state-and-local-governments-during-pandemic-recession

Bitler, M. P., Hoynes, H., & Iselin, J. (2020). Cyclicality of the U.S. safety net: Evidence from the 2000s and implications for the COVID-19 Crisis. *National Tax Journal, 73*(3), 759–780.

Burness, A. (2020). Colorado lawmakers bracing for coronavirus budget hit of up to $3 billion. *The Denver Post,* 9 April.

California Health Care Foundation (2021). *Unexpected growth in California health insurance during COVID-19 recession*. Retrieved May 4, 2022, from https://www.chcf.org/publication/unexpected-growth-ca-health-insurance-covid-19-recession/

Carlson, J. (2021). Chicago had $41,100 in debt per taxpayer before COVID-19, second to New York. *Illinois Policy*. Retrieved February 4, 2022, from www.illinoispolicy.org/chicago-had-41100-in-debt-per-taxpayer-before-COVID-19-second-to-new-york/

Chernick, H., Copeland, D., & Reschosvsky, A. (2020). The fiscal effects of the covid-19 pandemic on cities: An initial assessment. *National Tax Journal*, *73*(3), 699–732.

City of Philadelphia, Pennsylvania Controller's Office (2020). *Interactive: Revised FY21-FY25 Budget*. Retrieved February 4, 2022, from https://controller.phila.gov/philadelphia-audits/revised-fy21-fy25-budget/#/

Clemens, J., & Miran, S. (2012). Fiscal policy multipliers on subnational government spending. *American Economic Journal: Economic Policy*, *4*(2), 46–68.

Clemens, J., & Veuger, S. (2020a). Implication of the COVID-19 pandemic for state government tax revenues. *National Tax Journal*, *73*(3), 619–644.

Clemens, J., & Veuger, S. (2020b). *The COVID-19 pandemic and the revenues of state and local governments: An update American enterprise institute, economic perspectives*. Retrieved

February 4, 2022, from www.aei.org/wp-content/uploads/2020/09/The-COVID-19-Pandemic-and-the-Revenues-of-State-and-Local-Governments.pdf?x91208

Cleveland.com (2021). *Cuyahoga County home values increase 16% in 2021 reappraisal.* September 21 2021. https://www.cleveland.com/news/2021/09/cuyahoga-county-property-values-increase-16-in-2021-reappraisal.html

Congressional Budget Office (2020a). *An update to the economic outlook: 2020 to 2030.* Retrieved February 4, 2022, from www.cbo.gov/system/fi outlook.pdf.

Congressional Budget Office (2020b). *The budgetary effects of laws enacted in response to the 2020 coronavirus pandemic, March and April 2020,* 16 June. Retrieved February 4, 2022, from www.cbo.gov/publication/56403.

Dadayan, L. (2020a). COVID-19 pandemic could slash 2020–21 state revenues by $200 billion. *Urban-Brookings Tax Policy Center.* Retrieved February 4, 2022, from www.taxpolicycenter.org/taxvox/COVID-%2019-pandemic-could-slash-2020-21-state-revenues-200-billion.

Dadayan, L. (2020b). The COVID-19 effect: State sales tax receipts shrank $6 billion in May. *Tax Policy Center,* 14 July. Retrieved February 4, 2022, from www.taxpolicycenter.org/taxvox/covid-19-effect-state-sales-tax-receipts-shrank-6-billion-may

Federation of Tax Administrators (2020). State sales tax rate and food & drug exemptions (As of January 1, 2020). *Federation of Tax Administrators.* Retrieved February 4, 2022, from www.taxadmin. org/assets/docs/Research/Rates/sales.pdf.

Felix, A. (2020, May 13). COVID-19 challenges state and local government finances. *Federal Reserve Bank of Kansas.* Retrieved February 14, 2022, from www.kansascityfed.org/documents/5438/2020-eb20felix0513.pdf

FEMA. (2021). *Local Government Solutions Guide for COVID-19 and Beyond: Alternative Public Service Solutions.* Retrieved February 14, 2022, from www.fema.gov/sites/default/files/documents/fema_alternative-public-service-solutions_guidance_05-21-2021.pdf

Fiedler, M., Furman, J., & Powell, W. (2019). *Increasing Federal Support for State Medicaid and CHIP Programs in Response to Economic Downturns.* The Brookings Institution. Retrieved February 14, 2022, from www.brookings.edu/research/increasing-federal-support-for-state-medicaid-and-chip-programs-in-response-to-economic-downturns/

Fiedler, M., Young, C., & Adler, L. (2020). *What are the Health Coverage Provisions in the House Coronavirus Bill?* USC Brookings Schaeffer on Health Policy. Retrieved February 14, 2022, from www.brookings.edu/blog/usc-brookings-schaeffer-on-health-policy/2020/03/13/what-are-the-health-coverage-provisions-in-the-house-coronavirus-bill/

Gascon, C., & LaBelle, J. (2021). COVID-19 and states' revenues: An analysis. *Federal Reserve Bank of Saint Louis.* Retrieved February 4, 2022, from www.stlouisfed.org/publications/regional-economist/first-quarter-2021/COVID-19-states-revenues-analysis

Gordon, T., Dadayan, L., &Rueben, K. (2020). State and local government finances in the COVID-19 era. *National Tax Journal, 73*(3), 733–758.

Gorina, E., Maher, C., & Park, S. (2019). Toward a theory of fiscal slack. *Public Budgeting and Finance, 39*(4), 48–74.

Horner, D., & Ivacke, T. (2021). *Michigan local government officials report improved f iscal health after a year of COVID-19, but not yet back to prepandemic levels.* The Michigan Public Policy Survey. University of Michigan: The Center for Local, State, and Urban Policy. Retrieved March 24, 2022, from https://closup.umich.edu/sites/closup/files/2021-12/mpps-fiscal-health-2021.pdf

Investopedia (2021). *Coronavirus Aid, Relief, and Economic Security (CARES) Act.* Retrieved March 24, 2022, from https://www.investopedia.com/coronavirus-aid-relief-and-economic-security-cares-act-4800707

Joyce, P. G., & Prabowo, A. S. (2020). Government responses to the coronavirus in the United States: Immediate remedial actions, rising debt levels and budgetary hangovers. *Journal of Public Budgeting, Accounting & Financial Management, 32*(5), 745–758. doi:http://gsuproxy.govst.edu:2081/10.1108/JPBAFM-07-2020-0111

McKinsey & Company (2020). *The Great Consumer Shift: Ten Charts that Show How US Shopping Behavior is Changing*, 4 August. Retrieved February 14, 2022, from www.mckinsey.com/business-functions/marketing-and-sales/our-insights/the-great-consumer-shift-ten-charts-that-show-how-us-shopping-behavior-is-changing.

McNichol, E., & Leachman, M. (2020). *States Continue to Face Large Shortfalls Due to COVID-19 Effects. Center on Budget and Policy Priorities (CBPP).* Washington, D.C., 7 July. Retrieved February 1, 2022, from www.cbpp.org/research/state-budget-and-tax/states-continue-to-face-large-shortfalls-due-to-covid-19-effects

Mikesell, J. (2007). *Fiscal Administration: Analysis and Applications for the Public Sector* (8th ed.). Belmont, CA: Thomson Wadsworth.

National Association of State Budget Officers (NASBO) (2021). Fiscal survey of the states. *Fall.* Accessed February 16, 2021. https://higherlogicdownload.s3.amazonaws.com/NASBO/9d2d2db1-c943-4f1b-b750-0fca152d64c2/UploadedImages/Fiscal%20Survey/NASBO_Fall_2021_Fiscal_Survey_of_States_S.pdf

National Conference of State Legislatures. (2021). *State Budget Update: Winter 2021,* 12 March. Retrieved February 1, 2022, from www.ncsl.org/research/fiscal-policy/state-budget-update-winter-2021637511555.aspx.

National League of Cities (2020a). *Cities Prepared for Rainy Days, but Not a Fiscal Tsunami.* Washington, D.C., 8 June. Retrieved February 1, 2022, from www.nlc.org/article/2020/06/08/cities-prepared-for-rainy-days-but-not-a-fiscal-tsunami/

National League of Cities (2020b). *City Fiscal Conditions 2020.* Washington, D.C., 13 August. Retrieved February 1, 2022, from www.nlc.org/resource/city-fiscal-conditions-2020

New York State Comptroller (2021). *Fiscal Stress Monitoring System Municipalities: Fiscal Year 2020.* Retrieved February 1, 2022, from www.osc.state.ny.us/files/local-government/publications/pdf/fsms-municipalities-fiscal-year-2020-results.pdf

Pagano, M., & McFarland, C. (2020). When will your city feel the fiscal impact of COVID-19? *Brookings Institution*, 31 March. Retrieved February 1, 2022, from www.brookings.edu/blog/the-avenue/2020/03/31/when-will-your-city-feel-the-fiscal-impact-of-covid-19/?utm_source%C2%BCnewsletter&utm_medium%C2%BCemail&utm_campaign%C2%BCnewsletter_axiosam&stream%C2%BCtop

Poterba, J. (1994). State responses to fiscal crisis: The effects of budgetary institutions and politics. *Journal of Political Economy, 102*, 799–821.

Rivkin, D., & Karoub, J. (2021). Michigan local government officials report improved fiscal health after a year of COVID-19, but not yet back to pre-pandemic levels. *Michigan News, University of Michigan*, 16 December. Retrieved February 14, 2022, from https://news.umich.edu/michigan-local-government-officials-report-improved-fiscal-health-after-a-year-of-covid-19/

Roberts, L. (2020). Innovative program trains workers displaced by coronavirus. *Fairfield's Hamlethub*, 8 September Retrieved February 1, 2022, from https://news.hamlethub.com/fairfield/places/49564-innovative-program-trains-workers-displaced-by-coronavirus

Romm, T. (2020a). More than 2,100 U.S. cities brace for budget shortfalls due to coronavirus, survey finds, with many planning cuts and layoffs. *The Washington Post*, 14 April. Retrieved February 1, 2022, from www.washingtonpost.com/business/2020/04/14/cities-budget-cuts-coronavirus

Romm, T. (2020b). Over 700 cash-strapped cities halt plans to repair roads, water systems or make other key investments. *The Washington Post*, 23 June. Retrieved February 1, 2022, from www.washingtonpost.com/business/2020/06/23/cities-budget-infrastructure-cuts/

San Francisco Office of the Mayor. (2020). *Budget Outlook Update FY 2019–20 through FY 2023–24. City and County of San Francisco*. San Francisco, CA. Retrieved February 1, 2022, from https://sfcontroller.org/sites/default/files/Documents/Budget/Budget%20Outlook%20Report%20FY20-FY24.pdf.U.S.

Stewart, C. (2021). 'Astronomical increase' in property values hits some local homeowners. *Dayton Daily News*, February 21, 2021. Retrieved May 4, 2022, from https://www.daytondailynews.com/news/higher-tax-bills-due-as-astronomical-increase-in-property-values-hits-some-homeowners/SOKSRHJJNRAFDEJSCR7G4ZMBEI/

Tax Foundation (2020). *State rainy day funds and the COVID-19 crisis*. April 7, 2020. Retrieved March 24, 2022, from https://taxfoundation.org/state-rainy-day-funds-covid-19/

U.S. Bureau of Labor Statistics (2020). *Unemployment rate rises to record high 14.7 percent in April 2020*. Retrieved February 4, 2021, from www.bls.gov/opub/ted/2020/unemployment-rate-rises-to-record-high-14-point-7-percent-in-april-2020.htm?view_full

U.S. Census Bureau (2021). *Population*. Retrieved July 9, 2021, from www.census.gov/

U.S. Treasury (2021a). *Assistance for state, local, and tribal governments*. Retrieved February 1, 2022, from https://home.treasury.gov/policy-issues/coronavirus/assistance-for-state-local-and-tribal-governments

U.S. Treasury (2021b). *Coronavirus state and local fiscal recovery funds allocations to counties*. Retrieved February 12, 2022, from https://home.treasury.gov/system/files/136/Allocation-Methodology-for-Counties-508A.pdf

U.S. Treasury (2021c). *Coronavirus state and local fiscal recovery funds*. Retrieved February 1, 2022, from https://home.treasury.gov/policy-issues/coronavirus/assistance-for-state-local-and-tribal-governments/state-and-local-fiscal-recovery-funds

Whitaker, S. (2020). How much help do state and local governments need? Updated estimates of revenue losses from pandemic mitigation. *Federal Reserve Bank of Cleveland*, 29 June. Retrieved February 1, 2022, from www.clevelandfed.org/newsroom-and-events/publications/cfed-district-data-briefs/cfddb-20200629-updated-estimates-of-revenue-losses-from-pandemic-mitigation.aspx

White, D., Crane, S., & Seitz, C. (2020). *Stress-Testing States: COVID-19*. New York: Moody's Analytics.

8

INTRODUCTION TO THE CASE STUDIES

Introduction

To be able to better address fiscal stress, it is highly advisable to understand the roots of the problem in the first place. Fiscal stress can be triggered by a single event, but it does not evolve for one single reason; rather, a combination of multiple factors is usually responsible for the decline in a municipality's financial wellbeing. Different underlying conditions can make one municipality more financially vulnerable than others. The fiscal health of a city depends on economic, social, and institutional factors (Chernick & Reschovsky, 2013). Fiscal problems can originate from economic hardships, management crises (corruption, fraud, unqualified personnel, and such), political issues, institutional changes (such as tax and expenditure limits, changes in state aid, and others), declining population and other demographic fluctuations, and natural disasters (Honadle, 2003).

The infamous Orange County (CA) bankruptcy in 1994 resulted from risky investment decisions. It had a ripple effect on many local governments within the county, as the county treasurer invested not only county-own funds but also money of the cities, school districts, and other special districts within the county. The Detroit, MI bankruptcy and fiscal emergencies in Pittsburgh, PA; Flint, MI; and multiple other so-called legacy or rust-belt cities resulted from years of structural changes in the economy but were triggered mainly by the economic recession of 2008–2009. Corruption charges contributed to fiscal emergency situations in Miami, FL and the bankruptcy of Jefferson County, AL. Hurricane Katrina led to a substantial drop of New Orleans, LA's credit ratings. Problems with state employee retirement systems were at the heart of Detroit, MI; Vallejo, CA; and Prichard, AL bankruptcies.

DOI: 10.4324/b23117-8

We spent a lot of time and attention in the first chapters of this book discussing general causes of fiscal stress and potential solutions to the problems. While there are many commonalities, the nuances in causes, the flow, duration, and exit from every fiscal stress situation are unique and extensive. And, while general theoretical approaches are invaluable, case studies allow for studying and applying contextual information toward understanding the situation in more depth and from multiple angles. As such, case studies offer vigorous research, teaching, and learning opportunities. Case studies include a thorough review of facts to help the reader understand the causes of the fiscal stress problem, the decision-making process, the outcomes of implementation, lessons learned, and connections to public finance theories, concepts, policies, and tools relevant to the situation.

The following six chapters of the book present case studies of different degrees of fiscal stress and exits from it, from a mild fiscal distress in the city of Colorado Springs, CO to a major fiscal stress, the Act 47 recovery plan in Pittsburgh, PA, to the smaller bankruptcies in the city of Central Falls in Rhode Island and the City of Vallejo in California's San Francisco Bay Area, to the major bankruptcy cases in Detroit, MI and Jefferson County, AL. At the time of bankruptcy, Central Falls, RI had a structural deficit of over 6 million dollars and long-term debt of more than 63 million dollars (see Chapter 13). Jefferson County, AL (see Chapter 11) entered bankruptcy with 4.3 billion dollars in debt and Detroit, MI with a shocking 18.6 billion dollars in debt (see Chapter 9).

For the case studies, we chose one county and five cities of different sizes from six different states from around the United States (see Figure 8.1). The smallest city in the sample is Central Falls, RI with a population of 19,568. Central Falls happens to be also the smallest city in the smallest U.S. state. The most populated areas are Jefferson County, AL with a population of 658,573 and Detroit, MI with a population of 670,031 (2019 U.S. Census). Colorado Springs, Detroit, and Pittsburgh are three central cities. Central Falls is the suburb of the Providence, RI and Vallejo is the suburb of San Francisco, CA.

By studying several municipalities in depth we can identify similarities, trends, and differences in comprehending municipal bankruptcies and fiscal emergencies among selected cases. We can better explain the factors that contributed to fiscal stress or municipal bankruptcy. We can understand the elements of the institutional, political, and organizational contexts that were significant to fiscal stress or municipal bankruptcy in the selected cases. We can recognize what steps were taken by considered municipalities to improve budgeting and solve fiscal problems during and after fiscal stress or municipal bankruptcy.

The ultimate goal of this book is to provide practical recommendations on improving financial conditions of financially challenged municipalities. Unlike large-scale quantitative research, case studies are difficult to generalize to a larger population. Nevertheless, multiple case analyses offer a set of new propositions explaining why some practices to exit fiscal emergency or bankruptcy situations are adopted or not and what consequences of adopting or not adopting such

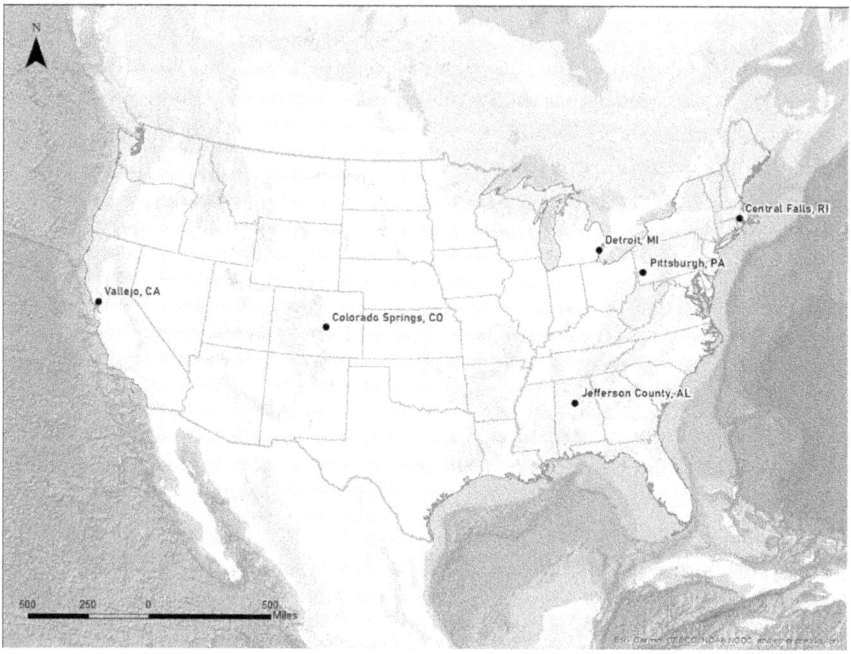

FIGURE 8.1 Map Showing the Selected Municipalities for Case Studies.

Source: Google Maps

practices are. This newly synthesized set of propositions should be empirically testable by future studies, yielding a theory of fiscal stress with a predictive capacity, especially at the local level. These case studies could be very helpful for communities suffering from a fiscal emergency or bankruptcy and help students and practitioners consider how to respond to fiscal stress. Every case discusses the causes of the fiscal emergency situation and the actions that municipalities execute to exit fiscal emergency or bankruptcy.

Chapter 9 is the case study of bankruptcy in Detroit, MI, the largest municipal bankruptcy in U.S. history. The main reasons for this bankruptcy were the decentralization of the auto industry (the dominant sector of Detroit's economy), economic conditions, a sharp decrease in population, and corruption. High gasoline prices and lower demand for American cars in the early 2000s further exacerbated economic and demographic difficulties of the city. Detroit experienced a significant drop in population (around 60 percent since the 1950s) and one of the nation's largest white flights (outmigration of white population). These and other factors resulted in low tax revenues, a structural budget deficit, an accumulation of substantial pension, and general obligation debt, which eventually led to a bankruptcy filing on July 18, 2013. An interesting peculiarity is that the city's exit from the bankruptcy was followed by – unprecedented by its novelty and extant public-private partnerships – a collaboration among the city, the state, philanthropy, and corporations.

The second case (Chapter 10) analyzes the fiscal distress of Colorado Springs, CO caused by the Great Recession of 2008–2009. It demonstrates extreme budget cuts, which included the removal of trash bins from its parks, the closing of recreational facilities, turning off streetlights, and other radical cutback measures. The response by the city to a rather mild fiscal distress situation might have looked excessive, but Colorado Springs serves as a good example of how an unfortunate fiscal situation can be resolved quickly and favorably if serious steps are taken right away at the onset of the fiscal hardships.

The third case (Chapter 11) provides an analysis of Jefferson County's bankruptcy. The main reasons for Jefferson County's misfortunes that led to bankruptcy were financial mismanagement, a wide-scale public corruption, and a staggering amount of debt. The majority of debt obligations were accumulated beginning in 2003 when the Environmental Protection Agency (EPA) accused Jefferson County of dumping raw sewage into neighboring rivers. The county issued and refinanced several bond issues to repair and expand its sewer system over the next several years. The renovation contracts did not result in required repairs, and more debt had to be issued to comply with EPA requirements. The head of the Jefferson County commission (later elected as a Mayor of Birmingham) was accused of bribery and cheating on sewer repair contracts (and their financing and other indictments) and was consequently arrested in 2008 and sentenced to 15 years in prison. The county applied for Chapter 9 bankruptcy protection on November 9, 2011. To exit the bankruptcy, Jefferson County had to increase sewer fees, renegotiate its debt obligations with creditors, and resort to severe budget cuts that led to the closing of many county facilities, laying off hundreds of public employees, and sizably reducing capital expenditures.

Chapter 12 discusses the causes of fiscal emergency in another legacy city – Pittsburgh, PA – and how the city and the state worked to solve fiscal problems. The recovery process in Pittsburgh was long and painful. The city spent over 14 years from December 29, 2003, to February 12, 2018 under the "severe financial difficulty" status as defined by the Pennsylvania Municipalities Financial Recovery Act (also known as Act 47). Pittsburgh introduced around 390 initiatives in the 3 recovery plans (2004, 2009, 2014) that addressed the city's financial management, collective bargaining, and budgeting issues.

Corruption charges and high legacy debt obligations – as with many other examples of financial misfortunes in other municipalities – were some of the major causes that led to the city of Central Falls, RI's bankruptcy discussed in Chapter 13. The state-appointed receiver applied for bankruptcy on August 1, 2011. The city of Central Falls relied on multiple strategies to exit bankruptcy, including property tax increases, extreme budget cuts, laying off as many as one third of all public employees, collecting higher service charges and fees, and reducing retirees' pension payments by approximately 55 percent. The city managed to strengthen its finances relatively quickly and exited bankruptcy in about 14 months. This municipal bankruptcy is considered one of the shortest ever.

Poor economic conditions and resulting lower tax revenues, the inability to increase tax rates due to tax limitations imposed by Proposition 13 in California, and consistently raising expenses on salaries and benefits (dictated by unions) led to three consecutive years of substantial budget deficits and the subsequent bankruptcy by the City of Vallejo, CA. After Vallejo filed for bankruptcy on May 23, 2008, the city underwent a major bankruptcy-related restructuring that included changes to retiree healthcare benefits, reworked lease obligations, reduced bond debt, made extreme budget cuts, deferred infrastructure spending, and underfunded development work from 2008 to 2011. The City of Vallejo additionally engaged in various budget reforms after bankruptcy, the most dramatic of them being a switch to participatory budgeting practices, where residents of the city take an active role in shaping the city's budget. Despite all positive changes, Vallejo is still not out of the woods as it continues to pay high Union-directed salaries, benefits, and pensions to current and former city employees.

The fiscal stress and bankruptcy processes across the case studies are summarized, compared, and contrasted in the last chapter of the book, Chapter 15. This chapter discusses possible reasons why some practices of exit from fiscal stress or bankruptcy are not always utilized. The chapter describes the obstacles in adopting these practices, such as the lack of legal capacity, insufficient technical expertise, corruption, or political infeasibility. This chapter shows how fiscal distress/bankruptcy practices are related to various political, economic, and public sector factors. It identifies the short-term and long-term, internal and external, and political and economic perspectives that may help explain fiscal stress and emergency situations by accentuating the generic aspects of the causes. The final chapter summarizes commonalities and presents differences in fiscal emergency or bankruptcy entrance and exit and, based on these, discusses measures that might be utilized by other municipalities that find themselves in similar situations. It is an integrative chapter that reflects on the literature and cases, then proposes a tentative theory of financial management and budgeting during fiscal emergency and bankruptcy and provides recommendations.

References

Chernick, H., & Reschovsky, A. (2013). *The Fiscal Health of U.S. Cities*. Lincoln Institute of Land Policy Working Paper. Retrieved January 4, 2022, from https://www.lincolninst.edu/publications/working-papers/fiscal-health-us-cities

Honadle, B. (2003). The states' role in U.S. local government fiscal crises: A theoretical model and results of a national survey. *International Journal of Public Administration, 26*(13), 1431–1472

9

CASE STUDY: CITY OF DETROIT

Introduction

20th-century Detroit

The city of Detroit, MI that, in the midst of the 20th century, served as the symbol of American optimism and prosperity, is no less of an icon today, only now as a symbol of urban decay. Deindustrialization, crumbling schools, racial tension, white flight, crime, a dysfunctional government, the foreclosure crisis, and wasteful spending are only some of Detroit's numerous problems.

> The chain of events leading to Detroit's current situation is bizarre and depressing. The city serves as a distorted realization of the American Dream, made manifest in a sprawling mess of low-rent tinderbox houses, a 'Gangsta Mayor' who used the city as his personal playground, and a legacy of inept governance in the context of the nation's largest industry.
>
> *(Kasdan, 2014, p. 1093)*

To understand how the city went from being an "Automotive Capital of the World" to a point where the fiscal health of Detroit spiraled down so much that the city became the case of the largest municipal bankruptcy in U.S. history, we should start from afar, perhaps a century ago. Since the early 20th century, when Henry Ford founded its car manufacturing company on Piquette Avenue in Detroit (later moved to Dearborn, the suburb of Detroit), followed by the other two major auto manufacturers, Chrysler and General Motors (GM), Detroit's economy has been heavily reliant on a single auto industry. It is estimated that in 1930 about two-thirds of Detroit's employment was in auto manufacturing and

DOI: 10.4324/b23117-9

related industries. Overreliance on a single industry has meant that city's business cycles have been also heavily dependent on the health of the auto industry.

The automobile industry was the principal factor in the city's population expansion from 285,784 in 1900, to 993,687 in 1920, to 1,568,662 in 1930 (ACIR, 1973, p. 18). Between the 1920s and the 1940s, Detroit was the fourth largest city in the nation by population. Its population peaked at 1.45 million in the 1950s (biggestuscities.com). The growth in Detroit's population went hand-in-hand with the growth of its wealth, real property values, bank resources, bank credits and deposits, postal receipts, mortgages recorded, and building permits. The assessed valuation of Detroit properties increased from 238 million dollars in 1900 to 3.775 billion dollars in 1930 (ACIR, 1973, p. 18).

During the Great Depression when demand for cars plummeted, Detroit's fiscal health deteriorated as well. The city had to take several painful steps in 1931 and 1932 to address its financial crisis. The operating budget was reduced, hundreds of city employees were dismissed, the salaries of those who stayed employed were cut by 10 percent for those who earned up to 4,000 dollars and 20 percent for those who earned more, and taxpayers were asked to pay their taxes in advance. In late 1932, when it became apparent that the city would have an operating cash deficit of 20 million dollars, Detroit got emergency legislation for a special issue of 20 million dollars of tax anticipation notes to pay public employees (PEW Charitable Trusts, 2013). The city defaulted on its bonds in 1933.

During World War II the production of vehicles for civilian use was rationed and reduced to a minimum to free up resource capacity to produce war equipment. In 1940 President Roosevelt announced that the U.S. would become "the Arsenal of Democracy" by producing tanks, ships, planes, weapons, ammunition, and other war necessities to arm allied powers during the war. With all the production capacity already available in the city, Detroit became the heart of "the Arsenal of Democracy".

> Ninety-one percent of all Army helmets were stamped in Detroit. Chrysler's Detroit Arsenal Tank plant in Warren, Michigan created half the tanks made in the U.S. By the summer of 1944, Ford's Willow Run plant completed one B-24 bomber every hour. General Motors was responsible for the greatest percentage of war materiel during the period. U.S. companies produced 2,665,196 vehicles of all types for military use by the end of the war.
>
> *(Encyclopedia of Detroit)*

350,000 people moved from other parts of the U.S. to Detroit to work for the car manufacturers (ibid). As the economy of Detroit boomed in the 1940s, so did the fiscal strength of the city. The upward trend continued for some time after WWII when the rationing ended and demand for civilian cars surged.

But, over time, as the automobile production process became more automated and auto manufacturers expanded their production from being almost exclusively concentrated in Detroit to other states, and as the price of gas climbed and demand for American cars declined, Detroit's financial position became more and more deplorable. Thomas Sugrue (2014), in his book *Origins of the Urban Crisis: Race and Inequality in Postwar Detroit,* argues that a gradual decline in Detroit's economy was mainly due to the decentralization that happened in the auto sector. Technological advancements and positive developments in supply chain management, transportation, and logistics allowed factories to be moved farther away from ancillary suppliers. In some cases, this provided access to cheaper labor markets, lower taxes, and other money-saving decisions. Such decentralization broke the power of unions. It also followed the trend of suburbanization within the region.

Great Recession

The Great Recession of 2008 and a further increase in gasoline prices around this time had extremely detrimental effect on the three largest auto manufacturers. Both Chrysler and GM filed for Chapter 11 bankruptcy protection in 2009, notwithstanding billions of dollars in federal bailout efforts of the three auto makers earlier that year and in late 2008. Despite much lower production, the automobile industry to this day plays an important role in Detroit's economy. In 1996, in a highly publicized event, Chrysler moved its headquarters from Detroit to Auburn Hills, MI. The move, however, was not instant and lasted several years, slowly but surely further contributing to the disinvestment and decline of Detroit. In 2002, 13.26 percent of all the assessed property value in Detroit belonged to Chrysler, which made the company the largest taxpayer in the city. When the recession hit, this number dropped to 6.73 percent in 2010 (Detroit's top taxpayer) and 1.17 percent in 2014, until Chrysler was no longer among the top ten taxpayers by 2020 (Detroit Comprehensive Annual Financial Report (CAFRs) for 2002, 2010, 2014, and 2020). GM was the fifth largest taxpayer in the city in 2009 with 1.4 percent of the taxable valuation of Detroit's property (Moody's Investors Services, 2017). The number of GM employees in Detroit also decreased by 40 percent around the same time (City of Detroit, 2014).

The depth of the socio-economic decline in Detroit that trailed the decline in the automotive industry, accompanied by racial disaggregation and white flight, is hard to comprehend (Encyclopedia of Detroit, 2020). The "Race Riot of 1943" and especially "the Uprising of 1967" (also known as "the 1967 Detroit Riot" or "the Detroit Rebellion") that is considered "the largest civil disturbance of twentieth century America" (Encyclopedia of Detroit, 2021), in addition to the continuing decentralization of the auto sector, led to unprecedented white flight from the city that had already started in the 1950s. The share of the population of color in Detroit increased from 16 percent in 1950 to 83 percent of the total

FIGURE 9.1 Abandoned Fisher Body 21 Factory in Detroit.

FIGURE 9.2 Abandoned Fisher Body 21 Factory in Detroit.

FIGURE 9.3 Fisher Body 21 Factory Neighborhood in Detroit.

population in 2014, while the population of the surrounding Oakland, Macomb, and Wayne counties are almost 85 percent white and only 8 percent black now (Phinney, 2018). The extent of the out-migration of the white population was staggering. Only about 36 percent of the population of the city was left by 2020 from its population peak in the 1950s (Detroit CAFRs for 2002 and 2020).

Table 9.1 provides the demographic, economic, and social situations in Detroit in 2010 and 2019.

Fiscal Stress Situation

In 2009, during the Great Recession, Moody's Investors Services (2010) claimed that Detroit's economy and demographic situations remained "one of the weakest in the nation". Detroit had the highest unemployment rate in the country, measured at 15.1 percent (Guzman, 2019). But the already dire situation spiraled down even further in the following years. By 2011 the unemployment rate reached a staggering 21.1 percent while per capita personal income was only 15,556 dollars (2020 CAFR). A high unemployment rate and lower personal income translated into much lower income tax revenues for the city. Per capita personal income tax collections in 2010 were only about 59 percent of what they were in 2000 (FISC).

TABLE 9.1 Demographic, Economic, and Social Situations in Detroit in 2010 and 2019

Population	
Population estimates, July 1, 2019, (V2019)	670,031
Population, Census, April 1, 2010	713,898
Race and Hispanic Origin	
White alone, percent	14.7
Black or African American alone, percent	78.3
Asian alone, percent	1.7
Hispanic or Latino, percent	7.7
Housing	
Owner-occupied housing unit rate, 2015–2019, percent	47.20%
Median value of owner-occupied housing units, 2015–2019, $	49,200
Median gross rent, 2015–2019, $	824
Education	
High school graduate or higher, percent of persons age 25 years+, 2015–2019, percent	81.00
Bachelor's degree or higher, percent of persons age 25 years+, 2015–2019, percent	15.30
Health	
With a disability, under age 65 years, percent, 2015–2019	15.3
Persons without health insurance, under age 65 years, percent	9.6
Economy	
In civilian labor force, total, percent of population age 16 years+, 2015–2019	54.4
Total accommodation and food services sales, 2012 ($1,000)	2,237,286
Total retail sales per capita, 2012, $	3,196,348
Income and Poverty	
Median household income (in 2019 dollars), 2015–2019	$30,894
Per capita income in past 12 months (in 2019 dollars), 2015–2019, $	$18,621
Persons in poverty, percent	35

Source: Table created by authors based on US Census, 2021 https://www.census.gov/quickfacts/detroitcitymichigan

A lower population means a shrinking tax base, hence a lower capacity to collect own source revenues and lower revenue sharing with the city from the state (the revenue sharing formula in Michigan is largely based on population count). Following the Great Recession of 2008–2009 the state also significantly cut regular state transfers to the city to cover its own deficit (FISC).

Property tax, the main source of revenue for many municipal governments and special districts, was also hit hard in Detroit as the city had 81,754 vacant housing units (22.2 percent of the total) in 2007 and 101,737 (27.8 percent of the total) in 2008. The median price of residential units sold between January and November 2009 was 12,439 dollars, down from 97,847 dollars in 2003 (Citizens Research Council of Michigan, 2010, p. 1). Leading toward bankruptcy, the per capita market value of Detroit properties between 2000 and 2014 was the lowest among the 150 largest cities in the U.S. (FISC). In 2012, 47 properties were listed for sale for under 500 dollars, 5 of them for a symbolic one-dollar price. Over half of homeowners did not pay property taxes in 2012. The median home values in the city were the lowest among all large U.S. cities. About 78,000 buildings in the city were blighted (Detroit Free Press, 2015). Since the property tax base was depleted, the city tried to boost its property tax collections by increasing tax rates. This resulted in the largest average effective property tax rate on commercial properties among the 150 largest U.S. cities and the second largest rate on median valued private homes (Guzman, 2019). In 2013 the property tax collections lowered by 13 million dollars compared to 2012 (Detroit Free Press, 2014a). Low property values and high property tax rates were not the only problems; the entire property tax system in Detroit is considered regressive, meaning that the homeowners of the lower valued properties pay higher effective property tax rates than the owners of the higher valued properties. Because of the regressivity concerns, in 2014 the city reappraised all the properties. But the efforts were reportedly not successful. The Berry (2020) study finds that the regressivity problem only worsened after reappraisal and the overall assessed value of Detroit properties went down in the following years. The regressivity of property tax appraisals even sparked the American Civil Liberties (ACLU) court case, spearheaded by a lawyer from the University of Chicago, Bernadette Atuahene (Atuahene, 2018).

Besides unfavorable socio-economic conditions, the amount of revenues that Detroit could raise to somehow improve its deteriorating financial conditions has been constricted by constitutional tax limitations in Michigan (Article IX § 26 of State Constitution).

The inadequacy of revenues was a big problem but, by itself, was only a drop in the sea compared to other more serious issues. Unable to secure sufficient current revenues to pay for ongoing needs, Detroit officials had to cut city services and borrow more and more funds continuing to submerge in higher debt. According to the official estimates, the city was 18.6 billion dollars in debt by the time it filed for bankruptcy. "People had to pay higher taxes for less services"; as a result, "people who had the capacity to pay taxes left, which left fewer tax dollars, fewer services, and the cycle continues" (interview with Matt Cullen[1]).

Issues with city pensions were the other notorious contributors to the bankruptcy. Since the 1980s, in a practice known as "13th month checks", instead of reinvesting excess revenues, the pension fund redistributed them back to beneficiaries (Stone et al., 2015). This was not a problem until the number of employees contributing to the pension system exceeded the number of retirees. By 2014, however, the number of pensioners in Detroit was twice the active city employees' count (City of Detroit, 2014). Current contributions to the pension plans were no longer sufficient to cover pensions and retiree benefits. In Fiscal Year (FY) 2013 (ended June 30, 2013), right before the bankruptcy filings, the city reported that 73.8 percent of the 193.4 million dollars of total benefit payments was spent on retiree benefits alone (ibid).

Concerns about retirement plans were not anew to the city administration and started well before bankruptcy. In 2005 Detroit already had about 1.7 billion dollars in deficit in its pension fund. Back then, the city was close to reaching its statutory debt ceiling, which allowed additional borrowing of no more than 660 million dollars. To work around the debt restrictions, the city created two nonprofit "service corporations" controlled entirely by the city that issued 1.44 billion dollars in certificates of participation (COPs; Chief Investment Officer, 2014). Eight hundred million dollars of issued COPs carried a variable interest rate and were converted to fixed rate securities using interest rate swaps (demos.org) that were meant to protect the city against high interest rates that were of concern at the time. The swap counterparties were Bank of America/Merrill Lynch and UBS. When the recession hit in 2008 and the Federal Reserve lowered interest rates to almost nothing, Detroit ended up owing 300 million dollars in interest payments to the two banks. The city tried to renegotiate swap agreements with the swap counterparties, but the attempts were not successful. Swap counterparties not only refused to lower the debt payments but also, seeing the deplorable state of Detroit finances, demanded the city to pledge casino revenues to secure swap payments. When the Detroit administration earmarked casino revenues to pay for swaps in 2009, the city lost one of its very few remaining stable revenue sources that could be used to pay for city services.

The deterioration of the city's finances coincided with political crisis. Mayor Kwame Kilpatrick was beset by a series of scandals, including an affair with his chief of staff they both had denied under oath. That led to perjury charges followed by assault charges, Kilpatrick's removal from office in 2008, a prison sentence, federal fraud and tax charges, and a federal grand jury indictment for racketeering, fraud, extortion, and tax evasion ("Former Detroit Mayor Kwame Kilpatrick Faces Major Corruption Charges", Christian Science Monitor, Dec. 18, 2010). In 2009 during the political corruption investigation, Detroit councilwoman Monica Conyers was also convicted of bribery charges and sentenced to 37 months in prison (Sharon Terlep, 2010).

Some of the remnants of poor leadership besides ill-made investment decisions were inadequate and delayed reporting of financial information on the true condition of the city that, for example, Moody's repeatedly complained about in their credit outlooks for Detroit (Moody's Investors Services, 2017).

Detroit Credit Rating Changes

In Chapter 2 we discussed how credit ratings may indicate the condition of municipal fiscal health. We can clearly see from the rating changes how the bankruptcy situation unfolded in Detroit. Rated at Baa1 by Moody's in the late 1990s, the ratings on Detroit's unlimited tax general obligation bonds slipped to Baa2 in late 2005 following the pension debt issuance, to Baa3 in 2008 as recession struck, and plunged to a "junk" status in 2009. In January 2009 Moody's lowered its Detroit rating to Ba2 and to Ba3 in August of the same year. As the city was approaching bankruptcy, the credit rating was lowered by two more notches to B2 in March 2012, to B3 in June 2012, to Caa1 in November 2012, to Caa2 on June 13, and then to Caa3 on June 17, 2013 citing the halt on debt payments as the reason for the downgrade. S&P similarly lowered the rating from BBB to BB in January 2009; further to B in March 2012; CCC- on June 12, 2013; CC on June 14, 2013; and C on July 18, 2013.

In June 2013, Detroit defaulted on 146.6 million dollars in pension contributions and debt payments. On July 18, 2013, the city filed for Chapter 9 bankruptcy, which received a lot of attention in the press as the case of the largest municipal bankruptcy ever in the United States. In October 2013, three months into bankruptcy, S&P further reduced the rating of the city to the lowest possible, D ("Default"). In 2014, Detroit defaulted on the other 81.6 million dollars in general obligations bonds. 56.6 million dollars of this debt was, however, insured and paid by insurers. By June 30, 2014, Detroit additionally defaulted on 261.8 million dollars in various pension contributions and 51.8 million dollars in limited tax GO bonds (City of Detroit, 2014).

However, as soon as the city exited bankruptcy on December 10, 2014, both Moody's and S&P began issuing issuer's rather than a general obligation rating to the city. On December 18, 2014, Moody's assigned a B3 issuer credit rating to Detroit. Moody's highlighted a reduction in long-term debt, stronger cash flow, positive management, and operational changes among other factors contributing to improved credit quality. In July 2015, Moody's increased the credit rating of the city to B2. And S&P issued its first since default B rating to the city.

Bankrupt City

As we discuss in Chapter 6, financially challenged municipalities tend to have lower credit ratings and cannot borrow funds at reasonable interest rates to address their operating or capital needs. When such municipalities borrow, financial constraints make it difficult to ensure scheduled payments to the creditors (if they use the pay-as-you-use approach to financing) or try to provide maintenance out of current revenues (using the pay-as-you-go approach). The lack of funding for required maintenance, replacement, and repair causes continuing deterioration of local infrastructure. This was clearly the case for Detroit.

By the time Detroit filed for bankruptcy, less than half of 88,000 streetlights were working due to staff shortages (the staffing of the Public Lighting Department dropped from over 800 in the 1970s to less than 100 by 2010), deteriorating infrastructure (from simple wire or lamp failure to deteriorating poles and substations), and theft (copper wires and transformer thefts; Kinzey, 2015). Garbage was often not picked up on a regular schedule, the bulk collection was substantively cut, and a recycling plan did not exist (Citizens Research Council of Michigan, 2010). Only 58 of 300 Detroit parks were open since the city was not able to maintain them (Detroit Free Press, 2014a). If this was not enough trouble for the ailing city, the Detroit Water and Sewerage Department (DWSD) had an overall debt of 6.4 billion dollars, mostly accumulated due to unfortunate investment decisions and 118 million dollars in unpaid utility bills and, as such, was unable to support aging sewer and water infrastructure. Consequently, in 2014 DWSD shut off water to about 30,000 households that were over 150 days delinquent on their water bill payments or owed more than 150 dollars to the city (We the People of Detroit Community Research Collective, 2016).

Bankruptcy Process

Michigan was one of the first states to conclude that the government should have a formal program for intervening in local financial crises. In 1990, the legislature enacted a law allowing the state to appoint emergency managers (EMs) in critical situations where a city or school district had no plan to resolve its budget problems and could not deliver services. Between 1990 and 2010 emergency managers were sent to seven cities in Michigan (Michigan Department of Treasury, 2020, 2021). Since 2009 emergency managers have been appointed to nine Michigan cities; six of these cities accounted for nearly half of the black population of the state (We the People of Detroit Community Research Collective, 2016).

In 2011, the Michigan state legislature strengthened the emergency managers' powers by allowing them to break union contracts to control rising labor costs and gave the state the authority to intervene earlier if officials determined through a financial review that a city is headed toward insolvency. This law was, however, viewed as unconstitutional by many in Michigan as EMs were appointed to manage struggling municipalities rather than elected by a popular vote and because EM position imposed additional costs on local governments without providing new revenue. After several lawsuits, the law was placed on the ballot on November 6, 2012, but referendum proposal did not pass the vote. Five localities, including Flint, however, already had an appointed EM during referendum. Then Governor Rick Snyder and the Michigan republican legislature proposed a new Emergency Manager bill in lame duck in December that now included a state appropriation of 75,000 dollars to pay for the EM. The new version of the law was approved by the republican house and senate on December 13, 2012 and signed into law by the Governor on December 27, 2012. Because the new bill included an appropriation for EM, it was not subject to further public referendum, despite the residents voting down the original law (Ballotpedia).

In March 2013, the situation in Detroit deteriorated so badly that then governor, Rick Snyder, declared a fiscal emergency in the city and named an emergency manager who effectively undertook the power of the city's then Mayor Dave Bing and the City Council. The emergency manager was chosen to be a Washington D.C. lawyer, Kevyn Orr, who was previously actively involved with other notorious bankruptcy cases, including Chrysler's bankruptcy. Unfortunately, with an estimated 18.5 billion dollars in debt, the city could not afford to pay its creditors. With no time to repair city finances, Orr made several attempts to negotiate a lower debt payment, but the debtors were not willing to accept the pennies on the dollar Orr offered them. On Thursday, July 18, 2013, Governor Rick Snyder approved Orr's bankruptcy petition submitted two days earlier. The same day the Chapter 9 Bankruptcy petition was filed in the official PACER system. The U.S. 6th Circuit Court of Appeals appointed Bankruptcy Judge Steven Rhodes to lead the case. U.S. District Chief Judge Gerald Rosen was appointed as federal mediator.

"Grand Bargain"

While bankruptcy protection gave some breathing room, the city desperately needed a lot of cash to pay pensions and benefits to its retirees, pay its creditors, and provide city services. Michigan lawmakers (especially conservative Republicans) actively opposed any bailout of the city by the state in order not to create a precedent and not believing city administration could properly manage monetary resources. Unable to raise any additional tax or non-tax revenues by itself and without a state support, the city had to be really innovative in securing funds to pay for its multiple debt obligations. The "bailout" came from multiple unexpected sources in what became known as the "Grand Bargain". The two big tasks of the emergency manager in the "Grand Bargain" were to try to cut city expenses on one side and raise revenues on another.

Negotiation with Creditors and Debt Restructuring

One of the first and most important steps in the "Grand Bargain" was renegotiating debt obligations with city creditors and pension funds. Pension obligations were one of the most sensitive topics for Detroit. On one side, at the time of bankruptcy the total share of pensions and healthcare obligations was about 40 percent of Detroit's budget and with no changes would increase to 60 and even 70 percent in several years (The Detroit News, 2018). On the other side, the pensions were not too high to start with and these were the payments to retired policemen, firemen, city administration, and other staff who devoted their lives to city service. Besides, pension payments are protected by the state constitution (Article IX, Section 24). In a number of painful steps, the city negotiated a 4.5 percent cut to general city pensions and the elimination of an annual cost-of-living adjustment (COLA). The pensions to retired police and firefighters remained intact, but their COLA was reduced from 2.25 percent to about 1 percent. The city also stopped providing retiree health benefits (from December 31, 2014; City of Detroit, 2014).

Negotiation with creditors was another central task of the emergency manager. Before the bankruptcy filing, Detroit had eight swap agreements (City of Detroit, 2013), owing close to 290 million dollars to Bank of America Merrill Lynch and UBS (Detroit Free Press, 2015). As mentioned earlier, Orr tried to lower the debt payments before the city filed for bankruptcy, but his attempts were mostly unsuccessful. After filing for bankruptcy, negotiations with the banks renewed and initially led to a 235-million-dollar deal (City of Detroit, 2013). This first deal, however, was rejected by Judge Rhodes as excessively high and citied the city's inability to make settlement payments. The city and the banks were back at the negotiation table. On December 24, 2013, the city agreed to pay 165 million dollars when banks refused to go any lower. On January 17, 2014, at the Bankruptcy Court hearings, "Judge Rhodes stunned the legal community by rejecting the second settlement as 'just too high a price to pay,' saying that the original debt was 'likely illegal'" (Detroit Free Press, 2015). Orr supported Judge Rhodes sentiment and threatened to sue the two banks a few weeks later. Eventually the city and the banks agreed to an 85-million-dollar payment stretched over time, which Rhodes authorized.

Financial Guaranty Insurance Company (FGIC) – another major creditor of the city – insured Detroit pension debt swap obligations and by the time of bankruptcy filing held 1.1 billion dollars in city debt. The city negotiated to pay FGIC just 13 cents on the dollar of the debt. FGIC also received the right to develop the Joe Louis Arena waterfront site and adjacent parking garage that the city agreed to demolish in 2017 with financial assistance from the state (Detroit Free Press, 2014a).

Detroit owed about 400 million dollars to another large creditor, the bond insurance company Syncora. The emergency manager negotiated to reduce this debt to 200 million dollars with most of it to be paid not in cash but in-kind, through the lease or purchase of some of the prime city-owned Detroit properties that Syncora offered to develop (like Grand Circus Park garage and others; Detroit Free Press, 2014b). Syncora also owned the American Roads company (sold it in 2018) that operates the U.S. portion of the Detroit-Windsor tunnel, the underwater tunnel that connects Detroit to Canadian Windsor (the Canadian portion of the tunnel is owned by the city of Windsor). The lease was set to expire in 2020 but, as a part of the bankruptcy negotiations deal with Syncora, the lease was extended to 2040.

Foundations

On the revenue raising side, one of the most notorious roles in the Grand Bargain was played by foundations. As mentioned earlier, Michigan politicians were reluctant to provide any state transfers to bail out the city. The own-source revenues were not nearly enough to cover even some of the essential city services. Basically, unable to raise funds anywhere else, Kevyn Orr approached presidents of several foundations. This was a very unusual request. Foundations are known for sponsoring research, education, healthcare, and other social matters but not for bailing cities or other private or public entities out of trouble. As the president of the New York-based Ford Foundation, Darren Walker initially reacted to Orr's request "Foundations fund the future. They don't pay for the mistakes of the past" (Detroit Free Press, 2015). Besides, everyone understood that Detroit was in big trouble and any help to the city would be expensive and presume some major donations. It took time and numerous negotiations and consultations to even wrap the minds of foundations' presidents and trustees around the fact that they might be contributing to something like this.

In a highly unusual move several months following the bankruptcy filing, nine private foundations collectively pledged an astounding 330 million dollars to Detroit. Of them, the Ford Foundation approved 125 million dollars, the Kresge foundation pledged one hundred million dollars, and the W.K. Kellogg Foundation pledged 40 million dollars. The smaller Community Foundation for Southeast Michigan (CFSEM), the Flint-based Mott Foundation, and the Detroit-based Hudson Webber, committed ten million dollars each. Thirty million dollars came from the Knight Foundation and twenty-five million dollars was raised by the Davidson Foundation (a full list of contributions and the names of contributing foundations is available at Ferris (2017)).

Detroit Institute of Art

Another interesting and very unusual aspect of Detroit bankruptcy is the involvement of the Detroit Institute of Art (DIA). When Detroit was approaching bankruptcy, a multibillion-dollar art collection at the city-owned Art Institute became a point of interest for both the city creditors and the emergency manager Kevyn Orr. The city did not have many assets that could be quickly converted into cash to pay for the pensions and other debts. Yet, the creditors and city administration realized way too well that Van Goghs, Picassos, and many other pieces of artwork owned by DIA are worth millions of dollars. All of a sudden, the Art Institute was in the center of bankruptcy negotiations and the DIA administration found itself on very unfamiliar ground when, instead of speaking of art, they had to attend countless meetings and negotiations on bankruptcy and city finances.

Expectedly, the DIA tried everything possible to keep its collection intact. They believed that selling art would discredit the museum in the eyes of private sponsors who may be then less willing to donate to the Institute and county officials who may discontinue county tax support.

Many numbers were floating around in negotiations about the potential contribution of the DIA in bailing the city out of bankruptcy. Eventually, after consultations with Michigan Governor Snyder, the DIA committed to raise 100 million dollars for the city in "the Grand Bargain". The three big automakers (Ford and GM contributed ten million dollars each and Chrysler six million dollars), DTE Energy and Quicken Loans (contributed five million dollars each), and multiple other corporations donated to the DIA fundraiser (see Ferris (2017) for the amounts and names of contributing corporations). In return to its contribution to the Detroit pension fund, the Art Institute received independence from the city and promises to expand its statewide programming (such as painting traveling shows), among other things (Detroit Free Press, 2014b).

The Michigan State

Now, with foundation and other money pouring in, it was the state's turn to make the step to Detroit recovery. The main task for the emergency manager and newly elected city administration was to convince lawmakers that the state should not take immediate action and contribute to recovery efforts, as the potential consequences might be losing even more money over higher welfare spending and likely legal actions over city pension cuts (Ballotpedia, 2012). The state eventually agreed to participate in the "Grand Bargain" and in June 2014 approved 195 million dollars in state transfers drawn mainly from the Michigan rainy-day fund and some from tobacco settlement funds.

In the "Grand Bargain" the foundations, the state, and the DIA collectively raised 816 million dollars for the city's pensions funds over the 20-year period (Detroit Free Press, 2014**c**).

Post-bankruptcy Restructuring

Outsourcing and Privatization of City Services

While the issues with the creditors and retirees were two of the highest predicaments of the Detroit bankruptcy case, the city had to address a number of other pressing matters. One of the most important tasks of the emergency manager was the assurance of adequate provision of future city government services whose quality was severely neglected for years leading to the bankruptcy. While a lot of funds were raised through the "Grand Bargain", they solved only one problem the city had (although the largest and most pressing one) as they were earmarked for retirement funds and could not be used for any other purposes. As mentioned earlier, the bankrupt city did not have sufficient current revenues to take care of city operations and deteriorating infrastructure and had very little, if any, ability to borrow, especially at decent interest rates.

One of Orr's solutions to the problems was outsourcing or privatizing several city services. While privatization is often criticized because of the loss of government control, cheating on contracts, and other issues, in the Detroit case privatization turned out to be a solution to many problems of the struggling city. Most of all privatization efforts raised cash for the financially strained city. Privatization also meant that agencies that now ran certain city operations independently could borrow at more preferred rates than the bankrupt city.

One of the earlier tasks of the emergency manager was the creation of an independent Public Lighting Authority (PLA) in February 2014. The PLA succeeded the city's Public Lighting Department. The PLA was not going to simply replace the bulbs and repair the lines, but they wanted to switch to energy efficient LED lights. It was decided to issue 160 million dollars in bonds to update the lighting system (Kinzey, 2015). The PLA estimated that with this money they could replace 50,000 streetlights. The PLA, however, as an independent of the city authority, was able to secure a better interest rate that allowed for increasing the number of streetlights to 65,000. The interest and principal on bonds had been paid from a user fee. New lights were estimated to reduce environmental emissions and save the city 2.4 million dollars a year. But probably the most notable effect from well-lit streets was a reduction in crime. In 2014 the overall number of violent crimes in the city was about 4 percentage points lower than in 2013, and the number of property crimes was lower by about 17 percentage points. In 2015, the number of violent crimes was an astonishing 57 percent of the 2013 rate, and the number of property crimes was only about 48 percent of the 2013 level (FBI, 2019).

Trash collection was another challenge that had to be urgently addressed. The city, under Kevyn Orr's motivation, hired two companies on a five-year contract for a slightly lower price than Detroit used to spend to run its own highly inefficient waste management program. Now the trash was collected weekly and bulk, seasonal items, and recycling were collected biweekly.

The next stop for Detroit was the complicated situation around tens of thousands of unpaid water bills, water shutoffs, and aging water infrastructure. The situation was complicated by the fact that the DWSD supplied water not only to the city of Detroit but also to surrounding counties. To bring the water system back to somewhat normal operations, the Detroit Water and Sewerage Department was the other agency that got privatized in 2014 under a 40-year lease contract with the Great Lakes Water Authority (GLWA) that is represented by the regional board. Under the agreement, GLWA pays the city 50 million dollars a year for a total of 2 billion dollars that are earmarked for maintenance of water infrastructure (We the People of Detroit Community Research Collective, 2016).

Corporate Efforts

While not a part of "the Grand Bargain", the contributions made by the private sector, including corporate and individual efforts in revitalization and beautification of the city, cannot be underestimated. As Matt Cullen mentioned during an interview, corporate leaders engaged in a very "aggressive way" to save the city. "For a period of time business led and philanthropy was right behind".

Probably some of the most notable contributions to the city come from Dan Gilbert, the chairman of JACK Entertainment who is currently considered the thirty-sixth-richest person in the world with 37.6 billion dollars in net worth according to the Bloomberg Billionaires Index (Matt Cullen is a close ally to Dan Gilbert). In 2010 Mr. Gilbert, a native Detroiter, moved the headquarters of his Quicken Loans, a mortgage lending company to downtown Detroit. This effort immediately brought 1,700 new jobs to the city. Today, Rock Ventures, the holding for Dan Gilbert's companies (which include, among others, two casinos in Cleveland, several sports teams, real estate companies, and others), is the number one employer in the city of Detroit with 17,887 employees and represents 8 percent of all employment in the city (City of Detroit, 2020). Following the city bankruptcy when demand and consequently the price of real estate in Detroit were extremely low, Dan Gilbert and affiliates purchased over 90 historical buildings and commercial properties in downtown Detroit (62 CBS Detroit, 2016) and invested heavily in their renovations. He also created a security force to coordinate security efforts and ensure public safety in the downtown area. Bedrock, another company owned by Dan Gilbert, now manages "more than 100 properties totaling over 18 million square feet" in Detroit (Bedrock Detroit, 2021). Around the time of bankruptcy Gilbert additionally co-chaired the Detroit Blight Removal Task Force that identified blighted areas in the city, prioritized their demolition, and funded blight elimination initiatives.

Mike Ilitch, a founder of the Little Caesars Pizza company and another native Detroiter, was also one of the key players for decades, contributing millions of dollars into the revitalization of Detroit. Ilitch and his wife purchased and revitalized a neglected Fox Theater in 1988 and a year later moved the Little Caesars headquarters campus next to it. In 1992, Ilitch purchased the Detroit Tigers baseball team. Since 2000, Ilitch and his wife have donated millions of dollars to Wayne State University in Detroit. The holding of all Ilitch companies is developing the *District Detroit* destination that incorporates five city midtown neighborhoods and includes, among other sports and entertainment facilities, the Little Caesars Arena, which opened in 2017, a home to the professional hockey team, the Detroit Red Wings and the basketball team, the Detroit Pistons (www.ilitchholdings.com/mike-legacy.html).

Another big private investor, John Hantz, introduced an urban agriculture vision into the city's post-bankruptcy recovery efforts. Mr. Hantz created the Hantz Woodlands company that invests money in demolishing dangerous structures, renovating and rehabilitating other buildings, cleaning weeds and debris from thousands of parcels in blighted areas of Detroit, and planting trees in empty spaces (Hantzfarms Detroit, 2021).

Private investments also poured from the other sources. Penske Corp., Quicken Loans Inc., General Motors Co., Ford Motor Co., Chrysler Group LLC, Blue Cross Blue Shield of Michigan, the Kresge Foundation, and Platinum Equity LLC collectively donated 8 million dollars to the city to buy 23 EMS and 100 police cars in early 2014. This effort allowed the city to substantively reduce response time to emergency calls (62 CBS Detroit, 2014).

In 2017, DTE Energy built Beacon Park in the heart of Detroit's downtown on a 1.2-acre lot. The Park features a two-story restaurant with roof-top dining, an open lawn that hosts food trucks, concerts, farmers' markets and other events, and a beautiful light installation (Empowering Michigan (2021). Beacon park. Retrieved from https://empoweringmichigan.com/beacon-park/faqs/).

While there have been multiple individuals contributing to Detroit's revival, there have also been numerous examples of collaborations between different corporations and philanthropy in Detroit recovery efforts (62 CBS Detroit, 2014, 2016). As Matt Mullins said, "People came together, and they worked together". Projects like "Invest Detroit", Detroit Riverfront Conservancy, the streetcar project, and others are some of the highlights of such joint actions that collectively played a sizeable role in recovery of the city.

The Invest Detroit fund was established in 1995 to attract and expand businesses and support real estate development in the city. 2010 marked the creation of the Invest Detroit Foundation that expanded from one to nine funds thanks to major contributions from Quicken Loans, the Ford Foundation, and multiple other corporations, banks, and foundations that also collectively manage the nonprofit. By 2020 Invest Detroit leveraged almost 2.9 billion dollars, subsidized 749 projects and businesses in Detroit, developed over six million square feet of commercial and retail space, created 5,070 housing units including 836 affordable housing units, and created or retained 12,848 jobs in the city (Invest Detroit 2020, report).

The Detroit Riverfront Conservancy, Inc. is a nonprofit organization that started thanks to a collaboration of various nonprofits, corporations (the Kresge Foundation and General Motors are the largest ones), numerous individual donors, the city of Detroit, and the county, state, and federal government organizations. The major purpose of the entity is the development and maintenance of Detroit's river-walk. When the project is completed, the entire Riverfront will be a five-and-a-half mile contiguous public walkway between the Ambassador Bridge and Gabriel Richard Park that connects multiple plazas, pavilions, and parks (Detroit Riverfront Conservancy, 2021).

Multiple philanthropic organizations and large corporations, including the Kresge Foundation, Quicken Loans, Penske, and others in partnership with the U.S. DOT and multiple state and local governments also joined to pursue an M-1 RAIL Streetcar initiative, known as the QLine Streetcar project (Lowe & Grengs, 2020). This project created 89 billion dollars in development (from an interview with Matt Cullen). The not-for-profit QLine railcar, the only privately run railroad system in the U.S., was open for public use in May 2017. A 3.3-mile rail system provides easy access to various points of interest in downtown Detroit (Qline Detroit, 2021). There is a view, however, that a streetcar project is a slower and less efficient alternative to a bus rapid transit and, while good for the city's development, is not beneficial for the transit-dependent population (King & Fischer, 2016).

Another positive outcome of these recovery efforts is that many of the development initiatives started in the downtown area but later expanded to other strategic neighborhoods in the city, slowly but surely bringing Detroit back to life (The Chief Financial Officer of Detroit, 2021). The recovery of Detroit is truly a collective effort. Not only big corporations and foundations but private individuals contributed a lot to Detroit's recovery. By late 2014, 225 city parks were open (up from 58 parks just over a year earlier) and maintained by multiple church and community volunteers who mowed the grass and removed trash and litter (Detroit Free Press, 2014a, 2014c).

Federal Grants

Thanks to a 25.9-million-dollar grant from the federal government to the Detroit Department of Transportation (DDOT), the city purchased 50 new busses in 2014. A federal program, the Hardest Hit Fund (HHF mentioned in Chapter 3), provided funding for the demolition of abandoned houses in the blighted areas of the city. 265 million dollars of federal funds were provided through the HHF program, which supported the demolition of 15,084 houses in Detroit (The Detroit News, 2020). The results of the program have been overwhelmingly positive. The office of Detroit's Chief Financial Officer reports that the affected areas have seen a 90 percent increase in property values, a 42 percent drop in fire load, and a 3 percent reduction in violent and property crime rates for every ten demolished houses. However, there were some corruption allegations related to the program and spending of funds, as well as raised environmental concerns.

Leadership

The last but absolutely not the least contributor to the rise of the city was the positive changes in the city and county administration. When the heavy lifting was done and the administration of the city was ready to be transferred from the emergency manager back to the mayor and the city council in late fall of 2014, strong leadership was crucial for the continuing recovery of the city. The newly elected city council and mayor of Detroit, Mike Duggan, started their term on January 1, 2014. "Mayor Mike Duggan came in. Very strong leader, vary capable, very operations' focused" (interview with Matt Cullen). As a mayor (reelected for a third term in 2021) Duggan has played one of the most crucial roles in Detroit's recovery.

> He oversaw the relighting of city streetlights, improved bus service and emergency response times while Detroit's emergency manager Kevyn Orr tended to the bankruptcy and finances. His administration has helped rebuild corridors in several key commercial districts, spearheaded a crackdown on blight and touts an ambitious, federally funded demolition effort that's torn down more than 14,200 blighted houses since May 2014.
> *(Ferretti, 2018)*

Wayne County (headquartered in Detroit) executive Warren C. Evans, who started his term on January 1, 2015, has been another important figure to administer recovery of the city of Detroit.

Conclusions

Countless issues with an overreliance of the city on a single auto industry, economic challenges, racial disaggregation and white flight, high deficit in the city's pension fund, unhealthy borrowing practices, and poor leadership are some of the most notable factors that led Detroit to bankruptcy. Years of bad fiscal habits and depraved overall economic and demographic conditions were not easy to overturn. But when the worst happened and Detroit applied for Chapter 9 bankruptcy protection, serious steps had to be made, quickly, to overturn the city's downward path. What put Detroit on the track toward recovery was unprecedented by the breadth and extensive collaboration among corporations, philanthropy, and the city. "As a community we didn't have good track record of collaborations at times. People would do their own thing" (interview with Matt Cullen). But too many people loved Detroit, were not ready to give up on it, and were willing to spend millions of dollars, volunteer countless hours, and devote a lot of their passion for the recovery of the city.

"Business, the city government, and philanthropy, a three-legged stool . . . all those people became aligned during the bankruptcy process" (interview with Matt Cullen). In the "Grand Bargain" among city creditors, foundations, and the state, the emergency administration managed to renegotiate and substantively lower the debt the city owed. The Detroit Institute of Art, multiple foundations, corporations, and the state collectively raised hundreds of millions of dollars for the bankrupt city.

During the recovery efforts a high emphasis was put on bringing people together. A lot of public spaces, such as Beacon Park, Campus Martius, or

FIGURE 9.4 "The Spirit of Detroit Monument".

FIGURE 9.5 Detroit Riverwalk.

FIGURE 9.6 Detroit Belle Isle.

Riverwalk, were brought to life for residents to meet and spend time together, to give a sense of community. Now

> people from the suburbs and the city, black and white, young and old, and rich and poor, they walk along with baby carriages, they are walking the dogs, they are doing things. They are interacting as a community in a very different way. That is probably one of the most profound changes in the city.
> *(interview with Matt Cullen)*

While there were many success stories in Detroit's recovery, not all actions and efforts can be deemed lucrative. One of the parties that perhaps lost the most in the bankruptcy process was thousands of Detroit retirees who devoted their lives to public service and after retirement received just a portion of the pensions and very little or none of the health benefits promised to them. An estimated 32,000 current and retired city employees were affected by pension and benefits cuts (The Detroit News, 2018). To alleviate the possibility of any future pension cuts, the city established the Retiree Protection Fund.

FIGURE 9.7 Port Detroit.

Note

1 Matthew (Matt) P. Cullen manages several large corporations and non-profits based mainly in Detroit, MI. He is chief executive officer of JACK Entertainment and a principal of Rock Ventures LLC. Matt Cullen also serves as volunteer President and CEO of the M-1 RAIL Streetcar initiative in Detroit, the chairman of Invest Detroit, and the vice chairman of the Downtown Detroit Partnership, and he is on the Board of Trustees of multiple other organizations. Mr. Cullen and his entities have been heavily involved with Detroit recovery efforts. He and Dan Gilbert (read about Dan Gilbert in the "Corporate Contributions" section) collectively invested hundreds of millions of dollars and developed and pursued dozens of projects aimed at Detroit revival. Mr. Cullen was interviewed on August 12, 2021 on contributions of corporate world to Detroit recovery efforts.

References

62 CBS Detroit (2014). *Detroit police get final group of donated patrol cars*, 9 April. Retrieved from https://detroit.cbslocal.com/2014/04/09/detroit-police-get-final-group-of-donated-patrol-cars/

62 CBS Detroit. (2016). *The David Stott building like a treasure hunt For Dan Gilbert's renovators*. Retrieved from https://detroit.cbslocal.com/2016/08/25/the-david-stott-building-like-a-treasure-hunt-for-dan-gilberts-renovators/

Advisory Commission on Intergovernmental Relations (ACIR) (1973). *City Financial Emergencies: The Intergovernmental Dimension*. Washington, D.C.: U.S. Government Printing Office.

Atuahene, B. (2018). "Our taxes are too damn high": Institutional racism, property tax assessment, and the fair housing act. *Northwestern University Law Review*, *112*(6), 1–23. Retrieved November 4, 2020, from https://scholarlycommons.law.northwestern.edu/nulr/vol112/iss6/10/

Ballotpedia (2012). Michigan Emergency Manager Referendum, Proposal 1 (2012). https://ballotpedia.org/Michigan_Emergency_Manager_Referendum,_Proposal_1_(2012)

Bedrock Detroit (2021). *Local businesses are the heart and soul of Detroit*. Retrieved May 3, 2022, from https://www.bedrockdetroit.com/press-releases/

Berry, C. R. (2020). *Center for Municipal Finance. 2020. An Evaluation of Residential Property Tax Assessments in the City of Detroit, 2016–2018*. Chicago, IL: University of Chicago.

Chief Investment Officer (2014). *Detroit Seeks Legal Relief over Interest Rate Swaps*, 3 February. Retrieved May 3, 2022, from https://harris.uchicago.edu/files/evalrespropertytaxasdetroit20162018.pdf

Citizens Research Council of Michigan (2010). *The fiscal condition of the city of Detroit*. Retrieved May 3, 2022, from http://crcmich.org/PUBLICAT/2010s/2010/memo1098.pdf

City of Detroit (2013). *Comprehensive annual financial report for the fiscal year ended June 30, 2013 (CAFR)*. Retrieved May 3, 2022, from https://detroitmi.gov/sites/detroitmi.localhost/files/migrated_docs/financial-reports/FY13%20City%20of%20Detroit%20Financial%20Statements%20-%20FINAL_1.pdf

City of Detroit (2014). *Comprehensive annual financial report for the fiscal year ended June 30, 2014 (CAFR)*. Retrieved May 3, 2022, from https://detroitmi.gov/sites/detroitmi.localhost/files/migrated_docs/financial-reports/Final%20CAFR.pdf

City of Detroit (2020). Comprehensive annual financial report for the fiscal year ended June 30, 2020 (CAFR). Retrieved May 3, 2022, from https://detroitmi.gov/sites/detroitmi.localhost/files/migrated_docs/financial-reports/Final%20CAFR.pdf

Detroit Free Press (2014a). *How Detroit's automakers helped a city exit bankruptcy*, Alissa Priddle. 10 November. Retrieved May 3, 2022, from https://www.freep.com/story/news/local/detroit-bankruptcy/2014/11/10/detroit-bankruptcy-ford-gm-chrysler-donation/18798399/

Detroit Free Press (2014b). *Why Detroit-Windsor tunnel plays key role in big Detroit bankruptcy deal*, Alissa Priddle. 10 November. Retrieved May 3, 2022, from https://www.freep.com/story/money/business/michigan/2014/09/10/why-detroit-windsor-tunnel-plays-key-role-in-big-detroit-bankruptcy-deal/15369749/

Detroit Free Press (2014c). *9 ways Detroit is Changing after Bankruptcy*, 9 November, 2014. Matt Helms, Joe Guillen, John Gallagher and JC Reindl. Retrieved May 3, 2022, from https://www.freep.com/story/news/local/detroit-reborn/2015/11/08/detroit-rising-life-after-bankruptcy/75085252/

Detroit Free Press (2015). *Detroit Rising: The DIA's $170 million challenge*, 21 November, 2015. Mark Stryker. Retrieved May 3, 2022, from https://www.freep.com/story/entertainment/2015/11/21/dia-after-grand-bargain-detroit-bankruptcy/75113624/

Detroit Riverfront Conservancy (2021). *Detroit riverfront*. Retrieved May 3, 2022, from https://detroitriverfront.org/riverfront.

Empowering Michigan (2021). *Beacon park*. Retrieved May 3, 2022, from https://empoweringmichigan.com/beacon-park/faqs/

Encyclopedia of Detroit (2020). *Arsenal of democracy*. Retrieved May 3, 2022, from https://detroithistorical.org/learn/encyclopedia-of-detroit/arsenal-democracy

Encyclopedia of Detroit (2021). *Uprising of 1967*. Retrieved May 3, 2022, from https://detroithistorical.org/learn/encyclopedia-of-detroit/uprising-1967

FBI (2019). *Uniform crime reporting*. FBI: UCR. Retrieved May 3, 2022, from https://ucr.fbi.gov/ucr.

Ferretti, C. (2018). Mike Duggan: Mayor instrumental to Detroit's turnaround. The *Detroit News*, 21 June. Retrieved February 5, 2022, from https://www.detroitnews.com/story/news/michigan/michiganians-of-year/2018/06/21/mayor-mike-duggan-michiganian-year-detroit-news-detroit-turnaround/672780002/

Ferretti, C. The Detroit News (2020). *Last Detroit house demolished in $265M blight-removal effort*, 14 August. Retrieved from https://www.detroitnews.com/story/news/local/detroit-city/2020/08/14/last-detroit-house-demolished-blight-removal/3349213001/

Ferris, J. M. (2017). *Detroit's Grand Bargain: Philanthropy as a catalyst for a brighter future*. Retrieved from Usc.edu.

Guzman, Tatyana (2019). Fiscal conditions of largest legacy cities. In *The Legacies of Legacy Cities: Continuity and Change amid Decline and Revival*. Pittsburgh, PA: University of Pittsburgh Press.

Hantzfarms Detroit (2021). *25,000+ hardwood trees planted. Creating truly liveable neighborhoods, one square mile at a time*. Retrieved from hantzfarmsdetroit.com

Kasdan, O. (2014). A tale of two hatchet men: Emergency financial management in Michigan. *Administration & Society*, *46*(9), 1092–1108.

King, D. A., & Fischer, L. A. (2016). Streetcar projects as spatial planning: A shift in transport planning in the United States. *Journal of Transport Geography, 54*, 383–390

Kinzey, B. (2015). *Restoring Detroit's street lighting*, September 2015. The United States Department of Energy. Retrieved November 4, 2021, from https://energy.gov/sites/prod/files/2015/09/f27/2015_restoring-detroit.pdf

Lowe, K., & Grengs, J. (2020). Private donations for public transit: The equity implications of Detroit's public – private streetcar. *Journal of Planning Education and Research, 40*(3), 289–303. doi:10.1177/0739456X18761237

Michigan Department of Treasury (2020). *Fiscal health indicators.* Retrieved July 9, 2021, from www.michigan.gov/treasury/0,1607,7-121-1751_47023-171423--,00.html
Michigan Department of Treasury (2021). *MI community financial dashboard.* Retrieved from !/dashboard/COUNTY/ https://micommunityfinancials.michigan.gov/#!/dashboard/COUNTY/
Moody's Investors Services (2010). *High Profile Ratings Update.* City of Detroit. New York, NY: Moody's Investors Services. Retrieved November 4, 2021, from https://www.moodys.com/credit-ratings-tab/DefaultResearch/600001576?orgname=Detroit-City-of-MI-&rdtid=Rating%20Update
Moody's Investors Services (2017). *US municipal bond defaults and recoveries, 1970–2016.* New York, NY: Moody's Investors Services.Retrieved November 4, 2020, from www.moodys.com/researchdocumentcontentpage.aspx?docid=PBM_1059508
PEW Charitable Trusts (2013). *The state role in local government financial distress.* Retrieved December 23, 2021, from www.pewtrusts.org/~/media/assets/2016/04/pew_state_role_in_local_government_financial_distress.pdf
Phinney, S. (2018). Detroit's municipal bankruptcy: Racialised geographies of austerity. *New Political Economy, 23*(5), 609–626.
Qline Detroit (2021). *Let's Get (Re)Started!* Retrieved December 23, 2021, from https://qlinedetroit.com/
Sharon Terlep (2010). Lawmaker's wife sentenced to jail. *The Wall Street Journal*, 11 March.
Stone, S. B., Singla, A., Comeaux, J., & Kirschner, C. (2015). A comparison of financial indicators: The case of Detroit. *Public Budgeting & Finance, 35*(4), 90–111.
Sugrue, T. J. (2014). *The Origins of the Urban Crisis.* Princeton, NJ: Princeton University Press.
The Chief Financial Officer of Detroit (2021). *The next step: Detroit aims to be free of residential blight by the end of 2024*, 31 May. Retrieved December 23, 2021, from https://detroitmi.gov/news/next-step-detroit-aims-be-free-residential-blight-end-2024
The Detroit News. Christine Ferretti (2018). *Detroit bankruptcy 'threw everything into chaos' for retirees*, 18 July. Retrieved May 4 2022, from https://www.detroitnews.com/story/news/local/detroit-city/2018/07/18/detroit-bankruptcy-retirees-reaction/783828002/
US Census (2021). *Detroit.* Retrieved May 4 2022, from https://www.census.gov/quickfacts/detroitcitymichigan
We the People of Detroit Community Research Collective. (2016). *Mapping the Water Crisis: The Dismantling of African-American Neighborhoods in Detroit.* Detroit, MI: We the People of Detroit Community Research Collective. Retrieved May 4 2022, from https://www.wethepeopleofdetroit.com/community-research

10

CASE STUDY: COLORADO SPRINGS, CO

Introduction

The case of Colorado Springs, CO is an example of the mildest fiscal distress, compared to the downfalls experienced by the other municipalities discussed in this book. In fact, despite internal fiscal and other resulting issues, the city managed to preserve its high credit ratings (at AA3 and AA2 by Moody's; S&P rated the city AA up until it withdrew the ratings in early 2009). But even a relatively small distress triggered substantial cuts to city services. While Colorado Springs is not a typical insolvent city in our sample, we present the case of Colorado Springs to show how quick and timely measures undertaken to improve the situation in the very beginning of a downfall, as well as the partnership with city residents, helped avoid potentially devastating consequences. Overall economic recovery in the country and additional revenues from the legalization of marijuana in the state also aided the recovery of the city.

Background Information

Colorado Springs was founded on July 31, 1871. It is the second largest city in Colorado, the most populous municipality in its home county, El Paso, and the forty-sixth largest city in the U.S. by population, with 416,427 residents in 2010 (U.S. Census Bureau, 2010). With a territory of 185 square miles, it is also the largest city in Colorado by area. Colorado Springs is a home rule (self-governing) municipality. It is in east central Colorado, situated on Fountain Creek, 60 miles (97 kilometers) south of Denver. More than 70 miles of on-street bicycle lanes thread their way across the city, and the city manages another 100 miles of urban trails for jogging and hiking.

DOI: 10.4324/b23117-10

FIGURE 10.1 The Road to Colorado Springs.

The 2010 Census reported that 78.8 percent of the population of the city was white, 16.1 percent Hispanic or Latino of any race, 6.3 percent Black or African American, 3.0 percent Asian, 1.0 percent descended from Indigenous peoples of the Americas, 5.5 percent of some other race, and 5.1 percent of two or more races (U.S. Census Bureau, 2010). The city is populated mainly by young individuals. The median age of city residents was 35 years old in 2010. Table 10.1 provides demographic and economic situations in Colorado Springs in 2010 and 2019.

Colorado Springs utilizes a strong mayor and city council system. The mayor serves as the city's chief executive and is responsible for proposing a budget, signing legislation into law, appointing departmental directors, and overseeing the city's day-to-day operations. Colorado Springs has been governed by Republican mayors since at least the 1970s, while the state has mostly been led by a Democratic governor and voted for Democrats in the past four presidential elections. The city council serves as the city's primary legislative body and is responsible for adopting the city budget, approving mayoral appointees, levying taxes, and making or amending city laws, policies, and ordinances (Ballotpedia, 2009).

The city has quite a diverse economy dominated by defense, the high-tech industry, and tourism. The city's largest employers are defense contractors like Northrop Grumman, Boeing, L3Harris Technologies, SAIC, ITT, General

TABLE 10.1 Demographic, Economic, and Social Situations in Colorado Springs in 2010 and 2019*

Population	
Population estimates, July 1, 2019, (V2019	478,221
Population, Census, April 1, 2010	417,221
Race and Hispanic Origin	
White alone, percent	78.5
Black or African American alone, percent	6.5
Asian alone, percent	2.9
Hispanic or Latino, percent	17.6
Housing	
Owner-occupied housing unit rate, 2015–2019, percent	59
Median value of owner-occupied housing units, 2015–2019, $	269,800
Median gross rent, 2015–2019, $	1,131
Education	
High school graduate or higher, percent of persons age 25 years+, 2015–2019, percent	93.9
Bachelor's degree or higher, percent of persons age 25 years+, 2015–2019, percent	39.9
Health	
With a disability, under age 65 years, percent, 2015–2019	9.8
Persons without health insurance, under age 65 years, percent	8.9
Economy	
In civilian labor force, total, percent of population age 16 years+, 2015–2019	64.7
Total accommodation and food services sales, 2012 ($1,000)	1,274,811
Total retail sales per capita, 2012, $	16,133
Income and Poverty	
Median household income (in 2019 dollars), 2015–2019	64,712
Per capita income in past 12 months (in 2019 dollars), 2015–2019, $	34,076
Persons in poverty, percent	11.7

* *The numbers are for 2019 if not specified otherwise*
Source: Table created by authors based on US Census, 2021

Dynamics, Lockheed Martin, and Bluestaq. A large segment of this industry is dedicated to the development and operation of various projects for space. Several military bases surround Colorado Springs. The city is also a home to the United States Air Force Academy and the Space Foundation.

In the 1980s, the city began to actively support the relocation of non-profit organizations. Colorado Springs was home to the national headquarters of more than 80 religious organizations, including the socially conservative Focus on the Family, which moved to the city in 1991. By 1993, Focus on the Family ran a 45-acre campus on the north side of the city, with 1,200 employees. Other similar groups followed, earning Colorado Springs the nickname of "the Evangelical Vatican" (Patton, 2010).

The Fiscal Distress Situation

The Revenue Shortage

Economic and consequent fiscal problems started in Colorado Springs before the Great Recession of 2008. The Colorado Taxpayer Bill of Rights (TABOR) law, implemented in 1991, advocated for the idea of smaller government and imposed an inflation-based cap on the amount of revenue the city can collect. Any revenue over that limit must be returned to taxpayers. That has kept the city government lean and small, even before 2009.

The high-tech and military sectors that were vital industries for the economy of Colorado Springs decreased their overall presence from about 21,000 to 8,000 employees between 2000 and 2006 (University of Colorado at Colorado Springs, 2006), dragging down economic growth and jeopardizing tax collections (see Table 10.2).

TABLE 10.2 Revenues and Expenditures in Colorado Springs from 2007 to 2010 (in 000's)

	2007	*2008*	*2009*	*2010*
REVENUE				
Property taxes, $	22,696	25,741	26,276	24,326
Operating grants and contributions $	22,918	15,004	19,290	24,111
Capital grants and contributions, $	263,274	122,531	101,615	156,253
Investment earnings, $	46,886	(4,879)	46,955	32,180
Gain on sale of assets, $	87	275	1,517	573
Other taxes, $	167,678	153,881	146,767	151,936
Charges for services, $	1,368,145	1,411,377	1,403,208	1,319,224
Total Revenue	1,842,862	1,715,866	1,710,650	1,800,835
EXPENDITURES				
General government, $	79,498	92,817	56,678	46,363
Public safety, $	126,768	123,712	145,664	150,429
Public works, $	79,445	69,909	83,648	61,480
Health and welfare, $	1,147	1,181	1,231	1,206
Culture and recreation, $	25,899	22,674	25,192	21,616
Total Expenditures	1,606,593	1,927,820	1,659,071	1,676,144
Net assets, beginning	2,922,032	2,685,763	2,710,068	3,005,208
Net assets, ending	2,685,763	2,710,068	3,005,208	3,137,968
Current and other assets	206,481	180,027	1,332,130	1,672,131
Capital assets	1,048,699	1,089,936	4,389,662	4,764,805
Total assets	1,255,180	1,269,963	5,721,792	6,436,936
Current liabilities	82,424	76,589	370,726	385,968
Long-term liabilities	135,842	139,046	2,345,858	2,912,973
Total liabilities	218,266	215,635	2,716,584	3,298,968
Net Assets	2,922,032	2,710,068	3,005,208	3,137,968

Source: Table created by authors based on CAFRs and annual budgets of the City of Colorado Springs (City of Colorado Springs, 2009, 2010, 2011)

The city, however, navigated these challenges well and remained fiscally strong until the Great Recession hit in 2008–2009. In late 2009, Colorado Springs faced a 28-million-dollar budget shortfall. Total tax and non-tax revenues were down from 2007 to 2008 by 127 million dollars, due primarily to decreases in capital grants and contributions by 141 million dollars and a decrease in sales tax collections (included in "other taxes" category in Table 10.2).

In 2008, the unemployment rate was between 4 percent and 6 percent, but in 2009, unemployment at the end of the year was 8.1 percent. Colorado Springs lost more than 23,000 jobs following the beginning of the recession. When people lose jobs, it negatively affects the tax base on one side and increases expenditures on the other. Table 10.2 provides the dynamic of expenditures and revenues in Colorado Springs from 2009 to 2012.

City's Actions to Exit Fiscal Emergency

Proposal to Increase Property Taxes

It should be mentioned that when the recession hit, Colorado Springs had the lowest property taxes in the nation. In 2008, the per capita property tax was only about 55 dollars. To compare numbers, in the United States, overall, the

> average county-level residential property tax burdens tend to be close to $1,000 per year. Between 2007 and 2011, 60 percent of counties had average tax burdens between $500 and $1,500. Fewer than 3 percent of counties had average property tax payments more than $4,000 and just nine counties had average property tax bills over $8,000.
>
> *(Harris & Moore, 2013, p. 5)*

When Colorado Springs faced the perspective of a substantial budget deficit, the city administration naturally sought to pass a property tax increase, Measure 2C, in November 2009 to avoid service impacts (Ballotpedia, 2009). According to this proposal, the annual property tax increase would be between 126 dollars and 210 dollars based on the average home price value of 262,000 dollars in the area. According to official estimates, the tax measure, if approved, had to generate 27.6 million dollars in additional revenue in 2010 and 46 million dollars in additional revenue in 2014 (Ballotpedia, 2009). The ballot language read as the following:

> Shall city taxes be increased $46,000,000 annually by increasing 2009 general property tax 6.00 mills, 1.00 additional mill per year for four years, continuing thereafter, constituting voter approved revenue change?

To support the tax measure, residents and city council members even formed the "A City Worth Fighting For" campaign. This group argued that "even with the full implementation of 2C in 2014, Colorado Springs will continue to have a low tax burden per capita, when compared to other similar size cities on the Front Range" (Ballotpedia, 2009).

Councilwoman Jan Martin, in a televised debate on October 7, 2009, claimed that the property tax increase would lead to a stabilization of the city revenue base and a lack of action would result in cuts to public facilities and services. Firefighters supported the debate, noting that at least 35 firemen positions would be cut in 2010 if the tax measure would not pass and funding was not provided sufficiently for the Colorado Springs Fire Department.

Residents opposing the property tax increase argued that Colorado Springs had issues with city spending. They pointed out that the city government claims multimillion-dollar shortfalls in their budget but then proceeds to spend millions on new capital utility projects within the same budget year.

A Colorado Springs Property Tax Increase, Measure 2C was ultimately defeated during elections on November 3, 2009, with only about a third of voters' support. According to Patton (2015), "the message from residents was clear: We'd rather suffer the cuts than spend more to avoid them".

Expenditures' Cuts

With no anticipation of additional tax revenues coming to cover the budget deficit, Colorado Springs had nothing to do but cut expenditures, which meant the city was about to face a reduction in many essential public functions. In 2009, city residents sent emails to the town council with the following suggestions: (1) close community centers, (2) reduce the size of the police department, (3) sell city-owned utilities, (4) sell the municipal hospital, and (5) decrease salaries and benefits of city employees. "The town council has been bombarded with emails telling it to close community centers. Letters to the local newspaper call for shrinking the police department and putting the city-owned utility up for sale. A commission is studying whether to sell the municipal hospital" (Eaton, 2010).

One of the first cost-cutting steps, as is often the case with fiscally challenged municipalities, was hiring freezes for city jobs, including firefighters, beat cops, drug investigators, and other essential positions. Colorado Springs additionally eliminated 197.75 existing positions, including 14 uniform positions in the fire department. The police department had 689 officers in 2006 and 609 in 2010. Most police departments in comparable cities would have 750 to 900 officers. The police department in Colorado Springs reduced the number of detectives who investigate property crimes, cut the number of officers assigned to the schools, and eliminated units that tracked juvenile offenders and caught fugitives. According to then Chief Richard Myers, the property detectives were cut by one-third, and the department completely wiped out some units, including its fugitive-investigation group; "We have eliminated entire street teams out of our regional drug unit. In 2011, we're significantly shrinking the number of school resource officers. Our specialty units are just imploding" (Patton, 2010). Not only manning but equipping a police department became a problem that could adversely affect public safety and safety of the police officers themselves.

The steepest budget cuts were in the parks, recreation, and cultural services department. Dozens of workers in the parks and recreation department were laid off. The city continued to manicure 13 big parks, 17 others received partial irrigation and maintenance, and the remaining 111 smaller neighborhood parks received minimum maintenance. The city eliminated maintenance of alleys and unpaved streets, stopped collecting trash from any parks, and even pulled out all the trash cans from them, replacing the trash bins with the signs asking parkgoers not to litter. Sports and other recreation programs were reduced or eliminated (Colorado Springs Budget, 2010). The city funded only four community centers and only in the first quarter of 2010 (Hillside, Meadows, West, Deerfield Hills) and closed six others, opened two of seven swimming pools (Aquatics and Fitness Center, Cottonwood Creek Recreation Center), and closed the remaining recreation and cultural facilities. Public restrooms were closed with signs on the doors: "NOTICE: Due to budget reductions, this facility is closed indefinitely" (Patton, 2010).

Colorado Springs turned off a third of its 24,512 streetlights. The city's goal was to save 1.2 million dollars on electric bills. The city officials later announced a streetlight adoption program "to help interested citizens reactivate streetlights that have been turned off over the past six weeks as part of a $1.2 million cost-saving measure" (City of Colorado Springs, 2010). It was calculated that a year of service of streetlights was 75 dollars for each residential light and 180 dollars for an arterial light in 2009 (Chanacon & Bean, 2009). Citizens could "adopt a streetlight" on their block and have it turned back on by paying a donation – between 100 dollars to 240 dollars, depending on the type of light (Patton, 2010). City officials announced that "streetlights that are turned off are wrapped with a strip of orange tape around the pole and many will have a red cap placed on top of the light pole. This will help citizens distinguish between lights turned off on purpose and those in need of repair. Adopted streetlights will have a strip of blue tape wrapped around the pole for identification". According to Eaton (2010), even these cuts had their fans, "while many people called to ask to have their lights turned back on, says Sue Skiffington-Blumberg, the city's spokeswoman, about 10% of the callers actually wanted their streetlights to go dark" (p. 3).

Colorado Springs had taken additional action to reduce expenditures in 2010: they eliminated the general fund portion of funding for transit routes; reduced funding for the City Auditor, Municipal Court, and City Attorney; and reduced the size of Human Resources, Budget, Procurement, and other departments. The city eliminated the Land Use public information counter, the neighborhood issue intervention/resolution, and economic development programs, reduced zoning inspections, eliminated strategic planning monitoring and reporting, and encouraged early retirements. These reductions resulted in 2010 general fund net savings of 24.4 million dollars.

To raise additional revenue, the police department auctioned off its three helicopters online.

Cooperation with Not-for-profit and Private Organizations

Colorado Springs was trying to get volunteers and the private sector to provide services the city could no longer afford. The *Wall Street Journal* wrote that

FIGURE 10.2 Colorado Springs City Hall.

Colorado Springs, "faced with dwindling revenues, intransigent voters and widespread distrust of government, this city of 400,000 has embarked on a grand experiment: It is trying to get volunteers and the private sector to provide services the city can no longer afford" (Eaton, 2010).

The examples of volunteering and public-private partnership in Colorado Springs came from a variety of different sources. In addition to the "adopt a streetlight" program discussed earlier, the city introduced an "adopt a trash can" initiative, where volunteers organized themselves to empty garbage cans in 128 neighborhood parks. Participants signed a contract with the city agreeing to make sure the cans get emptied and then tried to round up their neighbors to help. "Proud of Our Parks" residents' initiative had even set up websites that allowed 38 parks to communicate and post garbage pickup schedules. With volunteer help, the city was able to place back about one-third of the rubbish bins that were removed from municipal parks (Patton, 2010). The "adopt a trash can" initiative helped not only to reduce costs to taxpayers but also encouraged residents to be more connected to their parks and neighborhoods (Ermasova, 2014). Taxi drivers were recruited to serve as a second set of eyes for stretched police patrols. The private swimming programs were asked to operate municipal pools. City officials negotiated a deal with a big-box retailer that would allow residents to get discounts on riding mowers to voluntarily cut grass in the parks. The city discussed an "adopt a median" program to recruit residents to trim the medians with their own lawnmowers (Patton, 2010).

The volunteer activities and public-private partnership saved a community center that was run by a church and a museum. The Pioneers Museum raised enough money to keep its doors open for a year and to hire consultants to develop a plan for it to go private. The local brewery, Phantom Canyon Brewing Company, designated one of their beers to help fund the public fountain. The U.S. Olympic Committee donated 250,000 dollars over two years for sports programs, including summer camps at the community centers.

These volunteer activities and public-private partnerships became crucial for economic recovery. They encouraged community engagement, connected people in neighborhoods, and gave residents a sense of pride for helping their community and a sense of ownership in their neighborhoods. These initiatives helped to keep open spaces clean and promoted public safety. They undoubtedly also had a tremendous cost-saving effect.

Fiscally Distressed City

Expectedly, budget cuts and resulting downfall in service delivery created numerous problems. One big issue the city was facing was deteriorating capital infrastructure due to a decrease in public works and economic degradation. Spending on infrastructure projects essentially ceased, and the city faced a 700-million-dollar backlog in capital needs in 2010. Sixty percent of the city's roadways have gone more than a decade without being repaved (Patton, 2015).

It should come as no surprise that cuts in the police department and turned off streetlights sparked public safety concerns. Back in the day, Colorado Springs' police chief Richard W. Myers was noting that "people don't feel as safe. They're already telling us that, even if the numbers don't bear that out" (Cooper, 2010, p. 2). New York Times (2010) was writing that there was "a 23 percent chance that all patrol units in Colorado Springs will be busy when someone calls the police". Luckily for the city, the fiscal distress was not severe or prolonged enough, and safety concerns remained just concerns.

However, the reduction of municipal programs in Colorado Springs led to increased inequality at the neighborhood level. The closing of the community centers, after-school childcare and public swimming pools, and the elimination of affordable sports programs and summer day camps for low-income residents had, expectedly, a more detrimental effect for families in disadvantaged neighborhoods. Dave Munger, president of the Council of Neighbors and Organizations, which includes about 180 neighborhood groups in Colorado Springs, was one of those who aired the concern that neighborhoods with fewer resources would fare worse than those communities that are more affluent or better organized (Eaton, 2010; Neighborhood Scout, 2019). City Councilmember Jan Martin noted that "the parts of the community that can't afford services will continue to deteriorate, and the neighborhoods that can afford to pay for streetlights, parks, trash removal and medians will continue to prosper and be beautiful. I worry we're creating a city of haves and have-nots" (Patton, 2010).

The inequality problem was exacerbated by cutting bus services by 100,000 hours in 2009, meaning that buses quit running on nights and weekends and some routes were terminated altogether. The issue was especially pronounced in lower income neighborhoods where the vast majority of transit riders had no alternative way to get to work.

Other negative long-term consequences for the community, as with most other municipalities in a similar situation, were economic degradation of the city, brain drain (when professionals move to other areas), and a decline of the tourism industry.

Exit from the Fiscal Distress

Quick and dramatic cutback management measures, while extremely painful in the short run, prevented the city from experiencing continuing deterioration and a potential fiscal emergency in the future and promptly reversed the situation back on a positive growth track. National economic recovery and new revenues coming from marijuana taxes gave an additional positive boost to the city's fiscal health.

Since 2012, the city's high-tech industry, tourism, and service sectors started expanding again. The unemployment rate lowered from 7.3 percent in November 2013 to 4.8 percent in October 2014 and 3.9 percent in October 2015. From June 2015 to September 2018, Colorado Springs added an estimated 24,000 jobs (an average of 7,300 per year). There were 15,576 single-family homes sold in 2018 (Moix, 2019). The Colorado Springs economy has seen a significant diversification with the healthcare, professional and technical assistance, construction, and hospitality industries leading the growth. According to the Economic Forum's annual report, the city's gross metropolitan product (GMP) continued to outpace the national GDP by around one percentage point in 2018. Colorado Springs was among the top 25 percent in the nation in GMP growth at 3.7 percent in 2018.

On top of economic expansion, Colorado Springs received a new stream of revenues. Colorado made changes to the medical marijuana law in 2010 (Ludlum & Ford, 2011). The amendments to the law aimed to limit the number of dispensaries by enacting strict standards of who could apply for a dispensary license. Additionally, the new amendments reduced the number of medical marijuana doctor referrals for patients who truly need them by raising the standards and restrictions on the doctors themselves (Ludlum & Ford, 2011). The 2010 modifications also made medical marijuana subject to sales tax. On July 1, 2010, 230 medical marijuana related businesses with active sales tax licenses were allowed to continue operating in Colorado Springs. Application fees were 7,000 dollars to 15,000 dollars for medical marijuana centers and 1,000 dollars for infused product manufacturers. Registration fees were 5,200 dollars to 13,200 dollars for centers and 2,200 dollars for infused product manufacturers (Ermasova, 2020). Table 10.3 demonstrates the revenues and expenditures in Colorado Springs from 2011 to 2014.

In the 2012 election, new legislation was passed, effectively legalizing not only medical but recreational use of marijuana in Colorado. This brought even more revenue to Colorado Springs. According to the Colorado Amendment 64 Task Force's final report, applicants transferring from medical marijuana dispensaries to recreational marijuana dispensaries were required to pay a 500-dollar application fee (Regulation of Marijuana in Colorado, 2013). The report also stated that, after their first year, new applicants had to pay a 5,000-dollar application fee (Regulation of Marijuana in Colorado, 2013). Nonrefundable fees for dispensary applications ranged from 1,000 dollars to 5,000 dollars, with registration or annual fees typically between 5,000 dollars and 20,000 dollars. Total marijuana revenue has been collected from the 2.9 percent medical and recreational marijuana sales tax, the 10 percent retail marijuana special sales tax, the 15 percent marijuana excise tax, and the retail/medical marijuana application and license fee (Colorado Department of Revenue, 2015).

By late 2011, as sales tax revenues started to increase, the city restored many of the services that had been cut. Some streets lights came back on, and trash pickup resumed. Public restrooms and swimming pools reopened. By 2012, Colorado

TABLE 10.3 Revenue and Expenditures in Colorado Springs from 2011 to 2014 (in 000's)

	2011	*2012*	*2013*	*2014*
REVENUE				
Property taxes, $	24,474	22,897	24,284	22,863
Operating grants and contributions $	25,378	20,122	21,515	15,400
Capital grants and contributions, $	223,137	146,914	118,316	141,120
Investment earnings, $	4,784	20,196	5,173	5,914
Gain on sale of assets, $	748	0	996	327
Other taxes, $	158,830	167,025	175,825	188,951
Charges for services, $	1,445,281	1,328,437	933,402	985,095
Total Revenue	1,881,389	1,285,409	1,359,753	1,279,075
EXPENDITURES				
General government, $	48,067	58,618	57,777	66,869
Public safety, $	149,931	149,169	158,518	168,655
Public works, $	67,068	74,046	80,476	78,015
Health and welfare, $	1,214	1,274	1,058	1,083
Culture and recreation, $	21,789	22,238	22,344	27,009
Total Expenditures	1,544,104	1,721,414	1,246,674	1,237,593
Net assets, beginning	3,137,968	3,316,153	3,055,917	3,008,152
Net assets, ending	3,316,153	3,055,917	3,008,152	3,127,707
Current and other assets	1,662,979	1,368,940	1,899,267	1,541,182
Capital assets	4,990,626	4,819,872	4,983,185	5,247,661
Total assets	6,653,605	6,462,431	6,886,075	6,961,509
Current liabilities	380,494	675,048	287,136	553,680
Long-term liabilities	2,956,957	2,670,821	3,363,866	3,446,394
Total liabilities	3,337,451	3,406,514	3,758,368	3,953,357
Net Assets	3,316,154	3,055,917	3,127,707	3,008,152

Source: Table created by authors based on Audit Reports, CAFRs, and annual budgets of the City of Colorado Springs (2011, 2012, 2013, 2014)

Springs' reserve funds were at their highest level ever, which helped the city cope with devastating floods and wildfires, including the 2012 Waldo Canyon fire that destroyed nearly 350 homes in the area (Patton, 2015). By 2013, the city revenue was already back to pre-recession levels. As local sales tax revenues increased between 2012 and 2014, Colorado Springs made new hires in police, fire, parks, recreation, and cultural services departments (City of Colorado Springs, 2011, 2012, 2014).

In 2015, Colorado Springs brought back and maintained 275 acres of neighborhood parks. The city reestablished evening, weekend, and holiday bus services and extended their services to new locations (City of Colorado Springs, 2015). The 3,500 streetlights were turned back on. In 2015, Colorado Springs provided funding to open a new fire station – Station 21 (in Stetson Hills) and hire 42 new firefighters, 66 police officers, and 28 community service officers (City of Colorado Springs, 2015).

Colorado Springs' total budget for fiscal year 2016 doubled from just a year before to 528 million dollars (City of Colorado Springs, 2016). The general fund made up 267 million dollars of the budget that included 995,000 dollars in funding for 12 additional firefighters to staff the city's newest Fire Station #22, one million dollars in increased funding for the storm water control program, 3.2 million dollars in increased funding for employee pay increases, and 2.2 million dollars in increased funding for closed sworn police and fire pension plans (City of Colorado Springs, 2016).

In 2020, Colorado Springs ranked number 13 on the New York Times 52 Places to Go list and number 10 in TripAdvisor's Top 25 Trending Destinations. In 2018, U.S. News named it the most desirable place to live in the United States (US News, 2019). In 2018, Colorado Springs placed second on U.S. News' list of the 125 Best Places to Live in the USA (US News, 2019). "The fact is, as a result of unprecedented levels of public and private investment, Colorado Springs has taken its place among the great cities of America" said Colorado Springs Mayor John Suthers in his 2018 State of the City address (Moix, 2019). The Metropolitan Policy Program at Brookings found that Colorado Springs was the fastest-growing city for millennials (Brookings, 2019). Thumbtack's annual Small

FIGURE 10.3 Garden of the Gods. Colorado Springs.

Business Friendliness Survey named Colorado Springs to be the fourth most business-friendly city in the country (Thumbtack, 2019).

Conclusions

As it is often the case, multiple fiscal and economic factors contributed to Colorado Springs' downfall and subsequent recovery. The main reasons for the fiscal emergency situation in 2009–2011 were the tax limitations imposed by the local TABOR law, a high dependency on sales tax revenues, a high reliance on the military industrial complex, and, most importantly, the general economic downfall during the Great Recession of 2008–2009.

The local TABOR law imposes an inflation-based cap on the amount of revenue the city can collect. Any revenue over that limit must be returned to taxpayers. James and Wallis (2004) examined the effects of TABOR on Colorado in the decade after its adoption and found that it "severely limit[ed] [Colorado's] capacity to adjust to recessionary cycles" (p. 16). James and Wallis (2004) point out that TABOR brings with it a "ratcheting effect", resultant from a growth formula whereby the revenues that are allowable under TABOR are calculated using spending figures from the previous year. What this means is that Colorado is always locked-in to the results of the previous years and is not as able to "bounce back", (p. 30) from unforeseeable one-time economic downturns or other emergencies. While TABOR was designed to control government revenues and spending, it does not include adequate measures for responding to emergencies or downturns in the economy. Because of TABOR, during and immediately after the Great Recession in 2008–2011, Colorado Springs simply did not have enough financial reserves to cope with lower sales tax collections.

In an effort to decrease expenditures during fiscal emergency, Colorado Springs turned to a *cutback management* practice (see Chapter 5 for the discussion of main budgeting practices for fiscally challenged municipalities) by reducing many core public functions. The city substantially reduced the funding of parks, recreation, and cultural services departments (which led to the closing of city swimming pools, community centers, and minimal park maintenance among other measures), the fire department, and police department. The city turned off streetlights, encouraged early retirements, cut bus services, and decreased the salaries and benefits of city employees. McFarland, the director of finance and economic development programming for the National League of Cities (NLC) argued, however, that the Colorado Springs model cannot be a long-term solution in a fiscal emergency situation: "Cities need to get back to a basic level of delivering services, particularly in public safety" (Patton, 2010).

The Colorado Springs scenario played out in many other municipalities across the U.S. after the Great Recession. Revenues went back up to pre-recession levels and jobs were returning, but some fundamental problems remained. To avoid similar problems in the future, Colorado Springs needs to diversify its revenues and be less dependable on sales taxes that still generate around 50 percent of total revenues in the city. The COVID-19 pandemic created favorable conditions for another potential fiscal emergency situation: the local unemployment rate went from 3 percent in February 2020 to 12.6 percent in April of that year. City tax revenues decreased by 14 percent in March and 22 percent in April. Airport traffic declined by 90 percent in April 2020 (Beckman, 2020).

Remembering the lessons of previous fiscal emergencies, city officials have carefully monitored and managed revenue losses to help minimize the impact on the public. That included cutting 22 million dollars from the 2020 budget, a deferral of capital projects, and imposing a hiring freezes that resulted in 200 fewer employees in 2020 than in 2019 (Beckman, 2020). Without changes in tax policy and infrastructure, Colorado Springs will not be able to withstand the next downturn like the COVID-19 crisis any better than the fiscal emergency in 2009–2011. Without more thoughtful preparations for fiscal emergency, history may repeat itself when the next storm approaches.

References

Ballotpedia. (2009). Colorado Springs Property Tax Increase, Measure 2C. Retrieved January 12, 2021, from https://ballotpedia.org/Colorado_Springs_Property_Tax_Increase,_Measure_2C_(2009)

Beckman, A. (2020, September 17). *State of the City: Colorado Springs Remains Resilient Through Coronavirus and Economic Challenges*. Denver, CO: Colorado Public Radio. Retrieved March 1, 2021, from https://www.cpr.org/2020/09/17/colorado-springs-state-of-the-city-john-suthers-coronavirus-economy/

Brookings. (2019). *The Millennial Generation: A demographic bridge to America's diverse future*. The Brookings Institution. Retrieved March 1, 2021, from https://www.brookings.edu/research/millennials/

Chanacon, D., & Bean, J. (2009). Springs offers streetlight adoption program. *Gazette*. Retrieved March 10, 2020, from http://gazette.com/springs-offers-streetlight-adoption-program/article/95802#oFZs7VtC3ZHOG6JP.99

City of Colorado Springs (2009). *CAFR 2009 Colorado Springs, CO*. Retrieved March 1, 2021, from https://coloradosprings.gov/sites/default/files/finance/Accounting/cafrs/cafr2009final.pdf

City of Colorado Springs (2010). *CAFR 2010 Colorado Springs, CO*. Retrieved March 1, 2021, from https://coloradosprings.gov/sites/default/files/finance/Accounting/cafrs/cafr2010final.

City of Colorado Springs (2011). *CAFR 2011 Colorado Springs, CO*. https://coloradosprings.gov/sites/default/files/finance/Accounting/cafrs/cafr2011final.pdf

City of Colorado Springs (2012). *CAFR 2012 Colorado Springs, CO*. Retrieved March 1, 2021, from https://coloradosprings.gov/sites/default/files/finance/Accounting/cafrs/2012cafr.pdf

City of Colorado Springs (2013). *CAFR 2013 Colorado Springs, CO*. https://coloradosprings.gov/sites/default/files/finance/Accounting/cafrs/2013cafr.pdf

City of Colorado Springs (2014). *CAFR 2014 Colorado Springs, CO*. Retrieved March 1, 2021, from https://coloradosprings.gov/sites/default/files/finance/Accounting/cafrs/2014cafr.pdf

City of Colorado Springs (2015). *CAFR 2015 Colorado Springs, CO*. Retrieved March 1, 2021, from https://coloradosprings.gov/sites/default/files/finance/Accounting/cafrs/cafr2015final.pdf

City of Colorado Springs (2016). *CAFR 2016 Colorado Springs, CO*. Retrieved March 1, 2021, from https://coloradosprings.gov/sites/default/files/finance/Accounting/cafrs/cafr2016final.pdf

Colorado Department of Revenue. (2015). *2015 Colorado marijuana tax data*. Retrieved March 10, 2020, from https://cdor.colorado.gov/data-and-reports/marijuana-data/marijuana-tax-reports

Cooper, M. (2010). Governments go to extremes as the downturn wears on. *The New York Times*, 7 August. Retrieved March 10, 2020, from https://www.nytimes.com/2010/08/07/us/07cutbacksWEB.html

Eaton, L. (2010, April 13). Strapped city cuts and cuts. *Wall Street Journal*. Retrieved March 10, 2020, from https://www.wsj.com/articles/SB10001424052702303411604575168030083419748

Ermasova, N. (2014). Budget priorities of Colorado Springs during economic decline. *Case Study*. Retrieved March 10, 2020, from https://studylib.net/doc/18513565/budget-priorities-of-colorado-springs-during-economic-decline

Ermasova, N. (2020). Fiscal and health effects of U.S. Marijuana Legislation at the state level. *Journal of Social, Political and Economic Studies (JSPES)*, *45*(1–2), 151–177.

Harris, B. H., & Moore, B. D. (2013). *Residential property taxes in The United States Urban-Brookings Tax Policy Center,* 18 November. March 10, 2020, from https://www.taxpolicycenter.org/publications/residential-property-taxes-united-states

James, F. J., & Wallis, A. (2004). Tax and spending limits in Colorado. *Public Budgeting & Finance*, *24*(4), 16–33.

Ludlum, M., & Ford, D. (2011). Colorado's 2010 update to the medical marijuana law: Three problems, three solutions. *Mustang Journal of Law and Legal Studies*, *2*, 73–81.

Moix, C. (2019). *How's the economy? Strong and on the rise*. Retrieved November 1, 2019, from https://springsrelocationguide.com/hows-the-economy/

Neighborhood Scout (2019). *Colorado Springs*. Retrieved November 1, 2019, from https://www.neighborhoodscout.com/co/colorado-springs/crime

Patton, Z. (2010). Colorado Springs' do-it-yourself government. *Governing*, 30 August. Retrieved November 1, 2019, from https://www.governing.com/archive/colorado-springs-diy-government.html

Patton, Z. (2015). The Illusion of Cities' Recovery from the Recession. *Governing*. September. Retrieved November 1, 2019, from https://www.governing.com/archive/gov-recession-recovery-cities-colorado-springs.html

Regulation of Marijuana in Colorado (2013). *Task force report on the implementation of amendment 64*. Retrieved November 1, 2019, from https://digitalcommons.du.edu/cgi/viewcontent.cgi?article=1024&context=law_facpub

Thumbtack (2019). 2018 Small Business Friendliness Survey. *Thumbtack*. Retrieved November 1, 2019, from https://blog.thumbtack.com/our-10th-annual-small-business-friendliness-survey-29efaa6f5b

University of Colorado at Colorado Springs (2006). *Southern Colorado Economic Forum*. Retrieved November 1, 2019, from https://web.archive.org/web/20060825154303/http://web.uccs.edu/scef/data/scef/data/ForumPub2005.pdf

U.S. Census Bureau (2010). *American FactFinder – Results*. Retrieved March 10, 2020, from https://data.census.gov/cedsci/deeplinks?url=https%3A%2F%2Ffactfinder2.census.gov%2F

U.S. News (2019). 125 best places to live in the USA. *U.S. News*. Retrieved November 1, 2021, from https://web.archive.org/web/20170208023442/http://realestate.usnews.com/places/rankings/best-places-to-live

U.S. News (2019). The 25 most desirable places to live in the U.S. in 2018. *U.S. News*. Retrieved November 1, 2021, from https://realestate.usnews.com/real-estate/slideshows/the-25-most-desirable-places-to-live-in-the-us?slide=26

11

CASE STUDY: JEFFERSON COUNTY, AL

Introduction

Jefferson County, AL filed a Chapter 9 bankruptcy petition on November 9, 2011, with 4.23 billion in debt. This was the largest filing of any U.S. municipality before the infamous bankruptcy of the city of Detroit, MI in 2013. But, compared to Detroit, which spent less than 17 months under Chapter 9 bankruptcy protection, the bankruptcy in Jefferson County lasted for over 3.5 years. "Jefferson County has truly experienced a perfect storm of financial ineptitude, bribery and corruption, economic factors, a hostile public, and assaults from the legal community which have transpired to nearly ruin the most populous county in the State of Alabama" (Morris, 2011, p. 2).

Background Information

Jefferson County was founded in 1819 and named in honor of President Thomas Jefferson. It is the most populous county in the State of Alabama (the 2019 Population Estimates by the U.S. Census Bureau) and a home to the most populous city in the state, Birmingham, as well as 34 other municipalities. The county covers approximately 1,124 square miles and is divided into two divisions – the Birmingham and Bessemer Divisions, each having their own judicial district, courthouse, and county offices (Jefferson County, 2019). With a population of 674,271, Jefferson County is the center of the seven-county Birmingham-Hoover Metropolitan Statistical Area (MSA), which ranks as the fiftieth most populated area among the 384 MSAs in the United States (Jefferson County, 2022, p. 34). Jefferson County is considered the economic center of Alabama and encompasses around 18 percent of Alabama's total employment (Jerkins, 2022;

DOI: 10.4324/b23117-11

TABLE 11.1 Demographic, Economic, and Social Factors in Jefferson County in 2010 and 2019

Population	
Population estimates, July 1, 2019, (V2019)	658,573
Population, Census, April 1, 2010	658,466
Race and Hispanic Origin	
White alone, percent	53.1
Black or African American alone, percent	43.5
Asian alone, percent	1.8
Hispanic or Latino, percent	4.1
Housing	
Owner-occupied housing unit rate, 2015–2019, percent	62.7
Median value of owner-occupied housing units, 2015–2019	$159,100
Median gross rent, 2015–2019, $	900
Education	
High school graduate or higher, percent of persons age 25 years+, 2015–2019	90.1%
Bachelor's degree or higher, percent of persons age 25 years+, 2015–2019	33.4 %
Health	
With a disability, under age 65 years, percent, 2015–2019	11.1 %
Persons without health insurance, under age 65 years, percent	10.7%
Economy	
In civilian labor force, total, percent of population age 16 years+, 2015–2019	62.1%
Total accommodation and food services sales, 2012 ($1,000)	1,461,142
Total retail sales per capita, 2012, $	$15,385
Income and Poverty	
Median household income (in 2019 dollars), 2015–2019	$ 53,901
Per capita income in past 12 months (in 2019 dollars), 2015–2019	$ 32,098
Persons in poverty, percent	16.2

Source: Table created by authors based on U.S. Census Bureau (2021).

Morris, 2003). Table 11.1 provides demographic and economic information for Jefferson County in 2010 and 2019.

Roots of the Problem – the County Sewer System

At the heart of the financial struggles in Jefferson County was the local sewer system. In 1993, three residents filed a complaint against Jefferson County, followed by a Motion to Intervene issued by the Cahaba River Society in 1994. In 1996, Bart Slawson (an attorney specializing in environmental law), on behalf of the local residents, filed a lawsuit against Jefferson County, citing that the county sewer system was operating in violation of the Federal Water Pollution Control

Act, also known as the Clean Water Act. The complaint "contended that Jeffco illegally violated its permits through by allowing the bypass of raw sewage and semi-treated sewage to flow into the rivers at various treatment plants", along with "operating two unpermitted automatic discharges" and "failing or refusing to provide for repairs to the sewer collection system" (Morris, 2011, p. 55). The lawsuit alleged that, at the time of the filing, approximately 4,720 violations had occurred. The untreated wastewater containing raw sewage was dumped into the neighboring Black Warrior and Cahaba Rivers. The Cahaba River is the longest free flowing river in the State of Alabama and the main source of drinking water for the city of Birmingham. At a fine of 25,000 dollars per day, the suit sought approximately 118 million dollars in damages from the county (Morris, 2011, p. 44). Instead of a prolonged court battle, Jefferson County agreed to a settlement in November of 1996. In 1996, the United States District Court entered a consent decree that involved the county, the State of Alabama, the Environmental Protection Agency, and other plaintiffs in litigation over pollution caused by the Jefferson County sewer systems.

In an effort to end the lawsuit, Jefferson County agreed to assume all the sewer systems within its jurisdiction. This entailed acquiring 21 individual systems and thousands of miles of sewer line from other local governments (BE & K, 2003, p. 1). It took decades, if not a century, of neglect for sewer problems to deteriorate to the level they were in the 1990s, but, as the U.S. Court stated it, it took a "catastrophic event" for the county to make definitive actions to address the problem (U.S. Court, 2011, p. 3).

Jefferson County acquired sewer systems from the local governments without financial compensation by any of them and without investigation by the county of the systems' conditions. In addition to the acquisition of the existing municipal sewer infrastructure, the consent decree called for a three-phased approach to remedy the failings of the sewer system. In phase one, the county was required to develop a number of planning documents in order to identify and address the scope, methodologies, time frame, and resources needed to evaluate the County Collective System (U.S. Bankruptcy Court, 2011, p. 20). The second phase necessitated the county to analyze and report on the extent of rehabilitation needed for the county sewer system and the county's wastewater treatment plants in order to meet the Consent Decree (U.S. Bankruptcy Court, 2011, p. 21). The third phase of the Consent Decree included the actual implementation of the Waste Treatment System Capital Improvement Plan (WTSCIP).

In the beginning, things seemed to be moving in the right direction. Jefferson County's 1997–1998 capital budget included 50 projects from the Waste Treatment System Capital Improvement Plan (WTSCIP) and 54 additional sewer-related projects. The number of projects in the capital budget was more than double that required by the Consent Decree. (Morris, 2011, p. 52). However, in 2002, Jefferson County announced that the depreciation expense increased by 43 million dollars as a result of the 1.4 billion dollars in additional municipal sewer assets that the county acquired (Jefferson County, 2002, p. 26).

Besides high sewer-related expenses, in 2002, Jefferson County's governmental fund balances decreased by approximately 33 million dollars or 14.8 percent. The enterprise fund's equity decreased by 101 million dollars or 6.9 percent (Jefferson County, 2002). Over 22 million dollars was used for expansion of a courthouse and jail renovations, and another 4 million dollars was utilized for road construction. These expenditures were covered by the Capital Projects Funds. The county faced not only increasing capital but also operating expenses. Public safety experienced a large increase in personnel costs due to increased security needs at County facilities. In addition, 1.3 million dollars was paid for the contract to provide health services to jail inmates in 2002 (Jefferson County, 2002). On the revenue side, however, Jefferson County recorded only four million dollars in proceeds from the service charges and money received from other governments (Jefferson County, 2002, p. 18).

To cover increasing expenses, the county was issuing more debt. According to the U.S. Bankruptcy Court (2011), the majority of Jefferson County's debt between 1997 and 2003 was created by warrants issued to finance the construction and repair of a sewer system. Such warrants totaled almost 3.7 billion dollars during that period of time and had an unpaid principal balance of around 3.2 billion dollars. At the end 2002, the county had 268 million dollars outstanding in general obligation warrants and 2.437 billion dollars outstanding in sewer revenue bonds (Jefferson County, 2002, p. 27). In 2002, the interest expense on sewer revenue bonds was 114 million dollars, plus a 43-million-dollar additional depreciation expense on municipal sewer assets (Jefferson County, 2002).

The county issued and refinanced several bond issues to repair and expand its sewer system over the next several years. These special revenue warrants have been utilized for capital project financing such as water systems, sewer systems, and other needs. The special revenue warrants are attractive to municipal issuers because in Alabama such warrants do not require a vote by citizens, while bond issues do. The revenues of the sewer system were the sole source of repayment on the warrant debt, which, ironically, made residents pay for the mismanagement of the sewer systems by their municipalities (U.S. Bankruptcy Court, 2011). From a total of 876 million dollars designated to sewer repairs "about $315 million, 36 percent, went to initiatives not required by the court. Much of that money was used to build new lines and treatment services in growing and undeveloped areas" (Blackledge & Howell, 2003). Walsh (2012) describes one of the examples of such mismanagement of capital projects:

> Rather than replacing more than 2,000 miles of decrepit sewer pipes, the county dispensed contracts to build water treatment plants, pumping stations and administrative buildings, some on slag heaps left behind by closed steel mills. In an attempt to expand the system and add new ratepayers, the

> county tried to bore a giant tunnel beneath the Cahaba River, Birmingham's main source of drinking water. But the tunnel was so unstable that the endeavor was abandoned. The county spent millions just to extract the boring machine, which had become entombed underground.
>
> *(pp. 4–5)*

The tunnel cost 19 million dollars and is now called "the Tunnel to Nowhere".

Serious problems arose when the county entered into several risky financial transactions in the early 2000s, switching from close to 99 percent fixed interest rate bonds to nearly 95 percent auction rate securities.[1] The switch occurred when JPMorgan Chase was able "to persuade the county to agree to a bond deal with terms that included complicated interest-rate swaps.[2] Those swaps blew up during the financial crisis of 2008, leaving the county with even more debt than it had started with" (Walsh, 2012, p. 5). The auction rate securities market failed in February 2008 at the onset of the Great Recession of 2008–2009 and Jefferson County was stuck paying extremely high interest rates on these securities (U.S. Bankruptcy Court, 2011).

> The County's sewer system debt's fate was sealed, and default was likely to follow with respect to the warrants. Despite being a simplistic explanation, the County's use of auction rate warrants was essentially taking advantage of short-term interest rates to finance long term debt. To do this requires the existence of a market for short term debt refinancing, and when it became nonexistent, a critical part of the scheme collapsed.
>
> *(U.S. Bankruptcy Court, 2011, p. 7)*

Ultimately, it was not as much of a desire to save on interest payments but corruption among county officials that led to the switch to risky auction-rate securities. According to Morris (2011), "due to bribery, corruption, and general mismanagement, the costs for rehabilitating the sewer skyrocketed" (p. 1). Larry Langford, the former mayor of Birmingham, was the president of the Jefferson County commission when he orchestrated the refinancing of the sewer debt to avoid large rate increases on sewer customers. Langford presided over the Jefferson County Commission during the height of a series of variable rate auction and bond swaps that led to the run-up of the 3.2-billion-dollar debt. He was convicted of steering friends into the bond deals in exchange for bribes (Gates, 2010). "The political arena was spoiled by corruption, greed, and a lack of proper planning for growth. These factors coupled with negligence have led directly to the county's demise as a body politic" (Morris, 2011, p. 39). In October 2009, Langford was convicted on sixty-one federal charges for bribery, money laundering, mail and wire fraud, conspiracy, and filing a false tax return (Gates, 2010). Langford is serving a 15-year prison sentence in Kentucky. In addition to his time behind bars, Langford was sentenced to a three-year probation and ordered to pay nearly 367,000 dollars in financial penalties (Gates, 2010, 2014). Another County Commissioner, Gary White, was sentenced to ten years in federal prison and 44,900 dollars in fines and restitution for his role in the sewer scandal (Morris, 2011, p. 81). In October of 2006, another important party in the sewer scandal, the Director of Environmental Services Department, Swann, was convicted on 18 counts of "conspiracy, bribery and mail fraud" (WSFA, 2006). "Most of the charges revolved around Swann accepting bribes and services from various contractors on the sewer project" (Morris, 2011, p. 61). Swann was ultimately sentenced to eight years in prison and a "fine of $250,000 and $355,533 in restitution" (Gordon, 2010). In total, 17 people were convicted of bribery and fraud in the entire sewer scandal (PEW Charitable Trusts, 2013, p. 26).

The Fiscal Emergency Situation

Receiver

In July 2009, Jefferson County began missing due payments on its debt (Jefferson County, 2009, 2011, 2013). Howell-Moroney and Hall (2011) point out that

> following failed auctions for sewer debt in April 2008, major bond rating companies downgraded Jefferson County, Alabama's bond rating to D (default) triggering massive mandatory payments by the county to its creditors. At the time of writing, the county teeters on the brink of actual default and bankruptcy, unable to pay service on its $3.3 billion sewer debt portfolio. *(p. 232)*

The situation worsened further when forbearance agreements between the county and its creditors expired on September 30, 2009 (Morris, 2011). Before filing for Chapter 9 bankruptcy, Jefferson County tried to restructure its sewer system indebtedness by using a third party, a receiver. "John S. Young, Jr., LLC, a Delaware limited liability company, was appointed receiver for the County's sewer system and the Indenture Trustee was awarded a judgment of $515,942,500.11 against the County" (U.S. Bankruptcy Court, 2011, p. 8).

The receiver had full power and authority to effectively administer, operate, and protect the sewer system. These powers included the right to fix rates and charges, hire and lay off system staff, and terminate or modify outstanding system contracts and enter new ones. A court-appointed receiver, however, was not given greater powers than the municipality. According to the National Association of Bond Lawyers. (2015).

> the receiver faced the same legal and financial limitations as the County, including legal and practical limits to rate increases, federal environmental and employment mandates, state-law limits on hiring and contracting,

> and lack of support from the state legislature. The receiver did not raise rates and failed to broker a settlement and was divested of control by the County's bankruptcy filing.
>
> *(p. 13)*

In one of its first steps, John S. Young, Jr., LLC, the sewer receiver, laid off excessive employees and introduced a required training for the remaining employees on how to best maintain, repair, and improve the sewer system. The receiver captured about three million dollars in lost revenues by enforcing collections from non-paying customers and identifying consumers who hooked illegally onto the sewer system without paying Jefferson County.

The receiver additionally looked at various means of increasing revenue, including non-user fees and other fees on residents and businesses located in the county who were not connected to the sewer system. On November 1, 2011, the new Jefferson County commissioners agreed to increase the sewer rate of 8.2 percent per year for next three years (2012, 2013, 2014), followed by up to 3.25 percent per year increases after these three years. The average sewer rates increased over 300 percent since 1997 and would increase by an additional 527 percent. These sorts of increases would take the average monthly residential sewer bill of 63 dollars per month up to 360 dollars per month (571 percent increase) under the Indenture Trustee's wishes. Recognizing the economic and legal limits on potential rate increases, the receiver studied both the structure of the rates and the ability of users to pay increased rates. The plans to increase rates were, however, paused when the county filed for bankruptcy.

The County's Fiscal Problems

On September 16, 2011, the Jefferson County Commission approved a term sheet with the receiver, establishing the framework for a settlement with its sewer system creditors. But the settlement was never finalized, in part because the involved parties were not in agreement (U.S. Bankruptcy Court, 2011).

The fiscal problems amplified when the Alabama Supreme Court eliminated an occupation tax on workers' salaries in 2011. This tax provided more than a quarter of the county's general fund revenue (Wright & Chandler, 2009). Jefferson County lost over 75 million dollars a year when the occupational tax levied on incomes and a business license fee was found unconstitutional by the Alabama Supreme Court.

After failing at restructuring its sewer system indebtedness and losing a large part of its general tax revenues, the county closed many county facilities, including some of the county courts, laid off over 500 employees, eliminated overtime and sick days, cut work hours to as low as 32 per week for remaining hourly employees, and suspended hiring in many job classifications. Capital expenditures have been drastically reduced as have other expenditures.

Retirement funds were also not funded. According to the Jefferson County Commission Audited Financial Statement (2011), "the OPEB was zero percent funded. The actuarial accrued liability was $80,163,000, and the actuarial value of assets was $0, resulting in an unfunded accrued liability of $80,163,000" on September 30, 2011 (p. 108).

Jefferson County had a difficult time managing the fiscal emergency for one other reason. Alabama is a Dillion's Rule[3] state, and therefore the State Legislature determines how much authority counties can have. Under the Dillion's Rule system, Jefferson Country was acting under the state's permission to raise revenue. This proved to be very difficult, as many state lawmakers do not want their names to be associated with a tax increase and therefore are wary about giving counties permission to levy taxes. Additionally, Alabama, has a limited state government.[4] The state prioritizes limited government and lacks the experts needed to monitor local municipalities' financial situations and to provide expertise to help local governments in times of need (PEW Charitable Trusts, 2013, p. 25). Governors Robert Bentley and Robert Riley convened several meetings with county-elected officials and business leaders to find a solution to the fiscal emergency in Jefferson County. Governor Robert Riley also unsuccessfully tried to negotiate an agreement with the county's creditors (PEW Charitable Trusts, 2013).

Jefferson County Credit Rating Changes

As the situations with auction-rate securities, debt accumulation, and corruption unfolded, these negative events started to get reflected in the county's credit ratings. On March 27, 2008, Moody's lowered Jefferson County's issuer's credit ratings from Aa2 to Baa1. Later that year the ratings were lowered below the investment grade to Ba3 on July 31, 2008 and further down to B3 on September 25, 2008. On April 28, 2009, the rating fell to Caa1. A few months after the county applied for bankruptcy on November 9, 2011, Moody's lowered its credit ratings to the lowest point they have been at during the entire ordeal, Caa3. Jefferson County exited bankruptcy only on June 4, 2013 (Bloomberg, 2013; Church et al., 2013). It took credit rating agencies several more months to revise ratings. Moody's lifted the county rating to Ba3 on February 18, 2014, then to Baa3 on December 8, 2015, and to A3 on June 27, 2017. Moody's issuer's rating of Jefferson County has stayed that way since then.

County's Actions to Exit Bankruptcy

As is usually the case, the strategies used to bring the county out of bankruptcy included a mix of tax increases, renegotiations of debt obligations with the creditors, and extreme budget cuts.

Fees and Taxes

After the bankruptcy filing, the county's 8 senators and 18 representatives were split on proposals asking the GOP-controlled legislature to allow Jefferson County to impose new taxes that would help it cover the budget gap and resolve the bankruptcy faster. "Matt Fabian, a managing director of Municipal Market Advisors, call[ed] Alabama an example of 'state exacerbation' instead of 'intervention'" (PEW Charitable Trusts, 2013, p. 26).

After a failed attempt to increase sewer fees in 2011, Jefferson County filed a plan in federal court to exit the bankruptcy in part by trying to raise sewer fees again in June 2013. This time the residential rates were increased by 7.89 percent annually for four years and 3.49 percent afterward for the foreseeable future (Jefferson County, 2009, 2011). An additional five-dollar base charge began earlier, in November 2012, for all sewer customers. In the years 2012–2014, those user rates would match the residential user increases and decrease to 3.49 percent afterward for the foreseeable future. Based on this plan to exit bankruptcy, Jefferson County would be able to raise 14.7 billion dollars based on the sewer fees' collection to pay over the 40-year sewer revenue restructuring financing plan (Wright, 2019).

To provide a more complete picture of county revenues at the time of bankruptcy, it should be noted that besides increasing sewer fees, residents of Jefferson County faced sales taxes that are among the highest in the nation. Following the bankruptcy, the county additionally substantively increased its property tax rates. Jefferson County's sales tax rate is 1 percent, in addition to the 4 percent Alabama sales tax. Some cities and local governments in Jefferson County collect additional local sales taxes, which can be as high as 5 percent. Jefferson County's maximum sales tax rate of 10 percent is a higher maximum than 81 percent of Alabama counties and higher than 93 percent of counties nationwide (SalesTaxHandbook, 2022).

Tax revenues are not a function of the Jefferson County Board of Equalization (Jefferson County, 2016). Property values are based on the calculations of a computer-assisted mass appraisal system provided by the Alabama Department of Revenue's Appraisal Manual. The new appraisal manual adopted in 2015 led to an increase of property values and, consequently, a sharp increase of property taxes in Jefferson County in 2019 (Jefferson County, 2019). Pierre (2019) described the results of implementing a new appraisal manual in Jefferson County in 2019: "we found buildings where property taxes are going up in some cases 85 percent, and it's everything from small barbecue joints in places like Avondale to skyscrapers downtown. We found a skyscraper that their tax bill is going to go up by more than $500,000" (p. 1).

Negotiations with Creditors

The County was also able to renegotiate and lower the amount of debt obligations with creditors. Jefferson County issued 1.84 billion dollars in new debt obligations to refinance three billion dollars in sewer debt in 2011 (Wright, 2019). Jefferson County's lawyers were negotiating with roughly 4,000 creditors, from suppliers to hedge funds (Walsh, 2012).

Church et al. (2013) explained the negotiation process with creditors:

> JPMorgan Chase & Co., seven hedge funds and a group of bond insurers, which together hold $2.4 billion, or approximately 78 percent, of the sewer debt, agreed to support the plan. Under the plan, JPMorgan, which holds $1.22 billion of debt, will forgive $842 million. Taken together with a previous settlement, the bank will have agreed to pay the county and waive sewer obligations totaling $1.57 billion.
>
> *(p. 1)*

According to Wright (2019), it took 20 months for Jefferson County to reach a settlement with JPMorgan and other creditors in court. Since the November 2011 bankruptcy filing, the county has spent nearly 30 million dollars on attorneys and other advisers.

Expenditure Cuts

To pay its way out of bankruptcy, Jefferson County turned to radical austerity urbanism practices, among other measures. According to PEW Charitable Trusts (2013), Jefferson County laid off hundreds of workers, closed satellite courthouses, crammed its jails, stopped responding to minor traffic accidents, and reduced mowing, weeding, and repaving across the county. Overall, from 2011 to 2013, Jefferson County decreased expenditures by 119 million dollars (Jefferson County, 2011, 2013, 2015). Walsh (2012) described the results of these extreme budget cuts:

> One county jail here is so crowded that some inmates sleep on the floor, while the other county jail, a few miles down the road, sits empty. There is no money for the second one anymore. The county roads here need paving, and the tax collector needs help. There is no money for them, either. There is no money for holiday D.U.I. checkpoints, litter patrols or overtime pay at the courthouse. None for crews to pull weeds or pick up road kill.
>
> *(p. 1)*

The county went as far as to eliminate inpatient care at the public hospital due to fast-rising costs. The public hospital was reorganized beginning from 2013 as an ambulatory and urgent care facility (PEW Charitable Trusts, 2013, p. 24). Before that, in 2012, the commission voted to close the inpatient care unit at Cooper Green Mercy Hospital (Jefferson County, 2011, p. 141). In 2011, Jefferson County's Commission tried to sell the nursing home facility to a not-for-profit health care organization for 9.5 million dollars, but the agreement was not reached. In September 2011, the commission attempted to sell 238 licensed beds at the nursing home for 8.3 million dollars, but in this case, the Alabama State Health Planning and Development Agency opposed this sale. As Abott and Singla (2021) wrote about Jefferson County experiences during bankruptcy "Jefferson County has even canceled municipal elections scheduled for this August. It seems that there's no money for voting booths, either" (p. 2). Jefferson County's road crews are

> patching only big potholes; resurfacing can wait. The tax collector has laid off four agents, at a savings of $180,000. But the math of bankruptcy doesn't always work well. Last year, those four agents collected $2.7 million from delinquent taxpayers, so it's possible the county is losing money in this arrangement.
>
> *(Walsh, 2012, p. 7)*

Post-bankruptcy Improvements

While a lot of extreme measures were taken to exit bankruptcy, ongoing advances in budgeting and financial reporting practices, investment in capital infrastructure, economic development, and business attraction and retention are some of the key contributors to the continuing long-term improvements of the financial position of the county.

Improvements in Budgeting Practices

After exiting bankruptcy, Jefferson County put a lot of efforts into improving its budgeting practices. One of the positive developments in fiscal administration was the introduction of long-term revenues and expenditure forecasts. The revenues and expenditures are projected five years out beyond the budget year, based on a previous five-year trend now. The revenue forecasts remain very conservative (Jefferson County, 2022, p. 11).

To reduce financial risks, Jefferson County also tries to maintain a general fund reserve of approximately 10 percent of annual expenditures (Jefferson County, 2022b, p. 16). To ensure long-term financial health, Jefferson County has established three separate reserve funds (the Economic Uncertainty Fund, the Budget Stabilization Fund, and the Catastrophic Event Fund). As of September 30, 2020, the county's total cash reserve balance in these three emergency reserve accounts was approximately 36.1 million dollars.

To improve transparency, the Jefferson County, Alabama, information portal has been established by the Information Technology Department. This portal contains County Commission and Committee agendas and minutes, county news, audit, budget, and tax information, and a lot of other information and data related to county activities and regulations.

Infrastructure Development

Jefferson County used new and innovative ways to upgrade public infrastructure by encouraging regional cooperation in project implementation. At the end of fiscal year 2020, the Jefferson County Commission invested 2.45 billion dollars in a broad range of capital projects, including buildings, roads, bridges, public safety equipment, and sewer lines (Jefferson County, 2020, p. 18). Continued capital infrastructure maintenance and development is very important, because during and after bankruptcy it is more critical than ever to effectively prioritize where capital funding should be spent, weighing the costs and benefits of competing investments projects, and understanding the implications of deferred construction and maintenance. Some of the planned capital projects included renovations of the 2121 Building (high-rise office building) and the County Youth Detention facility (Jefferson County, 2020). Jefferson County prioritizes capital projects, based on the value of safe and secure rehabilitation, and it allocated 250,000 dollars to begin renovations for the county's Youth Detention facility. The county has allocated an additional 14.8 million dollars to construct a new animal control facility (Jefferson County, 2022b, p. 16). The costs of all roads that need extra work is upward of 160 million dollars from 2022 to 2026 (Jefferson County, 2020, p. 11). The Total Capital Road Construction Fund is projected to spend 16,550,681 dollars in 2022 (Jefferson County, 2020, p. 7).

Jefferson County developed a Master Plan in Environmental Services to govern sewer expansion needs and to plan for the next five years to resolve the stream water issues (Jefferson County, 2020, p. 29). Sewer rates have increased yearly and are expected to increase annually in the next 40 years, as the county repays sewer system creditors and to cover the cost of bringing the system into compliance with the Clean Water Act. "Costs of this undertaking are exceeding $3 billion (not counting interest payments), and the County is looking to refinance the sewer debt in 2023 Warrants" (Jefferson County, 2020, p. 29).

Economic Development and Business Attraction and Retention

Jefferson County is at the center of Alabama's automotive manufacturing region, with four auto makers within an 80-mile radius of downtown Birmingham. Some of Alabama's largest employers are based in Jefferson County, including the University of Alabama at Birmingham (UAB), Regions Financial Corp., and St. Vincent's Health System (Jerkins, 2022).

According to the City of Birmingham Comprehensive Plan (2018), the development of Birmingham's economy is shaped by its "economic building blocks": human resources, entrepreneurial climate and incentives, physical infrastructure, economic institutions, and general quality of life. Strengthening these economic building blocks is an essential focus for economic development success, with a particular emphasis on building the community's "human capital". Thornton (2020) pointed out the key advantages of Birmingham: "workforce training programs, which are a key component of the support system we have in place in Alabama to help companies in many different industries find and develop the skilled workers they need to achieve success" (p. 1). Alabama workforce training agency is the first state workforce training organization in the United States to earn international certification for its quality management system. Alabama's workforce training agency's economic impact on Alabama was calculated at seven billion dollars. The Jefferson County Workforce Investment Board (WIB) has similar responsibilities specific to Jefferson County, including planning, coordination, monitoring, and evaluation of workforce development services. It is managed and staffed by the Jefferson County Community and Economic Development Department (City of Birmingham Comprehensive Plan, 2018, p. 10.9). The full-service Career Center works closely with the Jefferson County WIB's Intensive Services Center, which subsidizes on-the-job training for newly hired workers and "provides career testing and counseling, supportive services referrals, and adult basic education, and can provide clients who are most in need of career skill development with Individual Training Accounts, which can be used to pay the costs of training by certified providers" (City of Birmingham Comprehensive Plan, 2018, p. 10.10).

Jefferson County, in cooperation with the cities within its boundaries, now puts a lot of effort in investing in economic development and business attraction and retention that includes: (1) streamlining the process of starting a business and doing business with the city, (2) providing incentives to startups and other small businesses, (3) providing incentives for vacant or derelict property renovations, (4) establishing a business retention service, (5) developing technology parks, (6) establishing a microloan program, and (7) improving transparency of existing programs and incentives (City of Birmingham Comprehensive Plan, 2018, p. 10.9).

The City of Birmingham Mayor's Office of Economic Development (OED), for example, describes such economic incentives as "business retention and expansion; administering the city's 10,000-acre Enterprise Zone; offering a number of federal, state, and local economic development financing programs; administering the city's Foreign Trade Zone; and offering sites to new and expanding businesses at city-owned industrial parks" (City of Birmingham Comprehensive Plan, 2018, p. 10.21). OED partners with the Birmingham Business Alliance, REV Birmingham, Urban Impact, Birmingham Construction Industry Authority, and the Jefferson County Development Authority. In 2012, the Innovation Depot, an award-winning 140,000 square-foot technology incubator, was created. It housed 84 companies with 460 employees in fields of life sciences and information technology. Harbert Venture Partners facilitates equity growth to early-stage information technology and healthcare companies primarily across the Southeastern U.S. The Regional Planning Commission of Greater Birmingham's Accounts Receivable Revolving Loan Fund provides low-cost, short-term working capital loans of up to 25,000 dollars to tenants of the Innovation Depot and the Bessemer Business Incubation System (City of Birmingham Comprehensive Plan, 2018, p. 10.15).

The city of Birmingham uses tax incentives, in some instances, for business recruitment, retention, and expansion. These are typically in the form of sales tax rebates over a period of years and cash grants. Birmingham "conducts economic impact analyses before deciding to grant incentives in order to ensure that they have a strong positive economic impact on the city. It also includes claw-back provisions if employment goals are not met" (City of Birmingham Comprehensive Plan, 2018, p. 10.22). As a result of these initiatives and economic incentives, Business Facilities magazine ranked Birmingham as one of the top cities for business climate among their size, and Alabama was placed fourth for business climate (Thornton, 2020).

In 2019, the County attracted 456 million dollars in capital investment along with 1,100 jobs (Jefferson County, 2020, p. 13). This included investing around ten million dollars annually in business development such as a 2.5-million-dollar commitment for the World Games 2022.[5] The World Games 2022 are planned to be held in Birmingham, AL from July 7 to July 17, 2022. Birmingham has announced that the World Police and Fire Games will be coming to the city in 2025 and would attract new businesses and tourists to the county. In 2019, Jefferson County attracted 456 million dollars in new capital investment and more than 1,100 jobs, according to the Alabama Department of Commerce (Thornton, 2020).

Jefferson County's economy is now also more diversified as healthcare, banking, and professional services emerged to become leading industries in the metropolitan area. Heavy industry continues to be an important component of the local economy as well. Automotive manufacturers like Mercedes-Benz, Honda, and Hyundai all have major automobile assembly facilities within an 85-mile radius of Jefferson County. The county's economy has benefited a lot from its proximity to these major manufacturing facilities (Nelson, 2021). The county's central southeast location became a central logistics hub for national retailers and service providers like Amazon, Lowe's Home Improvement, Home Depot, Buffalo Rock, and FedEx. In 2020, Amazon and FedEx announced major expansions in Jefferson County (Jefferson County, 2020, p. 13). In addition, the healthcare sector has become a primary driver of economic activity in the Birmingham-Hoover MSA and is anchored by the University of Alabama at Birmingham. The University of Alabama at Birmingham received over 300 million dollars in research awards from the National Institute of Health in 2020 (Jefferson County, 2020). According to the 2020 New and Expanding Industry Report, with 1,211 new jobs and about 362 million dollars invested in new and expanded projects, Jefferson County was number one in the number of jobs created (Jefferson County, 2020, p. 39).

Conclusions

Pollution of the two neighboring rivers, a failed market for auction-rate securities, the major bond instrument the county was using to borrow money for required sewer repairs and other infrastructure projects, financial mismanagement, corruption among county administration, and a staggering amount of debt are some of the major problems that led Jefferson County to bankruptcy.

To lower expenditures during bankruptcy, Jefferson County drastically increased sewer rates, closed many county facilities, laid off over 500 employees, eliminated overtime and sick days, cut work hours to as low as 32 hours per week for the remaining hourly employees, suspended hiring in many job classifications, and drastically reduced capital expenditures. Ultimately, taxpayers in Jefferson County are the ones who ended up paying for the mismanaged sewer system issues, in some cases costing more than 11,000 dollars per person. The debt from the sewer system crisis has been paid by taxpayers through higher residential sewer rates, high interest rates on sewer bonds, bond insurance, and an overall increase in taxes and fees for construction work. As a result of these extreme budget cuts, many negative consequences occurred, as there was a lack of funding for police, fire, libraries, and hospitals in Jefferson County.

During restructuring and exit from bankruptcy, Jefferson County implemented administrative innovations in budgeting, established three separate reserve funds, implemented long-term revenue and expenditure forecasting practices, created a five-year Capital Improvement Program, increased spending on capital projects, and invested heavily in economic development. Jefferson County maintains a fiscally conservative budgeting process. The county publishes a five-year strategic plan where one of main goals is to create quality infrastructure that is efficient and serves the community.

While the fiscal and underlying environmental issues and corruption struggles lasted for years, dramatic actions during the bankruptcy process and subsequent budget and economic reforms seem to bear fruit. Today, the county has restored its credit ratings and overall appears to be in much stronger shape and form.

Notes

1 Auction rate securities (ARS) are the long-term debt obligations with a variable interest rate that is reset regularly (typically every 7, 28, or 35 days) in a Dutch auction process. So, a rate is set at the lowest interest, at which buyers are willing to purchase all of the securities of potential sellers. ARS owners have the option to hold bonds regardless of new interest rate, bid to hold bonds at a specified rate, or request to sell regardless of the interest rate set at the auction. In February 2008 80% of the national auction rate securities market failed when there was insufficient demand for these securities from investors (no bidders) and the lead underwriters (Citigroup, UBS AG, Morgan Stanley, and Merrill Lynch), who acted as bidders of last resort in past declined to purchase them as well citing the liquidity concerns. As a result, investors in ARS were stuck with the securities that they were unable to sell since the market for these securities basically ceased to exist and "issuers were often stuck paying double-digit rates as the investors who remained in the market exacted a greater risk premium" (Ross, 2017).

2 Bond swap is when an investor chooses to sell one bond and subsequently purchase another bond with the proceeds from the sale in order to take advantage of the current market environment.

3 The Dillon Rule is the principal that local government only exercises (1) powers expressly granted by the state, (2) powers necessarily and fairly implied from the grant of power, and (3) powers crucial to the existence of local government.

4 Snider (2018) explained that limited government "means that there will be some spaces, some needs or hopes of the community or community members, that are not met by a central power. In states that don't deem limited government as a highly as Alabama, these gaps tend to be filled by government. In a state like Alabama, however, these spaces are befittingly left to be filled by the private sector" (p. 2).

5 The World Games is an 11-day international multi-sport event organized with the support of the International Olympic Committee.

References

Abott, C., & Singla, A. (2021). Service solvency and quality of life after municipal bankruptcy. *Journal of Political Institutions and Political Economy*, *2*(2), 249–280.

BE & K. (2003). *Jefferson County Program Review*. Birmingham, AL: Programmatic Review.

Blackledge, B., & Howell, V. (2003). Third of sewer costs not ordered by court. *The Birmingham News*, 10 June 10.

Bloomberg (2013). Jefferson County files to end Bankruptcy, Adjust Debt. *Bloomberg*, 1 July. Retrieved June 10, 2021, from https://www.bloomberg.com/news/articles/2013-06-30/jefferson-county-files-to-end-bankruptcy-adjust-debt

Church, S., Newkirk, M., & Edwards, K. (2013). Jefferson County, creditors reach deal to end bankruptcy. *Bloomberg*, 5 June. Retrieved January 12, 2021, from https://www.bloomberg.com/news/articles/2013-06-04/jefferson-county-reaches-deal-with-creditors-on-bankruptcy-exit

City of Birmingham Comprehensive Plan (2018). *Chapter 10 – Reinforcing the building blocks of the economy*. Retrieved February 20, 2020, from www.birminghamal.gov › uploads › 2017/08

Gates, V. (2010). Ex-Alabama mayor sentenced in sewer debt case. *Reuters*, 10 March. Retrieved January 12, 2021, from https://www.reuters.com/article/us-usa-alabama-langford/ex-alabama-mayor-sentenced-in-sewer-debt-case-idUSTRE6243GZ20100305

Gates, V. (2014). Alabama County Ratepayers Say Sewer Bankruptcy Settlement Too Pricey, *Reuters*, 21 July. Retrieved January 12, 2021, from https://www.reuters.com/article/usa-bankruptcy-jeffersoncounty/alabama-county-ratepayers-say-sewer-bankruptcy-settlement-too-pricey-idUSL2N0PW1SN20140721

Gordon, R. K. (2010). Judge orders garnishment from ex-Jefferson County environmental chief Jack Swann's retirement. *Alcom*, 19 February 2010. Retrieved February 19, 2022 from www.al.com/spotnews/2010/02/post_472.html; http://blog.al.com/spotnews/2010/02/post_472.html

Howell-Moroney, M. E., & Hall, J. L. (2011). Waste in the Sewer: The Collapse of Accountability and Transparency in Public Finance in Jefferson County, Alabama. *Public Administration Review*, *71*(2), 232–242.

Jefferson County (2002). *Comprehensive annual financial report 2002*. Retrieved January 12, 2021, from https://jeffersoncountyoh.com/static/documents/118/189133122002_Annual_Financial_Report.pdf

Jefferson County (2009). *Jefferson County Commission audited financial statement*. Retrieved January 12, 2021, from https://www.jccal.org/Sites/Jefferson_County/AppData/DocLib/Main/JeffersonCountyCommissionAuditFY2009.pdf

Jefferson County (2011). *Jefferson County commission audited financial statement*. Retrieved January 12, 2021, from https://www.jccal.org/Sites/Jefferson_County/AppData/DocLib/Main/2011ISSUEDJeffersonCountyCommissionFinancialStatements.pdf

Jefferson County (2013). *Jefferson County commission audited financial statement*. Retrieved January 12, 2021, from https://www.jeffcomo.org/Archive.aspx?AMID=38
Jefferson County (2015). *Jefferson County commission audited financial statement*. Retrieved January 12, 2021, from https://www.jccal.org/Sites/Jefferson_County/AppData/DocLib/Main/2015%20ISSUED%20Jefferson%20County%20Commission%20FS.pdf
Jefferson County (2016). *Jefferson County commission audited financial statement*. Retrieved January 12, 2021, from https://www.jccal.org/Sites/Jefferson_County/AppData/DocLib/Main/2015%20ISSUED%20Jefferson%20County%20Commission%20FS.pdf
Jefferson County (2019). *Property tax notices*. Retrieved January 22, 2022, from https://www.jccal.org/Default.asp?ID=1982&pg=Property+Tax+Notices
Jefferson County (2020). *Comprehensive annual financial report 2020*. Retrieved January 12, 2021, from https://www.jccal.org/Sites/Jefferson_County/AppData/DocLib/Main/FY2020%20CAFR%204.30.21%20Submitted.pdf
Jefferson County (2022). *Official operating budget 2022*. Retrieved January 12, 2022, from https://files4.1.revize.com/jeffersoncountynew/Budget/2022%20Budget/Budget%20in%20Brief.pdf
Jerkins, E. (2022). Jefferson County profile. *Birmingham Business Alliance*. Retrieved February 20, 2022, from https://www.birminghambusinessalliance.com/jeffersoncounty
Morris, L. (2003). *Jefferson County Program Review*. Birmingham, AL: Programmatic Review.
Morris, L. (2011). *Jefferson county, Alabama: A perfect storm of ethical, financial, political, and market failures*. [PhD Dissertation. Auburn, AL: Department of Political Science].
National Association of Bond Lawyers (2015). *Municipal bankruptcy: A guide for public finance attorneys* (3rd ed.). Retrieved October 12, 2021, from www.bradley.com/-/media/files/insights/publications/2018/12/municipal-bankruptcy-a-guide-for-public-finance-attorneys-3rd-edition.pdf
Nelson, A. (2021). Jefferson County Commissioners pass 2022 budget with no tax increase. *Courier Express*, 16 December. Retrieved January 12, 2021, from https://www.thecourierexpress.com/jeffersonian_democrat/news/local/jefferson-county-commissioners-pass-2022-budget-with-no-tax-increase/article_f5397a32-820d-5be1-adac-42cda862db96.html
PEW Charitable Trusts (2013). *The state role in local government financial distress*. Retrieved December 23, 2021, from www.pewtrusts.org/~/media/assets/2016/04/pew_state_role_in_local_government_financial_distress.pdf
Pierre, J. (2019). *Tax bills increase for many in Jefferson County*. Retrieved February 20, 2022, from https://birminghamwatch.org/tax-bills-increase-many-jefferson-county/Order of the Circuit Court of Jefferson County (2012, September 22). Jefferson County, Alabama. In 01-CV-2009¬02318.00 (465 B.R. 243, 249, Bankr. N.D. Ala. 2012).
SalesTaxHandbook (2022). *Jefferson County, Alabama Sales Tax Rate 2022*. Retrieved February 20, 2022, from https://www.salestaxhandbook.com/alabama/rates/jefferson-county
Snider, P. (2018). Limited government demands more, not less, of Alabama. *Alabama Policy Institute*, 28 August 2018. Retrieved February 12, 2022, from https://alabamapolicy.org/2018/08/24/limited-government-demands-more-not-less-of-alabama/
Thornton, W. (2020). Birmingham, Huntsville top cities for business climate. *Alcom*, 29 July 2020. Retrieved February 12, 2022, from https://www.al.com/business/2020/07/birmingham-huntsville-top-cities-for-business-climate.html

U.S. Bankruptcy Court (2011). *Northern District of Alabama Southern Division Case (No.: 11–05736-TBB).* Retrieved January 12, 2021, from https://casetext.com/case/mosley-v-jefferson-cnty-in-re-jefferson-cnty

U.S. Census Bureau (2021). *Jefferson County*. Retrieved February 12, 2022, from https://www.census.gov/quickfacts/jeffersoncountyillinois

Walsh, M. (2012). In Alabama, a County That Fell Off the Financial Cliff. *New York Times*, 18 February 2012. Retrieved January 12, 2021, from https://comebacktown.com/2012/02/20/in-alabama-a-county-that-fell-off-the-financial-cliff/

Wright, B. (2019). *One year ago, Jefferson County emerged from bankruptcy. Did Wall Street fleece the County Commission?* Retrieved January 12, 2021, from https://www.al.com/news/birmingham/2014/12/one_year_later_jefferson_count.html

Wright, B., & Chandler, K. (2009). *Occupational tax bill to save Jefferson County has flaws, lawyer for county*. Retrieved January 12, 2021, from https://www.al.com/spot-news/2010/12/judge_stops_jefferson_county_o.html

WSFA (2006). Former Jefferson County Environmental Services Director Found Guilty of Conspiracy, Bribery, and Mail Fraud. Retrieved February 12, 2022, from www.wsfa.com.

12

CASE STUDY: PITTSBURGH, PA

Introduction

A decline in population, inefficient tax structure, skyrocketing cost of post-employment health benefits for police and firefighters, unfunded pensions and workers' compensation programs' liabilities, and unsound fiscal management and budgeting were some of the factors that led the city to the fiscal emergency.

Overall, Pittsburgh spent over 14 years in fiscal emergency (so-called Act 47[1]) status from December 29, 2003, to February 12, 2018. While fiscal stress did not lead to bankruptcy, this is the longest case of a fiscal stress situation among the six considered case studies in this book. "An outmoded tax structure and out of budgetary gimmicks to meet its spending needs" were among the major factors leading to the Act 47 designation (Montarty, 2009, p. 3). According to the Allegheny Institute of Public Policy (2020), "at the close of 2003 when the city was a newly designated distressed community, the audited results for the general fund showed an operating deficit of $35 million with $349 million in revenues and $384 million in expenditures" (p. 2). Pittsburgh stood "on the precipice of full-blown crisis" in 2003 (Commonwealth of Pennsylvania, 2004).

The first version of the recovery plan for Pittsburgh was written by the state-appointed Act 47 oversight board and adopted by the city in 2004. The plan was amended in 2009 and 2014. The 2004 version of the recovery plan contained over 200 cost reduction or containment initiatives and steps to improve the equity and revenue-generating capability of Pittsburgh's tax structure. In total, around 390 initiatives were contained in the three recovery plans that addressed nearly all facets of city finance, collective bargaining, and budgeting practices. The Commonwealth of Pennsylvania created a separate overseer with its own broader powers that had to work alongside with the recovery coordinators. There were tax

DOI: 10.4324/b23117-12

FIGURE 12.1 Pittsburgh.

Source: Photo credit Alex Phillip

reforms that affected all city levies. In addition, a municipal pension's reform law included the possibility of a state takeover of Pittsburgh's pensions.

Background Information

Pittsburgh received its nickname of the "Iron City" or "Steel City" as a major iron and steel producer in the United States in the 19th and early 20th centuries (Guzman, 2019). Similar to other legacy cities, Pittsburgh has experienced a dramatic decline in population since 1960; in the case of Pittsburgh, the population drop was caused by a deminishing demand for steel. Between 1960 and 2019, the city's population decreased by 50 percent. Pittsburgh, PA had 604,332 residents in 1960, 334,563 residents in 2000, and only 300,286 residents in 2019 (U.S. Census Bureau, 2021). "Between 1970 and 1990, the region lost 158,000 manufacturing jobs, and over 289,000 residents. The economy's share of jobs in manufacturing fell from 28% to 12% over the same two decades" (Gradeck, 2003, p. 1).

Table 12.1 presents demographic and economic indicators for Pittsburgh in 2010 and 2019.

A decreased population, persistent unemployment, stagnant wages, and lagging property values were fueling budget shortages as a growing number of residents were relying on government social support.

TABLE 12.1 Demographic, Economic, and Social Situations in Pittsburgh in 2010 and 2019

Population	
Population estimates, July 1, 2019 (V2019)	300,286
Population, Census, April 1, 2010	305,704
Race and Hispanic Origin	
White alone, percent	66.8
Black or African American alone, percent	23.0
Asian alone, percent	5.8
Hispanic or Latino, percent	3.2
Housing	
Owner-occupied housing unit rate, 2015–2019	47.2
Median value of owner-occupied housing units, 2015–2019	125,000
Median gross rent, 2015–2019	958
Education	
High school graduate or higher, percent of persons age 25 years+, 2015–2019	92.9
Bachelor's degree or higher, percent of persons age 25 years+, 2015–2019	44.6
Health	
With a disability, under age 65 years, percent, 2015–2019	10.0
Persons without health insurance, under age 65 years, percent	6.1
Economy	
In civilian labor force, total, percent of population age 16 years+, 2015–2019	63.7
Total accommodation and food services sales, 2012 ($1,000)	1,306,229
Total retail sales per capita, 2012, $	13,413
Income and Poverty	
Median household income (in 2019 dollars), 2015–2019, $	48,711
Per capita income in past 12 months (in 2019 dollars), 2015–2019, $	34,083
Persons in poverty, percent	20.5

Source: Table created by authors based on U.S. Census Bureau (2021).

Pittsburgh's tax structure was blamed as one of the main contributors to the fiscal stress situation. In 1990, Pittsburgh reduced its income tax rates, which led to a persistent budget deficit in subsequent years. To address the budget deficit, the city privatized city water and sewer systems in 1995, which provided a short-term boost to the city's finances (Guzman, 2019). In 2003, Pittsburgh levied taxes on real estate, real estate transfers, parking, earned income, business gross receipts (business privilege and mercantile), occupational privilege, and amusements (Allegheny Institute of Public Policy, 2009, 2020). The state laws exempted businesses and non-profits from taxes. A 10-dollar occupational privilege tax that has remained the same for 38 years[2] for the city's financial hardships.

Similar to other municipal entities, the single largest expense of the city of Pittsburgh was employee wages and benefits, totaling approximately two-thirds of overall general fund expenditures – or 241.1 million dollars – in fiscal year (FY) 2003. Personnel expenditures – which include salaries, premium pays, fringe benefits, uniforms, and employer pension contributions – grew by 5–6 percent annually in FY2001 and FY2002, in contrast to revenue growth of below 1 percent (City of Pittsburgh, 2004, 2005, 2006, 2007; Commonwealth of Pennsylvania, 2004, p. 23). In 2003, Pittsburgh paid over 3.9 million dollars in "call-back" pay to firefighters and nearly 4.9 million dollars in general overtime, over and above police court premiums and firefighter call-backs (Commonwealth of Pennsylvania, 2004, p. 34).

Besides overwhelming personnel expenses, Pittsburgh was dealing with unfunded pensions and workers' compensation programs' liabilities. The general fund pension contributions were below 5.9 million dollars in FY2002 and were expected to reach nearly 17.2 million dollars in FY2004 (Commonwealth of Pennsylvania, 2004, p. 37). The city's actuary, Mockenhaupt Associates, indicated that the combined ratio of assets to the Actuarial Accrued Liability was 40.8 percent as of January 1, 2003. According to Fitch credit rating agency (2003), a funding ratio below 60 percent raises analysts' concerns about an issuer's fiscal future. The city's issuance of pension obligation bonds in 1996 and 1998 significantly improved the aggregate funding ratio from 18.2 percent in 1996 to 67.0 percent as of January 1, 2000. From January 2000 to December 2002, "the City's Combined Pension Trust Funds experienced a decline in net assets of more than $155.1 million, from $467.6 million to $312.5 million" (Commonwealth of Pennsylvania, 2004). As a result of this drop, Pittsburgh's funding ratio eroded to 59.3 percent in 2001, 50.7 percent in 2002, and 40.8 percent in 2003 (Commonwealth of Pennsylvania, 2004).

Unsound fiscal management and budgeting were another issue contributing to the downfall of Pittsburgh finances. City budgets often included optimistic scenarios of revenue estimates that were unlikely to be collected (Commonwealth of Pennsylvania, 2009). Many – but not all – revenue collection functions were administered by the Finance Department. But the collections of other revenues connected to the service provision were recorded in operational departments (Commonwealth of Pennsylvania, 2009). As such, there was no centralized way for the Finance Department to observe and manage the city of Pittsburgh's overall revenue collection process and results, including the aging of receivables, collection rates, and other indicators. The expenditure budget included no multi-year spending projections and only one year of historical actuals (Commonwealth of Pennsylvania, 2009). The greatest level of detail was provided on personnel, but overall, the budget did not have enough information for policy development and decision making. The accounting system was not used efficiently to manage revenue, other than to record collections. The data was recorded on a cash basis rather than the more conservative and recommended by GASB modified accrual basis.

The Fiscal Stress Situation

Thanks to unsound budgeting and financial practices, Pittsburgh had over 90 million dollars in deficit in 2002, 2003, and 2004 each (Guzman, 2019). The city was also unable to raise taxes as the State Legislature failed to approve a long-promoted city tax reform. In August 2003, the city laid off 446 employees, including nearly 100 police officers. The recreation centers and public swimming pools were closed. City services from police mounted patrol to salt boxes needed to deal with snow and ice in wintertime were eliminated (Commonwealth of Pennsylvania, 2004, p. 1). While not implemented, the city was entertaining the ideas of eliminating councilmember seats from nine to seven or even five, laying off fire officers, shifting certain payroll from the city to school district budgets, letting volunteers operate recreation centers, and cutting the work week from five to four days (McNulty, 2003).

Pittsburgh's credit ratings were downgraded repeatedly in October and November 2003. On October 15, 2003, S&P lowered the city of Pittsburgh's credit rating by five notches from "A-" to "BB" (junk rating) following the audit that expressed a growing concern about Pittsburgh's budget deficit and questioned the city's ability to operate unless it received an additional taxing authority from the state and the city council (S&P). Moody's also lowered the city's credit rating by five notches from A3 to Ba2, in the series of four credit rating events between October 2003 and October 2004. On November 7, 2003, FitchRatings downgraded Pittsburgh's credit rating from A- to BB, continuing on Rating Watch Negative: the absence of substantial progress toward budget resolution in a timely manner could result in further downgrade. The city already restructured 13 million dollars of debt service payments in 2003 to provide cash flow relief as it sought tax reform legislation from the commonwealth (FitchRatings, 2003). In 2004, Pittsburgh was the nation's only major city with below-investment-grade "junk bond" ratings.

Actual general obligation debt service grew from 55,314,000 dollars in 2002 to 71,230,000 dollars in 2003 with 86,231,000 dollars budgeted for 2004. The 30.9 million dollars or 56 percent increase between 2002 and 2004 represented a heavy additional burden for an already burdened budget (Commonwealth of Pennsylvania, 2004, p. 73). On March 1, 2004, Pittsburgh had an outstanding 577,680,000 dollars of the principal amount of tax-exempt general obligation debt issued for various capital purposes and 268,010,000 dollars of the principal amount of taxable general obligation pension bonds issued in 1996 and 1998 to fund portions of Pittsburgh's unfunded pension liability. From a credit and payment perspective, there is no difference between these two debt categories as both issues were paid from the city's general revenues (Commonwealth of Pennsylvania, 2004, p. 75). These bonds had a total principal amount of 845,690,000 dollars outstanding. Pittsburgh's forthcoming cash shortfall threatened pension payments and payroll in 2004. Without corrective action, Pittsburgh would "strain to pay its bills through the end of 2004 and mounting annual deficits would then grow from approximately $72 million in 2005 to nearly $115 million for FY2009 alone" (Commonwealth of Pennsylvania, 2004, p. 1).

First Recovery Plan

In response to the fiscal emergency situation, Pittsburgh filed for fiscal emergency status in accordance with the Pennsylvania's "financial distress" law, Act 47 of 1987 ("Act 47"). The request was reviewed by the Commonwealth's Secretary of Community and Economic Development and the city was placed in Act 47 status on December 29, 2003. Under Act 47, the distressed municipality must appoint a coordinator, typically an employee of the municipal district or an outside consultant (53 Pa. Stat. Ann. § 11701.221(d), 2017). Once appointed, the coordinator must quantify the financial deficits and give a public presentation as to his initial findings (53 Pa. Stat. Ann. § 11701.221(d), 2017). Based on these findings, the coordinator must then develop and carry out a plan for the municipality to reach financial stability. Municipalities that fail to adopt or implement the recovery plan will not receive loans or other payments from the Commonwealth. Pittsburgh had a unique position of both being in Act 47 status and under the direction of an oversight board (Montarty, 2009).

In February 2004, the Commonwealth of Pennsylvania created the Pittsburgh Intergovernmental Cooperation Authority (ICA), a five-member board that was charged with the task of overseeing Pittsburgh's finances. The city of Pittsburgh's administration worked with the ICA to develop the recovery plan. In 2004, the ICA identified multiple issues with reporting and estimating employees' compensations, issues with unfunded pensions, health care, workers' compensation programs' liabilities, and high debt burden. The 2004 Recovery Plan pursued the following objectives:

- restoring public safety and parks and recreation at new levels in consideration with the available resources and lower population
- improving cooperation between the City, Allegheny County, and neighboring municipalities
- using technology and private sector resources to gain efficiency in emergency medical transportation
- improving billing, fleet maintenance, and other areas
- improving flexibility and efficiency of management by changing work rules and collective bargaining agreements
- improving financial management and budgeting to create more transparent budget on an ongoing basis

To achieve the set objectives and navigate the city out of the fiscal emergency, the Act 47 Recovery Plan of 2004 was extremely detailed and specified about 200 initiatives aimed at direct budget cuts, cost-savings – such as outsourcing or intergovernmental cooperation – revenue generation, and general initiatives aimed at maintaining financial strength.

Budget Cuts

The initial Act 47 recovery plan suggested the following budget cuts:

1. 15 percent across-the-board cuts in the budgets for the mayor, city council and clerk, and the city controller
2. significant staffing reductions and station closures in the Fire Bureau based on the city's current population and fire protection needs, which presumed elimination of a minimum of 168 positions
3. elimination of a separate Engineering and Construction Department
4. targeted elimination of multiple programs and positions in other departments
5. freezing all employee wages for two years with subsequent 2.5 percent annual increases and restructuring benefits
6. no further benefit enhancements
7. moderation of growth in the salary base used for pension calculations, elimination of retiree health care for employees hired after December 3, 2004, extension of police cost sharing requirements for retiree medical premiums with City firefighters, reevaluation of the city pension contribution levels
8. government-wide reductions in materials, supplies, and miscellaneous contracts
9. limited restorations of services central to quality of life (recreation centers, pools, etc.)
10. elimination of cable TV production
11. reductions to the fleet.

(Commonwealth of Pennsylvania, 2004, pp. 5–6)

The Act 47 Recovery Plan of 2004 targeted containment of fast-growing employee compensation, applied to non-represented managers and union workers: (1) two-year wage freeze, (2) health benefits restructuring, including establishment of a 15 percent employee contribution to monthly premiums, (3) overtime and premium pay reductions, (4) enhanced workers' compensation controls, and (5) changes in benefits for future hires, such as the elimination of city-funded retiree health benefits, to improve long-term fiscal health.

The first recovery plan suggested reduction of overtime expenditures from the over ten million dollars budgeted in FY2004 (including police officer court premium pay and firefighter call-back pay) by at least ten percent. In addition, employees would no longer receive sick days, and existing sick banks would be frozen (Commonwealth of Pennsylvania, 2004, p. 42). Employees would also be required to use any previously accumulated sick days before other leave due to illness. Payment of unused sick leave on retirement, death, or other termination of employment shall not exceed 50 percent of the total days accrued (Commonwealth of Pennsylvania, 2004, pp. 42–43).

Outsourcing and Intergovernmental Cooperation

In addition to direct cost-cutting initiatives, the Act 47 Recovery Plan of 2004 laid down a number of cost-saving steps. One of them was the intergovernmental cooperation with Allegheny County and other regional governments that presumed: 911 call center merger, consolidation of purchasing, transfer of arson investigation to the county, transfer of pet licensing to the county, joint facility management and information technology management, and consolidation of tax collection. For example, the 911 merger meant that most of the city's 911 personnel, their salaries and operating costs, along with most of the city's 911 fee structure would be transferred to Allegheny County. This merger allowed Pittsburgh to avoid approximately 4.8 million dollars in capital expenditures on its 911 system. Instead, Pittsburgh invested only around 400,000 dollars on Computer Aided Dispatch (CAD), radio improvements, and moving expenses. The net capital expenditure savings was approximately 4.4 million dollars. Pittsburgh also saved over one million dollars in operating expenses each year (Commonwealth of Pennsylvania, 2004, p. 53).

The Act 47 Recovery Plan of 2004 proposed multiple outsourcing initiatives to improve efficiency of the following core services: fleet maintenance, EMS billing and collections, trash collection, custodial services, and animal control services.

Revenue Generating Initiatives

Another major focus of the first recovery plan was the development of new revenue streams. The General Assembly enacted tax reforms in 2004 by giving Pittsburgh the authority to levy a payroll preparation tax in exchange for the immediate elimination of the mercantile tax and the phase-out of the business privilege tax. The tax reforms increased the amount of the occupational privilege tax from 10 dollars to 52 dollars (the local services tax), created payroll tax, and to begin the phase-out of the business privilege tax that allowed multiple businesses operating in the city, including 24 of the 27 largest corporations, to avoid paying taxes (Intergovernmental Cooperation Authority, 2009). The amended tax laws also shifted a portion of the Pittsburgh Public Schools' share of the earned income tax to the city and reduced the maximum allowable parking tax rate in steps from its 50 percent rate in 2004 (Commonwealth of Pennsylvania, 2009). The deed transfer tax increased in late 2004.

Strengthening of Fiscal Management Practices

The main objectives of the first recovery plan were strengthened financial management practices and strategic investment in long-term fiscal health.

Specifically, it included the following initiatives: (1) establishment of pay-as-you-go capital funding to reduce reliance on debt (see Chapter 6 for the discussion of pay-as-you-go mechanism), (2) capitalization of a Productivity Bank revolving loan fund to finance projects that improved local governments' efficiency, (3) adoption of the best practices in municipal budgeting (enhanced interim reporting and midyear controls, etc.), (4) adoption of pro-active risk management tools, and (5) formalization of a Fund Balance policy toward the gradual rebuilding of prudent reserves (Commonwealth of Pennsylvania, 2004, p. 17).

Over a period of three to five years, beginning on January 1, 2005, Pittsburgh started to build and maintain undesignated Fund Balance reserves equivalent to at least 5 percent and up to 15 percent of annual revenues. The recovery plan predicted that Pittsburgh would start FY2005 with a fund balance of approximately zero. If things went as planned, the recovery plan would generate modest annual positive operating balances that would total to approximately 22.5 million dollars by 2009 or about 5.6 percent of general fund revenue (Commonwealth of Pennsylvania, 2009, p. 65).

The Act 47 Recovery Plan of 2004 additionally suggested that Pittsburgh produces an annual "popular budget" accessible to city residents and that the regular annual budget meet the criteria for application for the Government Finance Officers Association (GFOA) Distinguished Budget Presentation Award (Commonwealth of Pennsylvania, 2004, p. 60). The recovery plan specified that budget oversight shall be much more formal and rigorous. Departments should prepare a detailed revenue and expenditure plan by the beginning of January each year, showing the projected monthly progress for the year. Monthly updates shall be submitted to the Finance Department and head of the Office of Management and Budget, showing actual spending to date and revised projected spending for the year. Each department head and departmental budget officer shall meet with the Finance Director and other officials at quarterly intervals to review and discuss these reports, including year-to-date spending, expected overall result, and actions taken to control any potential overspending. This process could be managed as an extension to the CitiStat performance management system (CitiStat).[3] This initiative would require accurate and timely monthly reporting of financial results to the Finance Department from the Controller's Office. Within 45 days of the close of each quarter, the Finance Director and head of the Office of Management and Budget (OMB) shall compile and circulate a Quarterly Financial and Management Report detailing key budgetary metrics. The City's Quarterly Report shall include: details on the performance of major revenue sources and expenditure categories (current quarter, year-to-date, budget-to-actual, budget-to-projected actual, comparisons to prior year: year-to-date through the same period and year-end, narrative variance analysis), reports on key factors driving the budget (e.g., staffing levels by unit, filled vs. authorized positions, overtime by unit, leave usage by unit), cash flows, and brief updates on important management initiatives (i.e., deficit reduction initiatives; Commonwealth of Pennsylvania, 2009, p. 62).

The recovery plan additionally made a specific recommendation on how to centralize revenue collection and reporting. As mentioned earlier, many revenues were collected and recorded by individual departments, and it was difficult to estimate the total value of tax and non-tax collections. Before 2004, parking and parking-related issues for the city, for example, were fragmented among several different agencies, including the police department, parking authority, and traffic court. The parking authority issued parking tickets and managed approximately 8,000 parking meters. Unpaid parking tickets and adjudicating disputed tickets were handled by the District Justices in traffic court. The responsibility for some enforcement activities, including boot and tow activities, were handled by the police department. The Act 47 team recommended the integration of most parking-related enforcement functions into the Pittsburgh Parking Authority. Such consolidation facilitated elimination of redundant positions, streamlining work processes, and providing a platform for collection and outsourcing strategies (Commonwealth of Pennsylvania, 2004, p. 67).

Debt Management

The 2004 debt service payment obligation of 86.2 million dollars comprised almost 23 percent of the city's budgeted expenditures for 2004. Pittsburgh's obligation to pay debt service on its outstanding bonds represented one of the single largest impediments to the city's return to financial health and balanced budgets. The annual debt service on non-pension general obligation bonds was approximately 68 million dollars in each of the next 6 years, while the annual debt service on pension general obligation bonds was approximately 20 million dollars in each of the next 8 years. In December 2004, S&P raised the Pittsburgh credit rating back to the investment grade (BBB- by), citing a reduction in expenditures, an increase in revenues, and a balanced budget as the reasons for the upgrade. Moody's did not upgrade the city's rating to the investment grade (Baa3) until March of 2005.

The Act 47 team has recommended that the city designates up to an additional four million dollars per year toward pensions, explores the option of issuing pension obligation bonds, avoids future or retroactive pension enhancements, eliminates overtime calculation for pensions for the firefighters, and explores new defined benefit plans for new hires, among other recommendations (Commonwealth of Pennsylvania, 2009).

Second Recovery Plan – More Definitive Steps to Recovery

There were indeed multiple positive developments in Pittsburgh in the years following the Act 47 designation. In 2008, the public safety department, for example, accounted for an 11-million-dollar drop in expenditures thanks to a decrease in workers' compensation expenses (City of Pittsburgh, 2008, p. IX). On September 11, 2008, Pittsburgh closed a 66.8-million-dollar deal on bonds refinancing. The refinancing saved the city 2.9 million dollars in debt service costs over the next 9 years (City of Pittsburgh, 2008, p. XIV).

Encouraged by the positive developments in December 2007, the Pittsburgh city administration felt like the city progressed enough to exit the Act 47 oversight. The corresponding petition from the city council signed by the mayor was sent for approval to Pennsylvania's Secretary of Community and Economic Development. The Commonwealth gathered information and conducted a public hearing in April 2008 where multiple parties including city officials, union representatives, business community representatives, individual citizens, the Intergovernmental Cooperation Authority (ICA), and the Act 47 Coordinator presented testimony. In July 2008, the secretary determined that the city's status as a distressed municipality under Act 47 should continue. While acknowledging the city's progress under the 2004 Recovery Plan, the secretary concluded that there were still major issues with pensions and other post-retirement benefits, debt service, and legacy costs that threatened city finances. The secretary's ruling cited the importance of funding future capital needs and having a balanced budget throughout the five-year plan period in the next stage of the city's recovery.

Pittsburgh's unfunded pension liabilities were 523.9 million dollars on January 1, 2007. In fact, city pensions were funded at only 40 percent. Between January 2007 and November 2008, market declines resulted in losses of more than 100 million dollars in the city's investments, and revised estimates showed that the city's pensions were now only 29 percent funded. Plus, as of 2007, the city had fewer active employees contributing to the pension fund than retirees drawing benefits from it. City OPEB liabilities' valuations identified an unfunded liability of approximately 320 million dollars as of January 1, 2007 and determined that the city should make an annual required contribution (ARC) of 26.7 million dollars to OPEB (Commonwealth of Pennsylvania, 2009). In addition, Pittsburgh had to service a substantial annual debt (404.4 million dollars over the next 16 years) on pension obligation bonds issued in 1996 and 1998. In FY2008, debt service was the second highest line item after employee salaries and wages (84.9 million dollars). Debt service comprised nearly 20 percent of the city's annual revenue (City of Pittsburgh, 2008, 2009, 2010, 2011). As with its pension liabilities, the overall debt service in Pittsburgh was far higher than in comparable cities. Along with the high volume, the city's debt was largely non-callable, giving the city little flexibility in restructuring the payments in the near term. The remaining outstanding city general fund debt was 723.1 million dollars in early FY2009. To lower the debt, the city made a substantial effort in trying to avoid borrowing for capital initiatives (Commonwealth of Pennsylvania, 2009, p. 10).

In 2009 the original recovery plan was updated to include:

- "Continue to control expenditure growth, including employee compensation and benefit costs, so that City can direct more resources to meet the large remaining liabilities, especially the $523.9 million in unfunded employee pensions.
- Providing more funding for capital projects so the City can continue investing in infrastructure on a pay-as-you-go basis and pay down its remaining $723.1 million in outstanding General Fund debt obligations,
- Developing the processes and tools for budget, debt service and capital improvement plan management so ensure the City has collaborative process for deciding how to use its resources.
- Building public safety capacity, particularly in code enforcement through improved employee training, police patrol through civilianization, and rescue response through enhanced Bureau of Fire participation".

(Commonwealth of Pennsylvania, 2009, p. 6)

The Amended Recovery Plan of 2009 (second recovery plan) increased the city's contributions to the pension fund by 48 million dollars over the expenditures in the ICA-approved five-year plan. The Amended Recovery Plan gave Pittsburgh the flexibility to pursue different options to fund this contribution, such as leasing its parking garages. The city's pension funded ratio has increased significantly from where it stood a decade ago, rising from the mid-30 percent range to over 60 percent. The city tried setting aside money in the pension plans beyond its minimum obligation and dedicated parking charge revenues toward the plan. Pittsburgh established a trust fund to generate funds for post-retirement health care benefits for new hires that ended in 2005 (Allegheny Institute of Public Policy, 2009, 2020).

The Amended Recovery Plan of 2009 set up a collaborative process involving the Department of Finance, City Planning, Public Works, the Mayor's Office, the Controller's Office, and City Council that produced an annual capital budget and six-year capital improvement plan (CIP) for City Council's review and approval.

The second recovery plan's initiatives incited changes such as the revenue growth sustained by the payroll preparation tax, the higher local services tax, and the shifting of revenue from the school district and the property reappraisal. In 2010, Pittsburgh started to dedicate 13.4 million dollars of annual revenues from parking fees toward the pension fund and committed to setting aside 26.8 million dollars to address legacy costs by 2018 (Cook, 2018, p. 2) Allegheny County's property reassessment in 2012 increased the value of taxable real estate by 49 percent (Allegheny County, 2012). Thanks to an increase in the tax base, Pittsburgh was able to collect higher property tax revenues without increasing the rate.

Outside of improvements in fiscal performance, in 2009, the Act 47 team identified over 200 non-tax economic development initiatives, ranging in cost from 5,000 dollars to over 10 million dollars a year (City of Pittsburgh, 2011, 2014). Pittsburgh implemented an aggressive strategy to reclaim riverfront property and reuse industrial sites left behind by the decline of the steel mills. A variety of technology companies and university researchers moved their operations to the Pittsburgh Technology Center (City of Pittsburgh, 2008, p. I-4).

To attract families with kids to live in the city, the city, in cooperation with the Pittsburgh School District, created a Pittsburgh Promise program. The city obliged to provide up to 5,000 dollars per year in merit-based scholarships to any accredited postsecondary institution in Pennsylvania. In 2008, more than 650 students took advantage of this promise. And, by the end of 2019, Pittsburgh Promise funded 9,528 graduates from Pittsburgh Public Schools. Over 144.4 million dollars in scholarships had been given to facilitate attendance at 139 postsecondary schools (City of Pittsburgh, 2019, pp. 1–8).

Third Recovery Plan and Exit from the Fiscal Emergency

While Pittsburgh has experienced considerable progress in stabilizing their financial position and has achieved surpluses in the last several years, "legacy costs remain a serious concern and jeopardize the city's ability to maintain a sustainable operating budget without further action" (City of Pittsburgh, 2017, p. 5). The third recovery plan was approved and adopted in June 2014 after wide consultation with the administration, City Council, City Controller, and city labor unions. To be financially healthy, Pittsburgh needed to address the financial threat to the current employees and retirees who depend on these benefits and to the residents, businesses, and others who must pay for them in lieu of receiving current services. The goals of the third recovery plan remained largely the same: save costs, improve capital infrastructure, increase revenue without raising property taxes, and contribute to the pension fund without taking on more debt. Pittsburgh changed its spending model by treating 40 percent of the city's capital expenditures as operating expenses. The capital budget was dedicated to longer-lasting projects, like the upkeep of 137 city bridges (Commonwealth of Pennsylvania, 2014).

By 2016, Pittsburgh renegotiated seven of the city's nine collective bargaining agreements (City of Pittsburgh, 2017). The overall number of city employees decreased by 15 percent from January 2004 to January 2017, but with population also declining, the employee count per 1,000 residents fell only 7 percent.

According to the Rescission Report (2017), Pittsburgh had finally "structurally balanced its budget with recurring revenues consistently outpacing recurring expenditures. Over time, the City has adopted a series of financial management tools that will guide the decision-making of future leaders on fiscal issues to ensure budgetary stability" (City of Pittsburgh, 2017, p. 2).

In February 2018, the Secretary of Community and Economic Development concluded that Pittsburgh had complied with its recovery plan and that termination of the distressed status was due. In 2018, the city budget had 566.4 million dollars in revenue and 556.4 million dollars in expenditures (a 10-million-dollar operating surplus). Both revenues and expenditures grew faster than inflation (40 percent for the Pittsburgh area consumer price index), but the growth in revenues was greater (62 percent) than expenditures (44 percent). In 2019, the city's governmental funds had ending fund balances of 292.7 million dollars, an increase of 48.1 million dollars from 2018.

In 2019, Pittsburgh heralded a national marketing campaign named "Pull Up a Chair – You Are Welcome Here" to increase awareness of the city across the country, thereby promoting it as a world-class event destination. The campaign has won 13 national and regional awards and is credited with generating over two million dollars in additional tax revenues from hotel taxes. Travel ranked Pittsburgh fourth among "The 10 Most Welcoming Cities in the US". TravelPulse named the city as "Pennsylvania's Best Travel Destination", while Parade Magazine called Pittsburgh "one of the best cities for family vacations on a budget" (City of Pittsburgh, 2019, pp. 1–7). Multiple factors combine to make Pittsburgh an attractive destination for investors, including Pittsburgh's leading class of technical capabilities. In 2016, Pittsburgh ranked 144th out of 150 cities on financial stability and 117th on per capita spending (Allegheny Institute of Public Policy, 2020, p. 2).

Conclusions

Many issues contributed to poor fiscal health for Pittsburgh, such as: the decades of decline in steel mining, the major industry in Pittsburgh economy, followed by population decline, unemployment, lagging property values, heavy reliance on stagnant property tax values, and strong political and policy obstacles to raising tax rates. Pittsburgh accumulated a high amount of pension and bonded debt, which lowered the city's ability to issue new and service existing debt. In 2004, the city's credit ratings lowered to "junk" and the state designated the city in Act 47 fiscal emergency status. It took the city over 14 years and 3 recovery plans to exit the fiscal emergency.

In the case of Pittsburgh, the recovery plan was spelled out to the point in all three iterations of the document. Multiple cost-saving and cost-cutting strategies were implemented at the first recovery stage in 2004, including across-the-board cuts; significant staffing reductions and station closures in the Fire Bureau; elimination of a separate Engineering and Construction Department; government-wide reductions in materials, supplies, and miscellaneous contracts; targeted elimination of multiple programs and positions; two-year wage freeze; health benefits restructuring; overtime and premium pay reductions; etc. Because of these extreme budget cuts, there was no substantial funding for police, fire, libraries, parks, and hospitals in Pittsburgh.

Pittsburgh implemented cost-saving strategies, especially for the EMS and fire department, and it doubled the budget to demolish the city's abandoned buildings, among other cost-saving actions. Since the adoption of the 2004 Recovery

Plan, Pittsburgh has recorded positive annual operating results instead of the large deficits that were projected if no action had been taken.

During the second stage of restructuring and exit from fiscal distress, Pittsburgh implemented administrative innovations in budgeting, strengthened financial management practices, increased cooperation with local governments, private and non-for-profit organizations, and increased capital investments in infrastructure.

The three Recovery Plans of 2004, 2009, and 2014 incorporated multiple initiatives, such as:

- increasing cooperation with Allegheny County and other local governments
- reaching new collective bargaining agreements with all city unions
- improving training and organizational restructuring
- increased spending on the demolition of dangerous buildings
- competitive contracting of fleet, animal control, and solid waste selection services
- controlling expenditure growth across multiple departments
- improving presentation and financial reporting
- contributing funds toward capital projects on a "pay-as-you-go" basis

By the results of the three recovery plans, the operational deficits were eliminated, and the amount of outstanding debt and debt service were substantively reduced.

FIGURE 12.2 Pittsburgh.

Source: Photo credit Alex Phillip

The improvements in budgeting and financial management practices resulted in a smaller, yet more efficient, city government. Multiple economic development incentives increased attractiveness of the city for tourists and families with school-aged kids.

Notes

1 Read more about Act 47 further in this chapter and also in Chapters 2, 3, and 4 of this book.
2 Compared to ad valorem taxes, unit specific taxes, such as a ten-dollar occupation tax, lose the real value over time due to inflation. So the total tax revenues generated by unit-specific taxes shrink if the rate is not growing.
3 CitiStat is a recent performance management innovation claiming budgetary savings and improved performance, which were empirically tested across multiple jurisdictions, including Pittsburgh, Baltimore, and Houston. CitiStat is a method of strategic problem solving, a combined managerial and technical system, a major innovation, and a leadership strategy (Henry, 2003).

References

Allegheny County. (2012). *Property assessment*. Retrieved January 12, 2021, from www.alleghenycounty.us/real-estate/property-assessments/index.aspx

Allegheny Institute of Public Policy (2009). *Allegheny Institute Report #09–05*. Pittsburgh, PA. Retrieved January 12, 2021, from www.alleghenyinstitute.org/wp-content/uploads/components/com_reports/uploads/09-05.pdf.

Allegheny Institute of Public Policy (2020). Act 47 in Pittsburgh: What was accomplished? *Allegheny Institute of Public Policy*. Retrieved January 12, 2021, from www.alleghenyinstitute.org/act-47-pittsburgh-accomplished/

City of Pittsburgh (2004). *Comprehensive annual financial report city of Pittsburgh, Pennsylvania 2004*. Retrieved January 12, 2021, from https://pittsburghpa.gov/controller/annualreport

City of Pittsburgh (2005). *Comprehensive annual financial report city of Pittsburgh, Pennsylvania 2005*. Retrieved January 12, 2021, from https://pittsburghpa.gov/controller/annualreport

City of Pittsburgh (2006). *Comprehensive annual financial report city of Pittsburgh, Pennsylvania 2006*. Retrieved January 12, 2021, from https://pittsburghpa.gov/controller/annualreport

City of Pittsburgh (2007). *Comprehensive annual financial report city of Pittsburgh, Pennsylvania 2007*. Retrieved January 12, 2021, from https://pittsburghpa.gov/controller/annualreport

City of Pittsburgh (2008). *Comprehensive annual financial report city of Pittsburgh, Pennsylvania 2008*. Retrieved January 12, 2021, from https://pittsburghpa.gov/controller/annualreport

City of Pittsburgh (2009). *Comprehensive annual financial report city of Pittsburgh, Pennsylvania 2009*. Retrieved January 12, 2021, from https://pittsburghpa.gov/controller/annualreport

City of Pittsburgh (2010). *Comprehensive annual financial report city of Pittsburgh, Pennsylvania 2010*. Retrieved January 12, 2021, from https://pittsburghpa.gov/controller/annualreport

City of Pittsburgh (2011). *Comprehensive annual financial report city of Pittsburgh, Pennsylvania 2011*. Retrieved January 12, 2021, from https://pittsburghpa.gov/controller/annualreport

City of Pittsburgh (2014). *Comprehensive Annual financial report city of Pittsburgh, Pennsylvania 2014*. Retrieved January 12, 2021, from https://pittsburghpa.gov/controller/annualreport

City of Pittsburgh (2017). Municipalities financial recovery program – Act 47. *Rescission Report*. Retrieved January 12, 2021, from https://apps.pittsburghpa.gov/redtail/images/1000_2017_Rescission_Report_PFM_Final.pdf

City of Pittsburgh (2019). *Comprehensive annual financial report city of Pittsburgh, Pennsylvania 2019*. Retrieved January 12, 2021, from https://apps.pittsburghpa.gov/redtail/images/13424_FY_2019_ANNUALREPORT.pdf

Commonwealth of Pennsylvania. (2004). Municipalities financial recovery act, Recovery plan. *City of Pittsburgh, Allegheny County, Pennsylvania*. Retrieved January 12, 2021, from https://dced.pa.gov/download/Recovery%20Plan%20Final%20Filing%20June%2011/?wpdmdl=58398

Commonwealth of Pennsylvania. (2009). Department of community and economic development, governor's center for local government services. *Municipal Pension Handbook*. Retrieved January 12, 2021, from www.newpa.com

Commonwealth of Pennsylvania. (2009). *Municipalities Financial Recovery Act, Amended Recovery Plan, Department of Community and Economic Development, Governor's Center for Local Government Services*. Allegheny, PA: City of Pittsburg. Retrieved January 12, 2021, from https://dced.pa.gov/download/Final%20Pittsburgh%20Amended%20Recovery%20Plan/?wpdmdl=58400

Commonwealth of Pennsylvania. (2014). *Municipalities Financial Recovery Act, Amended Recovery Plan, Department of Community and Economic Development, Governor's Center for Local Government Services*. Allegheny, PA: City of Pittsburg. Retrieved January 12, 2021, from https://dced.pa.gov/download/city-of-pittsburgh-2014-amended-recovery-plan-adopted-2014–06–24-pdf/?wpdmdl=58397

Cook, S. (2018, February 25). *Rags to bridges: Pittsburgh's climb out of financial distress*. Retrieved January 12, 2021, from https://sites.law.duq.edu/juris/2018/02/25/rags-to-bridges-pittsburghs-climb-out-of-financial-distress/

FitchRatings (2003). Pittsburgh, PA. Retrieved January 22, 2021, from www.fitchratings.com/entity/pittsburgh-pa-3796

Gradeck, B. (2003). The Root of Pittsburgh's Population Drain. Pittsburgh, PA: Carnegie Mellon University Center for Economic Development Retrieved January 22, 2021, from https://www.heinz.cmu.edu/ced/file/pop-drain.pdf

Guzman, T. (2019). Fiscal conditions of largest legacy cities. In *The Legacies of Legacy Cities: Continuity and Change amid Decline and Revival*. Pittsburgh, PA: University of Pittsburgh Press.

Henry, V. E. (2003). *The CompStat Paradigm: Management Accountability in Policing, Business, and the Public Sector*. Flushing, NY: Looseleaf Law Publications.

Intergovernmental Cooperation Authority (2009). *A Summary Report of the Intergovernmental Cooperation Authority (ICA) and its Oversight Role with the City of Pittsburgh, 2004 to Present*. Philadelphia, PA: Intergovernmental Cooperation Authority. Retrieved January 22, 2021, from https://www.picapa.org/reports/

McNulty, T. (2003). *City Neighborhoods. Pittsburgh begs state for help with fiscal crisis*, 11 November. Retrieved January 12, 2021, from http://old.post-gazette.com/neigh_city/20031111murphy1111p1.asp

Montarty, E. (2009). *Chapter 9 bankruptcy: What it means for Pennsylvania's municipalities.* Retrieved January 12, 2021, from www.alleghenyinstitute.org/wp-content/uploads/components/com_reports/uploads/09-05.pdf

U.S. Census Bureau (2021). *Pittsburgh.* Retrieved February 12, 2022, from https://www.census.gov/quickfacts/pittsburghcitypennsylvania

13

CASE STUDY: CENTRAL FALLS, RI

Introduction

In August 2011, the City of Central Falls, Rhode Island petitioned a court for protection under Chapter 9 of the federal bankruptcy code. Central Falls emerged from bankruptcy just short of 14 months later, in October 2012. This city's bankruptcy is possibly the fastest Chapter 9 proceeding in U.S. history (Bidgood, 2012a).

The city made history, not only by becoming the only city in Rhode Island to ever go bankrupt but also because its financially struggling school district in the 1990s turned out to be the first district in the nation that, jointly with the city, requested for the state to take over. In 2010, the city schools were again in the news when the superintendent fired all its teachers who refused to work extra hours at no extra pay. In 2010, the school district was the worst performing in Rhode Island. In 2019, the Central Falls school district was finally in the news for a good reason, when it became the first local government in Rhode Island to implement participatory budgeting.

The fame of this smallest city in the state and the most densely populated city in the nation increased with the last three city mayors. The corruption accusations against the mayor Charles Moreau were one of the contributing factors to the city bankruptcy. The next mayor, James Diossa, became the mayor of Central Falls in 2012 at the age of 27, which made him the youngest and the first Latino mayor in Rhode Island history. The mayor after him, Maria Rivera, who assumed the office in 2021, is the first female mayor in Rhode Island's history and the only Latina mayor in the state.

DOI: 10.4324/b23117-13

FIGURE 13.1 Central Falls City Hall.

Background Information

Central Falls is a suburb of Providence, the capital of Rhode Island. With only 19,408 residents in 2010 (U.S. Census Bureau, 2010) and 19,568 residents in 2019 (U.S. Census Bureau, 2021) and an area of only 1.29 square miles, Central Falls is Rhode Island's smallest and most densely populated city. Originally inhabited by European immigrants, the population dynamics started to shift dramatically in the 1960s when skilled yet lower-paid Columbians and other Latino nationals had been brought to the town to work as weavers in textile mills, the major Central Falls industry. Today around 66 percent of the city residents are Hispanic or Latino. Table 13.1 provides demographic and economic information on Central Falls in 2010 and 2019.

TABLE 13.1 Demographic, Economic, and Social Situations in Central Falls in 2010 and 2019

Population	
Population estimates, July 1, 2019, (V2019)	19,568
Population, Census, April 1, 2010	19,408
Race and Hispanic Origin	
White alone, percent	48.5%
Black or African American alone, percent	12.7%
Asian alone, percent	0.6%
Hispanic or Latino, percent	劳66.4%
Housing	
Owner-occupied housing unit rate, 2015–2019	20.2%
Median value of owner-occupied housing units, 2015–2019	$159,100
Median gross rent, 2015–2019	$1,727
Education	
High school graduate or higher, percent of persons age 25 years+, 2015–2019	64.9%
Bachelor's degree or higher, percent of persons age 25 years+, 2015–2019	8.1%
Health	
With a disability, under age 65 years, percent, 2015–2019	15.1%
Persons without health insurance, under age 65 years, percent	劳18.2%
Economy	
In civilian labor force, total, percent of population age 16 years+, 2015–2019	61.6%
Total accommodation and food services sales, 2012 ($1,000)	10,858
Total retail sales per capita, 2012	$2,437
Income and Poverty	
Median household income (in 2019 dollars), 2015–2019	$32,982
Per capita income in past 12 months (in 2019 dollars), 2015–2019	$15,519
Persons in poverty, percent	30.2%

Source: Table created by authors based on U.S. Census Bureau, 2021

After being a predominantly textile mill town inhabited mostly by first- and second-generation immigrants for decades, it is not surprising that only 8 percent of Central Falls residents had a bachelor's degree or higher between 2015 and 2019. Only 7 percent of eleventh grade students were proficient in math, 55 percent in reading, and the four-year graduation rate from the Central Falls high school (CFHS) was 52 percent in 2007–2009 (Moore & Geoff, 2012, p. 1). Nearly 80 percent of CFHS students were eligible for free or reduced-priced lunch and 27 percent had limited English proficiency in 2010 (Rhode Island Department of Education, 2011).

More than 30 percent of the population of Central Falls lived below the poverty level in 2019. Over 18 percent of people under the age of 65 years lived without health insurance (Table 13.1). The median income of Central Falls households was 32,982 dollars in 2019, which is only about 48 percent of median household income in the U.S. (US Census).

The Origins of the Fiscal Emergency Situation

Donald W. Wyatt Detention Facility

After years of outsourcing textile production capacity and jobs to developing countries, textile mills in Central Falls were closing their doors one after another, and the city had to look for new sources of revenue. Central Falls was considered the poorest city in the state and was already nearly bankrupt in 1990, when the city received an attractive proposition to build a for-profit jail for nonviolent federal detainees that would guarantee a steady stream of money and jobs for Central Falls (Bernstein, 2008a, b). The jail had to provide a reliable income that would help the city avoid financial collapse.

To build the jail, named the Donald W. Wyatt Detention Facility (Wyatt), Central Falls issued 30 million dollars in revenue bonds and later refinanced this loan that required another 38-million-dollar bond issue (Bernstein, 2008b). The facility opened in 1993. As a federal jail, the Wyatt Detention Facility was tax-exempt, but the U.S. Marshals Service that owns the Wyatt Detention Facility was expected to make per diem payments that were earmarked to repay the jail bonds. The Wyatt Detention Facility paid Central Falls two to three dollars a day for each detainee (around 400,000 dollars per year). The revenues from the jail were used to pay Wyatt bonds and the balance was going to the city's general ledger.

The number of federal immigration detainees at the Wyatt Detention Facility increased after the September 11, 2001 attacks and the consequential tightening immigration procedures and requirements. In 2003, the Wyatt Detention Facility became one of 654 facilities used to temporarily house federal immigration detainees prior to transfer or deportation. The number of detainees transferred out of Wyatt Detention Facility to other Immigration and Customs Enforcement (ICE) facilities increased by over 800 percent between 2000 and 2008 (O'Brien,

2013, p. 531). As more illegal immigrants transferred through the facility, Central Falls Finance Department projected increasing revenues from this source and approved a 2005 expansion of Wyatt. 106 million dollars in bonds were issued to fund the jail expansion.

In December 2008, however, ICE halted the placement of federal immigration detainees at Wyatt due to an investigation surrounding the treatment of a Chinese computer engineer who died in custody at Wyatt. A lower number of detainees meant lower than forecasted revenues for the city (Bernstein, 2008a). Unfortunately, the Finance Department continued to budget revenues from Wyatt operations at previous levels, which contributed to the weakening of the city's fiscal position.

Budget Deficit

Central Falls' government struggled with staying fiscally sustainable and ran a budget deficit for years leading to bankruptcy (see Table 13.2). The Wyatt facility was hardly generating sufficient revenue to make payments to bondholders, leaving the revenue going to the city practically nonexistent (O'Brien, 2013). In addition to the cash flow problem with the Central Falls Prison Authority, the city had extremely high pension obligations.

On the revenue side, the city's total gross assessed property value dropped to about 524 million dollars from nearly 804 million dollars between fiscal years 2010 and 2011. Intergovernmental revenues received from the state of Rhode Island were down by 603,572 dollars (negative 15.1 percent) over FY2009 year, resulting from mid-year state budget cuts (City of Central Falls, 2011, 2012).

Total net assets declined from a negative 12,208,312 dollars in 2008 to a negative 22,044,762 dollars in 2010 and to a negative 27,309,406 dollars in 2011 (City of Central Falls, 2010, p. 3).

Unfunded Pensions and Long-term Debt Before Bankruptcy

The city of Central Falls adopted a definitive funding plan for pension obligations in 2007. The annual contributions appropriated by the city were, however, smaller than the actuary's required contribution (ARC). Every now and then, the city sold assets in the pension fund to meet current obligations and pay pension benefit recipients. This, along with less favorable returns on investments, led to a dramatic decrease in the pension trust funds. The total net assets of these funds totaled 8,734,522 dollars in FY2009, a decrease of 3,268,508 dollars compared to FY2008. At the same time, the combined unfunded actuarial accrued liability (UAAL) in the two pension funds was 69.3 million dollars as of July 1, 2008.

For the fiscal year (FY) ending on June 30, 2009, the total long-term debt for the city of Central Falls was 46.2 million dollars (Table 13.3). By FY2011 the total long-term debt was already 63,345,905 dollars (City of Central Falls, 2011,

TABLE 13.2 Revenue and Expenditures in Central Falls from 2008 to 2012

	2008	*2009*	*2010*	*2011*	*2012*
REVENUE					
Property taxes, $	9,898,722	10,392,152	10,548,712	12,403,485	13,353,506
Grants and contributions (unrestricted) $	5,438,368	4,544,796	3,822,314	2,395,363	2,630,919
Investment earnings, $	90,733	126,137	38,027	14,776	50,625
Gain on sale of assets, $	378,540	199,489	(143,920)	0	(21,645)
Miscellaneous, $	1,142,167	881,832	880,003	1,018,782	941,020
Total Revenue	16,858,530	16,144,408	15,145,136	15,832,406	16,954,425
EXPENDITURES					
General government, $	2,817,663	3,531,210	3,263,095	4,542,417	4,053,914
Public safety, $	6,400,991	7,171,004	7,211,017	6,347,094	5,432,818
Public works, $	1,663,997	1,678,913	1,666,599	1,466,618	1,633,886
Public Education, $	1,396,932	1,450,386	56,250,099	54,464,561	1,726,365
Recreation, $	647,886	741,716	747,088	519,331	488,874
Total Expenditures	21,708,379	24,174,794	78,898,559	77,283,900	16,891,895
Fund balance, beginning	–	3,962,264	5,063,602	8,059,934	7,005,934
Fund balance, ending	3,962,264	3,216,264	8,059,934	7,005,934	5,687,524
Current and other assets	8,534,950	6,063,286	10,235,214	16,612,701	11,764,001
Capital assets	27,160,801	25,341,994	25,014,520	27,694,369	24,581,633
Total assets	35,695,751	31,405,280	35,249,734	44,307,070	36,345,634
Current liabilities	5,560,958	3,921,598	4,224,223	10,216,633	5,902,823
Long-term liabilities	42,343,105	44,350,501	53,070,273	61,399,843	53,828,882
Total liabilities	47,904,063	48,272,099	57,294,496	71,616,476	59,731,705
Net Assets	(12,208,312)	(16,886,819)	(22,044,762)	(27,309,406)	(23,386,071)

Source: Table created by authors based on Audit Reports, CAFRs and annual budgets of the City of Central Falls (2009, 2010, 2011, 2012)

TABLE 13.3 The Total Long-term Debt for the City of Central Falls from FY2008 to FY2012

Long-term Debt	*2008*	*2009*	*2010*	*2011*	*2012*
Net pension obligation (NPO), $	21,838,061	24,522,605	32,836,481	31,205,040	30,688,474
Bonded debt (for school purposes), $	10,985,000	10,615,000	13,740,000	12,835,000	5,555,000
Bonded debt (for municipal purposes), $	8,700,000	8,555,000	8,275,000	7,985,000	13,740,000
Liability for compensated absences, $	1,881,045	2,097,545	1,926,782	3,206,081	164,695
Total, $	43,954,417	46,202,701	58,587,863	63,345,905	55,622,324

Source: Table created by authors based on Audit Reports, CAFRs and annual budgets of the City of Central Falls (2009, 2010, 2011, 2012)

p. 9). Despite the high debt obligations for a city of this size, Central Falls never missed a bond payment until 2012. It managed to stay current on the interest payments primarily by failing to fund pension funds (Fisher, 2013).

Bribery and Political Corruption

Another element that contributed to the fall of the city of Central Falls was the bribery accusation against the mayor. In Fall of 2012, Central Falls' Mayor, Charles Moreau, resigned and pled guilty to federal corruption charges (Bidgood, 2012b). Moreau used a scheme that involved offering lucrative contracts to board-up about 160 abandoned homes to his close friend and political supporter, Michael Bouthillette. The financially strained city paid Bouthillette 14,000 dollars to 16,000 dollars per home, when the average price for a board-up work was around 5,000 dollars per house. (NBC News, 2012). Mayor Moreau was sentenced to two years in prison and Mr. Bouthillette received three years of probation (Niedowski, 2013).

Central Falls School District

As per usual, the problems do not come one at a time. When Central Falls was on the brink of bankruptcy for the first time in the beginning of the 1990s, its school district was also so financially challenged that it made an unprecedented step in 1991 requesting the state to take over. In fact, it was the first school district in the nation to make such a request (Diegmueller, 1991).

As the struggling city was nearing bankruptcy again, the Central Falls School District was considered the worst in the state. To improve the quality of education, the district superintendent requested more hours of instructional support during the school year, summer tutoring, professional development, and other actions. When teachers refused to assume more work at no extra pay, on February 19, 2010, all district staff was fired. Moore and Geoff (2012) reflected about the situation, that for Central Falls school "teachers, staff, students, and families, the school year had been intense, unpredictable, emotional, and stressful" (p. 1). The Central Falls Teachers' Union and the school district reached an agreement only three months later, in mid-May of the same year to rehire the schools' faculty under certain conditions.

Central Falls Credit Rating Changes

As discussed, the downfall and the recovery of the municipal finances can be monitored through the changes in the city's credit ratings. Moody's Investors Service downgraded Central Falls' rating twice in May 2010, from Baa1 to Ba1 and again to B3 later that month citing "the city's weak financial position, mounting pension obligations, limited tax base, and low wealth levels" on top of the city's liquidity constraints (Moody's Corporation, 2010). The worsening situation with the pension plans lead to a further downgrade of the city's credit rating to Caa1 in June 2011 (Moody's Corporation, 2013). In fact, the city's fire and police pension fund was 92 percent unfunded in 2011. "By the time the city sought bankruptcy protection, its unfunded pension and retiree health obligations exceeded $80 million" (O'Brien, 2013, p. 534).

One day after the city applied for bankruptcy on August 1, 2011, Moody's placed Central Falls on review for another possible downgrade, which, however, never materialized. The city exited bankruptcy on October 24, 2012, and by October 26, 2012, Moody's had already upgraded the city's general obligation bond rating to B2 with a positive outlook. On November 16, 2012, Standard and Poor's bond rating improved to BB: "the upgrade reflects active state oversight of the city's financial operations and an approved six-year operating plan that maintains structural balance after the city emerged from Chapter 9 bankruptcy without defaulting on its long-term General Obligation debt" (Rhode Island government, 2012). On July 18, 2013, Moody's further upgraded the city's general obligation bond rating to B1 from B2 with a positive outlook. And, on June 27, 2014, the credit rating increased to Ba3 from B1, with a positive outlook reflecting on encouraging changes in the city's fiscal situation. Then, on May 26, 2015, Moody's upgraded the city's general obligation bond rating to Ba2 from Ba3, with a positive outlook. And, on March 5, 2015, Standard and Poor reaffirmed its BB rating for the city of Central Falls, with a positive outlook.

Bankruptcy Process

Rhode Island is the latest state in the U.S. to adopt bankruptcy regulations. As the situation in Central Falls deteriorated, it turned out that the state (at the time) had a very restricted ability to intervene. In fact, despite the fiscal emergency in the city, Central Falls did not even meet the eligibility requirements for the state limited intervention program. To respond to the looming fiscal crisis in Central Falls, Rhode Island adopted a bankruptcy authorization law on June 11, 2010 (read Chapter 4 for details about the Rhode Island bankruptcy process). The state appointed a receiver, a former Associate Justice of the Rhode Island Supreme Court, Robert Flanders, who, on behalf of the city, applied for the states' first ever Chapter 9 bankruptcy on August 1, 2011.

As it is usually the case in the fiscally challenged cities, the costs of bankruptcy-related restructuring falls primarily "on taxpayers (already some of the poorest residents of the state) and current and former public employees" (O'Brien, 2013, p. 542). Indeed, the city's 133 retirees had their pensions cut by up to 55 percent, with pensioners now getting an average of 16,626 dollars a year (McDonald & McLaughlin, 2011; McGowan, 2013; O'Brien, 2013). The pension of former Central Falls acting fire chief, Gerard Dion, for example, dropped from over 75,000 dollars annually to just over 34,000 dollars (Nesi, 2011). According to Orson (2013),

> state officials say they convinced the stakeholders of their sincerity through transparency: showing the retirees the numbers and building the case that they would otherwise eventually lose benefits altogether. Also, key was a signed pledge by city officials that they would not cut pension benefits again for at least five years.
>
> *(p. 1)*

Layoffs of city employees was another important cost-cutting step (Burton, 2011). The city of Central Falls employed 174 individuals in May 2010. The number of city staff was reduced by 33 percent to 118 employees in 2012. In the fire department, the minimum number of active-duty firefighters per shift was lowered from 9 to 7, straining the agency that goes on about 5,000 runs per year (Bidgood, 2012a). Russ (2012) highlighted more extreme budget cuts in Central Falls:

> Mayor Charles Moreau started cutting the city's workforce after asking for a judicial receiver in May 2010. City employees now total 116, down from 174. The city's only community center was shut, cutting 32 positions. The library was also closed, reopening later under nonprofit management. While positions were cut, base salaries rose. On average, city employees made $41,650 annually before the bankruptcy. Today, Central Falls employees earn an average base salary of $47,500. And they'll get annual 2.5 percent raises for at least the next five years, said Gayle Corrigan, the receiver's chief of staff.
>
> *(p. 1)*

In addition to expenditure cuts, the receiver introduced a 4 percent property tax rate increase. "With the annual 4 percent property tax hikes through 2017,

Central Falls expects its revenue collections to grow from $16.6 million in fiscal 2013 to $19.8 million in 2017" (Russ, 2012, p. 1). The state also helped the bankrupt city to overcome its challenges, by offering Central Falls a one-time allocation of 2.6 million dollars in 2012 to soften the impact of public pension benefit cuts on retirees over 5 years.

In September 2012, a federal judge approved a plan allowing the city to come out of bankruptcy after only 13 months. "It's record time, and record efficiency", said Judge Frank Bailey, a federal bankruptcy judge who led Central Falls bankruptcy case. "In a way, I think this is an example – for not only Rhode Island, but maybe the nation – on how to run a Chapter 9" (Bidgood, 2012a). Within two months, the credit-rating agencies raised Central Falls' rating.

Financial Situation After the Bankruptcy Process

Table 13.4 illustrates the improvements in Central Falls' fiscal situation between 2013 and 2019. The city's revenues have been increasing, mostly thanks to lower delinquency and higher property tax rates. Expenditures, after a dramatic cut during bankruptcy, remained quite stagnant. In addition to expenditure cuts and revenue increases after exiting bankruptcy, the city of Central Falls implemented certain innovative budgeting approaches, made steps to strengthen fiscal responsibility as well as budgetary transparency and citizens' engagement, and increased investments in capital infrastructure, affordable housing, and economic development.

Central Falls created a new city website (www.centralfallsri.gov) to improve government transparency and accessibility of information for residents in 2019. This new website, among other uses, is utilized to communicate spending of federal stimulus funds during the COVID-19 pandemic. In 2019, when the city began receiving federal recovery dollars, a community-based advisory committee was created to support the efficient use of such funds.

Central Falls' local government increased investments in capital infrastructure, public safety equipment, affordable housing for residents, and economic development. Additionally, Central Falls is working to transfer ownership of the city's deteriorating sewer infrastructure to the Narragansett Bay Commission. The city is also working on repairing and repaving roads and sidewalks, as well as continuing to fix school buildings and planning to build new high school. In 2021, a three-day Housing Summit identified more than a dozen housing projects that can directly create jobs and develop safe, affordable housing for residents. The FY2022 budget will invest 50,000 dollars into a new Affordable Housing Fund.

Central Falls' FY2022 budget has a strong commitment to building a local city government that works better for its residents. The FY2022 budget recognizes the incredible hardships Central Falls' residents and businesses have faced

TABLE 13.4 Revenue and Expenditures in Central Falls from 2013 to 2019

	2013	*2014*	*2015*	*2016*	*2017*	*2018*	*2019*
REVENUE							
Property taxes, $	13,659,898	13,307,776	13,362,074	14,895,636	15,078,492	16,645,560	15,287,652
Grants and contributions (unrestricted) $	2,726,709	2,677,982	2,504,076	2,476,125	2,253,918	2,970,744	2,919,265
Investment earnings, $	21,092	9,354	4,953	8,669	343	8,982	7,180
Fees/non-tax income, $	1,303,732	1,288,854	145,061	258,307	890,792	1,017,447	1,161,276
Total Revenue	13,761,169	16,947,260	18,374,714	20,383,317	21,195,030	26,998,554	23,230,544
EXPENDITURES							
General government, $	3,068,862	2,263,650	3,512,480	2,705,590	4,331,316	4,888,232	3,276,888
Public safety, $	7,345,742	6,448,481	7,539,864	7,807.359	7,623,890	8,600,393	8,178,430
Public works, $	1,633,318	1,680,556	2,822,067	2,456,989	2,552,101	2,379,083	2,011,156
Public recreation/planning, $	426,813	178,008	517,679	678,426	933,072	1,201,031	807,907
Municipal debt service, $	2,087,818	2,570,841	687,848	1,212,290	514,876	283,666	2,320,015
Retirement, $	2,012,585	2,404,151	3,349,320	2,296,007	2,384,148	1,561,630	2,631,303
Total Expenditures	18,407,204	16,681,165	20,439,457	19,076,737	20,398,342	19,408,569	19,926,966
Net Position	(4,646,035)	266,095	(2,064,743)	1,306,580	1,073,146	5,594,410	3,303,578
Fund balance, beginning	5,867,524	6,541,563	7,112,610	6,806,842	8,124,644	3,025,377	2,946,676
Fund balance, ending	6,541,563	7,112,610	6,806,842	8,124,644	3,025,377	2,946,676	2,979,118
Current and other assets	10,613,856	12,097,877	10,911,451	10,477,047	6,538,378	7,890,805	6,266,354
Capital assets	20,335,708	18,468,194	17,276,529	17,236,989	19,437,048	20,875,561	19,968,249
Total assets	30,949,564	30,566,071	28,187,980	27,714,036	25,795,426	28,766,366	26,234,603
Current liabilities	3,954,739	4,004,068	2,606,133	3,285,701	4,661,495	5,900,251	4,181,968
Long-term liabilities	52,583,771	51,409,584	57,131,169	46,107,898	41,942,337	40,030,339	38,151,629
Total liabilities	56,538,510	55,413,652	59,737,302	49,393,599	46,603,832	44,984,666	42,333,597
Net Assets	(25,588,946)	(24,869,325)	(23,823,884)	(22,517,304)	(21,265,871)	(20,795,138)	(19,374,081)

Source: Table created by authors based on CAFRs, Audit Reports, and annual budgets of the City of Central Falls (2013, 2014, 2015, 2016, 2017, 2018, 2019)

during the pandemic and includes no anticipated tax increases (City of Central Falls, 2022). The proposed FY2022 budget aims to improve the quality of life in the city's neighborhoods. The budget would create a new community garden and parks, programs for older residents like senior concerts and picnics with seniors, and organized physical activities in the park. The city is planning to build a new Community and Senior Center (City of Central Falls, 2022). The city of Central Falls' Mayor Rivera highlighted that the FY2022 budget recognizes the steps that the local government needs to take to recover, build, and thrive, stating that: "behind every decision made in this budget, I asked, 'Is this best for our residents?' These fiscally responsible decisions will make a better today and a brighter tomorrow. I am confident this budget and its priorities are the best path forward to helping our city recover and rebuild" (City of Central Falls, 2022, p. 2).

Innovations and improvements came not only in the city itself but also in its school district. In 2019, Central Falls started the implementation of the participatory budgeting process in its schools, in which decisions on the allocation of a portion of the budget are made by the students, rather than school administrators (Jordan, 2010). In 2019, the city allocated 10,000 dollars to its high school, and students and parents were asked to identify and prioritize projects to fund and later to vote on their funding. In 2021, the participatory budgeting project was expanded to the entire school district to decide how to allocate 100,000 dollars in COVID-19 relief funds (Brown University, 2022).

Pension Funds and Debt Administration After Bankruptcy

In an effort to reverse the negative consequences of several years when Central Falls failed to contribute to its pension funds, the city began to make annual contributions into the Central Falls Pension Plan beginning in FY2012, to amortize the unfunded liability over a number of years and make these pension funds viable and safe for retirees in the future. Under the new plan, the ARC is projected to be less than the Pay-As-You-Go ("PAYGO") costs until 2027, so the city of Central Falls will essentially be paying more than the annual required contribution, which will result in a reduction of its "net pension obligation" on its statement of net position.

These efforts are already proving to be effective. The total net position of the city's pension trust funds amounted to 9,988,434 dollars in FY2018, an increase of 818,166 dollars compared to FY2017. The total net position of the city's pension trust funds grew even further to 11,474,800 dollars in FY2019, an increase of 1,486,366 dollars compared to FY2018.

At FY2013, the total long-term debt for the city of Central Falls was 54.5 million dollars, and it decreased to 44.5 million dollars in FY2018 and to 40.4 million dollars in FY2019 (Table 13.5).

TABLE 13.5 The Total Long-term Debt for the City of Central Falls from 2013 to 2019

Long-term Debt	*2013*	*2014*	*2015*	*2016*	*2017*	*2018*	*2019*
Net pension obligation (NPO), $	30,393,625	30,071,448	35,623,954	26,955,151	27,691,403	27,643,554	30,667,028
Net OPEB Liability, $	4,945,000	3,005,494	3,144,940	3,228,211	3,267,708	5,435,000	3,936,768
Bonded indebtedness (for municipal purposes), $	12,785,000	7,020,000	6,665,000	6,290,000	5,895,000	3,936,768	4,975,000
Liability for compensated absences, $	162,391	232,980	214,315	257,820	274,824	376,814	439,970
Total, $	54,585,803	53,392,141	57,131,169	46,107,898	44,489,819	42,648,020	40,380,626

Source: Table created by authors based on CAFRs, Audit Reports, and annual budgets of the City of Central Falls (2013, 2014, 2015, 2016, 2017, 2018, 2019)

FIGURE 13.2 Central Falls.

Conclusions

Central Falls faced several obstacles to fiscal stability. It was heavily reliant on property taxes with stagnant property tax values and some of the highest property tax rates in the state. Gross assessed property value dropped by 35 percent between fiscal years 2010 and 2011. The city also made a wrong decision to expand one of its money-making projects, the jail, for nonviolent federal detainees. Central Falls overestimated budget revenues from Immigration and Customs Enforcement (ICE) that pays a fixed rate for every federal immigration detainee housed in the jail. While the city provides infrastructure for the jail, the ICE payments are hardly sufficient to cover the service of bonds that were issued to expand the detention facility with basically nothing adding to the city's general budget. Corruption on the local government level was also one of the reasons for mismanagement of capital projects in the city of Central Falls.

The city of Central Falls used multiple "financial gimmicks" to try to artificially balance its budget prior to bankruptcy, mainly by including overly optimistic forecasts of revenues from the Donald W. Wyatt Detention Facility (Wyatt) and underfunding pensions (by 69.3 million dollars as of July 1, 2008). During bankruptcy, the city of Central Falls further reduced retirees' pension payments by approximately 55 percent, fired one-third of public employees, collected higher

TABLE 13.6 Central Falls Crime Rate from 2008 to 2018

Years	*Central Falls*	*RI*	*USA*
2018	430.21	219.14	380.56
2017	500.28	234.17	394.86
2016	653.63	239.13	397.52
2015	776.20	242.99	373.74
2014	687.25	219.92	361.55
2013	675.12	257.27	369.13
2012	733.47	252.97	387.75
2011	614.89	246.13	387.06
2010	540.80	257.38	404.50
2009	545.57	254.27	431.88
2008	583.92	252.76	458.61
2007	605.80	229.15	471.77
2018	430.21	219.14	380.56

Source: Microtrends, 2022

service charges and fees, and dramatically cut municipal services. The property tax rate increased by 4 percent. O'Brien (2013) highlighted that "the burden of correcting the city's finances fell solely on the shoulders of retirees and taxpayers – the status of bondholders, insurers, and even the city's defined benefit plans was unaffected or improved following bankruptcy" (p. 547).

In Central Falls, the fiscal emergency created a domino-like effect when a lack of funding for police, fire, library, hospital, prison, and sanitation services resulted in higher crime rates as well as overcrowded prisons and hospitals. The Central Falls crime rate for 2015 was 776.2 per 100,000 people, a 142.3 percent increase from 2009 (Table 13.6).

After exiting bankruptcy, the city continued reforming its budgetary system. Central Falls strengthened their fiscal responsibility by continuing to fund the pension fund at 100 percent and investing in Other Post-Employment Benefits (OPEB) for future retiree health care benefits, improved fiscal transparency and engagement by creating a new website, and increased investments in capital infrastructure, affordable housing, and economic development. The city has even encouraged and allocated money for its school district to implement participatory budgeting practices there.

References

Bernstein, N. (2008a). City of Immigrants Fills Jail Cells with its Own. *New York Times*, 27 December. Retrieved December 12, 2021, from www.nytimes.com/2008/12/27/us/27detain.html?pagewanted=%20all&_r=2&

Bernstein, N. (2008b). Detention Center Facing Inquiry Will Get No More Immigrant Detainees. *New York Times*, 6 December. Retrieved December 12, 2021, from www.nytimes.com/2008/12/06/nyregion/06detain.html

Bidgood, J. (2012a). Plan to End Bankruptcy in Rhode Island City Gains Approval, *The New York Times*, 7 September. Retrieved December 12, 2021, from www.nytimes.com/2012/09/07/us/central-falls-ri-to-emerge-from-bankruptcy.html

Bidgood, J. (2012b). Rhode Island: Central falls mayor quits and is to plead guilty to corruption. *N.Y. TIMES*, 20 September. Retrieved December 12, 2021, from www.nytimes.com/2012/09/20/us/rhode-island-central-falls-mayor-quits-and-is-to-plead-guilty-to-corruption.html.

Brown University (2022). *Participatory budgeting in central falls school district*. Retrieved July 12, 2022, from https://static1.squarespace.com/static/5f0622a32fc85336b0183fe8/t/618d1c5e60f440244bbc6da2/1636637805345/VCP+REPORT+FINAL+V4+%281%29.pdf

Burton, P. (2011). Central falls' fiscal woes resonate. *The Bond Buyer, 377*(33561), 7–9.

City of Central Falls (2009). *Basic financial statements and supplementary information with report of independent auditors*. Retrieved December 12, 2021, from www.municipalfinance.ri.gov/documents/data/audits/2009/Central%20Falls_2009.pdf

City of Central Falls (2010). *Basic financial statements and supplementary information with report of independent auditors*. Retrieved December 12, 2021, from https://municipalfinance.ri.gov/sites/g/files/xkgbur546/files/documents/data/audits/2010/Central-Falls_2010.pdf

City of Central Falls (2011). *Basic financial statements and supplementary information with report of independent auditors*. Retrieved December 12, 2021, from www.centralfallsri.gov/sites/default/files/fileattachments/finance/page/3023/central_falls_fy_2011_audit.pdf

City of Central Falls (2012). *Basic financial statements and supplementary information with report of independent auditors*. Retrieved December 12, 2021, from http://www.municipalfinance.ri.gov/documents/data/audits/2012/Central%20Falls_2012.pdf

City of Central Falls (2013). *Basic financial statements and supplementary information with report of independent auditors*. Retrieved December 12, 2021, from https://d3n8a8pro7vhmx.cloudfront.net/centralfalls/pages/90/attachments/original/1410985813/FY13-Audit.pdf?1410985813

City of Central Falls (2014). *Basic financial statements and supplementary information with report of independent auditors*. Retrieved December 12, 2021, from www.centralfallsri.gov/sites/default/files/fileattachments/finance/page/3023/central_falls_fy_2014_audit.pdf

City of Central Falls (2015). *Basic financial statements and supplementary information with report of independent auditors*. Retrieved December 12, 2021, from www.municipalfinance.ri.gov/documents/data/audits/2015/CentralFallsAudit2015.pdf

City of Central Falls (2016). *Basic financial statements and supplementary information with report of independent auditors*. Retrieved December 12, 2021, from www.centralfallsri.gov/sites/default/files/fileattachments/finance/page/3023/central_falls_fy_2016_audit.pdfFinance

City of Central Falls (2017). *Basic financial statements and supplementary information with report of independent auditors*. Retrieved December 12, 2021, from https://d3n8a8pro7vhmx.cloudfront.net/centralfalls/pages/47/attachments/original/1557950484/Central_Falls_FY17_Final_Audit.pdf?1557950484

City of Central Falls (2018). *Basic financial statements and supplementary information with report of independent auditors*. Retrieved December 12, 2021, from www.municipalfinance.ri.gov/documents/data/audits/2018/Central-Falls-6-30-18-Audit.pdf

City of Central Falls (2019). *Basic financial statements and supplementary information with report of independent Auditors*. Retrieved December 12, 2021, from https://municipalfinance.ri.gov/sites/g/files/xkgbur546/files/documents/data/audits/2019/Central-Falls-2019-Audit.pdf

City of Central Falls (2022). *Central falls Mayor Rivera proposes FY2022 budget to help city recover, rebuild.* Retrieved December 12, 2021, from www.centralfallsri.gov/finance/page/central-falls-mayor-rivera-proposes-fy2022-budget-help-city-recover-rebuild-0

Diegmueller, K. (1991). Troubled R.I. district becomes first to request state takeover. *EdWeek*. April 3. Retrieved December 12, 2021, from https://www.edweek.org/education/troubled-r-i-district-becomes-first-to-request-state-takeover/1991/04

Fisher, D. (2013). Muni Bankruptcies Set Up War Between Pensioners and Bondholders, *Forbes*, 3 April. Retrieved December 12, 2021, from www.forbes.com/sites/danielfisher/2013/04/03/muni-bankruptcies-set-up-war-between-pensioners-and-bondholders/

Jordan, J. (2010). Schools, union reach tentative deal. *The Providence Journal*, 17 May 2010. Retrieved December 12, 2021, from www.factiva.com,

McDonald, M., & McLaughlin, D. (2011). Dire Finances Force R.I. City into Bankruptcy. *Bloomberg*. Retrieved December 12, 2021, from www.bloomberg.com/news/articles/2011-08-01/-dire-situation-forces-rhode-island-city-of-central-falls-into-bankruptcy

McGowan, D. (2013, March 12). Judge gives ok to providence pension deal. *WPRI*. Retrieved December 12, 2021, from www.wpri.com/dpp/news/local_news/providence/judge-gives-ok-to-providence-pension-deal

Microtrends (2022). *Central Falls RI Crime Rate 1999–2018*. December 12, 2021, from www.macrotrends.net/cities/us/ri/central-falls/crime-rate-statistics

Moody's Corporation. (2013). *Central Falls, Ri – Moody's research reports may 2010-july 2013*. Retrieved December 12, 2021, from www.municipalbonds.com/bonds/moodys_reports_by_issuer/153447/

Moore, S., & Geoff, M. (2012). *Central Falls High School* (Case study. PEL – 068. May, 11, 2012). Boston, MA: Harvard Business School Publishing.

NBC News (2012). Mayor of Bankrupt central falls, RI, Resigns, set to plead guilty to corruption. *NBC News*, 19 September. Retrieved December 12, 2021, from http://usnews.nbcnews.com/_news/2012/09/19/13964989-mayor-of-bankrupt-central-falls-ri-resigns-set-to-plead-guilty-to-corruption

Nesi, T. (2011). *C. Falls slashes dozens of pensions by 55%; One Gets Cut $41K*, *WPRI*, 2 September. Retrieved December 12, 2021, from http://blogs.wpri.com/2011/09/02/c-falls-slashes-dozens-of-pensions-by-55-one-gets-cut-41k/.

Niedowski, E. (2013). Former Central Falls Mayor Gets Two Years in Prison. *Boston.com*, 12 February. Retrieved December 12, 2021, from www.boston.com/news/local/rhode-island/2013/02/12/former-central-falls-mayor-gets-years-prison/Fb98rVGBsl2u7nDTE18 yIO/story.html

O'Brien, M. (2013). *Central Falls Retirees v. Bondholders: Assessing Fear of Contagion in Chapter 9 Proceedings*. Boston, MA: Boston University School of Law. Retrieved December 12, 2021, from https://scholarship.law.bu.edu/faculty_scholarship/194/

Orson, T. (2013). *The Bond Buyer's 2nd Annual "Symposium on Distressed Municipalities," March 18–19, 2013*. Providence, RI: R.I. GEN.LAWS §45–121. Retrieved December 12, 2021, from http://webserver.rilin.state.ri.us/Statutes/title45/45-12/45-12-1.HTM.

Rhode Island Department of Education (2011). *Statistical tables central falls high school 2009–2010 school year, Rhode island department of education web site*. Retrieved December 22, 2021, from www.ride.ri.gov/applications/statistics.aspx

Rhode Island Government (2012). *City of central falls bond rating upgraded to "BB" by standard and poor's rating services*. Retrieved December 12, 2021, from www.ri.gov/press/view/17987

Russ, H. (2012, September 3). Bankruptcy saves tiny Rhode Island city but leaves scars. *Reuters*. Retrieved December 12, 2021, from www.reuters.com/article/us-usa-rhodeisland-centralfalls-bankrupt/bankruptcy-saves-tiny-rhode-island-city-but-leaves-scars-idUSBRE88300220120904

U.S. Census Bureau (2010). *Central Falls (City) Quick facts (2010)*. Retrieved March 7, 2021, from http://quickfacts.census.gov/qfd/states/44/4414140.html

U.S. Census Bureau (2021). *Central Falls (City) Quick facts (2019)*. Retrieved March 7, 2021, from www.census.gov/quickfacts/centralfallscityrhodeisland

14

CASE STUDY: VALLEJO, CA

Introduction

The city of Vallejo, California filed for protection under Chapter 9 of the United States Bankruptcy Code in May 2008. The city exited bankruptcy three and half years later, on November 1, 2011. The after-bankruptcy restructuring involved budget reforms and administrative innovation, in addition to budget cuts and increasing of taxes and fees. The city of Vallejo underwent many reforms in order to create a more stable city budget, including the introduction of participatory budgeting, which Vallejo was the first to implement on a city-wide basis (Davidson, 2018).

According to Davidson (2020), one of the difficulties involved in assessing post-recession urban restructuring in Vallejo is that "key budget problems have not often become central policy concerns. Extreme fiscal stress does not therefore necessarily convert to extreme remedial action (e.g. austerity), even despite continued, potentially bankruptcy-inducing, budget problems" (p. 536).

Background Information

The City of Vallejo, California, is located on the northern edge of the San Francisco Bay and at the southern end of Napa Valley. Vallejo, California is in southern Solano County, approximately 30 miles northeast of San Francisco. With a population of 121,097 in 2008, Vallejo was the largest city in Solano County and the forty-seventh most populous city among California's 478 cities. The city of Vallejo was incorporated in March 1868 (City of Vallejo, 2008). The city operates under a city charter that was originally adopted in 1911 and last amended in November 2000. The charter provides for a council-manager form of government (City of Vallejo, 2008).

DOI: 10.4324/b23117-14

TABLE 14.1 Demographic, Economic, and Social Situations in City of Vallejo in 2010 and 2019

Population	
Population estimates, July 1, 2019, (V2019)	121,692
Population, Census, April 1, 2010	115,914
Race and Hispanic Origin	
White alone, percent	35.3
Black or African American alone, percent	20.3
Asian alone, percent	23.8
Hispanic or Latino, percent	26.3
Housing	
Owner-occupied housing unit rate, 2015–2019,%	55.5
Median value of owner-occupied housing units, 2015–2019	370,000
Median gross rent, 2015–2019	2,005
Education	
High school graduate or higher, percent of persons age 25 years+, 2015–2019	88
Bachelor's degree or higher, percent of persons age 25 years+, 2015–2019	25.8
Health	
With a disability, under age 65 years, percent, 2015–2019	8.4
Persons without health insurance, under age 65 years, percent	5.8
Economy	
In civilian labor force, total, percent of population age 16 years+, 2015–2019	63.5
Total accommodation and food services sales, 2012 ($1,000)	147,888
Total retail sales per capita, 2012	$9,742
Income and Poverty	
Median household income (in 2019 dollars), 2015–2019	$69,405
Per capita income in past 12 months (in 2019 dollars), 2015–2019	$31,230
Persons in poverty, percent	12.6

Source: Table created by authors based on US Census, 2021

Table 14.1 provides information about demographic and economic situation in the city of Vallejo in 2010 and 2019.

In 2019, 12.6 percent of the population of Vallejo lived below the poverty level. Only 25.8 percent of residents had a bachelor's degree or higher (percent of persons ages 25 years and up) in 2015–2019. More than 5.8 percent of people under age 65 in Vallejo lived without health insurance.

Mare Island

For decades, Vallejo's economy was dominated by its largest employer, the U.S. Navy, located in the city's Mare Island. The Navy commenced its operations in

Mare Island in 1851. In fact, this was the first destination for the Navy on the west coast. In the 1990s, the Mare Island shipyard employed around 7,000 people. Most of its military personnel and many civil employees lived on the island.

The Mare Island Navy Shipyard was decommissioned in 1996. But,

> The federal government did not just walk away. It provided hundreds of millions of dollars for the Navy to "remediate" the island, which contained old munitions, PCBs, radioactive materials, and more. The Navy entered a cooperative arrangement with Vallejo, the state of California, the Lennar Corporation of Miami, and Weston Solutions to fast-track remediation and development. Vallejo's goal was to replace all the lost jobs by 2010.
>
> *(White, 2012, p. 62)*

The plan included the redevelopment of 1,400 out of 5,000 acres of Mare Island with the rest to become parks and natural areas (White, 2012). Two years after the naval shipyard's closing, Mare Island indeed experienced some redevelopment and cleanup. The development company Lennar Corporation and one of its subsidiaries (Weyerhauser) combined to develop the roughly 650 acres that embraced the shipyards and part of the naval base and to prepare building sites and infrastructure for a planned 1,400 homes and apartments. Development was supposed to provide 8,000 jobs.

Some industry and manufacturing have moved to Mare Island (like Alco and American Defense). But redevelopment efforts were far from where they supposed to be. Lennar Corporation was criticized "for not acting aggressively enough to attract more development, or for discouraging certain businesses to locate on Mare Island" (York, 2008, p. 1). "Ruined and empty buildings far outnumber those that are occupied" (White, 2012, p. 64). White (2012) further discusses how

> Over the last decade the base has declined into a kind of industrial Pompeii. A recent quixotic attempt to make it a national park went nowhere: the National Park Service considered even a mostly cleaned-up island too toxic to touch. Mare Island is a partial ruin among other ruins.
>
> *(p. 57)*

Property Tax Revenues

Throughout the 1990s and early 2000s, the city still managed to balance its general fund budget thanks to a booming housing market that helped to boost city's revenues (Davidson, 2018). The "property-related taxes grew by 47% between 2000 and 2005, whereas all other revenues grew in the same period by 22%" (Davidson, 2020, p. 528). Between 2002 and 2007 Vallejo's property tax assessments doubled and associated permit fees grew at similar rates.

Labor Costs

As is always the case with city and county governments, labor costs were the city's single largest expenditure. The majority of labor contracts were held by four unions: the International Association of Fire Fighters (IAFF), the Vallejo Police Officers Association (VPOA), the International Brotherhood of Electrical Workers (IBEW), and the Confidential, Administrative, Management and Professional Employees. The city was obligated to compensate public workers according to their respective collective bargaining agreements (CBAs). These obligations included that the terms of employment could not be adjusted without explicit agreements with the respective unions. In 1970, following a set of labor disputes, Vallejo committed to using binding arbitration to settle labor disputes. This arrangement pegged CBA salaries to tax collections of surrounding municipalities. "Salaries are adjusted annually through formulas in the employee labor agreements. Public Safety salaries are adjusted by a formula tied to the average annual change in a 14 City Bay area pool, and other employee salaries tie to a Consumer Price Index (CPI)" (City of Vallejo, 2009, p. 9).

So, between 1970 and 2010, if the city could not agree on terms with labor unions, an arbiter would apply a pre-defined formula (Davidson, 2020). In the end the city never won an arbitration case and continued to see labor costs take up a larger proportion of general fund revenues. In 1993, the Citizen's Budget Advisory Committee (CBAC) predicted that, sooner or later, without radical reform of the public employee compensation structure, the City of Vallejo would face bankruptcy.

In 2002–2003, the Vallejo general fund supported 512 fulltime equivalent (FTE) employees. The salaries and benefits associated with CBAs accounted for roughly three quarters of Vallejo's general fund expenditures. Police salaries and benefits ranged between 35 percent and 40 percent of total expenditures from 2002 to 2007. Fire service salaries and benefits constituted between 16 percent and 19 percent of the city's total expenditures from 2002 to 2007. In 2006–2007, Vallejo's labor costs increased by 11 percent while revenues grew only by 2.6 percent (Mayer, 2008a). In 2007–2008, when the recession hit, the budget became really difficult to balance as the city's revenues dropped and expenditures continued to grow thanks to built-in salary increases (Davidson & Kutz, 2015, p. 1448).

Around 20 percent of the general fund was dedicated to service and supply expenses, such as vehicle and street maintenance. The remaining funds were allocated to "internal transfers" such as general fund debt services (Tanner et al., 2008, p. 12).

The Fiscal Emergency

The City of Vallejo struggled to stay fiscally sustainable after 2008 when the Great Recession brought additional fiscal problems to the city.

> Vallejo's property-related and sales taxes' revenue growth stopped. Vallejo's property and sales tax revenues collapsed by 30 and 20% respectively when

> the housing bubble burst, on the eve of the Great Recession, finally pushing the city over a financial cliff that it had been skirting for some time.
>
> *(Peck, 2014, p. 36)*

Vallejo's median home prices decreased from 471,000 dollars in 2006, to 164,300 dollars in 2010 (Davidson, 2020). According to Davidson (2020),

> Vallejo's housing market collapsed, with per-square foot housing costs declining from $270 in 2007–2008 to $121 in 2009–2010 and, consequently, property-related taxes stopped growing.
>
> Declining property values, i.e. property tax base, coupled with strict statutory and constitutional property tax caps imposed by Proposition 13[1] in California, resulted in decreasing property, income and excise tax revenues. Since that time, many local governments have relied increasingly upon other revenue tools to finance local services, most notably: assessments, property-related fees, and a variety of small general-purpose taxes (such as hotel, business license, and utility user taxes).
>
> Between 2007–2008 and 2008–2009, Vallejo's General Fund revenues declined from $83.1m to $78.2 [million].
>
> *(p. 528)*

In 2008, the City of Vallejo had projected 85 million dollars in general fund revenues in 2007–2008 but ended up collecting only about 76 million dollars.

Table 14.2 provides the dynamic of expenditures and revenues in the city of Vallejo from 2007 to 2008.

By the end of the fiscal year, on June 30, 2008, Vallejo's general fund recorded a third consecutive year of budget deficits. The City of Vallejo's general fund was suffering a 13.4-million-dollar shortfall in 2007 (Table 14.2). Besides the general fund, unreserved and undesignated fund balances also dropped from 9.9 million dollars on June 30, 2005, to 797,195 dollars on June 30, 2008 (City of Vallejo, 2009, p. 8).

Expenditure Cuts

The next step for the struggling city was to cut the expenses. The City of Vallejo decreased the expenditures by 28.6 million dollars from 2007 to 2008 (Table 14.2). Community development expenditures decreased to 33 million dollars in 2008, from 45 million dollars in 2007 primarily due to a 12 million dollar decrease in federally funded hazardous remediation expenditures at the former Mare Island naval base. The city cut 2.2 million dollars in fire expenses by closing 2 of the city's 8 fire stations in March 2008 as a part of the general fund's fiscal emergency budget reductions. To mitigate growing per-unit employee costs, unable to reduce salaries due to Union contracts, the work force paid out of the general fund was reduced by 18 percent, from 494 to 407 employees between

TABLE 14.2 Revenues and Expenditures in City of Vallejo from 2007 to 2008 (in thousands $)

	2007	*2008*
REVENUE		
Charges for services, $	150,362	131,362
Operating grants and contributions $	50,790	40,864
Capital grants and contributions $	10,155	7,878
Property taxes, sales and others, $	50,170	55,786
User utility, $	12,474	13,501
Miscellaneous, $	20,534	46,005
Total Revenue	294,758	295,588
EXPENDITURES		
Development services, $	2,839	3,252
Community development, $	44,541	33,499
Fire services, $	29,683	27,465
Police services, $	41,702	43,074
Public works, $	24,422	25,984
Total Expenditures	308,176	283,556
Fund balance, beginning		(13,418)
Fund balance, ending	(13,418)	12,032
Current and other assets	280	241.8
Capital assets	703	683.3
Total assets	983	925.1
Current liabilities	66.5	51.7
Long-term liabilities	292	236.9
Total liabilities	358.5	288.6
Net Assets	624.5	636.5

Source: Table created by authors based on Audit Reports, CAFRs and annual budgets of the City of Vallejo (2008, 2009)

2004 and 2008 (City of Vallejo, 2007, 2008, 2009). In 2007 alone, the City of Vallejo reduced staffing from 464.7 full time employees (FTE) to 427.6 FTE. The staff cuts came in about equal parts from police and fire departments.

Through the formula used to calculate automated salary increase, public safety salaries were estimated to grow "by 24% during the four-year period from July 1, 2006, until the end of the contract period on June 30, 2010. IBEW salaries were estimated to increase by 13% and management salaries by 9% over the same contract period" (City of Vallejo, 2009, p. 9). In February–March 2008, the City of Vallejo failed negotiations with the Vallejo Police Officers Association and the International Association of Fire Fighters to restructure collective bargaining agreements to ensure solvency. In 2008, the obligations to employee salaries and benefits alone exceeded the entire general fund revenue and the city's budget faced a 23-million-dollar deficit.

Another challenge Vallejo faced was the maintenance of the city's aging public buildings, streets, and roads. The city's estimated annual cost of maintenance and repair for the buildings, streets, and roads was eight million dollars in 2010, but the city only had financial resources to fund 10–30 percent of this requirement annually (City of Vallejo, 2011).

"Financial Gimmicks"

In the absence of substantial reserves, a shrinking property tax base, and the inability to raise new revenues due to the state-wide restrictions imposed by Proposition 13, in 2008 Vallejo turned to "financial gimmicks" or "phantom balancing tricks" by transferring five million dollars from dedicated funds to the general fund, in attempt to balance the latter. This included a transfer of 1.7 million dollars of unrestricted cash balances from the vehicle replacement fund, 1.7 million dollars from the sale of Marine World, and 1.5 million dollars from other sources (City of Vallejo, 2009, p. 11). As of June 30, 2008, all unrestricted and available balances from other funds had been depleted.

Another attempt to artificially balance its budget was the sale of the city's share in the aforementioned Marine World Park. The Marine World Africa USA theme park relocated to Vallejo in 1988. The park was owned by the nonprofit Marine World Foundation until it defaulted on its debt to the city in 1996 and its ownership was transferred to Vallejo in 1998. In 1999, the park became co-owned by the city and Six Flags and its name changed to Six Flags Marine World. Revenue sharing agreements between the city and Six Flags brought Vallejo nearly three million dollars in 2005–2006, 1.45 million dollars in 2006–2007, and 1.68 million dollars in 2007–2008 (Colliver, 2009). Fiscal struggles made Vallejo sell a city-owned portion of the park to Six Flags on July 31, 2007, and the park was renamed into Six Flags Discovery Kingdom. In conjunction with the sale, the city was able to retire 56 million dollars of debt: 1.4 million dollars of the net proceeds from the sale, plus 385,000 dollars released from a related debt service resulted in one-time 1.7-million-dollar transfer to the city's general fund. While the sale of the park provided a much needed boost to the city's budget in 2008, it eliminated the annual stream of revenue for Vallejo. Since Six Flags became the solo owner of the park, the city receives only 2.5 percent in admission fees, with only 265,000 dollars in fees in 2007–2008, resulting in a "net annual loss in excess of a million dollars to the General Fund" (City of Vallejo, 2008, p. viii). The park is still the second largest employer, the second largest property taxpayer, and among the top sales tax payers in Vallejo (City of Vallejo, 2020).

Vallejo's Bankruptcy

In the face of economic recession, without any reserves that the city could use to sustain its operations during the Great Recession, waiting for the revenues to (hopefully) bounce back when the economy recovers, with limited opportunities to raise taxes due to state constitutional restrictions, and burdened by labor contracts locked in through 2010, the city determined in early May of 2008 that it was no longer able to meet its contractual obligations. Because of balanced budget requirements enacted by both the state and the city, the general fund would have lacked the legal authority to continue paying for services after July 1, 2008.

On May 23, 2008, the city filed for Chapter 9 of the United States Bankruptcy Code seeking an opportunity to adjust its debts (City of Vallejo, 2009). Back in the day, New York Times called Vallejo "Broke Town, U.S.A.". White (2012) writes about this time:

> Everything but the city's boundaries and its unemployment rate of about 15 percent seems to be shrinking. A bankrupt Vallejo has had to discharge public employees. Its population has declined. Its taxable retail sales have shrunk from $721 million in 2004 to $526.5 million in 2009. Its property tax and utility tax revenue are declining.
>
> *(p. 65).*

Table 14.3 provides the timeline of the City of Vallejo's bankruptcy.

Mare Island

In addition to the city's own bankruptcy, the financial situation in the city was further undermined when Lennar Mare Island LLC, a part of a 21-company real estate partnership that provided cleanup and redevelopment of Mare Island after the Naval shipyard closure in 1996, also filed for Chapter 11 bankruptcy on June 8, 2008. According to York (2008), this bankruptcy "filing, which included Lennar Mare Island and a number of its subsidiaries, was 'absolutely a concern' to Vallejo" (p. 1). The city was left with expensive time-pressing hazardous cleaning, redevelopment, and repurposing to do in the Island and no money for that in the

TABLE 14.3 Timeline of Vallejo Bankruptcy

Date	*Event*
May 6, 2008	City council votes unanimously (7–0) to file for Chapter 9 bankruptcy.
May 23, 2008	The City of Vallejo files for Chapter 9 bankruptcy
June 8, 2008	Lennar Mare Island LLC files for Chapter 11 bankruptcy, taking $4.5 million out of city 2008/2009 budget.
September 8, 2008	The City was ruled to be eligible for Chapter 9 relief by bankruptcy court
September 1, 2009	Judge Michael McManus approves rejection of Vallejo's CBAs with the International Brotherhood of Electrical Workers under Chapter 9
November 1, 2011	Federal Bankruptcy Court (Solano County) releases the City of Vallejo from Chapter 9 bankruptcy.

budget whatsoever. "Mare Island, which was supposed to provide revenue for the city, drains Vallejo's nearly exhausted resources" (White, 2012, pp. 65–66).

Labor Costs and Negotiations with the Unions

The Chapter 9 filing provided the city and its creditor constituencies, including employees and bond holders, with time to renegotiate settlements with an objective of long-term fiscal stability (City of Vallejo, 2009). The city restructured various general fund obligations and certificates of participation. Vallejo also renegotiated collective bargaining agreements with employee unions and reduced services as part of the bankruptcy plan.

On September 8, 2008, the bankruptcy court ruled that the city was eligible for Chapter 9 relief. That order was appealed by three of the city's four labor unions, one of which subsequently withdrew its appeal, following a settlement with the city on a labor contract amendment in January 2009. The fourth labor union also entered into a post-petition labor contract amendment. The Bankruptcy Appellate Panel of the Ninth Circuit affirmed the lower court's eligibility ruling on June 26, 2009. On July 6, 2009, the two remaining employee organizations filed a notice of appeal to the United States Court of Appeals of the Ninth Circuit (City of Vallejo, 2009). On February 3, 2009, the bankruptcy court ruled that bankruptcy law governed the rejection of the employee collective bargaining agreements. The court has not yet ruled on whether the two remaining contracts should be rejected (City of Vallejo, 2009).

During the entire bankruptcy process, Vallejo came to new agreements with police, fire, and public administrator unions. The International Brotherhood of Electrical Workers (IBEW) was the only union to reject a collective bargaining agreement (City of Vallejo, 2013). Davidson (2020) pointed out that reforms made to Vallejo's CBAs during bankruptcy did not, however, result in significant fiscal restructuring. The police union negotiated a 7 percent salary increase for 2011. In 2010, Measure A was placed on the election ballot asking residents if they wanted to remove binding arbitration with labor unions from the City Charter. Measure A was approved by 51 percent of voters and created the conditions necessary for the city to dispute CBA terms (Davidson, 2020).

Other Expenditure Cuts

With already extreme cuts in place before applying for bankruptcy, Vallejo had to tighten its belt even more between 2008 and 2011. In the Fiscal Year (FY) 2009–2010 alone the FTE positions paid from the general fund were reduced from 407 to 330 (City of Vallejo, 2009, 2010). During the bankruptcy process, Vallejo either suspended debt payments or paid lower interest rates on its general obligation debt:

> For the period from May to July, 2009, facing further revenue shortfalls, the City suspended all General Fund principal and interest payments. Payments resumed on August 1, 2009, at a 2% interest rate. As of July 2010, as part

> of an updated 5-year business plan, General Fund interest payments were again suspended. The new 5-year business plan includes deferring principal payments for three years from July 2010 until June 2013.
>
> *(City of Vallejo, 2010, p. 45)*

As it is usually the case during municipal bankruptcy, debt obligations secured by restricted "special revenues", such as water and improvement bonds, were treated as secured obligations and were paid in full as long as those special revenues were sufficient to meet debt service. The city was also able to refinance its water bonds in 2013.

The extreme budget cuts resulted in staff shortages, deferred infrastructure spending, underfunded development work, and a general decline of community services. Bankrupt Vallejo could not borrow money for capital expenditures, including expenditures for maintaining streets or replacing aging police cars and fire trucks.

Between FY2007–2008 and FY2009–2010, general fund revenues dropped 18 percent. "Police staffing was reduced by 47% and 42% reductions in Fire staffing resulted in closure of three fire stations" (City of Vallejo, 2012, p. 9). These budget cuts led to increased response times to fires and medical emergencies, and a rise in the violent crimes' rate. In 2013, the crime rate in Vallejo rose by twelve percent compared to 2010. In 2019, the crime rate in Vallejo was two times higher than the U.S. average and higher than in 96.8 percent U.S. cities (City-Data, 2022).

After over three years in bankruptcy, the Federal Bankruptcy Court (Solano County) approved Vallejo's restructuring plan and made changes to retiree healthcare benefits (that were now capped at 300 dollars per retiree, per month, resulting in a 75- to 100-million-dollar reduction in the city's long-term liabilities), reworked lease obligations (resulting in a 47 percent reduction in interest obligations, an estimated savings of 23 million dollars), and reduced bonded debt liability (unsecured creditors received between 5 and 20 cents on the dollar) (Davidson, 2020). On November 1, 2011, the Federal Bankruptcy Court released the City of Vallejo from Chapter 9 bankruptcy. "The city saved $34 million by avoiding paying a portion of interest costs on its bonds and rejecting expensive labor agreements, but it spent more than $13 million on legal fees, which counteracted the savings" (PEW Charitable Trusts, 2013, p. 11).

Post-bankruptcy Restructuring

Some of the changes that started in Vallejo during bankruptcy continued for years after. For example, labor costs negotiations with unions are still in place. A temporary sales tax increase adopted in 2011 was voted to become permanent in 2017. The idea of a participatory budget process first introduced in 2011 was adopted at the elections – along with the sales tax increase – and approved by the city council in April 2012.

Controlling Labor Costs

In addition to more manageable increases in labor costs negotiated with labor unions, the City of Vallejo focused on cutting post-employment benefits (OPEBs). In 2014, the city agreed to additional minor reforms to CBAs with its public administrator and firefighters' unions, cutting 83 million dollars from long-term OPEBs. The city adopted the year-by-year contract terms with the police union, including salary freezes and an increase in police staffing using only new revenues. The contract terms, however, maintained relatively generous CBA conditions that the city had negotiated with the police union in 2011. The police union also filed a lawsuit seeking to reclaim 12 million dollars in OPEB reductions imposed on retirees during bankruptcy (Davidson, 2020).

Although Vallejo's budgetary problems were dominated by an extremely high proportion of revenues dedicated to labor-related expenditures, labor reforms have proven to be difficult. The structural budget issues that led to Vallejo's bankruptcy have still not been resolved. In Vallejo's 2015–2016 budget, spending on salaries and benefits were 40,541,300 dollars and 31,911,955 dollars, respectively. In the 2017–2018 budget, salaries and benefits were at approximately the same proportion of general fund revenues as they were prior to bankruptcy. By 2021–2022, the City of Vallejo budgeted salaries are up 2 percent and benefits are a whopping 24 percent higher. To this day, the city also still experiences difficulties in addressing pension liabilities.

Sales Tax Increase

In 2011, Vallejo's City Council proposed a new one percent sales tax to fund economic development and infrastructure improvement. In November 2011, Measure B was placed on the ballot:

> To enhance funding for 9–1–1 response, police patrols, firefighter and paramedic services, youth and senior programs, street and pothole repair, graffiti removal, economic development, and general city services, shall the sales tax be raised one percent, expiring after ten years, with all revenue legally required to stay in Vallejo?

Vallejo's residents were asked to approve a term-limited sales tax increase that would generate annually an estimated 9–10 million dollars in new revenues. Measure B passed with 50.43 percent of voters' approval rate in November 2011. In 2017, Vallejo's residents voted to make the sales tax increase permanent. The effective combined sales tax in Vallejo increased from 7.375 to 8.375 percent (with 6 percent California State sales tax, 0.25 percent Solano County tax, 1 percent City of Vallejo tax, and 1.13% special tax rate). It has been the highest sales tax rate in Solano County (both cities of Fairfield and

Vallejo in Solano County have an 8.375 percent combined sales tax rate now). The sales tax represents about 13 percent of the city's general fund revenues, which, when adopted, provided a substantial and much-needed boost to the city's discretionary revenues.

In the first full year of Measure B adoption, the 37 percent of the 11.5 million dollars in new revenues was allocated to "Participatory Budgeting", 18 percent to "Infrastructure Enhancement", 16 percent to "Reserves and Pension Liability Paydown", 13 percent to "Public Safety Preservation/Enhancement", and other causes (Davidson, 2020). Since 2014, Measure B has increasingly been used to fund public safety, in particular police and fire personnel. By July 2016, Measure B revenues were supporting 22 sworn officers at an annual cost of 4.74 million dollars. Most of these officers were involved in field operations and with the Crime Reduction Team. Measure B also funds a police cadet program (100,000 dollars per year), two communications officer positions (159,832 dollars per year), and two Code Enforcement Officers (217,947 dollars per year). In the fire department, Measure B revenues fund 11 positions including the Deputy Chief and 10 Firefighters (1,137,770 dollars per year). Measure B funds are also used to keep open a sixth firehouse in Vallejo. Measure B revenues have therefore restored much of the emergency services previously subject to budget cuts. According to Davidson (2020), "the staffing of police and fire departments using Measure B revenues also created a budgetary problem. Measure B is a resident-approved sales tax which was due to expire after 10 years" (p. 530).

Participatory Budgeting (PB)

Participatory budgeting (PB) is a budgeting approach in which community members decide how to allocate a part of a city budget. The introduction of participatory budgeting to Vallejo was initially proposed by the City Councilman Marti Brown in 2010 and included in Measure B vote together with proposition to introduce a 1 percent city sales tax. On April 7, 2012, the City of Vallejo's council approved, with a four to three vote, the city-wide 3.4-million-dollar participatory budgeting process. Vallejo contracted an external consultant, a Participatory Budgeting Project, to organize the first cycle of the participatory budgeting process.

Vallejo began the PB process by assembling a 21-member steering committee, made up of representatives from local civic organizations and residents. The committee then established a process of how to develop consultation with the community, ultimately leading to residents voting on a set of fully developed proposals. In the first round of funding, the City Council approved 12 projects that received the most votes.

Vallejo's PB rulebook establishes project eligibility, timelines, participation rules, and PB roles and responsibilities. The rulebook set out four PB goals: (1)

improve our city, (2) engage our community, (3) transform democracy, and (4) open up the government (City of Vallejo, 2012, 2015).

The process of public consultation and decision-making in Vallejo's participatory budgeting had restored transparency and built the trust between the city administration and residents (City of Vallejo, 2015). Unfortunately, the city has gradually rolled back its commitment to the project since 2013 (Davidson, 2020). Thirty-seven percent of Measure B funds were initially allocated for participatory budgeting. In 2016–2017 this share was less than 10 percent of Measure B revenues. In 2017–2018, participatory budgeting received just one million dollars, which equates to seven percent of Measure B revenues. Most of this one million dollars was spent on routine infrastructure and emergency service operations. According to Davidson (2020), both city staff and residents complained that this spending did not correspond to the original ameliorative intentions of the program.

Reducing Fiscal Risks

To reduce long-term fiscal risks and to better guide budget decisions, Vallejo specified five major principles: (1) maintain a minimum of five percent reserves of general fund expenditures (a positive general fund balance), (2) conservatively project revenues, (3) use Measure B revenues only to augment existing services or rebuild reserves, (4) adopt the standard accounting practices and a five-year financial forecast, and (5) continue contributions to reduce OPEB's long-term liabilities and address maintenance deficiencies (City of Vallejo, 2013).

In response to the set objectives, in 2016, the size of City of Vallejo's reserves constituted 15 percent of expenditures (City of Vallejo, 2017). The city underwent extensive reforms in management and budgeting practices. These involved conservative revenue forecasting, the adoption of standard accounting practices, and a five-year financial forecasting. These reforms made the budget process more transparent and accountable. The reduction of OPEB liabilities further supported budget accountability.

In 2014–2015, Vallejo had the first structurally balanced budget in ten years. This budget received the Government Finance Officers Association (GFOA) Financial Reporting Award in 2014 and, for the first time ever, received an Unqualified Audit Opinion in the same year (City of Vallejo, 2016).

Repairing and Improving the City's Infrastructure

Many of the projects in post-bankrupt Vallejo focused on repairing and improving the city's infrastructure, with the other projects funding educational and social service improvements. The first cycle of funding in FY2012–FY2013 was used to renovate athletic fields, improve the look of downtown buildings, administer animal spay and neutering programs, and improve downtown street lighting. The second cycle of funding in FY2013–FY2014 targeted improvement in school meals, supported summer jobs program for city youth, subsidized school band, funded the repairs of city sidewalks, and subsidized the replacement of a fire service vehicle. The third cycle of funding in FY2014–FY2015 supported youth basketball and youth fire academy, funded purchase of tablets for afterschool programs, and subsidized roads' repairs. The fourth cycle in FY2015–FY2016 predominantly funded pothole repairs and an upgrade to the police department's communications room (Davidson, 2018). According to Davidson (2018), "In 2012–13, PB generated 60 potential projects for vetting by City staff. By 2016–17, this number has shrunk to 19" (p. 561). The overall service improvements in Vallejo were substantial: "streets are now being paved, parks renovated, senior citizen centers improved, and government administration made more efficient" (Davidson, 2020, p. 531).

Conclusions

Revenue-expenditure imbalance, a lack of a diversified economy, economic downswing and diminishing tax revenues during the Great Recession (Davidson & Kutz, 2018; Davidson & Ward, 2014; Peck, 2012), unsound financial management (Glaeser & Ponzetto, 2013), negative effects of the California state-wide restrictions imposed by Proposition 13 (Bardhan & Walker, 2011), increasing labor costs, zero reserve balances, and outstanding short-term operating loans collectively indicated impending financial trouble in Vallejo.

Vallejo tried to renegotiate labor contracts with the unions and actively cut expenses even prior to bankruptcy. During the bankruptcy process from 2008 to 2011, Vallejo further deepened budget cuts (including deferred maintenance of capital infrastructure) cut the police force by 42 percent and firefighters by 47 percent, and decreased expenditures for maintaining streets or replacing aging police cars and fire trucks. Following bankruptcy, perhaps the most notable budgetary reform in Vallejo was introduction of participatory budgeting. Participatory budgeting was intended to make the City of Vallejo's budgeting more efficient, accountable, and transparent.

Despite all the positive developments with the city budgeting and financial situation, Vallejo failed to resolve a structural deficit problem. Measure B revenues, participatory budgeting, and GAAP accounting have improved the city's fiscal health but largely left the collective bargaining agreements (CBA) and other post-employment benefit (OPEB) liabilities unaddressed, one of main reasons for bankruptcy in 2008 (Davidson, 2020; Mayer, 2008a,b). According to Davidson (2020), Vallejo's extreme fiscal stress involved "radical reform (i.e. bankruptcy) without the pain of real reform (i.e. addressing structural budget problems)" (p. 536).

In contrast to other case studies that we considered in this book, where localities were not only able to successfully exit the fiscal crisis but also structurally reformed their budgeting and financial practices to maximally protect their grounds against possibility of future downfalls, Vallejo succeeded in balancing its budget, but researchers, such as Hicken (2014) or Davidson (2020), are still predicting the city's second bankruptcy.

Note

1 Proposition 13 in California is one of the earliest and most strict revenue constraints among all the states. It limits the municipal ability to increase property taxes, the major source of revenue for most local governments. Proposition 13 additionally specifies that any local tax imposed to pay for specific governmental programs – a "special tax" – must be approved by two-thirds of the votes.

References

Bardhan, A., & Walker, R. (2011). California shrugged: Fountainhead of the great recession. *Cambridge Journal of Regions, Economy and Society*, *4*, 303–322.

City-Data (2022). *Vallejo crime rate 1999–2020*, 22 February 2022. Retrieved from www.city-data.com/crime/crime-Vallejo-California.html

City of Vallejo (2007). *Annual City Budget, 2007–2008*. Vallejo, CA: City of Vallejo. Retrieved December 12, 2021, from www.cityofvallejo.net/city_hall/departmentsdivisions/finance/financialreports

City of Vallejo (2008). *CAFR 2008*. Vallejo, CA: City of Vallejo. Retrieved December 12, 2021, from www.cityofvallejo.net/city_hall/departmentsdivisions/finance/financialreports

City of Vallejo (2009). *CAFR 2009*. Vallejo, CA: City of Vallejo. Retrieved December 12, 2021, from www.cityofvallejo.net/city_hall/departmentsdivisions/finance/financialreports

City of Vallejo (2010). *CAFR 2010*. Vallejo, CA: City of Vallejo. Retrieved December 12, 2021, from www.cityofvallejo.net/city_hall/departmentsdivisions/finance/financialreports

City of Vallejo (2011). *CAFR 2011*. Vallejo, CA: City of Vallejo. Retrieved December 12, 2021, from www.cityofvallejo.net/city_hall/departmentsdivisions/finance/financialreports

City of Vallejo (2012). *Annual city budget, 2013–2014*. Vallejo, CA: City of Vallejo. Retrieved December 12, 2020, from www.cityofvallejo.net/city_hall/departmentsdivisions/finance/financialreports

City of Vallejo (2013). *Annual city budget, 2013–2014*. Vallejo, CA: City of Vallejo. Retrieved December 12, 2020, from http://vallejoca.hosted.civiclive.com/common/pages/DisplayFile.aspx?itemId=17938041

City of Vallejo (2015). *Participatory Budgeting in Vallejo summaries, cycles 1–4*. Retrieved December 12, 2020, from www.ci.vallejo.ca.us

City of Vallejo (2016). *CAFR 2016*. Vallejo, CA: City of Vallejo. Retrieved December 12, 2020, from http://vallejoca.hosted.civiclive.com/common/pages/DisplayFile.aspx?itemId=17938047

City of Vallejo (2017). *CAFR 2017*. Vallejo, CA: City of Vallejo. Retrieved December 12, 2020, from http://vallejoca.hosted.civiclive.com/common/pages/DisplayFile.aspx?itemId=17938049

City of Vallejo (2020). *CAFR 2020*. Vallejo, CA: City of Vallejo. Retrieved December 12, 2021, from https://vallejoca.hosted.civiclive.com/our_city/departments_divisions/finance_department/financial_reports

Colliver (June 14, 2009). *Bankruptcy Filing Won't Close Vallejo Six Flags*. San Francisco: Chronicle. Retrieved February 26, 2022, from www.sfgate.com/bayarea/article/Bankruptcy-filing-won-t-close-Vallejo-Six-Flags-3295258.php

Davidson, M. (2018). *Participatory budgeting, austerity, and institutions of democracy*. Retrieved December 12, 2020, from http://wordpress.clarku.edu/mdavidson/files/2019/08/Davidson-2018-Participatory-Budgeting-Vallejo.pdf

Davidson, M. (2020). Extreme municipal fiscal stress and austerity? A case study of fiscal reform after Chapter 9 bankruptcy. *Environment and Planning C: Politics and Space, 38*(3), 522–538. doi:10.1177/2399654419872218.

Davidson, M., & Kutz, W. (2015). Grassroots austerity: Municipal bankruptcy from below in Vallejo, California. *Environment and Planning A: Economy and Space*, *47*(7), 1440–1459.

Davidson, M., & Kutz, W. (2018). *Cities under Austerity*. Albany: SUNY Press.

Davidson, M., & Ward, K. (2014). "Picking up the pieces": Austerity urbanism, California, and fiscal crisis. *Cambridge Journal of Regions. Economy and Society,* 7(1), 81–97.

Glaeser, E., & Ponzetto, G. (2013). *Shrouded costs of government: The political economy of state and local public pensions* [Working Paper18976]. National Bureau of Economic Research, Cambridge, MA. Retrieved December 12, 2020, from www.nber.org/papers/w18976

Hicken, M. (2014). Once bankrupt, Vallejo still can't afford its pricey pensions. *CNN Money*. Retrieved April 25, 2019, from http://money.cnn.com/2014/03/10/pf/vallejo-pensions/index.html

Mayer, S. (2008a). *Declaration of Susan Mayer in Support of Motion for Approval of Rejection of Collective Bargaining Agreements Case No. 2008–26813 In re*. City of Vallejo: United States Bankruptcy Court, Eastern District of California.

Mayer, S. (2008b). *Declaration of Susan Mayer in Support of the Statement of Qualifications under Section 109(c) Case No. 2008–26813 in Re*. City of Vallejo: United States Bankruptcy Court, Eastern District of California.

Peck, J. (2012). Austerity urbanism. *City*, *16*(6), 626–655.

Peck, J. (2014). Pushing austerity: State failure, municipal bankruptcy, and the crises of fiscal federalism in the U.S.A. *Cambridge Journal of Regions, Economy and Society*, 7(1), 17–44.

PEW Charitable Trusts (2013). *The state role in local government financial distress*. Retrieved February 22, 2022, from www.pewtrusts.org/~/media/assets/2016/04/pew_state_role_in_local_government_financial_distress.pdf

Tanner, J., Whittom, C., & Stout, R. (2008). *City of Vallejo, Council Communication* (Updated information regarding the condition of the General Fund and consideration of a resolution approving the filing of a petition under Chapter 9 of the United States Bankruptcy Code Case No. 2008–26813 In re). City of Vallejo: United States Bankruptcy Court, Eastern District of California.

York, J. (2008). Lennar Mare Island petitions for Chapter 11 bankruptcy. *Times-Herald*, 9 June. Retrieved February 22, 2022, from www.timesheraldonline.com/2008/06/09/lennar-mare-island-petitions-for-chapter-11-bankruptcy/.

White, R. (2012). Deconstructing Mare Island. Reconnaissance in the ruins. *Boom: A Journal of California*, *2*(2), 55–69.

15

CONCLUSIONS AND A THEORY OF FINANCIAL MANAGEMENT AND BUDGETING DURING FISCAL EMERGENCY AND BANKRUPTCY

Introduction

We placed a lot of emphasis in this book on the understanding of financial management and budgeting practices in different municipalities before, during, and after bankruptcy and fiscal stress. The last six chapters were devoted to an in-depth analysis of case studies representing various intensities of fiscal stress from a rather quick and relatively mild fiscal distress situation in Colorado Springs, CO, to the longest among studied municipalities fiscal emergency situations in Pittsburgh, PA that lasted over 14 years, to the largest municipal bankruptcy in U.S. history, the bankruptcy of Detroit, MI. An understanding of commonalities and differences in fiscal stress and bankruptcy practices across the six municipalities can provide a foundation toward a theory of financial management and budgeting during fiscal emergency and bankruptcy.

This chapter summarizes what we learned from the studied cases in terms of the causes of the fiscal stress, steps taken to exit it, and the consequences of such stress for municipalities. These findings will allow local and state governments officials to compare the various techniques and methods of planning, budgeting, and financing during fiscal stress or bankruptcy in search of what might work for their specific situation.

Common Causes of Fiscal Stress

An understanding of the causes of fiscal stress is extremely important in averting fiscal emergency. By looking at the warning signs and mistakes made by others, municipalities can be better prepared not to repeat the same slipups and find themselves in similar unfortunate situations.

DOI: 10.4324/b23117-15

Although the causes of default and the means of subsequent recovery varied among the individual municipalities, it is definitely possible to distill common elements from the case studies. The studied municipalities generally exhibited similar signs of deterioration during fiscal stress, including increasing blight and more abandoned properties, a low demand for housing, deserted neighborhoods, inactive downtowns, a high proportion of low-income households, a high share of unskilled workers, a shrinking tax base, cutbacks of city services, and increasing taxes and fees.

In one case study after another, we additionally observed certain underlying conditions that can cause fiscal emergency in local governments. Revenue-expenditure imbalance, national and regional economic downswings, unsound financial management, a negative impact of state tax limitations on municipal ability to raise additional revenues at the time of need, diminishing revenues, increasing expenditures, mismanagement of large infrastructure projects, growing reliance on short-term borrowing to provide liquidity for current operations, an underfunded locally administered retirement system, "financial gimmicks", corruption, and other common problems indicated impending financial trouble in all case studies.

The Impact of National and Regional Economic Downswings

Deindustrialization and changing tastes in the economy were at the core of the long-term problems in the fiscal emergency or bankruptcy cases we studied. Whether this is a decentralization of the auto sector, by far the most major employer and taxpayer in Detroit; or declining demand for steel, with steel mills staying at the heart of Pittsburgh's economy; or the outsourcing of textile production to developing countries and the closing of textile mills in Central Falls, RI, the major employer in that city; or closure of the Navy base, the major employer in Vallejo, CA, in all examples industrial changes were some of the major causes of long-term fiscal imbalance.

While a changing economy undermines the overall fiscal strength of municipalities, it is usually environmental jolts that push struggling municipalities over the fiscal cliff. In four out of six case studies we presented in this book, economic recessions were these jolts. The Great Recession of 2008–2009 was the strong last force leading Detroit, MI; Vallejo, CA; and Jefferson County, AL to bankruptcy, and Colorado Springs, CO to a fiscal distress situation. The lock-downs caused by the COVID-19 crisis, for example, pushed Springfield, AL to apply for bankruptcy (not one of our case study cities).[1]

Revenue–Expenditure Imbalance

Each studied city was dealing with budget deficits for years leading to fiscal emergency. The gap between expenditures and revenues was at least 5 percent of revenue in each case study. Both shrinking revenue and increasing expenditures caused budget deficits to grow out of control. Prior to the Great Recession of 2008–2009, most of the case study cities became financially vulnerable by permitting debt service to become a large percentage of total receipts.

Revenue Side of Fiscal Stress

On the revenue side, there were both economic and legal limitations that substantially constrained revenue collections in the sample of the studied cities.

Economic Limitations

Of the economic limitations, the common source of financial distress was a shrinking tax base caused by departure or downsizing of the major employers, outmigration of population, increasing unemployment, and diminishing property tax values. We observed a direct positive correlation between the severity of fiscal crisis and the shrinking tax base in every fiscal emergency or bankruptcy case considered in this book.

Legal Limitations

The legal limitations created by state-imposed statutory and constitutional tax caps cannot be blamed for the cause of fiscal emergency or stress in the studied local governments. However, they certainly did not make situation easier when fiscally challenged municipalities were looking for ways to raise additional revenues at the time of extreme need. Thirty-eight states in the U.S. have some sort of tax limitations (see Chapter 3). All municipalities in our sample come from these 38 states. Proposition 13 in California, Taxpayer Bill of Rights (TABOR) in Colorado, and the Headlee Amendment in Michigan have perhaps some of the strictest restrictions on local governments.

Expenses Side of Fiscal Stress

The main contributors to growing expenses were mainly ever-increasing labor costs, legacy costs, and debt service.

Personnel Expenses

Since municipalities do not generally produce goods but are mainly involved in service-oriented activities, it is of no surprise that personnel expenses, including wages, salaries, and benefits, constitute a major part of local government expenditures. In Pittsburgh, salaries and wages made up about two-thirds of general fund expenditures in FY2003 – the year when the city was officially designated as fiscally stressed – and grew by 5–6 percent annually in FY2001 and FY2002, in contrast to revenue growth of below 1 percent (see Chapter 12).

Labor expenses were not merely a contributing factor but are often at the core of fiscal distress, especially if their increase is not under control as, for example, in the case of Vallejo. Poorly constructed and negotiated contracts with powerful labor unions in Vallejo have led to unmanageable increases in personnel expenses in this city that became one of the primary causes of bankruptcy and continuing fiscal distress to this day. In FY2002–2003 collective bargaining agreements accounted for about three-quarters of all general fund expenditures in Vallejo. In 2008 when the city applied for bankruptcy, labor costs alone exceeded the entire general fund revenues (see Chapter 14).

Legacy Costs

In the attempts to deal with current fiscal hardships, cities often tried to push costs down the road by offering generous pensions and retiree health benefits in leu of current salary increases. As time passed and the financial situation further deteriorated, municipalities in one case after another were unable to afford "the costs of both current and future employees" (from an interview with professor Mikesell, published by Alan Greenblatt in NPR on June 29, 2012). An underfunded, locally administered retirement system was an important reason for fiscal stress in Detroit, Pittsburgh, Vallejo, and Central Falls. Central Falls' unfunded pension and retiree health obligations exceeded 80 million dollars in 2012. Central Falls' fire and police pension fund was 92 percent unfunded in 2011. The pension costs had become the primary driver of the city's financial problems in Detroit, where in 2014 the number of current employees was only half of the number of the city's retirees (Chapter 9). Detroit paid its employee retirement system bills through pension bond sales. Aa a result, Detroit's long-term obligations rose to nearly 15 billion dollars by 2012 (City of Detroit, 2012, p. 14). Pittsburgh's overall debt was incurred to fund previously existing pension obligations. In FY2008 at about 20 percent of revenues, pension debt service was the second highest line item after wages and salaries on Pittsburgh budget.

Economic and Social Factors

On the expense side, the same economic and social factors that shrunk the tax base lead to an increase in per capita expenditures. Detroit, Pittsburgh, and other legacy cities were expanding when in their better days and experienced an influx of population. With structural changes in the economy and subsequent outmigration, the cities whose infrastructure was built to accommodate much larger populations now had to continue providing city services, even in largely abandoned neighborhoods. "Not only are abandoned properties subject to higher maintenance and demolition costs incurred by the local government, but they are also frequent sites for vandalism, arson, and other crimes that require deployment of police, fire, and other government resources" (Guzman, 2018, p. 12). High unemployment and poverty rates in the studied cities also mean that municipalities have high expenditures on social services.

Unsound Financial Management

We find the evidence of unsound fiscal management practices in different shapes and forms in every case study we covered in this book. Poor financial mismanagement has, in fact, become one of the major contributors to the rapid deterioration of fiscal health in the studied cities.

Jefferson County, for instance, had several examples of fraudulent spending on its account, building new sewer lines and treatment services in undeveloped areas or when, in attempt to attract new clientele, the county spent 19 million dollars to bore a sewer tunnel beneath the Cahaba River. The tunnel was very unstable, and the work was eventually abandoned halfway through the project. The tunnel was even called "the Tunnel to Nowhere" (Walsh, 2012) in an analogy with Alaska's "Bridge to Nowhere".

We discuss multiple other examples of what we consider unsound financial management, like deceptive borrowing practices, "financial gimmicks" or the practice of funding operating expenditures with long-term debt, and administrative corruption and bribery, in the following sections.

Deceptive Borrowing Practices

The practice of funding recurring operating expenses with debt is really shaky and leads to fiscal unsustainability in the long term, when future taxpayers have to assume not only their own debt but also the past debt. Public financial practices consider it "healthy" for municipalities to issue debt to finance infrastructure projects, because such projects generate benefits for years to come, and it is okay to finance them over a long period of time. It is also considered "healthy" to borrow short term, in anticipation of coming revenues (if the tax collection period is approaching, say, for a property tax that is collected twice a year, or if a locality is expecting a federal grant, for example) if a municipality is experiencing short-term liquidity problems. But it is considered not "healthy" when municipalities use long-term borrowing to cover structural deficits. Once again, by doing so, municipalities simply shift their fiscal problems onto future generations, undermining fiscal sustainability (Mikesell, 2007). We discussed how Detroit and Pittsburgh were relying on pension bonds. In other cases, it is sometimes hard to say whether municipalities used borrowed funds to finance their operating versus capital needs, but we observed an increase in overall debt issuance in many cases prior to bankruptcies.

In fact, municipalities even used certain "tricks" to bypass debt ceilings or required voters' approval for the debt issue. Jefferson County issued special revenue warrants, instead of bonds, which do not require voter approval in Alabama (while bonds do). Vallejo and Detroit relied on Certificates of Participation (COPs) instead of bonds for the same exact purpose. Outstanding COPs worth 94 million dollars in Vallejo in 2007 were over half of 180 million dollars in overall debt outstanding (City of Vallejo, 2008). Detroit went even further. While approaching its state-imposed debt limitations, to be able to continue borrowing Detroit not only switched to COPs but also created two nonprofit "service corporations" to issue debt for the city. These corporations issued 1.44 billion dollars in COPs in 2005 on behalf of the city.

Detroit and Jefferson County also converted a large portion of their COPs or warrants into complicated interest rate swaps, which were meant to protect both cities against high interest rates. But, when the recession hit in 2008 and the Federal Reserve lowered interest rates to almost nothing to stimulate the economy, the municipalities ended up owing millions of dollars to the banks that carried corresponding debt (mainly America/Merrill Lynch and UBS for Detroit and JPMorgan Chase for Jefferson County). Jefferson County had close to 5.4 billion dollars in swaps, and Detroit had about 800 million dollars (Chapters 9 and 11). Both Detroit and Jefferson County were criticized for engaging in complicated swap transactions that administration of the municipalities did not fully understand. Banks were criticized because, in search of their own benefits, they failed to explain all potential side effects of such transactions, yet they had moral obligation to do it.

Mismanagement of Large Infrastructure Projects

Even before discussing how to finance capital projects, municipalities often made incorrect decisions about undertaking certain capital projects in the first place. Central Falls' bankruptcy was due, in large part, to bad decisions by elected officials about the expansion of the Wyatt Detention Facility. Jefferson County officials were engaged in a pattern of issuing risky debt for sewer facilities that desperately needed repairs.

"Financial Gimmicks"

In the face of a budget deficit, municipalities often resort to some sort of financial "gimmicks" or "maneuvers" to artificially balance their operating budgets. Municipalities have relied on anything from overly optimistic revenue forecasts, including low delinquency rates, reclassification of certain operating expenses into capital, and delaying payments to issuing the COPs or warrants to circumvent voter approval requirements discussed earlier.

The City of Central Falls, RI included overly optimistic forecasts of revenues coming from the Donald W. Wyatt Detention Facility (Wyatt). Such "rosy" forecasts led to additional bond issues for the expansion of Wyatt (106 million dollars in bonds) in 2005. High revenue forecasts never materialized, and the city has been hardly able to cover the bond service, let alone get extra general fund revenues anticipated from the jail operations.

The 2010 budget of the City of Detroit contained 275 million dollars in revenues from the securitization of the Detroit Windsor Tunnel, the city's parking, and the public lighting systems, none of which actually materialized.

The "rosy" revenue forecasts were consistently a part of Pittsburgh budgets. Compared to "one-shot" revenue-boosting ideas in Detroit and Central Falls, Pittsburgh did not have a good way to account for tax and non-tax revenues among finance and operational departments in general. So, overall general fund revenues were often overestimated.

The City of Vallejo, CA turned to a couple other "one-shot" practices trying to balance its 2008 operating budget. First, Vallejo sold its share of ownership of what is now known as the Six Flags Discovery Kingdom animal theme park in 2007. The sales eliminated 56 million dollars in debt in park bonds and generated a one-time 1.7 million dollars in net receipts for the city. While these one-time earnings from the sale of city assets provide a much-needed revenue boost to fiscally challenged municipalities in the short-run, they eliminate a consistent source of income in the long-term. Vallejo estimated, for example, that it would lose over a million dollars annually from the park sale (Vallejo CAFR, 2008). Besides, such sales are usually made in a hurry, which may result in a lower sale price.[2] The second one-time budget manipulation was a transfer of five million dollars from several dedicated funds to the general fund in 2008 in an attempt to balance the latter.

The problem with "phantom balancing" tricks is that the structural budget deficit problem is not getting addressed. Just like when municipalities offer generous retirement benefits in lieu of higher salary, financial "gimmicks" also simply defer the costs to the future. In addition, temporary "solutions" to budget balancing further destabilize an already shattered fiscal situation. We consider financial gimmicks as a special case of unsound financial management practices.

Public Corruption

Bribery and corruption contributed to bankruptcy of Central Falls, RI, where Mayor Charles Moreau was convicted on federal corruption charges. The mayor of Detroit, MI Kwame Kilpatrick and Councilwoman Monica Conyers were also convicted of bribery and corruption. While in the first two cases corruption played some – but not a major – role in these cities' bankruptcies, the corruption and bribery allegations were for sure at the heart of bankruptcy in Jefferson County, AL. In Jefferson County, the county officials were involved in fraudulent deals that fueled 3.7 billion dollars in sewer debt, and at the same time, the required sewer repairs were hardly made. Larry

TABLE 15.1 Causes of Fiscal Emergency/Bankruptcy Situations in Studied Municipalities

	Colorado Springs, CO	*Detroit, MI*	*Vallejo, CA*	*Central Falls, RI*	*Pittsburgh, PA*	*Jefferson county, AL*
Revenue-expenditure imbalance	x	x	x	x	x	x
National and regional economic downswings	x	x	x	x	x	x
Unsound financial management and risky bond issues	x	x	x	x	x	x
Negative state influence on tax revenues	x	x	x	x	x	x
Mismanagement of large infrastructure projects		x	x	x		x
Underfunded locally administered retirement system		x	x	x	x	x
Corruption		x	x	x		x
"Financial gimmicks"		x	x	x		x

Langford, the former mayor of Birmingham and the president of the Jefferson County Commission, was convicted on 61 federal charges for bribery, money laundering, and corruption. Another County Commissioner, Gary White, has been sentenced to ten years in federal prison. Overall, 17 people were convicted of bribery and fraud in the sewer scandal that was one of main causes that led to bankruptcy.

Table 15.1 provides a comparative analysis of main causes of fiscal emergency/bankruptcy situations in studied municipalities.

Budgeting and Administrative Steps During Fiscal Emergency and Bankruptcy

Now that we discussed the most common causes of municipal fiscal stress, we review the six case studies to synthesize budgeting, fiscal, and administrative approaches municipalities employed to exit fiscal emergency or bankruptcy.

Extreme Budget Cuts

Perhaps the first and most painful step in every fiscal stress situation was the dramatic cut in expenditures that consequently resulted in downsizing and delays in provision of essential services for the residents and diminishing quality of life.

Personnel and Retirement Expenses

As we discussed earlier, labor costs are usually the most expensive line item in municipal budgets. It comes as no surprise that, in the face of imminent crisis, cities and counties start slashing their budgets with personnel cuts. All municipalities in our case studies, regardless of the severity of fiscal stress, turned to layoffs, encouraged early retirements, decreased salaries of current employees and pensions of retired city workers along with benefits for both, or instituted hiring freezes in attempts to balance their budgets.

Just to name a few examples, during bankruptcy restructuring the number of Central Falls' city employees reduced by 33 percent. Vallejo decreased their police force by 42 percent and firefighters by 47 percent. Jefferson County laid off over 500 employees, cut work hours for remaining hourly employees, and instituted hiring freezes in many job classifications.

Central Falls successfully negotiated salary and benefit reductions with its employee unions.[3] Jefferson County eliminated certain benefits for its employees, such as overtime and sick days. Pittsburgh reduced overtime expenditures for firefighters and instituted two-year wage freezes and eliminated sick days for all. There were some changes to salaries and benefits in Vallejo as well, but negotiations with the unions in Vallejo were less successful. Nevertheless, the city was still able to cap healthcare benefits at 300 dollars per employee, which led to 75–100-million-dollar reduction in the city's long-term liabilities.

Central Falls negotiated a reduction of retirees' pension payments by approximately 55 percent, arguing that it was better to receive something than nothing at all. In Detroit, pensions were not high in the first place, but the city still negotiated a 4.5 percent cut to pensions of general retirees and an elimination or reduction of annual cost-of-living adjustments. Both Detroit and Pittsburgh proposed the elimination of all retiree health benefits. By 2016, Pittsburgh renegotiated seven of the nine collective bargaining agreements.

Negotiation with Creditors and Debt Restructuring

An overwhelming amount of debt service was one of the major causes of all studied bankruptcy cases for Detroit, Central Falls, Vallejo, and Jefferson County. So, expectedly, not only the renegotiation of labor contracts but also the debt obligations was a primary task during bankruptcy processes.

The city and the banks agreed to an 85-million-dollar payment of about 290 million dollars that Detroit owed to Bank of America Merrill Lynch and UBS. The city negotiated to pay Financial Guaranty Insurance Company (FGIC), another major city creditor, just 13 cents on the dollar of the debt. FGIC also received the right to develop the Joe Louis Arena. The 400 million dollars of debt to Syncora was lowered to 200 million dollars with most of it to be paid not in cash but in-kind, through the lease or purchase of some of the prime city-owned Detroit properties that Syncora offered to develop (Chapter 9).

When Jefferson County filed a Chapter 9 bankruptcy it had about 4.23 billion dollars in debt. Jefferson County lawyers renegotiated the debt payments with roughly 4,000 creditors. JPMorgan, for example, the major holder of the county's (sewer) debt, agreed to forgive 842 million dollars of 1.22 billion dollars of Jefferson County debt.

Vallejo's renegotiation of lease obligations resulted in a 47 percent reduction in interest, for an estimated savings of 23 million dollars. The reworking of debt obligations with bond holders resulted in a reduction to 5–20 cents per dollar on unsecured debt.

Infrastructure and Other Cuts

To cut expenses, all discussed municipalities also reduced many core public functions in parks, recreation, and cultural services, fire, police, and other departments. Recreational facilities and community centers were closed, summer programs were eliminated, garbage was not collected on time, recycling programs ceased to exist, and parks were only partially maintained. Vallejo could cover only about 10–30 percent of maintenance and repair costs of the streets, roads, and buildings. Colorado Springs turned off streetlights, closed public restrooms, eliminated maintenance of alleys and unpaved streets, and removed trash cans from public parks. During bankruptcy, arts and recreation programs were terminated in Vallejo. Jefferson County's officials closed some courts, eliminated inpatient care, and reorganized a hospital as an ambulatory and urgent care facility. The Detroit Water and Sewerage Department (DWSD) shut off water to close to 30,000 households that were delinquent on their utility bills. Central Falls closed its only library and community center. And Pittsburgh closed community centers and swimming pools.

These findings are consistent with Peck's conclusions (2014) that "municipalities feeling financial stress should work as hard as possible, accepting as much pain as they and their constituents, creditors and employees can endure, to avoid [this] path" (p. 21).

Consequences of Severe Cuts

It should come as no surprise that reduced funding for police, fire, libraries, hospitals, prisons, community centers and swimming pools, and sanitation services resulted in some of the serious negative consequences for the studied municipalities. Detroit, Central Falls, and Vallejo reported higher crime rates during and immediately following their bankruptcies. In 2013, the crime rate in Vallejo, for example, rose by 12 percent compared to 2010. Several years later, in 2019, the crime rate in Vallejo was still two times higher than the U.S. average and higher than in 96.8 percent U.S. cities. In Central Falls the crime rate in 2015 increased by 142.3 percent from 2009. Detroit reported that residents were stealing even the copper wires and transformers from the streetlights. Overcrowded hospitals in Central Falls and Jefferson County and overcrowded Jefferson County prison, increased response times to fires and medical emergencies and soaring foreclosure rates in Detroit, dire needs for infrastructure repairs, and rising inequality within the communities are some of the other numerous examples of adverse effects of extreme budget cuts.

Increasing Taxes and Fees

Tax increases were not easy to administer due to the tax limitations discussed earlier. However, during fiscal emergencies and bankruptcies the states gave permission to municipalities to institute tax increases or allowed adding corresponding measures to ballots. Central Falls collected higher service charges and fees and increased property tax rates by 4 percent. Vallejo introduced a new one percent sales tax (increasing a combined state and local sales tax rate from 7.375 percent to 8.375 percent). Jefferson County increased its property tax rates and residential sewer rates by 7.89 percent annually for four years and by 3.49 percent afterward for the foreseeable future. Colorado Springs had new revenues coming from marijuana taxes. Pittsburgh's recovery plans included such revenue-generating initiatives as higher local services tax and dedicating annual revenues from parking taxes toward the pension fund.

State Transfers

State grants are not commonly featured during fiscal stress to discourage bad or risky financial practices by municipalities. Sometimes states, however, stepped in and provided some funds to help municipalities financially during bankruptcy. Michigan approved a 195-million-dollar state transfer to Detroit in June 2014. Rhode Island offered a one-time allocation of 2.6 million dollars in 2012 to Central Falls.

Public-private Partnerships

Public-private partnerships (PPP), while emphasized in several cities during fiscal stress (for example, the Central Falls public library was run by a nonprofit during this city's bankruptcy process), became really important in Detroit and Colorado Springs.

Detroit was exceptional in its extent of involvement in partnerships among the city, foundations, the Detroit Institute of Art, corporations, and residents that jointly raised hundreds of millions of dollars for the city and provided other in-kind benefits to bail the city out of bankruptcy. In fact, nine private foundations collectively raised 330 million dollars for Detroit's recovery. The Detroit Institute of Art committed to raise an additional 100 million dollars for the city. By late 2014, 225 city parks were open (up from 58 parks just over a year earlier) and maintained by multiple church and community volunteers who mowed the grass and removed trash and litter. The involvement of the corporate world was also beyond imaginable. Dan Gilbert, the owner of Quicken Loans, moved its company's headquarters to Detroit in 2010. Dan Gilbert and affiliates, during and after bankruptcy, purchased and renovated dozens of historical buildings and commercial properties in downtown Detroit, created thousands of new jobs for the city. Dan Gilbert and multiple other individual investors and corporations helped identify and fund blight removal, purchased and renovated various landmarks in the city, developed commercial and retail spaces and new residential areas, launched the Streetcar project in downtown Detroit, completely redeveloped the city's iconic riverfront, funded the purchase of police cars and fire trucks, donated money to the university, and have been involved in countless other initiatives (discussed in Chapter 9).

In Colorado Springs, the administration of the city promoted an "adopt a streetlight" program, in which residents could make a monetary donation to turn city lights of their choice back on. They also started an "adopt a trash can" initiative, in which residents signed a contract with the city to empty trash cans in city parks and an "adopt a median" program, in which residents were recruited to mow medians with their own lawnmowers. Taxi drivers were recruited to "police" streets, and the city negotiated discounts on riding mowers for residents to voluntarily cut grass in the parks. A local church and a museum ran a community center. Chapter 10 discusses multiple other PPP examples in Colorado Springs.

More Efficient Budgeting

Vallejo established new guiding budgeting principles such as maintaining a minimum 5 percent reserve based on the bankruptcy five-year business plan. The city resorted to conservative revenue estimates and created a five-year financial forecast. Pittsburgh's Recovery Plan introduced a more formal and rigorous budget oversight. Under this Pittsburgh recovery program, departments prepare a detailed revenue and expenditure plan, showing the projected monthly progress of how the department will live within its approved budget throughout the year. Each department head and departmental budget officer must meet with the finance director and other officials at quarterly intervals to review and discuss monthly reports, including year-to-date spending, expected overall results, and actions taken to control any potential overspending. The Pittsburgh's Quarterly Report started to include details on the performance of major revenue sources and expenditure categories, reports on key factors driving the budget, cash flows, and deficit reduction initiatives. In November 2020, Jefferson County published a five-year strategic plan. All municipalities in our cases continued to use the cost-saving strategies even after exiting fiscal emergency or bankruptcy.

Participatory Budgeting

Participatory budgeting is not a common budgeting process for U.S. municipalities, but it found its way in post-bankruptcy Vallejo and to some extent in Central Falls, which allocates a small proportion of the city budget to its schools specifically for participatory budgeting efforts.

Vallejo began the participatory budgeting process by assembling a steering committee, made up of representatives from local civic organizations and residents. Vallejo uses city-level participatory budgeting to allocate one to three million dollars per year from a new voter-approved sales tax to various programs, services, and public improvements (Scholars Strategic Network, 2015). Vallejo's residents 16 and older can vote, regardless of past convictions or citizenship status. The committee established a process with which to develop community consultation, ultimately leading to residents voting on a set of fully developed proposals, including public capital projects.

Capital Investments

After many years of underfinancing capital infrastructure, the studied municipalities started to invest back in public infrastructure and address maintenance deficiencies. One of Jefferson County's major goals in their five-year strategic plan was to create quality infrastructure that is efficient and serves the community (Jefferson County, 2020, 2022). Jefferson County invested 2.45 billion dollars in 2020 alone in capital projects, including buildings, roads, bridges, equipment, and sewer lines. Colorado Springs had unprecedented levels of public and private investment in capital infrastructure projects following its fiscal distress. The other four studied cities similarly reported higher infrastructure expenditures following the exit from the fiscal emergency or bankruptcy.

Privatization and Contracting-out

The privatization of government assets is one of the cost-saving and fundraising initiatives municipalities often use to overcome fiscal challenges. The problem with privatization is that local governments lose control of certain important government functions, and while they make money on the sale of the assets in the short-run, they lose a consistent source of revenue in the longer-term. For bankrupt cities whose credit ratings are low and the ability to borrow is slim, privatization, however, opens opportunities to fund aging and neglected infrastructure projects as organizations that acquire government functions receive their own rather than city's credit ratings and are therefore able to borrow at a lower interest rate than bankrupt municipalities.

In Detroit, a brand new independent Public Lighting Authority (PLA) was created in February 2014 to succeed the city's public lighting department. The sewerage department was the other agency that got privatized in 2014, under a 40-year lease contract with the Great Lakes Water Authority (GLWA). The city additionally contracted-out its trash collections to two companies on a five-year contract.

Other Cost-saving Incentives

We discussed earlier how costly blighted areas are to the cities. So, blight removal becomes one of the essential cost-cutting steps for municipalities. During its fiscal emergency, Pittsburgh doubled the budget to demolish the city's abandoned buildings. Detroit created a task force that helped identify blighted areas, prioritize what needed to be demolished, and decided how demolitions would be financed. In another cost-cutting step, Jefferson County, for example, upgraded their public infrastructure by encouraging regional cooperation with projects.

A Theory of Financial Management and Budgeting During Fiscal Emergency and Bankruptcy

In Chapter 5 we discussed how, in the face of fiscal emergency and bankruptcy, municipalities use *Austerity Urbanism* practices, by severely slashing their expenses, which negatively affects the quality of life. Another budgeting theory during severe fiscal emergency or bankruptcy is the use of the more deliberate *Pragmatic Municipalism* ideas that incorporate more innovation, restructuring, and tax increases. We observe a mixed use of both budget theories in the six studied municipalities in a different shape and form and with a different degree of intensity. In one case after another, we saw, however, a definitive pattern of municipal responses to fiscal emergency at different stages of its occurrence and expansion. In fact, we observed the three definitive stages before, during, and after the fiscal crisis, every one of which incorporates certain distinctive features and strategies. We call the three strategies used at the three steps a "HEI" or "Haphazard Strategy" at the first stage, followed by "Emergency Strategy" at the second stage, and finally the "Innovative Strategy" at the third and final stage (see Figure 15.1).

First Stage: Haphazard Strategy

We observed three general stages of municipal response during fiscal stress among all six case studies. Actually, the first stage starts even prior to the emergency, when municipalities approach fiscal emergency or bankruptcy. In this stage, they launch cutback practices, and while these are tremendously painful, they are not nearly as extreme in this stage as they are when the municipality is already in a fiscal emergency or bankruptcy. Municipalities at this point try to raise tax revenues – usually unsuccessfully thanks to state tax limitations – and to renegotiate debt and

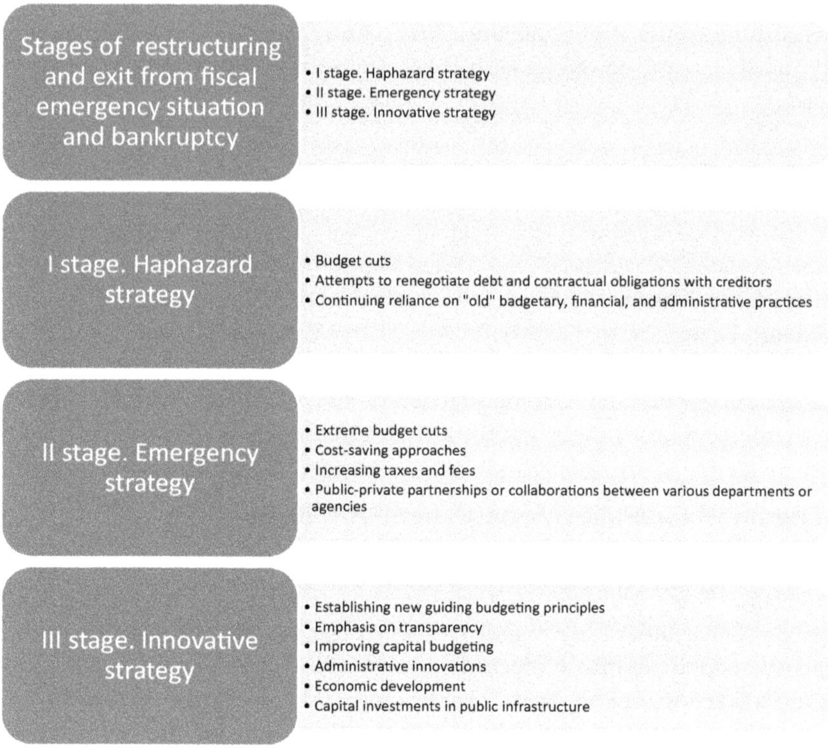

FIGURE 15.1 Stages of Restructuring and Exit from Fiscal Emergency Situation and Bankruptcy.

other contractual obligations with their creditors. In this early stage, municipalities usually do not engage in any innovative or transformative budgetary practices and continue to use old budgeting and administrative approaches that caused the financial problems in the first place. We call this stage the "*Haphazard Strategy*" of our theory of financial management and budgeting during fiscal emergency and bankruptcy.

Second Stage: Emergency Strategy

In the second stage, fiscally challenged municipalities usually get hit by some kind of environmental jolt and find themselves in a fiscal emergency or bankruptcy situation. The constructive steps to recovery start at this stage that we call the "*Emergency Strategy*". Our findings here are consistent with suggestions of other scholars, that the transformation process is even more rapid and drastic in the case of an environmental jolt (Meyer, 1979, 1980, 1982, 1994; Meyer & Goes, 1988; Meyer & Rowan, 1977; Meyer et al., 1990; Ermasova, 2012, 2013, 2020; Fehr, 2011). During bankruptcy or fiscal emergency, municipalities resort to the extreme budget cuts discussed earlier in Table 15.2. This strategy cannot be a long-term solution in fiscal emergency situations because municipalities need to get back to a basic level of delivering public services, particularly related to safety, social insurance, and economic development. This stage is additionally characterized by positive changes in budgeting and administrative innovations, such as cost-saving public-private partnerships or collaborations between various departments or agencies. In this stage, municipalities usually receive state permission or get voters' approval to raise taxes.

Table 15.2 compares some of the major common elements of the Emergency Strategy observed in studied municipalities.

TABLE 15.2 Emergency Strategy of Restructuring and Exit from Fiscal Emergency Situation and Bankruptcy in Studied Municipalities

	Colorado Springs, CO	*Detroit, MI*	*Vallejo, CA*	*Central Falls, RI*	*Pittsburgh, PA*	*Jefferson county, AL*
State-appointed fiscal manager		x		x	x	x
Tax increases	x	x	x	x	x	x
Cuts of employees	x	x	x	x	x	x
Decreased in salaries and benefits of city employees	x	x	x	x	x	x
Reducing retiree payments and healthcare benefits		x	x	x	x	x
Renegotiation of debt		x	x		x	x
Refinancing of bonds			x			x
Reduced parks maintenance	x	x	x	x	x	x
Cut bus services	x	x	x	x	x	x
Turned off streetlights	x					
Closing of municipalities facilities	x	x	x	x	x	x
Underfunded development work	x		x			x
Decrease of infrastructure projects financing	x	x	x	x	x	x
Decreased maintenance of municipal infrastructure		x	x	x	x	x
Bulldozing of empty lots		x		x		
State transfers		x			x	
Revised agreements with police, fire, and public administrator unions			x		x	

Source: Created by authors

Third Stage: Innovative Strategy

We call the third stage of response to fiscal emergency and budgeting the "*Innovative Strategy*" stage. The problem-oriented, innovative strategy embraces municipality's organizational, budgeting, and fiscal actions. During this stage, while still enduring a long and difficult path to recovery, municipalities already do not experience the pressures of bankruptcy and fiscal emergency. In this stage municipalities no longer resort to austerity urbanism practices and simply continue to implement the innovative ideas initiated in the second stage and come up with new financial management and administrative principles. In this third stage, the studied municipalities establish new guiding budgeting principles to direct their budget decisions, start maintaining minimum reserves, create strategic five-year investment plans, and establish longer-term (often five-year) financial forecasts, rely on more conservative revenue estimates, and adopt standard accounting practices. The innovative stage of capital budgeting, for instance, is characterized by

> increasing the planning period, using long-term or medium-term planning, developing formal mechanisms to set aside funds for preserving existing facilities, using special computer programs to increase automation of the process, increasing collaboration between agencies, and linking capital planning decisions to statewide performance goals and strategic plans.
>
> *(Ermasova, 2013, p. 124)*

Collectively such innovations lead to higher transparency and accountability in government operations. In this stage municipalities also heavily invest in their rebranding, initiating marketing campaigns to attract and retain younger residents and businesses and to host various big events in the city.

Table 15.3 compares some of the major common elements of the Innovative Strategy observed in studied municipalities.

Figure 15.2 summarizes our tentative theory of financial management and budgeting during fiscal emergency and bankruptcy. It connects the extent to which a municipality undertakes due diligence in its decision making during a fiscal emergency situation to possible antecedents and outcomes.

Conclusions and Practical Recommendations

We wrote this book attempting to understand the common causes of fiscal misfortunes and trying to learn how municipalities change their public management and budgeting practices before, during, and after fiscal emergency and bankruptcy. We discussed theoretical aspects of fiscal health and fiscal misfortunes. Then, we studied specific cases of different degrees of fiscal stress in five cities, Detroit, MI; Pittsburgh, PA; Vallejo, CA; Colorado Springs, CO; and Central Falls, RA and one county, Jefferson County, AL. This chapter summarized our

TABLE 15.3 Innovative Strategy of Restructuring and Exit from Fiscal Emergency Situation and Bankruptcy in Studied Municipalities

	Colorado Springs, CO	*Detroit, MI*	*Vallejo, CA*	*Central Falls, RI*	*Pittsburgh, PA*	*Jefferson county, AL*
Increasing accountability and transparency	x	x	x	x	x	x
Creating five-year strategic plans	x	x	x		x	x
Increasing investments in public infrastructure	x	x	x	x	x	x
Promoting economic development	x	x	x	x	x	x
Marketing campaigns to increase attractiveness of the city	x				x	x
Increasing public-private partnerships	x	x		x	x	
Participatory budgeting			x	x		
Establishing reserve funds			x			x
Controlling labor costs	x	x		x	x	x
Reducing fiscal risks	x	x	x	x	x	x
Adoption of standard accounting practices	x	x	x	x	x	x
Projecting revenues conservatively	x	x	x	x	x	x
Implementation of five-year financial forecast	x	x	x		x	
Improving maintenance of capital infrastructure	x	x	x	x	x	x
Increasing financial transparency			x		x	x
Preparing monthly, quarterly Financial and Management Reports					x	
Attracting tourism	x	x			x	
Using cost-saving strategies	x	x	x	x	x	x

Source: Created by authors

understanding of the common causes of municipal fiscal problems, consequences of fiscal misfortunes, and steps municipalities take to exit them. In the following sections, we offer some general recommendations for how to deal with fiscal emergencies. We already provided similar recommendations in the first theoretical chapters of the book. Recommendations now are based strictly on the observations made by comparing and contrasting the six selected case studies.

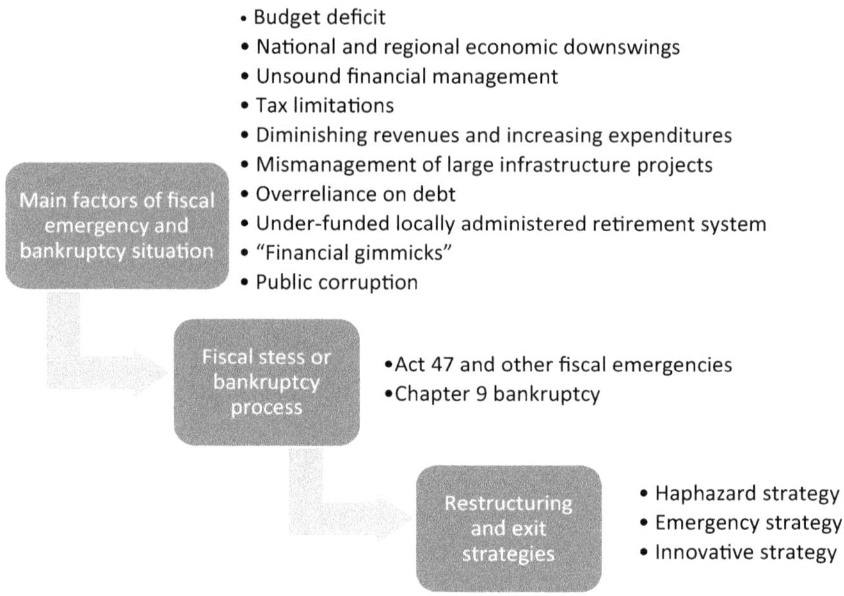

FIGURE 15.2 A Tentative Theory of Financial Management and Budgeting During Fiscal Emergency and Bankruptcy.

Recommendations

Understand the Causes

The first and, we believe, the most important step in addressing fiscal difficulties and ultimately exiting a fiscal emergency is to understand the roots of the problem. What happened? Which economic, demographic, financial, and political factors created or contributed to the issue? How did the situation develop and why? Only when we understand the roots can we find the best solutions that would fit a municipality's own unique situation, its history, demographics, industrial composition, and political structure.

Healthy Reserves

We emphasize in Chapter 3 and observe in all case studies the importance of reserves, rainy-day, or other emergency funds. We discussed repeatedly how it takes a long time for problems to develop, but it is usually an environmental jolt, such as an economic recession, natural disaster, or world pandemic that pushes the fiscal situation off the cliff when conditions deteriorate to the point of no return. It is difficult or simply impossible to foresee the coming of environmental jolts, but the existence of healthy reserves can cushion a municipality against such unexpected falloffs and prevent more severe problems in future.

Economic Development Incentives

Many of the economic development incentives discussed in Chapter 4 were successfully used in the considered case studies. Pittsburgh and Jefferson County established Enterprise Zones. Jeffco provides sales tax incentives to businesses on both the city and the county levels. Detroit, among other incentives, used money provided by the Federal Hardest Hit Fund (HHF) and designated 18 areas in the city as Renaissance Zones, Michigan's version of Enterprise Zones. All states represented in our case studies now offer Historic Preservation Tax Credits (HPTC), Michigan since 2020, California since 2019, Alabama since 2017, Pennsylvania and Rhode Island since 2013, and Colorado since 1990. Multiple other economic development incentives have been employed by studied municipalities on their recovery paths. These and numerous other incentives we discussed in Chapter 3 have proven to be successful in the studied cities and are encouraged to be used to promote economic development, business expansion and retention, and ultimately fiscal health, as well as to facilitate an exit from fiscal stress situations.

Citizens' and Corporate Participation

We found involvement of residents and corporations housed in the city to be very beneficial for the recovery efforts. The feeling that you do something important for your city, that your decisions and actions really matter, create a sense of ownership. With correct motivation, people showed a willingness to help from within, not simply to criticize and wait for the situation to get better. We observe extraordinary examples, when private parties donated millions of dollars to the recovery of Detroit, created fundraising, or simply rolled their sleeves up to aid with recovery efforts in Colorado Springs, Detroit, and Central Falls.

Participatory Budgeting

Participatory budgeting is a special case of such citizenry involvement. Participatory budgeting introduced by the City of Vallejo and by Central Falls schools following bankruptcy demonstrated that municipalities could improve transparency and engagement of residents when they use participatory budgeting. The participatory budgeting process increases residents' involvement in the adoption of the budgets, ensures their much-needed trust in budget accuracy and fairness, improves accountability and transparency in governance, empowers residents to take a more active role in their communities, increases municipal government efficiency, and reduces corruption. Volunteers in participatory budgeting efforts in

Vallejo felt more connected to officials and appreciative of the complex work they do (Scholars Strategic Network, 2015). Greater inclusion allows people in poor and marginalized communities to voice previously ignored needs. It increases social justice by providing a voice for traditionally excluded members of the community in decision-making processes and prioritization of capital projects.

State Involvement

State involvement with municipal finances, such as states' early fiscal monitoring systems, training and expert advice to the financial officials, and other state involvement discussed in Chapter 3 is definitely helpful in ensuring fiscal health and preventing fiscal stress in the first place. More strategic and in-depth state involvement when the situation spirals down without control, addressed in Chapters 4 and 5, was also found crucial. The appointment of a receiver, overseer, or fiscal emergency manager was one of the most important steps to improve a seriously undermined situation in Detroit, Pittsburgh, Jefferson County, and Central Falls. While not a panacea for every situation, the quickly adopted bankruptcy law in Rhode Island in response to fiscal emergency in its smallest city, Central Falls, led to perhaps the shortest municipal bankruptcy ever, which only lasted about 14 months.

We found that, on the other side, state-imposed tax limitations restricted local governments' ability to withstand financial stress, while debt limitations and balanced budget requirements simply made localities find creative ways to avoid them.

We are not advocating against any of the state-imposed limitations and would actually argue that such limitations are a crucial part of fiscal control and a responsible government. However, the states should be more diligent in identifying and patching any loopholes in the public budgeting and finance system, such as limiting the use of certificates of deposit or warrants in favor of regular bonded debt or requiring more conservative revenue estimates to avoid "rosy" budgeting scenarios. The language about potential tax increases at the time of severe need might also benefit from being more relaxed.

Open Budget Presentation and Budget Process

Another observation from the case studies that we feel should be applied to policy recommendations is more open budget presentations and higher transparency in the budgeting process in general. Transparency and openness go in line with many other recommended efforts we discuss here, but we believe it is so important that it should be additionally emphasized in a separate category. Such openness creates a more responsible use of taxpayers' money, less opportunity for public corruption, and, we believe, reduces the likelihood of fiscal problems deteriorating to the point of no return.

Long-term Planning for Capital Infrastructure Needs

The following two recommendations refer specifically to the capital budgeting process. During bankruptcy or fiscal crisis, municipalities should place additional emphasis on the planning and execution of preventive maintenance. The studied municipalities emphasized the necessity to increase a planning period, use long-term or medium-term planning, develop formal mechanisms to set aside funds to preserve existing facilities, use computer programming to increase automation of the process, increase collaboration between departments, and link capital planning decisions to strategic plans.

Local governments should develop comprehensive, multi-year capital improvement plans that indicate which facilities need maintenance, renovations, and replacement. To develop such plans, it would be beneficial to create an automated system that provides:

- current data on the conditions of buildings, roads, etc. and the degree of their usage, so that decisions could be made more rigorously
- a method for objectively setting priorities across the portfolio
- project planning tools that turn requirements into actions
- reporting tools that will give both finance and facilities departments the data they need.

We suggest that the long-term investment plan should clearly describe an entity's performance gap, the resources needed to bridge it, and a clear justification for new acquisitions proposed for funding, with links of proposed investments to a municipality's long-term strategic goals. Complementing the long-term vision, local governments should also identify a short list of priority projects, considering opposing policy goals, existing infrastructure needs, and budget constraints.

Development of Asset Management Programs

We suggest shifting the decision-making process from reactive to proactive based on the development of asset management programs. Municipalities should use the facility self-assessment practices that employ a consistent, repeatable process for internal staff. By leveraging existing facility resources to quickly assess assets of all types and portfolios of all sizes, organizations can greatly enhance the management of facilities. The self-assessment process should be rapid and cost-effective, resulting in data that can identify "hot spots" within the portfolio that require a more detailed professional condition assessment and help develop quick budgetary estimates. A good facility self-assessment also maintains data captured in previous years (University of Wisconsin-Madison Transportation Information Center, 2001).

Better Coordination Between Operating and Capital Budgeting

All selected cases demonstrated that municipalities could obtain significant benefits by improving their coordination between the capital and operating budget processes during fiscal emergency and bankruptcy. The same set of program needs drives both capital and operating budget requests, and the two budgets affect each other. Projects and spending approved in the capital budget influence future operating budgets, as principal and interest on capital borrowings are paid out of operating funds. Decisions made in the operating budget to improve or expand services can necessitate the future expansion of capital facilities or the acquisition of new equipment. Dual budgeting practices balance the budget office's workload and reduce the amount of information that must be processed by lawmakers at any time. The separation of the capital and operating budgets encourages government capital formation. If, however, a government has a separate staff dedicated exclusively to capital budget matters, then preparing the two budgets concurrently is not merely feasible but highly preferable.

We hope this book explained well what the fiscal stress is and how to deal with it based on specific examples and theories from literature. We hope students in the budgeting and public finance field, researchers, and practitioners find the book useful in explaining causes and finding solutions to numerous fiscal problems.

Notes

1 Environmental jolts are not always related to economic recessions. For example, historical flooding and destruction of the city by Hurricane Katrina and subsequent levees' failure led to the downgrade of the New Orleans, LA credit rating to "junk".

2 Chicago famously privatized Chicago Skyway, a toll road in the heart of Chicago, in 2005 and parking meters in 2008. The Skyway was leased for 99 years for 1.83 billion dollars in 2005. And in June 2016 the remaining 89-year lease on the toll road was resold to another private company for 2.8 billion dollars (Chicago SunTimes 2016). In 2009 the Inspector General estimated that the meters were also sold for less than half of what they were worth, and in 2010 Forbes concluded that the selling price was ten times less than what the meters were worth (In these Times, 2015). Besides, if the city needs to remove a meter to repair a road under it, or closes the portion of the road with meters for a festival, to repair a broken street light, or for any other reason, the city is required to pay the fair market price to the meters' owner for the time the meter was down.

3 To deal with fiscal emergency in San Jose, CA asked its employees to accept salary cuts for ten consecutive years for as high as 10 percent in 2011. The number of city employees in San Jose also dropped from 7,400 to 5,400 in these ten years (Greenblatt, 2012).

References

City of Detroit (2012, December 28). *Comprehensive annual financial report city of detroit, Michigan 2012*. Retrieved December 12, 2020, from https://detroitmi.gov/Portals/0/docs/finance/CAFR/Final%202012%20Detroit%20Financial%20Statements.pdf

City of Vallejo (2008). *CAFR 2008*. Vallejo, CA: City of Vallejo. Retrieved December 12, 2021, from www.cityofvallejo.net/city_hall/departmentsdivisions/finance/financialreports

Ermasova, N. (2012). *Capital budgeting at the state level: An empirical analysis from the economic downturn through the present*. [PhD Dissertation, SPEA, IU].

Ermasova, N. (2013). Capital budgeting in the states after the great recession. *State and Local Government Review, 45*(2), 119–130.

Ermasova, N. (2020). The 35 years of public capital budgeting: A review and future research agenda. *Public Finance and Management, 20*(4), 1–32.

Fehr, S. (2011). *Pittsburgh and Harrisburg: A tale of two deep-in-debt cities, stateline*, 20 October. Retrieved December 12, 2020, from www.pewstates.org/projects/stateline/headlines/pittsburgh-and-harrisburg-a-tale-of-two-deep-in-debt-cities-85899375281

Greenblat, A. (2012). How To Avoid Bankruptcy (If You're A City). NPR. June 29, 2012. Retrieved January 12, 2021, from https://www.npr.org/2012/06/28/155902510/how-to-avoid-bankruptcy-if-youre-a-city

Guzman, T. (2018). Cost-benefit and fiscal impact analysis of Ohio historic preservation tax credit (OHPTC). *Journal of Benefit-Cost Analysis, 9*(2), 342–373.

Jefferson County (2020). *Comprehensive annual financial report 2020*. Retrieved January 12, 2021, from https://www.jccal.org/Sites/Jefferson_County/AppData/DocLib/Main/FY2020%20CAFR%204.30.21%20Submitted.pdf

Jefferson County (2022). *Official operating budget 2022*. Retrieved January 12, 2022, from https://files4.1.revize.com/jeffersoncountynew/Budget/2022%20Budget/Budget%20in%20Brief.pdf

Meyer, A. D. (1982). Adapting to environmental jolts. *Administrative Science Quarterly, 27*, 515–537.

Meyer, A. D., Brooks, G. R., & Goes, J. B. (1990). Environmental jolts and industry revolutions: Organizational responses to discontinuous change. *Strategic Management Journal, Summer special Issue 11*, 93–110.

Meyer, A. D., & Goes, J. B. (1988). Organizational assimilations and innovation: A multilevel contextual analysis. *Academy of Management Journal, 31*, 897–923.

Meyer, J. W. (1980). The world polity and the authority of the nation-state. In Bergesen, A. (Ed.), *Studies of the Modern World-System* (pp. 109–137). New York: Academic Press.

Meyer, J. W. (1994). Rationalized environments. In Scott, R., & Myer, J. (Eds.), *Institutional Environments and Organizations* (pp. 28–54). Newbury Park, CA: Sage.

Meyer, J. W., & Rowan, B. (1977). Institutionalized organizations: Formal structure as myth and ceremony. *American Journal of Sociology, 83*, 340–363.

Meyer, M. W. (1979). *Change in Public Bureaucracies*. Cambridge: Cambridge University Press.

Mikesell, J. (2007). *Fiscal Administration: Analysis and Applications for the Public Sector* (8th ed.). Belmont, CA: Thomson Wadsworth.

Peck, J. (2014). Pushing austerity: State failure, municipal bankruptcy, and the crises of fiscal federalism in the USA. *Cambridge Journal of Regions, Economy and Society*, 7(1), 17–24 doi:10.1093/cjres/rst018

Scholars Strategic Network (2015). *How Participatory budgeting strengthens communities and improves local governance*, 14 December. Retrieved December 12, 2020, from https://scholars.org/contribution/how-participatory-budgeting-strengthens-communities-and-improves-local-governance

University of Wisconsin-Madison Transportation Information Center (2001). *PASER Manual*. Madison, USA: University of Wisconsin-Madison. Retrieved December 12, 2020, from https://interpro.wisc.edu/tic/document-type/publications/paser-manuals/

Walsh, M. (2012). With no vote, taxpayers stuck with tab on bonds. *The New York Times*, 25 June. Retrieved December 12, 2020, from www.nytimes.com/2012/06/26/business/surprised-taxpayers-are-paying-for-bonds-they-did-not-vote-on.html?pagewanted=all

INDEX

For Product Safety Concerns and Information please contact our EU representative GPSR@taylorandfrancis.com
Taylor & Francis Verlag GmbH, Kaufingerstraße 24, 80331 München, Germany

www.ingramcontent.com/pod-product-compliance
Ingram Content Group UK Ltd.
Pitfield, Milton Keynes, MK11 3LW, UK
UKHW020316270926
475702UK00050B/723
9781032349374